The Political Economy of J.H.G. Justi

Ulrich Adam

The Political Economy of J.H.G. Justi

PETER LANG
Oxford · Bern · Berlin · Bruxelles · Frankfurt am Main · New York · Wien

Bibliographic information published by Die Deutsche Bibliothek
Die Deutsche Bibliothek lists this publication in the Deutsche Nationalbibliografie; detailed bibliographic data is available on the Internet at ‹http://dnb.ddb.de›.

British Library and Library of Congress Cataloguing-in-Publication Data: A catalogue record for this book is available from *The British Library*, Great Britain, and from *The Library of Congress*, USA

ISBN 3-03910-278-8
US-ISBN 0-8204-7205-0

Hochfeldstrasse 32, Postfach 746, CH-3000 Bern 9, Switzerland
info@peterlang.com, www.peterlang.com, www.peterlang.net

Contents

Acknowledgements

Writing this book would have been impossible without the help of numerous individuals. Above all, I would like to express my gratitude to Istvan Hont for the patience and time he took to discuss the work with me at every stage of my research. I would also like to thank Michael Sonenscher and Keith Tribe for commenting on an earlier draft of this study. Hilary Brown, Jonathan Conlin, and Nigel De Souza kindly helped with corrections to the final version. I am greatly indepted to Traute Petersen who has supported and encouraged my historical studies for many years. This study is dedicated to her.

I would like to acknowledge the generous financial support from the following trusts and institutions: the European Trust of Cambridge University, the Kurt Hahn Trust, the Cambridge Political Economy Society, the Ellen McArthur Fund, the Sir John Plumb Charitable Trust, and Gonville and Caius College.

Brussels, May 2005 ULRICH ADAM

Abbreviations for principal sources

Gesammelte Schriften	*Gesammelte politische und Finanzschriften*, 3 vols, I+II (1761), III (1764)
Grundfeste	*Die Grundfeste zur Macht und Glückseligkeit der Staaten*, 2 vols, I (1760), II (1761)
Grundriss	*Der Grundriss einer guten Regierung* (1759)
Leben Brühls	*Leben und Charakter des Königl. Polnischen und Churfürstl. Sächsischen Premier-Ministre Grafens von Brühl*, 3 vols, I (1760), II (1761), III (1764)
Manufakturen und Fabriken	*Vollständige Abhandlung von denen Manufakturen und Fabriken*, 2 vols, I (1758), II (1761)
Natur und Wesen	*Natur und Wesen der Staaten* (1760)
Polizeiwissenschaft	*Grundsätze der Polizeiwissenschaft* (1756)
Psammitichus	*Psammitichus*, 2 vols, I (1759), II (1760)
Staatswirtschaft	*Staatswirtschaft*, 2 vols, I+II (1755)
Steuern und Abgaben	*Ausführliche Abhandlung von denen Steuern und Abgaben* (1762)
System des Finanzwesens	*System des Finanzwesens, nach vernünftigen Grundsätzen und Regeln ausführlich abgehandelt* (1766)
Vergleichungen	*Vergleichungen der europäischen mit den asiatischen und andern vermeintlich barbarischen Regierungen* (1762)

Chapter One
Introduction

Johann Heinrich Gottlob von Justi (1717–1771) is universally recognised as one of the founders of modern German political and economic thought. In 1798, a quarter of a century after Justi's death, the economist Heinrich Bensen paid tribute to him, claiming 'that even today he is commonly assumed to be the leading voice in this field.'[1] Twentieth-century interpretations have been no less enthusiastic. Justi has been called the creator of German political economy (*Staatswirtschaft*), 'the builder of the first system of financial theory in Germany' and the 'inventor of modern theory of administration'.[2] He has been praised for having composed the most important eighteenth-century textbook on economic policy-making (*Polizeiwissenschaft*)[3] and for having brought Cameralism to perfection.[4]

1 Heinrich Bensen, *Versuch eines systematischen Grundrisses der reinen und angewandten Staatslehre für Kameralisten* (3 vols; Erlangen, 1798–99), I, 21.

2 Keith Tribe, *Governing Economy. The Reformation of German Economic Discourse 1750–1840* (Cambridge: Cambridge University Press, 1988), p. 275; Karl-Theodor von Inama-Sternegg, 'Der Akzisenstreit deutscher Finanztheoretiker im 17. und 18. Jahrhundert', *Zeitschrift für die gesamte Staatswissenschaft* 21 (1865), 515–545 (p. 543); Ernst Klein, 'Johann Heinrich Gottlob von Justi und die Preussische Staatswirtschaft', *Vierteljahrsschrift für Sozial- und Wirtschaftsgeschichte* 48 (1961), 145–202.

3 Michel Foucault, 'La technologie politique des individus', in: *Dits et écrits*, edited by Daniel Defert, François Ewald, and Jacques Lagrange (4 vols; Paris: Gallimard, 1994), IV, 813-828 (p. 825).

4 Barbara Stollberg-Rilinger, *Der Staat als Maschine* (Berlin: Duncker & Humblot, 1986), p. 79. Other scholars praised Justi for having composed 'the most mature discussion of the separation of powers concept in Germany before the French Revolution' (Hans Fenske, 'Gewaltenteilung', in: *Geschichtliche Grundbegriffe*, edited by Otto Brunner, Werner Conze, Reinhart Koselleck (8 vols; Stuttgart: Klett-Cotta, 1972–97), II, 932–958 (p. 939)), for having offered 'the most penetrating attack ever made on the balance of power idea' (Matthew S. Anderson, 'Eighteenth-Century Theories of the Balance of Power', in:

Joseph Schumpeter listed Justi as a theorist who 'saw the practical argument for laissez-faire no less clearly than did A. Smith'. Justi's ideal bureaucracy, Schumpeter asserted, 'while guiding and helping where necessary, was always ready to efface itself when no guidance or help seemed needed'. In particular, Justi

> was much more concerned than A. Smith with the practical problems for government action in the short-run vicissitudes of his time and country and with particular difficulties in which private initiative fails or would have failed under the conditions of the German industry of the time. His laissez-faire was a laissez-faire plus watchfulness, his private-enterprise economy a machine that was logically automatic but exposed to breakdowns and hitches which his government was to stand ready to mend.[5]

Despite these positive assessments no comprehensive study of Justi's theories has yet been undertaken.[6] There are some obvious reasons for this. The sheer size of his oeuvre and his tortuous biography have presented the greatest obstacles.[7] Justi's writings include philosophical, literary, technological, geological, chemical, physical, as well as political and economic works. By nature a keen and fast writer, eager to get involved in all sorts of intellectual quarrels and debates, Justi published continuously over a span of thirty years, in the

Studies in Diplomatic History – Essays in Memory of David Bayne Horne, edited by Ragnhild Hatton and Matthew S. Anderson (London: Longman, 1970), pp. 183–198 (p. 191)), for having 'produced one of the most systematic eulogies of China known to have been written during the period of the *rêve chinois*' (Johanna M. Menzel, 'The Sinophilism of J.H.G. Justi', *Journal of the History of Ideas* 17 (1956), 300–310 (p. 300)), and for having been an early advocate of higher education for women (Amalia Holst, *Über die Bestimmung des Weibes zur höhern Geistesbildung*, edited by Berta Rahm (Zurich: Ala, 1983; originally: Berlin: Heinrich Fröhlich, 1802)).

5 Joseph A. Schumpeter, *History of Economic Analysis* (London: Routledge, 1954), p. 172.

6 Notwithstanding his reputation as the leading political economist of mid-eighteenth-century Germany, Justi has been missed out in the standard anthology on early-modern German political thinkers: *Staatsdenker im 17. und 18. Jahrhundert. Reichspublizistik, Politik, Naturrecht*, edited by Michael Stolleis (Frankfurt/M.: Metzler, 1987).

7 See Table 2.

course of which he edited numerous periodicals and translations and produced fifty-eight independent works, many of them multi-volumed and available in different editions in his lifetime.[8]

Lacking a systematic overview, subsequent commentators reconstructed Justi's ideas according to principles that were alien to his thinking. By contrast, this study aims to offer for the first time an in-depth exploration of Justi's life, his oeuvre, and that intellectual and historical environment in which he developed his ideas, demonstrating that Justi, rather like Sir James Steuart, was a political economist of considerable calibre whose ideas make full sense in their eighteenth-century context. This book sheds fresh light on Justi himself, but also aims to reassess the role of mid-eighteenth-century German intellectual achievements in the shaping of the European political economy in general.[9]

Previous scholarship saw Justi exclusively as a representative of Cameralism, defined as the specifically Austrian-German version of Mercantilism which had never been influenced by or had an impact on broader European intellectual discourse.[10] Only the late Ernest Lluch

8 Justi's last book, *Geschichte des Erdkörpers*, was finished only weeks before his death.

9 Apart from Albion Small's *The Cameralists – the Pioneers of German Social Polity* (Chicago: University of Chicago Press, 1909) and Keith Tribe's *Governing Economy* (1988), mid-eighteenth-century German political economy has remained 'virtually a lost chapter' in Anglo-American histories of the Enlightenment. Except for a brief passage from his *Steuern und Abgaben* in Monroe's *Selections from Economic Literature Prior to Adam Smith* (1927), Justi's writings are only available in German. Cf. Arthur Eli Monroe, *Early Economic Thought – Selections from Economic Literature Prior to Adam Smith* (Cambridge/Mass.: Harvard University Press, 1927), pp. 378–399.

10 Cf. Ingomar Bog, 'Mercantilism in Germany', in: D.C. Coleman (ed.), *Revisions in Mercantilism* (London: Methuen, 1969), pp. 162–189; Walter Braeuer, 'Kameralismus und Merkantilismus – ein kritischer Vergleich', *Jahrbuch für Wissenschaftsgeschichte* 1990, 107–111; Jutta Brückner, *Staatswissenschaften, Kameralismus und Naturrecht* (Munich: Beck, 1977); HansJoachim Braun, 'Economic Theory and Policy in Germany 1750–1800', *Journal of European Economic History* 4 (1975), 301–322; Erhard Dittrich, *Die deutschen und österreichischen Kameralisten* (Darmstadt: WBG, 1974); Thomas Riha, 'German Political Economy: The History of an Alternative Economics', *International Journal of Social Economics* 12 (1985), 2–25; Louise Sommer,

argued that Cameralism was in fact fully embedded in the wider European discussions of the time. Lluch maintained that it was inappropriate to explore eighteenth-century Austro-Prussian political economy under a nationally limited scope and to view it as the point of departure for distinctively 'German' modes of thinking in either economic thought (*Nationalökonomie*) or political theory (*Sonderweg*).[11] In so doing, he demolished the myth of the eighteenth-century 'Austrian-German' intellectual isolation, demonstrating that numerous translations made cameralistic works accessible to thinkers throughout the whole of Europe, including Adam Smith and Genovesi, and highlighted the key role that Austro-Prussian writings played in the formation of political and economic theories in eighteenth-century Russia and Spain.[12]

Lluch, however, was only concerned with the effects of Cameralism on other nations and wrote nothing about the influences operating in the opposite direction, i.e., the impact of contemporary European writings on mid-eighteenth-century German thinkers. In my analysis of Justi's political economy, I will make use of Lluch's comparative approach, but apply it in the opposite direction and explore the key role that contemporary foreign writings played in forming Justi's theoretical positions. In so doing, I intend to show how profoundly the

Die österreichischen Kameralisten in dogmengeschichtlicher Darstellung (Aalen: Scientia, 1967. Originally: Vienna, 1920); Mack Walker, 'Rights and Functions: The Social Categories of Eighteenth-Century German Jurists and Cameralists', *Journal of Modern History* 50 (1978), 234–251.

11 Ernest Lluch, 'Cameralism beyond the Germanic World: a Note on Tribe', *History of Economic Ideas* 5 (1997), 85–99. Lluch's findings rely on Kenneth E. Carpenter's *Dialogue in Political Economy – Translations from and into German in the 18th Century* (Boston: Baker Library, 1977).

12 Ernest Lluch, 'Der Kameralismus, ein vieldimensionales Lehrgebäude: Seine Rezeption bei Adam Smith und im Spanien des 18. Jahrhunderts', *Jahrbuch für Geschichte* 2000, 133–156. Justi's influence abroad is indeed impressive. The numerous translations of his works into French, Russian, Spanish, and Dutch give ample proof of the wide and immediate 'international' impact of his ideas, as do the reviews in the *Journal Encyclopédique*. The first obituary of Justi appeared in 1777 in a French journal (*Observations sur la physique, sur l'histoire naturelle, et sur les arts* 12 (1777), 323). See the bibliography at the end of this study.

narrow understanding of the term 'Cameralism' has handicapped past Justi scholarship. Although Justi was familiar with seventeenth-century German theorists like Seckendorff, Becher, Hörnigk, and Schröder, their significance for his intellectual formation was far less than has hitherto been assumed. Rather than viewing Justi as a quintessentially German thinker, I will argue that he was in fact firmly entrenched in the wider European intellectual context of the time and modelled his ideas primarily on those of contemporary west European, i.e., French and Anglo-Scottish, authors.

The attempts to position Justi on one side of a binary divide between Mercantilism and Liberalism have constituted another major handicap of previous studies.[13] Most modern analysts undertake a neat classification of economic thinkers prior to Adam Smith according to the degree to which these thinkers seem to have promulgated 'Smithian' doctrines, such as free trade and non-intervention by the state, and thus try to determine to what extent they contributed to a teleological movement in economic thought that culminated in the publication of *The Wealth of Nations* in 1776. As a result, secondary-literature assessments are often characterised by the hasty imposition of anachronistic labels on writers of the so-called pre-classical period, referring to them as either 'mature mercantilist' or 'early liberal' thinkers. Forcing Justi into either one of these frameworks is not satisfactory. Justi's political economy drew on an immense variety of (mostly French) sources and is far too multifaceted to be identified tidily with either one of these 'schools' of economic thought. In order to make sense of his writings and enable an adequate understanding of his views on issues such as state intervention or monopolies one needs to relate his analysis to the stage of economic development in Germany at the time he wrote and to the particular political situation of

13 Michael Sonenscher recently highlighted the problematic application of the term 'Mercantilism' to eighteenth-century economic realities: 'Fashion's Empire: Trade and Power in Early 18th-Century France', in: *Luxury Trades and Consumerism in Ancien Régime Paris: Studies in the History of the Skilled Workforce*, edited by Robert Fox and Anthony Turner (Aldershot: Ashgate Publishing, 1998), pp. 231–254 (p. 232).

Europe in the 1750s, rather than considering them to be analogous to Smithian or modern discussions of economic development.[14]

Justi's ultimate aim was to lower state intervention to a minimum, but non-interventionism was not an option in his own age. His analytical concepts, empirical generalisations, institutional assumptions, and policy prescriptions were designed for a particular phase of economic development in Germany that was marked by corporate privileges, institutional bottlenecks, and the absence of a large mercantile class. Most importantly, they were designed with an explicit political goal in mind: to close the gap between the German states and more advanced countries such as England, Holland, and France. To realise this ambitious goal, Justi accepted government intervention as an indispensable tool of transition. He focused on the way the state could help to abolish underdevelopment. Governmental authority was badly needed to enforce a greater liberation of domestic markets, which seemed a prerequisite of commercial success. Justi consequently devoted large portions of his writings to the specific ways of eliminating feudal constraints and moral prejudices against economic activity. As Hans Freudenberger remarked, government intervention was a tool 'to remove obstructions that traditional society had for decades and centuries created for itself'.[15]

Justi made a considerable effort to establish comprehensive rules and guidelines for public finance and governmental expenditures, and developed practical principles of modern administrative management. The focal point of his enquiries was the reform of the state itself. Justi

14 As Keith Tribe has complained, most historians of economics usually approach past thinkers by applying much the same analytical criteria to their writings 'as they would to modern publications – as if they were simply research papers published in modern journals with a readership composed of a community of scholars' (Tribe, *Governing Economy*, p. 7). For similar assessments see: Hubert C. Johnson, 'Theory of Bureaucracy in Cameralism', *Political Science Quarterly* 79 (1964), 378–402 (p. 378); Donald Winch, *Riches and Poverty. An Intellectual History of Political Economy in Britain, 1750–1834* (Cambridge: Cambridge University Press, 1996), p. 30.

15 Hermann Freudenberger, 'State Intervention as an Obstacle to Economic Growth in the Habsburg Monarchy', *Journal of Economic History* 27 (1967), 493–509 (p. 496).

was convinced that the transition from a traditional society, with its strict hierarchy of ranks, into a modern commercial society was impossible without substantial political change. Assuming a clear-cut separation between his economic and political ideas, previous commentators failed to see that for Justi, as for Montesquieu, Hume or Smith, politics and economics were tightly intertwined and mutually dependent features that could not be studied in isolation from each other. By contrast, this study demonstrates that in concentrating on the question of how governmental institutions could best facilitate the transition from pre-market to market societies, Justi addressed both a political *and* an economic problem.

In the literature, Justi's political theory is invariably misunderstood. The question of what was his preferred form of government has been a constant object of dispute which has produced two opposing interpretations: scholars were unable to decide whether Justi was a blind defender of unlimited monarchical power or, quite the contrary, whether he was a proto-democratic thinker who demanded popular participation in governmental affairs.[16] Scholars critical of enlightened absolutism took Justi's support to it as a proof of a distinctively German, authoritarian and anti-democratic attitude to politics and labelled

16 Albion Small denied that a final answer to the question could be found. In his view, Justi's eclectic political views did not indicate a clear preference for a particular form of government. Small remarked that it 'would be easy to cull out of Justi's books sentences, from which we might infer that he was, in the last analysis, a full-fledged democrat' while such inference would 'be as unwarranted as the contrary conclusion' that Justi 'manifested no democratic opinions or sympathies' at all (Small, *The Cameralists*, p. 401). According to Small, Justi's judgement of political ends, for instance, read 'almost like fundamental democracy'. On the other hand, he believed that if Justi's passages on the English constitution 'were read without checking them up by the rest of his political philosophy, the conclusion would be necessary that he was in favour of a form of government more like that of England in the Victorian period than that of the Stuarts'. Then again, Small pointed out, Justi explicitly praised enlightened absolutism in numerous other passages as the most effective form of government.

thinkers like him intellectual forerunners of the German *Sonderweg.*[17] Especially for those historians

> whose consciousness was formed during or soon after World War II, when the aftermath of the fascist nightmare and the growth of Communist totalitarianism made it extremely difficult to find any form of authoritarianism palatable, the role ascribed to governmental benevolence in eighteenth-century apologies for absolutism seemed highly dubious.[18]

The opposing view holds that Justi is best seen as a full-fledged liberal and a daring intellectual pioneer of the modern republican regime whose ultimate aim was to overcome traditional monarchical rule.[19]

This study refutes both these interpretations and argues instead for a more differentiated view of Justi's political theory. Recent supporters of the proto-democratic position have based their stance on a terminological misunderstanding. They quoted Justi's dual use of the term 'republic' (*Republik*) for both proper republics (*eigentliche Republiken*) and monarchies (*Republiken*) in support of their claim of his crypto-republican attitude. But Justi's use of the term 'republic' did not have an anti-monarchical connotation. Quite the contrary, by extending the use of the term 'republic' also to monarchical regimes Justi aimed to highlight his conception of a modern monarchy against earlier views that portrayed the king as 'possessing' the state (*dominium imminens*) or as being justified in pursuing private ends that went contrary to the welfare of the people. He thus attempted to

17 Leonard Krieger, An Essay on the Theory of Enlightened Despotism (Chicago and London: The University of Chicago Press, 1975); Harm Klueting, *Die Lehre von der Macht der Staaten: das außenpolitische Machtproblem in der 'politischen Wissenschaft' und in der praktischen Politik im 18. Jahrhundert* (Berlin: Duncker & Humblot, 1986).

18 Charles W. Ingrao, 'The Problem of "Enlightened Absolutism" and the German States', *Journal of Modern History* 58 (1986), 161–180 (p. 168).

19 Marcus Obert, *Die naturrechtliche 'politische Metaphysik' des Johann Heinrich Gottlob von Justi (1717–1771)* (Frankfurt/M.: Lang, 1992); Uwe Wilhelm, 'Das Staats- und Gesellschaftsverständnis von J.H.G. von Justi: ein Beitrag zur Entwicklung des Frühliberalismus in Deutschland', *Der Staat* 20 (1991), 234–251; Thomas Würtenberger, 'An der Schwelle zum Verfassungsstaat', *Aufklärung* 3 (1988), 53–88.

underline the obligation of the prince to further popular welfare (*salus populi suprema lex*) and to reinforce the view that the ruler was not allowed to pursue interests different from those of the nation at large.

Justi left no doubt as to his firm inclination towards monarchical government, provided it was modernised and transformed. In his earliest works, *Kurzer systematischer Grundriss* and *Staatswirtschaft*, Justi had not even been concerned with extensive discussions of the particular advantages or disadvantages of other governmental regime-types. Although he mentioned the mixed English constitution positively within them, he stressed that he had written both works under the explicit presupposition of an absolute monarchy:[20] and in subsequent treatises he had absolute monarchies in mind. It was not until *Der Grundriss einer guten Regierung* and *Natur und Wesen der Staaten*, that Justi – under the influence of Montesquieu and other French thinkers – started to discuss the institutional nature of proper republics (democracies and aristocracies) in detail. Yet proper republics (*eigentliche Republiken*) were, in Justi's view, small city states in the tradition of ancient Greek poleis whose complex constitutional arrangements could not be enforced by the larger territorial states of Europe. Among 'all the weak and fragile edifices of civil constitutions that have been erected by man' monarchy always remained Justi's preferred form of government.[21]

Justi's theory of modern kingship must be understood against his perception of French reform debates over absolutism, and particularly against his reading of Montesquieu's *The Spirit of the Laws*. Viewed from such an angle it is evident that, contrary to the claims of the *Sonderweg* view, Justi was highly sensitive to the necessity of limiting central monarchical power through constitutional safeguards. Justi's principal political problem was how to centralise power in modern monarchical government so effectively that the threat of despotism could be avoided.[22] His model of modern monarchy was designed to

20 *Staatswirtschaft* I, Preface.

21 *Vergleichungen*, p. 333.

22 Justi was a harsh critic of contemporary princely rule. Throughout numerous grim polemics, which are among the strongest and most original passages of his oeuvre, he portrayed the horrors and dangers of despotism. Due to the exces-

avoid French policy mistakes of the past such as Louis XIV's ruinous bellicosity and the financial mismanagement of the public debt under the Regency. By developing an updated French model of monarchy for the German states Justi hoped that they could escape the failures that bedevilled the history of France.

Justi considered a systematic reform from above as the most suitable means to accomplish the swift transformation of the German states. Influenced by Haugwitz's centralising reforms in Austria, he became an ardent proponent of the modernisation of government. Justi opposed Montesquieu's way of reforming the monarchy which envisaged a revival of aristocratic power.[23] He put no faith in the intermediary power of the nobility and the Estates summits and wanted to replace them by meritocratic schemes of representation. Equally, he saw the need for a profound reorganisation of the role and functions that the monarch and his ministers performed in the new central administration. His proposals for improved royal education and the creation of departmental councils were designed to guarantee governmental moderation. By putting a definite end to princely arbitrariness Justi believed his model of modern monarchy could enable the German states to catch up with their more developed Western rivals.

In the following chapters Justi's ideas are explored from different angles. In the next chapter, I present essential information about Justi's life, his oeuvre, and that intellectual and historical context in which he developed his ideas, identifying those authors who were

sively narrow textual focus of the studies of Obert and Wilhelm, such passages have led to an erroneous assumption that Justi rejected monarchy as such, although it is obvious that his criticism merely served to bolster his advocacy of a reformed modern commercial monarchy that granted civil liberty and economic advancement.

23 Recent analyses of Justi's political thought falsely believed that only minor, trivial disagreements existed between Justi's positions and those of his French counterpart (e.g. Frank Herdmann, *Montesquieurezeption in Deutschland im 18. und 19. Jahrhundert* (Hildesheim: Olms, 1990)). In contrast to this, Justi's contemporaries, like Heinrich Godfried Scheidemantel (the editor of the second edition of *Natur und Wesen der Staaten* in 1771) were fully aware that Justi 'refuted Montesquieu' (*Natur und Wesen*, p. 173, note by Scheidemantel).

most influential in his thinking. The third chapter focuses on the European power struggle of the 1750s as the principal driving force behind Justi's theoretical enquiries. I discuss Justi's post-Machiavellian vision of foreign policy and his polemics against the doctrine of the balance of power because they epitomise his vision of the interrelations between economic advancement and international political standing.

The fourth and fifth chapters offer a detailed analysis of Justi's theory of modern kingship. Throughout them, I explain how Justi tried to secure modern monarchy effectively against both princely and ministerial despotism by ascribing new roles to the aristocracy, the prince, and the administrative apparatus. In the final chapter, I turn to Justi's ideas on economic policy and commercial advancement in agriculture, industry, manufactures, domestic and foreign trade, demonstrating how his economic thought relates to, and depends on, his own political model of modern monarchy.

Chapter Two
Justi's life and oeuvre

Justi developed his ideas in a time of dramatic change that was dominated by the European power struggle that followed the War of the Austrian Succession (1748) and was reignited with the Seven Years War (1756–63). The aim of this chapter is to explore Justi's historical and intellectual surroundings and to establish what impact they had on his thinking. The poor quality of existing accounts of his life renders this undertaking particularly important. The disappearance of Justi's papers makes it almost impossible to establish the precise array of his personal contacts and the influence they might have had in stimulating or nourishing his ideas. From the appearance of the first obituary in the *Observations sur la physique, sur l'historie naturelle et sur les arts* in 1777 right up to the first serious biography by Frensdorff (1903) gossip about Justi's private life occupied his biographers more than a serious exploration of the few facts that are definitively known about him.[1]

Before Frensdorff, writers on Justi mostly subscribed to Friedrich Nicolai's verdict that Justi was nothing more than an 'academic adventurer' (*gelehrter Abenteurer*) whose unsteady, hectic, and profoundly 'unscholarly' life was of a piece with his confused, eclectic writings.[2] As a result, Justi appears as a somewhat eccentric figure in the history of German political and economic thought. The vague, yet thoroughly pejorative and moralistic tone of earlier accounts of Justi's life rendered a proper exploration of his thought impossible.

1 Ferdinand Frensdorff, *Über das Leben und die Schriften des Nationalökonomen J.H.G. von Justi* (Glashütten: Auvermann, 1970. Originally: Göttingen, 1903).

2 Previous accounts portrayed in great detail Justi's divorce from his first wife in Göttingen and concentrated on highly uncertain incidents, like Justi's alleged imprisonment in Württemberg in 1757 (after having criticised the local Duke's monetary policy in his writings). This incident seems to have been invented after Justi's death.

Although Frensdorff disproved some of the more ridiculous and erroneous claims and discovered new details in hitherto unaccessed archival material, he was nevertheless unable to shed fresh light on key periods of Justi's life, in particular his stays in Vienna and Denmark. By and large, Frensdorff reinforced the standard image of Justi's 'puzzling and adventurous life' that seemed to disqualify him as a serious thinker. He also failed to investigate intellectual influences on Justi and concluded that his life remained wrapped in obscurity and intrigue. Thus the standard preconception of Justi as a confused graphomaniac survived up to to the present day.

In contrast to these assessments, I want to suggest that there was nothing dramatically unusual about Justi's lifestyle, and that it was far less confused than hitherto assumed. I divide Justi's biography into four periods: first, his youth and early literary activities in Dresden up to the move to Vienna in 1750; second, the formative years in Austria up to the publication of the *Staatswirtschaft* in 1755; third, the highly productive eight years up to 1763 which saw the publication of his mature works on political economy; and last, the final years of his life in the Prussian service. I will focus especially on the two middle periods.

Youth and early literary activities

Justi was born in 1717 in the village of Brücken in Thuringia. Not much is known about the first twenty-four years of his life except that he received his education at the nearby *Gymnasium* in Quedlinburg.[3] In 1741–42, at the beginning of the War of the Austrian Succession, he served in the Saxon Army as secretary to lieutenant colonel Wiegand Gottlob von Gersdorff. According to Justi, it was Gersdorff

3 The rediscovered church register in Brücken shows that Justi was baptised on 28 December 1717. It disproved the long-held assumption – still to be found in numerous publications and library catalogues – that Justi was born in 1720 (cf. Frensdorff, *Über das Leben und die Schriften*, p. 21).

who first turned his mind towards literature and academic studies. Gersdorff became Justi's patron and granted him generous financial support for studying law at Wittenberg University between 1742 and 1744. Justi graduated with a dissertation on the law of military desertion and then returned to be private secretary to Gersdorff. The colonel, however, was killed shortly afterwards in the battle of Hohenfriedberg (4 June 1745).[4] After Gersdorff's death Justi settled as a freelance writer and journalist in Dresden where he began to edit his first monthly periodical, the *Ergetzungen der vernünftigen Seele*, and published his first book, *Die Dichterinsel*, 'a combination of *Utopia* and satire feebly resembling Swift's *Gulliver*'.[5] The novel met with favourable reviews, one of them by Gottsched.[6] Two years later, Justi moved to Sangerhausen where he settled as a lawyer and became legal advisor to the court of Saxe-Eisenach. As noble status was crucial in his profession, Justi decided to adopt the title of 'von' Justi. This was by no means an unusual move for ambitious young men at the time.

While at Sangerhausen, Justi first achieved moderate fame when his attack on Leibniz, entitled *Invalidity and Falseness of the Monads* (1747) won the essay-prize of the Prussian Academy.[7] In the ensuing controversy Justi defended his essay against Gottsched and Wolff. Wolff in particular called Justi a 'shameless rabble-rouser' (*unverschämter Rabulist*). According to Wolff, Justi owed the Prussian Aca-

4 *De fuga militiae* (Wittenberg: Johann Friedrich Schlomach, 1745). Justi returned to the issue in later writings. Cf. 'Von den Ursachen und Bestrafungen der Desertion', in: *Gesammelte Schriften* I, 192–198.

5 Albion Small, *The Cameralists – the Pioneers of German Social Polity* (Chicago: Chicago University Press, 1909), p. 287. *Ergetzungen der vernünftigen Seele aus der Sittenlehre und der Gelehrsamkeit überhaupt* (6 vols; Leipzig: Bernhard Christoph Breitkopf, 1745–1748). *Die Dichterinsul nach ihren verschiedenen Landschaften und denen darinnen befindlichen Städten und Einwohnern sowohl als nach dererselben Gottesdienst, Staats- und Kriegsverfassung unpartheyisch beschrieben benebst einem Lob- und Heldengedichte* (Leipzig und Wittenberg: Johann Friedrich Schlomach, 1745).

6 Beatrice Roesch-Wanner, *J.H.G. von Justi als Literat* (Frankfurt/M.: Lang, 1993), p. 13f.

7 *Dissertation qui a remporté le prix proposé par l'Academie royale sur le système des monades avec le pièces qui ont concouru* (Berlin: A. Haude and J.C. Spener, 1748).

demy's decision solely to the famous mathematician Euler, who was widely known for his hostility to Wolffian philosophy.[8] Indeed, Euler, Maupertius, and Merian, the Newtonians in the Academy, were Justi's greatest supporters. The heated discussions over the subject lasted for nearly a year during which, according to a contemporary testimony, 'everybody at court and in the city of Berlin talked about nothing else but monads'.[9]

Move to Vienna

His growing reputation helped Justi in establishing contact with the man who effectuated his sudden move to Vienna in early 1750: Count Frederick William von Haugwitz. Haugwitz's importance for Justi can hardly be overestimated. Justi became private tutor to Haugwitz's eleven-year-old son Otto Carl.[10] Through his acquaintance with the Austrian minister he came into direct contact with the immense challenge that the European power struggle posed to contemporary governments, particularly to the Habsburg monarchy as the most backward of the great monarchies in Europe. It was his encounter with Haugwitz that turned Justi away from literary and juridical pursuits and towards political and economic questions.

Justi arrived in Vienna in early 1750 following Haugwitz's 'revolution' of 2 May 1749, the so-called 'first great administrative reform' of Maria Theresa's reign. Carried out 'almost as a *coup d'état*' after the end of the War of the Austrian Succession by the Empress, her husband, and a handful of close advisers headed by

8 Frensdorff, *Über das Leben und die Schriften*, p. 374.

9 Hans-Heinrich Müller, *Akademie und Wirtschaft im 18. Jahrhundert: agrarökonomische Preisaufgaben und Preisschriften der Preussischen Akademie der Wissenschaften* (Berlin: Akademie-Verlag, 1975), p. 85f.

10 Justi had secured his post as private tutor to Haugwitz's son probably before leaving Sangerhausen.

Haugwitz, the changes aimed at a speedy and unprecedented centralisation of monarchical power in Austria and Bohemia.[11]

Haugwitz's reforms were a direct response to Austria's defeat in the Silesian Wars and were designed to support Habsburg aspirations to survive as a major power. The rude shock of the Prussian invasion in the Silesian Wars and the threat of collapse to which the Habsburg Monarchy had been exposed had strengthened Maria Theresa's determination to carry out the radical administrative reforms proposed to her by Haugwitz. The principal aim was to seize political and financial control from the Estates and unite them under a Prussian-style royal administration that endowed the ruler with greater control.

In Austria, the central government departments looked after provincial interests, and, while they quarrelled with each other, both united against the revenue claims of the *Hofkammer*. In many cases, the Estates simply bribed ministers to get what they wanted. As a result, the *Länder* enjoyed practical autonomy.[12] The administrative chaos with the Estates, the impotent *Hofkammer*, ministers protecting their own *Länder*, and the continuous quarrels between the different departments repeated itself on the economic level, where

> parochial guild practices, highly localised to a town or county, contended with central governments that were grappling with national budgetary problems, striving for greater planning efficiency and already taking on some of the features of modern economies.[13]

11 Detailed information on the reforms by Haugwitz is given in: P.G.M. Dickson, *Finance and Government under Maria Theresia* (2 vols; Oxford: Clarendon Press, 1987), particularly I, 222–232 and II, 1–35; Hans Haussherr, *Verwaltungseinheit und Resorttrennung vom Ende des 17. bis zum Beginn des 19. Jahrhunderts* (Berlin: Akademiverlag, 1953); Friedrich Walter, *Die theresianische Staatsreform von 1749* (Vienna: Verlag für Geschichte und Politik, 1958).

12 'The royal writ ran in the Bohemian lands only if the *Obrist-Kanzler* approved. The Austrian lands virtually governed themselves. Hungarians, despised as rebels, were excluded from the ministry' (Dickson, *Finance and Government*, II, 3).

13 Eva Balázs, *Hungary and the Habsburgs 1765–1800. An Experiment in Enlightened Absolutism*, translated by Tim Wilkinson (Budapest: Central European University Press, 1997), p. 7.

The absence of financial data and of government statistics on population, foreign trade, and social structure dangerously weakened the monarchy in an age of growing international competition.

To address these issues Haugwitz had already drafted a kind of master plan for a unitary body of control in his memorandum 'Fernere ohnmassgebliche Gemüthsmeinung' in December 1747. He had put his emphasis less on the reduction of the role of the Estates than on the necessity of procuring a much higher *Contribution* (military tax) for defence purposes even in peacetime. Haugwitz argued that a dramatic revenue increase was vital for the future survival of the Habsburg Empire. Otherwise, he warned, Bohemia and Moravia would soon be lost to Prussia just as Silesia had been. Haugwitz calculated that a peacetime army of 108,000 men in the central lands would cost no less than 15m florins a year.[14] This sum stood in remarkable contrast to the mere 9m florins in total that had been raised in 1743.[15]

According to Haugwitz, a reform of the central financial administration was the key to solving the revenue problem. In his view, the antiquated provincial administrative apparatuses 'constituted an internal enemy fully as dangerous to the Crown as the more obvious enemies without'.[16] If the Estates were excluded from political and financial administration in all provinces, a substantial increase of revenue could be expected. His plans met with open hostility in parts of the Viennese administration, particularly in the Estates-loyal *Hofkanzlei*. The Bohemian Chancellor Count Friedrich Harrach responded to Haugwitz's ideas with a powerful and clever counter-memorandum. Although he agreed with Haugwitz's demand that the military budget needed to be dramatically increased, his plan differed on the question of how these additional sums could be raised. Harrach wanted to leave responsibility for fiscal administration with the Estates. His plan 'put maximum fiscal power into the hands of the Bohemian and Austrian

14 In addition to this, a further 50,000 troops were to be stationed in the Austrian Netherlands and Italy, paid by increased budgets there.

15 The financing of the enhanced sums for the military had become even more difficult in the Habsburg territories since Silesia as one of the major contributors to the royal exchequer had been lost to Frederick.

16 Dickson, *Finance and Government*, I, 223.

Estates, at a time when Haugwitz and the Empress were determined to reduce their independence'.[17]

The struggle between Harrach and Haugwitz was decided in favour of the latter at the memorable Privy Conference (*Kronrat*) of 29 January 1748. Despite the resistance of most of her ministers, Maria Theresa was resolute in her approval of Haugwitz's plans. In an emotional account of the session in her memoir of 1750, the Empress freely expressed her anger and frustration at the spirit of particularism in her *Länder* and severely criticised the narrow-minded attachment of the landed aristocracy to their local regions. She directly blamed the military debacles of the 1740s on the Estates.[18]

Haugwitz was ordered to negotiate ten-year agreements (*Decennal Recesse*) with Bohemia and Lower, Upper, and Inner Austria for a new military tax.[19] Chaired by Haugwitz, a *Hauptdeputation* was established in 1748 that had jurisdiction over all the central lands outside those of the Hungarian Crown. Its principal task was to administer financial contributions and supervise the activities of the local *Deputationen*, which were set up simultaneously in Bohemia and the Austrian *Länder*. These committees reported directly to the *Hauptdeputation* and were charged with oversight of military supply, troop movements, and garrisoning, with the assessment and collection of the *Contribution*, and with cameral revenue.

Although the *Hauptdeputation* had effectively strengthened the central government in giving it direct control over military taxes for the first time, its creation presented only a preliminary arrangement, which required further institutional reforms if it was to become a

17 Dickson, *Finance and Government*, II, 13.

18 *Politische Testamente*, edited by Josef Kallbrunner (Vienna: Verlag für Geschichte und Politik, 1952), p. 49. Maria Theresa put complete confidence in Haugwitz. A native of the now conquered part of Silesia he had, in Maria Theresa's words: 'Out of loyalty and faith left everything in Silesia and stood by me in evil times.' Uprooted, thrown completely upon the mercy of the court at Vienna for his success in life, he was an ideal civil servant. 'He was', wrote Maria Theresa, 'truly sent to my Providence.'

19 Contrary to this, only three years could initially be obtained in Styria and Krain. Carinithia even refused any form of agreement, whereupon Maria Theresia simply imposed the new tax-rate there *jure regio*.

permanent institution. In a memorandum drawn up in the autumn of 1748, Haugwitz reminded the Empress that further steps were needed to curb the influence of the Estates-dominated *Hofkanzlei*, which still operated as a significant counterweight to the *Hauptdeputation*. The coexistence of these institutions, he maintained, hampered the prompt execution of orders and endangered the reforms made so far.

Haugwitz's ideas formed the theoretical background for the reforms on 2 May 1749. In a series of royal *Handbilleten*, Maria Theresa announced the unification of political (*brachium*) and financial (*cameralia*) power under a central council. These steps were taken by right of royal prerogative, without consulting the Estates or the ministers concerned. The Austrian and Bohemian chancelleries were dissolved and their judicial responsibilities transferred to a new central High Court, the *Oberste Justizstelle*. The fiscal and political autonomy of the Austrian and Bohemian *Länder* was united under the central administration of the newly established *Conferenz in Internis* which replaced the *Hauptdeputation*.[20]

The *Conferenz in Internis* was obviously intended by Haugwitz and the Empress as

> a forum in which royal will, intent on reforming finance, the army, education, the law, economic life, even the church, could be deployed against the forces of conservatism and resistance, both at the centre and provincially [...] In this way, the reassertion of monarchical power which both of them saw as essential to Austrian survival, and revival, was meant to acquire institutional force.[21]

As purely monarchical apparatuses, in which the Estates had no voice, the representatives and chambers on regional level were directly

20 The *Conferenz* was serviced by a *Directorium in Publicis et Cameralibus*, with Haugwitz as president. Despite the formally superior standing of the *Conferenz in Internis*, real power immediately passed into the hands of the *Directorium in Publicis et Cameralibus*. Since the *Conferenz* was an advisory council that lacked executive power and discussed only those issues that had been prepared in advance by the *Directorium*, Haugwitz was effectively in charge of affairs. Even though the former president of the Bohemian chancellery and old rival of Haugwitz, Count Harrach, was made first councillor of the *Conferenz*, the latter was *de facto* deprived of all power.

21 Dickson, *Finance and Government*, I, 225.

subordinated to the council.[22] By abandoning the distinction between royal and Estates-governed finance these steps upset the traditional balance of power between prince and Estates in favour of the crown. As levying direct and indirect taxes became the task of the central government, the near-monopoly of the Estates in matters of taxation was broken. And even though Haugwitz's demands to abolish the *Hofkammer* and make financial control entirely unitary in the Habsburg lands were not realised, the reformed state subsequently proved more capable of supporting Austrian aspirations as a great power and her aim of competing with the modern economies of England, Holland, and France.

Intimately acquainted with the reforms and driven by the hope of a permanent post, Justi was eager to demonstrate his skills to Haugwitz and other Viennese officials in a couple of political and alchemical pamphlets published in the first half of 1750. Haugwitz (who had little time for purely theoretical considerations) took a particular liking to him. The writings show that Justi had fully grasped the fundamental economic dilemma of the Habsburg monarchy, being a backward agrarian society with traditional pretentions to 'great-power' status, yet lacking a strong economic footing and the effective administrative system that its competitors elsewhere in Europe were developing.

Justi's 1750 writings dealt with Austrian domestic economic advancement and Habsburg political interests. In *Das entdeckte Geheimnis der neuen Sächsischen Farben*, Justi presented a scientific discovery which could help boost the underdeveloped domestic economy of the Habsburg territories. Justi claimed he had invented a cheap artificial substitute for indigo that he was ready to sell to the Viennese administration. In his essay entitled *Von denen Materien zu dem unechten Porcellan* he announced he had found a new formula for the production of china that would be cheap enough to serve the

22 The provincial *Deputationen*, which answered to the *Conferenz*, and oversaw financial and army affairs locally, were renamed *Repräsentationen und Cammern*, an example of Haugwitz's penchant for neologism.

ever-growing needs of the middle class.[23] Justi was also keen to demonstrate his political and juridical expertise. In his pamphlet *Abtretung eines Reichs-Lehns*, he vehemently defended Austrian claims over those Italian possessions (Parma, Piacenza, Guatalla) that had been handed over to the Infante Don Philip of Spain, the son of King Philip V, in the Peace Treaty of Aachen in 1748.[24] In so doing, he tried to lend support to the official court position that Parma, Piacenza, and Guatalla had remained fiefs of the Holy Roman Empire and so had stayed formally under the supreme legal dominion of imperial rule. Justi's writings had the intended effect. A suitable post for him was soon found in an area that had received growing attention during the reforms initiated by Haugwitz: the education of civil servants.

The *Theresianum* Academy and its sister institution, the Savoy Knights Academy – soon to be followed by the Diplomatic Academy in 1754 – had been established in 1746 and 1749 respectively for the purpose of training civil servants of noble descent.[25] The *Theresianum* was primarily designed for sons of the Hungarian aristocracy. By 1750, the Viennese authorities (and Haugwitz in particular) had become painfully aware that both acquaintance with the German language as an efficient instrument of administrative communication as well as a rudimentary understanding of financial and economic issues had become key qualifications for future civil servants.[26] In-

23 *Das entdeckte Geheimnis der neuen Sächsischen Farben benebst einigen Betrachtungen von dem Vorzug und der Theorie dieser neuen Färbekunst* (Vienna: Kraus, 1750). 'Von denen Materien zu dem unechten Porcellan', in: *Gesammmelte chymische Schriften*, I, 321–332.

24 *Abhandlung von der Abtretung eines Reichs-Lehns in den Frieden mit auswärtigen Mächten worinnen zugleich erwiesen wird, dass die Herzogthuemer Parma, Placenc und Guatalla, ohngeachtet der in dem Aachischen Frieden an den Durchl. Infant Don Philipp beschehenen Abtretung, annoch wirkliche Reichs-Lehen sind* (Frankfurt/Leipzig/Nuremberg: Peter Conrad Monath, 1750).

25 Cf. Eugen Guglia, *Das Theresianum in Wien: Vergangenheit und Gegenwart* (Vienna: Böhlau, 1996).

26 It was recognised that a unified style and usage of German in the Habsburg territories would support the centralising aims of Haugwitz's reforms. This attitude is best reflected in a royal decree of 1752 that ordered the diploma for

fluenced by similar contemporary endeavours, such as Johann Jakob Moser's state and chancellor academy in Hanau (founded in 1749) and, once again, Prussia – where Frederick William I had created university chairs for Cameral Sciences in Halle and Frankfurt an der Oder as early as in 1727 – Haugwitz was determined to implant German rhetoric and modern economic thought at the *Theresianum.*[27] Count Khevenhüller, the curator of the *Theresianum*, shared Haugwitz's views and suggested in an address of 10 August 1750 the appointment of a professor 'who not only teaches the adult youth a pure German writing-style, but also instructs them in composing reports in a concise, clear, and orderly manner'. Khevenhüller pointed out that as part of a newly established course called *Collegium Oeconomicum-Provinciale* this professor would also need to lecture on public finance and general economics.[28]

With Haugwitz's personal protection and the favourable reception of his recent publications, Justi was tailor-made for the post. On August 23, he was appointed professor at the *Theresianum*. Although Justi was keen in later years to lay emphasis on his Protestant faith, he must have converted to Catholicism before taking up his professorship.[29] On November 16 Justi delivered his inaugural lecture under the title *Rede von dem unzertrennlichen Zusammenhang eines blühenden Zustandes der Wissenschaften mit denjenigen Mitteln, welche einen Staat mächtig und glücklich machen* (*On the inextricable link between the flourishing of science and the means that render a state powerful and happy*) which he organised around the pressing issues of the day:

promotions of rank in both the Austrian and Bohemian lands to be henceforth composed in German according to a standard scheme.

27 Johann Stephan Pütter's sketch from 1749 for an academic curriculum in public law at the University of Göttingen and Georg Heinrich Zincke's 'Gedancken und Vorschläge von einem auf Universitäten auf die Cameral-Wissenschaften einzureichtenden besondern Collegio Statuum Europae Camerali' (*Leipziger Sammlungen* 3 (1746), 941ff.) had a similar aim.

28 Quoted from: Hans Haussherr, *Verwaltungseinheit und Resorttrennung vom Ende des 17. bis zum Beginn des 19. Jahrhundert* (Berlin: Akademieverlag, 1953), p. 80.

29 To be admitted to a governmental post in Austria, Protestants were required by a decree to take a form of oath that went against their religion (Balàzs, *Hungary and the Habsburgs*, p. 41).

the achievement of great-power status, economic advancement, and the implementation of administrative reforms.[30]

Viennese reaction to his inaugural lecture was ambivalent. Judging from contemporary comments, Justi was anything but a gripping lecturer. In a letter to Gottsched, the Viennese poet and civil servant Franz Christoph Scheyb remarked that Justi had rushed through his lengthy manuscript and had barely been understandable to his audience. Scheyb acknowledged the quality of Justi's lecture; however, its impact would have been far greater had it been pre-circulated in a written form.[31] Hoping for such an impact, Justi published the lecture shortly afterwards.[32]

Haugwitz's ultimate intention was to complement Justi's rhetoric classes with economic and financial courses. As initially suggested by Khevenhüller, Justi was asked by Haugwitz to develop a detailed syllabus for a new course in economics and public finance at the *Theresianum*. He drew up a meticulously detailed plan for lectures on politics, administrative science, trade, manufacturing, public finance, and taxation, called *Kurzer systematischer Grundriss aller Öconomischen und Kameralwissenschaften*. For the first time, the *Kurzer systematischer Grundriss* reveals Justi's idea of a theoretical system of political economy. It prefigured the framework of the *Staatswirtschaft* and all of his subsequent publications. Greatly admired by Haugwitz and approved by the ministry on 26 June 1752, the *Kurzer systematischer Grundriss* served as the textbook for Justi's economic classes.

Haugwitz's high estimation of Justi was manifested in the latter's earnings. In addition to his initial salary of 1000 florins per year Justi was granted a further 500 florins on 1 November 1750 'because of his great commitment', and again a further 500 florins on 1 November of

30 *Rede von dem unzertrennlichen Zusammenhang eines blühenden Zustandes der Wissenschaften mit denjenigen Mitteln, welche einen Staat mächtig und glücklich machen* (Vienna: Johann Thomas Trattner, 1750). The lecture is reprinted in: *Gesammelte Schriften* II, 129–175.

31 Hilde Haider-Pregler, *Des sittlichen Bürgers Abendschule: Bildundgsanspruch und Bildungsauftrag des Berufstheaters im 18. Jahrhundert* (Vienna: Jugend und Volk, 1980), p. 406.

32 (Vienna: Joh. Thomas Trattner, 1750).

the following year. Within less than two years Justi had become one of the best-paid academics in Vienna.[33] In addition to his educational duties, Justi was asked by the Viennese authorities to prepare surveys on mining projects and studies on how to further sericulture in the Habsburg countries.[34] In his capacity as professor at the *Theresianum*, Justi was also appointed to the newly established censorship commission headed by Maria Theresa's close confidant and doctor, Gerhard van Swieten. The commission's task – previously carried out by the Jesuits – was to determine which foreign books were to be allowed a free circulation in Austria.

Notwithstanding his success and personal contact with the two most influential men in Vienna at the time, Haugwitz and van Swieten, Justi soon became discontented with his post. The constraints imposed upon his teaching by the governmental authorities were the first setback in his hitherto mercurial rise. Justi's plan to extend his teaching from theoretical to practical courses – as was customary at the faculties of Protestant universities – and thus combine theory and practice, teaching and research, brought him into conflict with Viennese officials. Justi had asked for access to registrars' offices and archives and planned to interview councillors and ministers. But the *Directorium* and the *Hofkommerzienrat* denied his request. In their view, the available economic data and the general process of policy- and decision-making, particularly in regard to taxation, were matters of too great importance to be communicated to a foreigner or divulged to students and the public. The science that Justi conceived was grounded in large-scale empirical investigation and local case studies. 'But this kind of information was considered top secret in view of the international competition and therefore was not available to him.'[35]

33 Gustav Marchet, *Studien über die Entwicklung der Verwaltungslehre in Deutschland* (Munich: Oldenbourg, 1885), p. 319.

34 One of these studies, entitled 'Explicit instruction in the cultivation of silkworms and the winning of silk for the Imperial-Royal hereditary lands', was later published in Justi's journal *Neue Wahrheiten*. His articles on sericulture were reviewed in: *Göttingische Anzeigen von gelehrten Sachen* (1754), 523 & (1756), 338f.

35 Grete Klingenstein, 'Between Mercantilism and Physiocracy – Stages, Modes, and Function of Economic Theory in the Habsburg Monarch', in: *Early Modern*

Justi was seriously upset by this rejection, which he perceived as an act of petty-mindedness. The incident coincided with further disappointments. Justi began to complain about his lack of authority at the *Theresianum* and lamented the meagre motivation of his twelve students who, judging from Scheyb's letters, 'do not listen to him, and can hardly wait for the end of the lesson'. According to Scheyb, they regarded Justi's lectures as artificial nonsense, showed him no respect and, in short, refused to learn from him.[36]

Further confrontation cropped up with the Jesuits. Though Justi befriended the reform-minded Jesuit Father Frantz who was in contact with members of the Jesuit mission to China and first drew his attention towards Du Halde's *History of China*, he was targeted by conservative hard-liners of the order.[37] As a recent convert Justi raised their suspicions. Moreover, as representative of the new 'godless' science of economics, Justi's lectures at the *Theresianum* painfully reminded the Jesuits of their waning influence over Austria's education system. The Jesuit director of the *Theresianum* attacked Justi's newly established *Collegium Oeconomicum-Provinciale* as superficial humbug. In his view, there was no real need for teaching the cameral and police sciences since 'Austria had been prosperous a long time without anything of that sort.' If people remained pious and said their prayers 'God will bless the country without such fuss.'[38] As a result, Justi felt more and more restricted in his academic and business endeavours. In later works he painfully recalled the hostile attitude of the

Austria, edited by Charles W. Ingrao (West Lafayette: Purdue University Press, 1994), pp. 181–214 (p. 196). Justi published his request for access to registars' offices and archives in 1754: *Auf höchsten Befehl an Sr. Röm. Kaiserl. und zu Ungarn und Böhmen Königl. Majestaet erstattetes allerunterthänigstes Gutachten von dem vernünftigen Zusammenhange und practischem Vortrage aller Öconomischen und Cameralwissenschaften* (Leipzig, 1754). Interestingly, Joseph von Sonnenfels quoted from Justi's earlier plea in 1765 when he sent an unsuccessful petition to Maria Theresa for the same purpose.

36 Haider-Pregler, *Des sittlichen Bürgers Abendschule*, p. 468.

37 Father Frantz first raised Justi's interest into this issue and helped him with his historical essay on the conjectural origin of the Hungarian nation.

38 *Grundriss*, p. 324.

Jesuits, whom he even accused of having ordered 'spies to watch and listen at the doors and windows of my lecture room'.[39]

The Jesuits' hostility was aggravated by Justi's strenuous advocacy of Montesquieu in the memorable battle over *The Spirit of the Laws* in the censorship commission. The fight is one of the rare cases in which the inner proceedings of the commission were laid open. In 1750, two years after its first publication, but before the reform of the censorship commission by van Swieten, *The Spirit of the Laws* was put on the index of prohibited books by the Viennese Jesuits. Montesquieu himself complained about what appeared to his eyes to be unfair treatment of his book in a letter to the imperial envoy, the Marquis of Stainville, on 27 May 1750. He blamed the Jesuits for the decision and accused them of trying to undercut the authority of the Viennese Court and abuse the reputation of the Empress for their own ends. But Montesquieu's complaint had no immediate effect.

In the aftermath of the Haugwitz reforms, however, the censorship regulations were altered. In the summer of 1751, the Jesuits were stripped of their censorship privileges and replaced by the commission under van Swieten. Van Swieten tried hard to keep the Jesuits out of the new council altogether, but Maria Theresa insisted on their presence. He managed nonetheless to weaken their influence significantly. The new commission was made up of nine members: three professors (among them, Justi), two jurists, a representative of the archbishop, two Jesuits, and van Swieten himself. As a first step, van Swieten abolished the customary practice of assigning books to individual members and leaving it to their discretion whether to admit or prohibit their circulation. According to van Swieten's new regulation, arguments for and against a particular book now had to be discussed openly in one meeting and had to be followed by a majority vote on it in the next. In addition to this, van Swieten reserved for himself the veto on philosophical works while he transferred the veto rights for theological treatises from the Jesuits to the archbishop.

Thus equipped, van Swieten personally urged the reversal of a number of prior verdicts, particularly the prohibition of *The Spirit of the Laws*. Justi and his two professorial colleagues opted straightaway

39 *Staatswirtschaft* I, 119.

for an unrestricted authorisation of *The Spirit*. Van Swieten, the jurists, and the archbishop followed their recommendation. Because of 'ambiguous passages on the Christian faith' the two Jesuits, however, insisted on a restricted circulation among scholars and men of learning only. The conflict escalated due to a tactical move by the Jesuits. The Jesuits' provost nominated different censors for each meeting of the commission, so that the case had to be discussed anew each time. Thus the vote on *The Spirit* had to be constantly postponed. Van Swieten complained bitterly to the Empress. Ultimately, she forced the Jesuits to give a final statement on the subject. Urged by van Swieten she disregarded Jesuit opposition and personally decided the quarrel in favour of *The Spirit* in March 1753.[40] Well informed about the case by his friend in Vienna, the Abbé Guasco, Montesquieu welcomed the step and declared himself a 'veritable admirer' of van Swieten.[41]

The controversy over Montesquieu undermined Justi's position at the Jesuit-led *Theresianum*. As to many foreign visitors, Vienna must have seemed to him 'to be intellectually backward, stifled by Jesuit censorship and surfeited with religious observance'.[42] Justi's problems and frustrations were aggravated by the unsatisfactory course of his mining activities which threatened to destroy his reputation altogether. He raised great expectations about a silver mine next to the lower Austrian village of Annaberg, but the actual output proved to be much lower. Sensing disaster, Justi hastily sold his shares of the mining company back to the Empress and decided to turn his back on Austria. This departure, at some point in the second half of 1753, was sudden, as is shown by the fact that Justi was never formally dismissed from his chair at the *Theresianum*.

40 'Wegen dem Buch Esprit des Loix ist wegen selben nicht mehr zu reden in der Kommission und denen Buchführern zu erlauben, es zu verkaufen.' Quoted from: August Fournier, 'Gerhard van Swieten als Censor', *Sitzungsberichte der philosophisch-historischen Classe der k.k. Akademie der Wissenschaften in Wien* 84 (1876), 387–466 (p. 415).

41 Letter of March 5, 1753. Cf. Fournier, 'Gerhard van Swieten', p. 415, note 2; Grete Klingenstein, *Staatsverwaltung und kirchliche Autorität im 18. Jahrhundert* (Vienna: Verlag für Geschichte und Politik, 1970), p. 161.

42 Derek Beales, *Joseph II* (Cambridge: Cambridge University Press, 1987), p. 32.

In the next one and a half years Justi systematically digested his Viennese experience. He briefly settled in Mansfeld, Erfurt and Leipzig where he began to edit his new journal, the *Neue Wahrheiten*. A good deal of his time was spent preparing his grammatical and economic lectures for publication. In 1755, his guide for official letter-writing, entitled *Anweisung zu einer guten deutschen Schreibart*, and the economic treatise *Staatswirtschaft* appeared, both of which enjoyed considerable success as academic textbooks.[43]

Via Göttingen, Copenhagen, and Altona to Berlin (1755–1763)

Justi's rising reputation had not escaped the attention of the Hanoverian prime minister and Rector of the University of Göttingen, Baron von Münchhausen. In the summer of 1755, he appointed Justi as Director of Police and Royal British Mining Counsellor in Göttingen. The position allowed Justi to give private courses in his preferred subjects to students of the university. During the following two years, Justi lectured in Göttingen on the 'history of modern commerce', on agricultural issues and on *Polizeiwissenschaft*. He published his *Grundsätze der Polizeiwissenschaft* as a textbook for his Göttingen lectures in 1756. In addition to this, he offered personal tuition on economics and public finance to anyone interested. Justi also became member of the Academy of Sciences in Göttingen and in this capacity read and judged contributions to the competitions of the Academy.[44]

It was at this time that Justi started his systematic study of contemporary French works in the Göttingen library. In his new periodical, the *Göttinger Policey-Amts-Nachrichten*, Justi offered regular reviews of recent French works on literary, political, economic

43 In the same year, Justi also published a widely-noted treatise on coinage: *Entdeckte Ursachen des verderbten Münzwesens in Teutschland* (Leipzig: Bernhard Christoph Breitkopf, 1755).

44 Müller, *Akademie und Wirtschaft*, p. 73.

and agricultural issues.[45] Most importantly, Justi began his critical re-reading of Montesquieu. In order to develop his anti-Montesquieuian stand, he began to take up the arguments of Montesquieu's French opponents. Triggered by the 'renversement des alliances' between Austria and France in the same year, Justi swiftly adopted a decisively pro-English and pro-Prussian position in his political pamphlets, with which he first tried to please the Hanoverian, then the Prussian administration. Although he had won a considerable reputation by the mid 1750s, Justi apparently did not establish close contacts with his academic colleagues Johan Stephan Pütter (1725–1807) and Jacob Schmauss (1690–1757) in Göttingen, and it is doubtful whether his lectures exerted a lasting impact upon the further development of statistical studies and *Staatswissenschaften* within the university, as critics claim.[46] Such *ex post facto* assumptions rest on speculation rather than clear evidence. It seems that Justi remained an outsider ready to leave Göttingen at a moment's notice.

Justi must have heard of the ongoing discussions among Danish government officials about the great colonisation project in Jutland and sensed that his expertise might be welcome. Trouble with his professorial colleagues at the university and the divorce from his first

45 The translation of a French article on population in his periodical *Neue Wahrheiten* shows that Justi was an attentive reader of the *Journal Oeconomique* ('Ursachen der Bevölkerung und Entvölkerung von Deutschland', *Neue Wahrheiten* II, 8, 140ff. The original article had appeared in the *Journal Oeconomique* of October 1754). At about the same time Justi started a debate with Sussmilch about mortality rates in cities and rural areas (Frederick S. Crum, 'The Statistical Work of Sussmilch', *Publications of the American Statistical Association* 7 (1901), 1–46 (p. 44)).

46 Hans-Erich Bödeker, 'Das staatswissenschaftliche Fächersystem im 18. Jahrhundert', *Wissenschaften im Zeitalter der Aufklärung*, edited by Rudolf Vierhaus (Göttingen: Vandenhoeck & Ruprecht, 1985), pp. 143–162; '"Staatswissenschaften" and Political Economy at the University of Göttingen: the Scottish Influence', *Transactions of the Eighth International Congress on the Enlightenment* 3 (= *Studies on Voltaire and the Eighteenth Century* 305) (Oxford: The Voltaire Foundation, 1992), 1881–1884. Hans-Georg Herrlitz and Horst Kern (eds.), *Anfänge Göttinger Sozialwissenschaft: Methoden, Inhalte und soziale Prozesse im 18. und 19. Jahrhundert* (Göttingen: Vandenhoeck & Ruprecht, 1987), p. 79.

wife fostered his decision to leave. In early 1757 he sent several of his essays on agricultural reform to the Danish minister Count Bernstorff. Bernstorff's reaction was positive. Under the growing threat of a French occupation of Göttingen in July 1757, Justi accepted Bernstorff' s invitation and set out for Copenhagen.

Justi's task in Denmark was to determine whether the government's plan to reclaim the Jutlandic heath for agricultural purposes was feasible and, if so, develop proposals on how to carry it out in practice.[47] For this purpose, Justi travelled the peninsula widely in the following six months. In his final report (*Gutachten*) for the Danish government, drawn up immediately after his move to Altona (in close vicinity to Hamburg) in early 1758, Justi came to the devastating conclusion that in 'all states, in which agriculture flourishes, one has done the exact opposite of what is happening in Denmark'.[48] If, he argued, the Danish government really wanted to carry out the colonisation it would need to break radically with the existing agricultural practices in the country. Justi developed his ideas mainly along the lines of pre-physiocratic French works, such as Ange Goudar's *Les intérêts de la France mal entendus* (1756), which described English agricultural practices as exemplary. He demanded liberation for the future colonists from personal feudal servitude and from any form of corvée. Justi pointed out that only if the peasants actually owned their land they would contribute efficiently to the overall advancement of agriculture. For the colonisation process he also recommended avoiding all forms of common village property, and generally advised the government against the creation of villages as corporate entities. Ideally, the peasants would live scattered, each on their own modest parcels of land.

47 Justi's influence on the colonisation of Jutland is discussed in: Otto Clausen, *Chronik der Heide- und Moorkolonisation im Herzogtum Schleswig-Holstein (1760–1765)* (Husum: Husum Verlag, 1981) p. 19f; Wolfgang Prange, *Die Anfänge der großen Agrarreformen in Schleswig-Holstein bis um 1771* (Neumünster: Karl Wachholtz, 1971), pp. 465–467 and pp. 650–662.

48 *Alleruntertänigstes Gutachten wegen Anbauung der jütländischen Heiden* (Preface written in Altona, March 10, 1758), in: *Öconomische Schriften*, II, 246–310.

Justi was confident that the colonisation would be of great benefit to the Danish state if these guidelines were observed. The land was obviously fertile. As in his Viennese inaugural lecture, in his report Justi recurrently highlighted the political need for domestic economic advancement. Inner colonisation, he claimed, would surpass territorial enlargement through war. With the cultivation of the heath the Danish king could achieve a great conquest without bloodshed. Over 10,000 families could be settled. And although the state needed to raise a million florins for the colonisation project in advance, the initial investment would pay off soon. Even if the new subjects were granted a ten-year exemption, the monarch could tax them afterwards, so that the entire sum would be regained after a maximum of fifteen years. Justi's affirmative report positively influenced the government's decision in favour of the colonisation of the entire Cimbrian peninsula from Holstein to Jutland in the same year. In 1759, the Danish authorities started to seek colonists from the south of Germany, and within the following four years no less than 573 colonial farms were established.

Once settled in Altona, Justi began his seven-year-long efforts to attain Prussian employment – an aim that explains much of his activity as a pro-Prussian war pamphleteer. Shortly after his arrival he became acquainted with the Prussian envoy in Hamburg, Johann Julius von Hecht. Hoping for an official post or some other form of support, Justi started to negotiate with Hecht over an eventual move to Berlin. In his endeavours to join Prussian services Justi even turned down a Danish offer for an appointment as Norwegian Mining Officer in Bergen.[49] As Justi told Hecht in a letter dated 29 January 1758, he planned to buy an estate in the greater Berlin area on which he could make useful experiments and give an example of a 'perfect, English-style agriculture'.[50] Justi hoped for a Prussian offer, stressing in the

49 Georg-Christoph von Unruh, *Subjektiver Rechtsschutz und politische Freiheit in der vorkonstitutionellen Staatslehre Deutschlands* (Hamburg: Hansischer Gildenverlag, 1969), p. 11.

50 Mittenzwei, *Preussen nach dem Siebenjährigen Krieg. Auseinandersetzungen zwischen Bürgertum und Staat um die Wirtschaftspolitik* (Berlin: Akademie Verlag, 1979), p. 224.

letter that he would not be able to move without some form of financial support. Hecht recommended Justi in his regular reports to Berlin. On 20 March 1758 the Prussian minister Finkenstein answered Justi's requests. He asserted that the ongoing war did not allow for an appointment. However, once fighting had ended there would be good chances for attaining a post. In the meantime, Justi would be welcome to settle in Prussia at his own expense.

As no end to the war was in sight, Justi decided to stay in Altona for the time being. Lacking official employment, he produced an unprecedented literary oeuvre over the following five years.[51] He started with re-editing the *Staatswirtschaft*, whose first edition had sold out by the end of 1757. The second edition shows the strong influence of Montesquieu. Justi took up Montesquieu's distinction between republics, monarchies, and despotic states instead of sticking to the Aristotelian division of forms of government (into monarchy, aristocracy, and democracy) which he had used throughout the first edition. In Altona Justi also began his ambitious translation project of the *Arts et métiers* volumes of the *Encyclopédie*, and published the *Vollkommene Abhandlung von denen Manufakturen und Fabriken* which he had composed in the course of his journeys for the Danish government. In the following year Justi finished the initial volume of his 'mirror of princes' novel *Psammitichus* and, most importantly, published his first major political treatise, *Der Grundriss einer guten Regierung*, which contained a systematic dissection of Montesquieu's arguments in the *The Spirit of the Laws*. With his two famous war pamphlets *Die Chimäre des Gleichgewichts in Europa* and *Die Chimäre des Gleichgewichts der Handlung und der Seefahrt* he joined the greater European debate over the balance of power problem and the attainment of a stable peace in Europe.

Encouraged by the mathematician Leonard Euler in his hopes for an official position in Prussia, Justi moved to Berlin in the spring of 1760. Owing to his remarkable reputation, Justi, according to the otherwise hostile comments of Friedrich Nicolai, was received with great respect upon his arrival. Nonetheless, his efforts to find employ-

51 See Table 2. At that time, Justi possibly got to know the later Danish prime minister Struensee who lived in Altona.

ment still did not bear fruit. To save money, Justi settled in Bernau in the north of Berlin. During the following five years, he continued to live off his royalties and dedicated his time primarily to writing and carrying out all sorts of practical agricultural and chemical experiments. Justi finished the second volume of *Psammitichus*, published his other major treatise on politics, *Die Natur und das Wesen der Staaten*, as well as *Die Grundfeste*, a vastly expanded version of his *Grundsätze der Polizeiwissenschaft*. In addition to this, Justi reissued his earlier periodical articles in a number of essay collections and by compiling a dictionary of economics.[52] Commissioned by the Berlin authorities, he also composed several pro-Prussian war pamphlets as well as his famous anti-Saxon epistolary novel *Leben und Charakter des Grafen von Brühl*.[53]

In the following year, Justi gained notoriety among Berlin intellectuals with his sudden attack on Lessing's *Literaturbriefe*. Edited jointly with Thomas Abbt, Moses Mendelssohn and Friedrich Nicolai, Lessing's *Briefe, die neueste Literatur betreffend* was a moralizing weekly styled in the tradition of English journals like *The Spectator*. By 1761 it had won rapid acclaim for the unusual sharpness and wit of its articles on recent German literature. The clash was triggered by Abbt's devastating review of Justi's *Psammitichus*.[54] Abbt's critique was not wholly unjustified. From a literary critic's point of view, Justi's work is clearly anything but a masterpiece. In Abbt's eyes, Justi's attempt to excel in the genre of historical novel writing had thoroughly failed. According to him, Justi's painstaking endeavours to make the novel's plot appear historically accurate were ludicrous. The fictional character of the book, he maintained, was all too visible throughout. Nicolai himself referred to it as just another example of those 'miserable semi-novels' of the time.[55] It indeed makes more sense to view the book chiefly as a political and

52 *Gesammelte Schriften, Öconomische Schriften, Gesammelte chymische Schriften, Historische und juristische Schriften, Moralische und philosophische Schriften, Scherzhafte und satyrische Schriften.*

53 See the bibliography for a full list of Justi's pro-Prussian war pamphlets.

54 In letters 196 + 197 of part XII of the *Literaturbriefe*.

55 Friedrich Nicolai, 'Fortsetzung der Berliner Nachlese', *Neue Berlinische Monatsschrift* 2 (1802), 340–358 (p. 349).

economic treatise presenting Justi's ideas within the idealised, pseudo-historical framework of ancient Egypt, rather than as a work of literature. Justi himself may have sensed the literary shortcomings of the book. Yet this did not lessen his rage upon reading Abbt's review. Instead of writing a direct reply to Abbt, Justi decided in favour of a more subtle form of attack. Anxious to remind Frederick the Great of his presence (and unemployed status) in Berlin, he hastily composed a letter to the king, in which he complained bitterly about the journal's disrespectful tone, and boldly demanded its immediate prohibition.

In his letter, Justi of course cited reasons other than personal offence and professional advancement for addressing the king. Abbt's review, he briskly declared, had 'not the least influence' on his decision to raise objections against the *Literaturbriefe*.[56] As a patriotic citizen, however, he felt obliged to protest against the way that the Christian religion as well as works by Gottsched, Moser, Voltaire, Rousseau, and Frederick himself were ridiculed in the journal.[57] Since the king was away on campaign the letter did not reach Frederick, who might have treated it with greater indifference than his subordinate officials did. Struck by Justi's vastly exaggerated accusations, which implied a violation of existing censorship rights, they took the incident more seriously. Nicolai and Moses Mendelssohn were immediately interrogated, and the *Literaturbriefe* promptly banned. It took the authorities five days to work out that Justi's allegations were false and privately motivated. The episode was quickly resolved. By royal decree the *Literaturbriefe* were allowed publication again in the following week.

Shortly after the incident, Justi won the essay prizes of the Bavarian Academy of Sciences in both historical and philosophical classes, upon which the Academy's director Osterwald offered Justi

56 Nicolai, 'Fortsetzung der Berliner Nachlese', p. 347.

57 Justi's letter to Frederick the Great, dated 10 March 1761, is reprinted in: Gotthold Ephraim Lessing, *Briefe, die neueste Literatur betreffend*, edited by Wolfgang Bender (Stuttgart: Reclam, 1972), pp. 344–350. For the quarrel see also: Wolfgang Martens, 'Literatur und "Policey" im Aufklärungszeitalter. Aufgaben sozialgeschichtlicher Literaturforschung', *Germanisch-Romanische Monatsschrift* 31 (1981), 404–419; Richard Thiele, *Thomas Abbts Anteil an den Briefen, die neueste Literatur betreffend* (Halle, 1880).

the post of president of the institution, which carried an annual salary of 3000 florins. Still hoping for a permanent post in Berlin, however, Justi twice turned down the offer.[58] Justi instead used it as a means to press the Prussian government to employ him. In a letter to the Berlin authorities, Justi announced that he was about to leave for Munich. Pointing at the typical bigotry and narrow-mindedness of Catholic countries that had contributed to his departure from Vienna a decade earlier, Justi stressed he would ultimately prefer a Prussian post to the Bavarian one. Boldly, Justi asked for employment as financial councillor (*Geheimer Finanzrat*) in the General Directory. The Prussian authorities remained unmoved. Although they rewarded Justi with an annual pension of 200 florins for his pamphleteering during the war, he had to wait a further four years, during which his health, particularly his eyesight, declined rapidly. Justi kept up his high annual literary output until 1763. He now began to focus primarily on public finance and taxation. The *Ausführliche Abhandlung von denen Steuern und Abgaben* of 1762 was followed by the more extensive *System des Finanzwesens*, which appeared in 1766, although it had been written three years earlier.

Final years (1765–1771)

In July 1765, Justi was finally named Prussian Inspector of Mines, Glass, and Steel Works. With Justi's appointment, Frederick wanted to take direct control of the government-owned iron and steel manufactures, which had been rented to private entrepreneurs in previous years. Most of the rental agreements expired that year, and Justi was supposed to take over the manufactories and administer them on behalf of the Prussian state. By that time, however, a failed operation

58 Müller, *Akademie und Wirtschaft*, p. 85. Unruh, *Subjektiver Rechtsschutz und politische Freiheit*, p. 11.

on his cataracts had left Justi almost fully blind.[59] He encountered great difficulties in his practical day-to-day work, difficulties that were further aggravated by quarrels with colleagues and superiors in the Prussian administration. In his endeavour to build new ironworks in the province of Neumark, Justi not only had to fight the resistance of local bureaucrats, who regarded him as an outsider and intruder; his projects were also regarded with growing hostility in the General Directory. Though sensing the opposition to him and his plans, he nevertheless tried to push through the practical realisation of his departmental projects.

His work for the Prussian state ended abruptly. Justi was accused of misappropriating government funds, arrested on 15 February 1768 and imprisoned in Küstrin.[60] His property was seized. Despite his poor health, he categorically refused the assistance of a lawyer and decided to defend himself. Justi was convinced that he had been framed by envious rivals and remained confident that he would be able to prove his innocence. Much speculation has been dedicated in the literature on Justi to the question of his guilt. Most accounts simply take his innocence for granted. Some even portray Justi as a martyr of liberty, whose bold political statements figured as the true reason behind the imprisonment.[61] This latter assumption is clearly erroneous. The trial was concerned with the slackness of accounting practices in Justi's department: his political views played no role in it. It seems that it was Justi's secretary, Virmitz, who had had his hands in the till. Whether Justi himself profited from these dealings or was unaware of them will

59 Contemporary anecdotes have it that Justi rejected the appointment because of his blindness. Promising Justi an amanuensis, Frederick is believed to have responded with the following answer: 'He has reason. Eyes I will give him' ('Er hat Verstand. Augen will ich ihm geben'). Justi's alleged rejection of the offer seems unlikely after his reinforced efforts for Prussian employment. The veracity of the incident remains doubtful.

60 As the prison had been demolished by Russian troops in August 1758 Justi lived under surveillance in the nearby *Stockhaus*.

61 Horst Schmidt, 'Johann Heinrich Gottlob von Justi, ein vergessener Vertreter der deutschen Aufklärung des XVIII. Jahrhunderts, und Russland', *Wissenschaftliche Zeitschrift der Martin-Luther-Universität Halle-Wittenberg; Gesellschafts- und Sprachwissenschaftliche Reihe* 2/1961, 273–279.

probably never be known. In either case, Justi was clearly overwhelmed by the responsibilities of his post. Even if he had wanted to (and it is doubtful that he did), his blindness would have effectively prevented him from supervising his department sufficiently closely.[62]

Assuming that he died before the final verdict in Küstrin on 21 July 1771, much speculation has been dedicated in the literature to the question of Justi's guilt. However, a hitherto ignored reminiscence of the *Literaturbriefe* incident in the *Berlinische Monatsschrift* of 1802 by his old adversary Friedrich Nicolai provides in fact a clear answer: according to Nicolai, Justi had been released in April 1771 and had moved back to Berlin, where he died soon after.[63]

Justi's writings

Justi's inaugural speech in Vienna figured as the starting point for his political and economic enquiries. In it, Justi argued that under modern conditions, external political power primarily rested on commercial success. Military victory over a dominant economic power seemed increasingly implausible. A state's wealth and power no longer depended on traditional quantitative features, such as the number of inhabitants, territorial expansion, or the possession of gold and silver. On the contrary, since all European states had started to make renewed efforts to bolster their political standing with commercial success, the rise or decline of nations now depended predominantly on the quality of their economic policy. The general condition of science and learning within a country, Justi emphasised, determined whether a state would be able to elaborate a feasible competitive economic strategy for national survival. Once developed, the rigid implementation of such a strategy required a modern monarchical regime with a well-

62 Cf. Mittenzwei, *Preussen nach dem Siebenjährigen Krieg*, pp. 223–229.

63 Nicolai, 'Fortsetzung der Berliner Nachlese', p. 349. Upon Frederick the Great's order, Justi's children were granted places in the royal orphanage at Potsdam.

arranged central administration. Underlining his own new role as the state's instructor of civil servants, Justi concluded that the excellence of national administration rested to a considerable extent on the quality of the training given to its civil servants. The two key insights of the lecture – the vital importance of commercial policies for national survival in a market-based competitive world and the realisation that economic theories required political reform for successful implementation – were to emerge as the hallmarks of the *Staatswirtschaft*, his first treatise which appeared in 1755.[64]

Dedicated to Maria Theresa, Justi's explicit aim in composing the *Staatswirtschaft* was to offer a complete set of policies to enable Habsburg Austria to become a commercial power and compete with Prussia, France, and England, just as he had envisioned it in his inaugural lecture. The *Staatswirtschaft* is, however, not the chief work of Justi's oeuvre in political economy. It was, in effect, an early and rather undeveloped book.[65]

64 The term *Staatswirtschaft* (literally: state economy) is equivalent to the English 'political economy' or the French 'économie politique' and does not, as previous interpretations assumed, denote a specifically German form of political economy that laid particular stress on the active regulative function of the state in economic affairs. This can be seen from contemporary German translations of French and English works. For instance, James Steuart's *Inquiry into the Principles of Political Economy* (1767) was translated by Christoph Friedrich Schott as *Untersuchung der Grundsätze der Staats-Wirtschaft* (Tübingen: Cotta, 1769–1772). In the same way, A. Niemann in his *Grundsätze der Staatswirthschaft* (Altona, 1790) directly linked the term *Staatswirtschaft* to 'économie politique' and 'political oeconomy' (Keith Tribe, *Governing Economy. The Reformation of German Economic Discourse 1750–1840* (Cambridge: Cambridge University Press, 1988), p. 133). Likewise, Justi's term *Die Kommerzien* is the German adaptation (in plural) of the French 'Le commerce', which in the mid-eighteenth-century had a far wider meaning than today and served in contemporary literature as terminological synonym for what is now defined as economics. As Antoin Murphy has pointed out, the term economics 'had not, at this time [in the 1750s], been given its modern meaning' (Antoin E. Murphy, *Richard Cantillon – Entrepreneur and Economist* (Oxford: Clarendon Press, 1986), p. 248).

65 Due to Ernst Klein's (mistaken) assumption that Justi said all he had to say in his *Staatswirtschaft*, subsequent studies have ignored Justi's other works on political economy (Ernst Klein, 'Johann Heinrich Gottlob von Justi und die

In the *Staatswirtschaft*, Justi presented for the first time his fourfold division of political economy into political theory (*Staatskunst*), domestic policy (*Polizeiwissenschaft*), public finance (*Kameralwissenschaft*), and trade theory (*Commercienwissenschaft*).[66] Justi used political theory proper (*Staatskunst*) at the outset as a vital underpinning of his economic and fiscal ideas. The state occupied a crucial role in his thought. According to him, detailed theories on trade, industry, and taxation amounted to empty speculation without a fundamental understanding of the nature of politics. Nothing, Justi held, could be securely established in economics 'if one does not constantly look back to the nature of civic institutions (*bürgerliche Verfassungen*)'.[67] Even the seemingly apolitical science of public finance was in the highest degree political, since it determined 'the very existence and coherence (*Zusammenhang*) of the state'. In a similar way, Justi was clear about the fact that commerce, manufactures, agriculture, and governmental economic policy were only 'supporting means of political power, yet not its primary reason'.[68] Justi's somewhat abstract 'contribution to the politicisation of the German Enlightenment', which Horst Dreitzel has spoken of, was thus in fact the very specific politicisation of German economic thought.[69]

Justi's *Staatswirtschaft* already indicated his ambitious publication-plan for the following eight years. He announced his intention to offer separate treatises on each of the four major branches of political economy. His later books can indeed be explained in view of this statement: *Der Grundriss einer guten Regierung* (1759), *Natur und Wesen der Staaten* (1760), and *Vergleichungen der europäischen mit den asiatischen und andern vermeintlich barbarischen Regierungen* (1762) are primarily dedicated to political theory, elaborating his

Preussische Staatswirtschaft', *Vierteljahrsschrift für Sozial- und Wirtschaftsgeschichte* 48 (1961), 145–202 (p. 146)).

66 See Table 1. An abridged version of this scheme can already be found in Justi's *Gutachten* (Leipzig, 1754).

67 *Natur und Wesen*, Vorrede. Quoted from: Small, *The Cameralists*, p. 400.

68 *Natur und Wesen*, p. 404f.

69 Horst Dreitzel, 'Justis Beitrag zur Politisierung der deutschen Aufklärung', in: *Aufklärung als Politisierung – Politisierung der Aufklärung*, edited by Hans Erich Bödeker and Ulrich Herrman (Hamburg: Meiner, 1987), pp. 138–177.

model of modern monarchy through a critical dissection of Montesquieu's *Spirit of the Laws*. Parallel to this, Justi's *Grundsätze der Polizeiwissenschaft* (1756) and its later extension, *Die Grundfeste zur Macht* (1760/61), chiefly dealt with questions of economic policy, while the *Ausführliche Abhandlung von denen Steuern und Abgaben* (1762) and *System des Finanzwesens* (1766) explored fiscal issues. Lastly, the *Abhandlung von denen Manufakturen und Fabriken* (1758/61) and the collected *Ökonomische Schriften* (1760/61) were dedicated to practical economic questions.

In a further aspect the *Staatswirtschaft* marked a crucial turning point in Justi's thinking. Shortly after its publication, Justi embarked on his project of dissecting *The Spirit of the Laws*. With the help of the Göttingen library he also began to follow contemporary Parisian debates closely. His numerous translations and review-essays show that he was a diligent observer of French intellectual life.[70] In order to make his textbooks more competitive Justi was keen to integrate the latest fashionable debates and ideas within them. The heavily annotated second edition of the *Staatswirtschaft* in 1758 shows that in three years Justi had abandoned many of his original views from his Austrian period.[71]

Next to Montesquicu, Justi was particularly influenced by Vincent de Gournay and the circle of economists associated with him, the most important contributors to French economic thought in the 1750s. Soon after his appointment as *intendant du commerce* in 1751, Gournay had assembled an informal circle of like-minded thinkers whose activities he animated by circulating his manuscripts among them. The group, which was far more loose and heterogeneous in their views than the later physiocratic school, numbered around fifteen

70 All of Justi's writings give ample proof of his active involvement into contemporary intellectual life. Apart from academic textbooks, Justi's publications between 1755 and 1763 were reviews of recently published books, personal contributions to larger literary debates, and price essays for various German academies. Justi also became chief editor of the German translation of the *Arts et metiers* volumes published by the Parisian Academy of Sciences, which dealt with all sorts of agricultural, technological, and microeconomic questions.

71 As the main text remained unaltered, the numerous notes in the second edition of *Staatswirtschaft* oftentimes contradict the claims of the earlier version.

members and included the leading minds of the time. Veron de Forbonnais, Turgot, Montaudoin de la Touche, Claude Jacques Herbert, Simon Clicquot-Blervache, Henri Duhamel de Monceau, and Georges Butel-Dumont belonged to it, as did Montesquieu's son Jean Baptiste, the Abbé Morellet and the Abbé Coyer. From 1753 until the time of Gournay's death in 1758, the group wrote for a short period under Gournay's tutelage about 'le commerce en général'.[72]

The Gournay circle initiated an extensive programme of publications on economic questions which aimed to change French attitudes towards economic theory and policy. It started in 1753 with the publication of several new works as well as a number of French translations of Spanish and English treatises.[73] 1754 saw the publication of Forbonnais's *Elements du commerce* and the French translation of Hume's *Political Discourses*, both of which contributed greatly to economic discussions in France. The belated publication of Richard Cantillon's *Essai* in 1755 (originally written in 1735) was also part of the publication programme of the Gournay group. Turgot later alluded to these publication efforts in his *Éloge de Gournay*, speaking of 'that propitious fermentation of thought on these important questions [...] which sprang up two or three years after M. de Gournay had been Intendant of Commerce'.[74]

The French writings of the time provided Justi with crucial arguments to define his anti-Montesquieuian stand. In his contribution to the French debate on commercial nobility in 1756 (which was also

72 Simone Meyssonier, *La Balance et l'Horloge. La genèse de la pensée liberale en France au XVIIIe siècle* (Montreuil: Les Editions de la Passion, 1989), p. 179f.

73 These works include: Abbé Carlier, *Dissertation sur l'Etat du Commerce en France* (Paris, 1753); Veron de Forbonnais, *Considérations sur les Finances d'Espagne* (Paris, 1753); Don Bernardo de Ulloa, *Rétablissement des Manufactures et du commerce de l'Espagne*, translated by Plumard de Dangeul (Paris, 1753); Charles King, *Le négoicant anglais*, translated by Veron de Forbonnais (Paris, 1753); Geronimo de Ustariz, *Théorie et pratique du commerce et de la marine*, translated by Veron de Forbonnais (Paris, 1753). Cf. Meyssonnier, *La Balance*, p. 181.

74 Anne Robert Turgot, 'In Praise of Gournay', in: *The Economics of A.R.J. Turgot*, edited and translated by P.D. Groenewegen (The Hague: Nijhoff, 1977), pp. 20–42 (p. 33).

initiated by the Gournay group) he developed the nucleus of his political model of modern monarchy which he was to extend in subsequent years in his three major political treatises, *Der Grundriss einer guten Regierung* (1759), *Natur und Wesen der Staaten* (1760), and *Vergleichungen* (1762). Within them, Justi pointed to the need to modify the prevailing governmental form of monarchical absolutism by adding to it safeguards against arbitrary acts of the monarch which, in the past, had proven deleterious to the rise of national trade and industry. *Der Grundriss einer guten Regierung* – which is not available in a modern edition and has been undeservedly ignored by scholars – marked Justi's most ambitious attempt to elaborate his constitutional reform proposals. It is a critical dissection of Montesquieu's claims, as is Justi's most extensive treatise on politics, *Natur und Wesen der Staaten*, which he himself called an improved version of *The Spirit of the Laws*.[75]

Justi further elaborated his model of modern monarchy in the *Vergleichungen* (1762) in which he rejected Montesquieu's assessment of China as an example of oriental despotism. He berated Montesquieu for doubting the veracity of Jesuit reports and for lending too much credence to the tales of merchants who, in Justi's view, had evaluated everything according to their own narrow standards of greed. Justi based his own account mainly on Du Halde's *Description de l'Empire de la Chine* (1733) and highlighted the excellence of many governmental practices in China in order to show that a moderate absolute monarchy could be realised without the existence of a feudal aristocracy. To bolster his thesis, Justi also included extensive discussions of other Asian regimes, which, again, were drawn primarily from contemporary French sources.[76]

Justi hoped for an effective limitation of absolute monarchical rule by a reformed education of the prince. In a similar way to how he

75 *Natur und Wesen*, Vorrede.

76 Around two thirds of the text of Justi's *Vergleichungen* consist of German translations of French accounts of Asia and China such as Simone de La Loubères *Du royaume de Siam* (1691), Charles Rollins's *Histoire ancienne* (1730–38), Claude François Lambert's *Recueil d'observations curieuses* (1749) and François Marie de Marsy's *Histoire moderne* (1755ff.).

had designed *Natur und Wesen der Staaten* as 'an improved version of *The Spirit of the Laws*', Justi designed his mirror of princes novel *Psammitichus* (1759/60) as an updated version of Fénelon's *Telemachus* (1699). Justi admired Fénelon's anti-absolutist politics, but rejected his fervent opposition to luxury. Contrary to Fénelon, Justi made his ideal king Psammitichus apply neo-Colbertist, pro-urban, pro-manufacturing, and pro-luxury policies in order to translate his country into a modern monarchy.[77] Despite its literary shortfalls, *Psammitichus* is of considerable importance for a thorough understanding of Justi's political and economic thought, as many of his ideas on modern monarchy and commercial advancement are expressed in it in a clear, albeit idealised, form.[78]

In his economic treatises, and particularly in *Die Grundfeste* (1760), Justi also had recourse to contemporary French works. He discussed Melon's *Essai politique sur le commerce* (1733) and Mirabeau's *Ami des hommes* (1756) and showed familiarity with Montaigne, la Bruyère, la Boethie, and Voltaire. In addition, Justi was a close reader of the *Journal oeconomique*, the *Encyclopédie*, and was well acquainted with Rousseau's two *Discourses* (1750/54). Apart from French authors, Justi was also familiar with English and Scottish writers such as Hobbes, Temple, Bolingbroke, Mandeville, and Hume, whose *Essays* (1752) influenced his monetary theory.

77 Apart from *Telemachus*, Justi seems to have been influenced by Fénelon-styled works such as the Chevalier de Ramsay's *Voyages de Cyrus* (1727) and the Abbé Terrasson's *Sethos* (1731).

78 Contrary to Lieselotte Kurth's claims ('Historiographie und historischer Roman: Kritik und Theorie im 18. Jahrhundert', *MLN* (1964), 337–362), I believe it makes more sense to view *Psammitichus* primarily as an idealised presentation of Justi's political and economic claims rather than as an historical novel. No previous study of Justi's political economy has taken *Psammitichus* into account.

Chapter Three
The European power struggle of the 1750s

The German economy

In France there was widespread agreement among writers in the 1750s that the country had to redouble its efforts to catch up with the economically more developed England and to preserve its standing as the prime political power of the Continent. Heated debates focused on the nature (and possible repercussions) of political and economic reforms. Many political observers, including the Gournay group, were convinced that France needed to model itself on the English approach. Anglomania was rife in France, and the English works on trade were cited 'as a suitable means for surreptitiously attacking what was believed to be wrong in France'.[1]

The growing international pressure was felt even more strongly in the states of the Holy Roman Empire, most of all in Habsburg Austria. Comparisons with more advanced countries (such as England, Holland, and, above all, France) inspired a widespread desire to progress commercially and militarily. Through his intimate knowledge of the Haugwitz reforms Justi was painfully aware that Europe after the War of the Austrian Succession had entered into a gigantic contest in which the country with the highest economic development was most likely to win. He repeatedly stressed in his oeuvre that Holland and England were by far the richest and most advanced nations of the time. Both countries enjoyed a superior level of socio-economic development thanks to their dominant position in maritime trade, their higher degree of urbanisation, and their more sophisticated cultivation

1 Antoin E. Murphy, *Richard Cantillon. Entrepreneur and Economist* (Oxford: Clarendon Press, 1986), p. 313.

of land.[2] In comparison, France, having initiated and achieved substantial economic progress at the time of Colbert, was in several respects more backward than its maritime competitors.

Germany, with the exception of some Protestant territories in the north, offered a gloomy economic picture.[3] Justi lamented that only 'very few countries of our fatherland can say of themselves that they have a flourishing economy and a sufficient amount of money within them'.[4] None of these flourishing states could be found in the Catholic south of the Empire. Justi ascribed much of this backwardness to historical negligence and to a stubborn adherence to traditional, economically disadvantageous practices. Throughout the previous centuries, and particularly during the last two decades, when England and France had undertaken ever greater efforts to foster commerce and had enjoyed remarkable economic progress in turn, the Germans had devoted even less diligence to the question of how to undertake profitable trade.[5] History showed that it had not always been so. In sharp contrast to Germany's current misery, Justi drew an idyllic picture of the glorious Hanseatic past in the fourteenth and fifteenth centuries when north German cities prospered due to their dominant trading position in the Baltic. To be sure, as trade routes had changed with the Spanish and Portuguese discoveries in the New World the Hanseatic past could not simply be revived. However, as Justi pointed out, modern manufacturing and new agricultural techniques offered feasible alternatives for the German states to regain a strong trading position in Europe.[6]

In Justi's view, the neglect of industrial advancement in Germany in the distant as well as more recent past was even more regrettable and embarrassing given that the natural preconditions for trade were by no means worse than in France. Measured by the social

2 *Physicalische und politische Betrachtungen über die Erzeugung des Menschen und Bevölkerung der Länder* (Breslau: Neue Buchdruckerey, 1769), p. 79; *Manufakturen und Fabriken* I, 19 + 182.

3 *Manufakturen und Fabriken* I, 186.

4 *Grundfeste* I, 620.

5 *Grundfeste* I, 580.

6 *Der handelnde Adel, dem der kriegerische Adel entgegengesetzt wird*, Vorrede.

and juridical standing of the peasantry many German principalities were in fact far better off than France. Yet although

> the natural fertility of most of these countries is sufficiently known, although the fertile soil could nourish two or three times as many people, and although many German states have an advantageous location close to the sea and navigable rivers, trade and exchange are nevertheless down in most of them.[7]

Justi emerged convinced that an immense potential for economic growth lay dormant within the German states. They could 'be far better cultivated if only serious measures were undertaken to encourage commerce and industry [within them]'.[8]

Justi's theoretical investigations focused on finding a quick but safe way to realise Germany's potentials. This was not an easy task. Particularly in the manufacturing sector, Justi stressed, the 'English, the Dutch, and the French have such a great head-start [...] that a nation that is just beginning will hardly be able to compete with them'.[9] Nevertheless he remained confident that catching up with advanced neighbouring states was possible even for underdeveloped nations. Taking the encouraging seventeenth-century example of France into account, he believed that a sophisticated programme of social, political, and economic reforms could soon unleash the enormous dormant potential of the German states. To remind his readers of the highly flexible nature of commerce, he repeatedly quoted the example of Queen Elizabeth I's prohibition of wool exports to the Netherlands, which had forced Dutch weavers to settle in England and had contributed significantly to the country's subsequent economic rise. The German territories could catch up with their Western neighbours by the help of similar means.[10]

7 *Grundfeste* I, 620.

8 *Polizeiwissenschaft*, p. 69.

9 *Manufakturen und Fabriken* I, 27f. Justi's emphasis on the difficulties of economic development from relative backwardness within an internatinonal competitive surrounding made his ideas particularly attractive to eighteenth-century thinkers in Russia and Spain and explains the considerable impact of his works in both countries.

10 As the reviewer of Justi's *Vollständige Abhandlung von denen Manufakturen und Fabriken* remarked in the *Journal Encyclopédique* the work was primarily

Justi designed his own political economy to be a plan that would enable the greater German territories to undergo profound growth similar to that by which France had caught up with England and Holland in the seventeenth century. But he was painfully aware of the serious breakdowns and crises to which France had been subject in previous decades due to political and administrative mismanagement. The great commercial successes under Colbert in the early phase of Louis XIV's reign had been ruined by Louis's bellicosity which had virtually bankrupted the state. John Law's management of the war-induced national debt under the Regency had added a further disaster. Although Justi (like many contemporaries) regarded Law's system as a serious attempt at financial innovation and as a considerable endeavour to free French policy from the suffocating constraints of the national debt, he was aware that the practical application of Law's designs had thoroughly failed, not because the idea behind them was fundamentally defective, but because the projectors, along with their political backers, were overambitious and corrupt. By and large, France had nonetheless overcome her initial backwardness and had managed to draw level with Holland and England in certain areas, above all in manufacturing.[11]

As a model the French way held the greatest appeal, in so far as its starting and finishing points offered the closest similarities to the current and aspired stage of economic development in the German territories. In Justi's view, a careful analysis of France's advancement under Colbert promised to yield valuable insights into how to tackle the problem of Germany's underdevelopment. The crucial question was how to ensure that the political mistakes of France would not be repeated in the German states during their 'French-style' process of hauling themselves up. In other words, if the transformation of the German states into 'commercial societies' was to be successful, they had to avoid French pitfalls – external pitfalls, like warfare, and in-

designed to come up with proposals on how German manufacturers could become more competitive in Europe (*JE* 1758 VII, II, 107–116 (p. 108)).

11 Although France had started manufactures far later than England or Holland, it had brought them 'within a short period of time to perfection and foreign sales' (*Manufakturen und Fabriken* I, 28).

ternal ones like despotism, excessive taxation, a soaring public debt, and monetary collapse. Given the rising international competition in Europe, the avoidance of these pitfalls was, in effect, crucial to their long-term survival.

Warfare, empire, and foreign trade

Justi was acutely aware of the new eighteenth-century economic limits to politics that were 'set by the imperative need of modern nations to succeed in international trade'.[12] Since a country's power rested first and foremost on the condition of its commerce, the encouragement of trade had become a vital part of governmental prudence.[13] Throughout his writings, Justi laid particular stress on these new economic constraints confronting the modern statesman. The advent of substantial international trade had led to a remarkable shift in the traditional balance of power.

The idea that economic excellence had turned into something like an 'affair of state' (as Hume once put it) was fundamental for Justi's post-Machiavellian vision of international politics. Justi shared Montesquieu's ideas about *doux commerce*, particularly his famous assessment that one 'has begun to be cured of Machiavellianism, and one will continue to be cured of it'.[14] Like Montesquieu, he boldly declared that 'it is common knowledge by today that the Machiavellian principles are of no worth whatsoever', given that militarism and despotism increasingly seemed to fail in the new age of international trade: the former over-exhausted the economic power of a

12 Istvan Hont, 'Free Trade and the Economic Limits to National Politics', in: Istvan Hont, *Jealousy of Trade – International Competition and the Nation-State in Historical Perspective* (Cambridge/Mass. and London: The Belknap Press of Harvard University Press, 2005) pp. 185–266 (p. 185).

13 Cf. *Grundfeste* I, 519: '[N]obody doubts any longer that trade is the soul of a state and that its power and happiness primarily depend on the condition of its commerce'.

14 *Spirit of the Laws* 21, 20.

country, and the latter suppressed the skills and industry of the subjects.[15] Modern rulers did not gain power any longer by force, malice, or suppression of their subjects, but rather through active support of the latter's welfare. In numerous critical references to *The Prince* (and favourable quotations of Frederick's *Anti-Machiavel*, which occurred particularly in the works from 1758/59 when Justi was seeking Prussian employment) Justi claimed that Machiavelli had sacrificed the prince's real interests for 'reason of state'. Political suppression by military force was a short-term device. For long-term political success depended on national economic excellence – which could not be brought about by force. Condemning Machiavelli's *Prince*, Justi maintained that one had learnt 'from experience' that 'a depopulated country and the extreme suppression of its inhabitants do not make a prince powerful'. A poor country would always be marked by 'the poverty of its ruler'.[16]

Justi pointed out that the altered circumstances of his time required a radical break with conventional policies. The prime means for achieving formidable external strength had shifted from large armies and territorial conquest to internal economic improvement and the avoidance of destructive warfare. Justi took up the Fénelonian idea, modified by Frederick and Voltaire in the *Anti-Machiavel*, that internal development was a far more sophisticated form of aggrandisement than conquest. Frederick and Voltaire had argued that economic advancement and domestic improvement could alter the balance of power much more quickly and much more profoundly than territorial enlargement. In modern international competition military strength was no longer a primary goal of statecraft *per se*, but a natural (though still crucial) by-product of domestic economic strength.

Justi presented the two pillars of his political economy – modern monarchy and competitive economic policies (*Polizeiwissenschaft*) – as stringent deductions from his post-Machiavellian outlook of international politics. For a proper understanding of Justi's programme for domestic political and economic reform, one needs to explore first his views on the European struggle for power and on the implications of

15 *Natur und Wesen*, p. 74.

16 *Natur und Wesen*, p. 74.

modern trade for the notion of reason of state. Accordingly, I begin my enquiry into Justi's thought with an analysis of his international political theory.

The international struggle for power

Justi's repeated polemics against warfare echoed the ideas of Fénelon, Melon, and Montesquieu.[17] He shared Fénelon's assumption that there was never a war, 'even a successful war, which did not cause more harm than good to the state' considering 'how many families it ruins, how many men it kills, how it lays waste to and depopulates all countries and how it authorises licence'.[18] Any kind of war would give rise to a spiral of detrimental repercussions in the participating countries and hence could not be in the true interest of any state. Trade and war, by their nature, followed contrary logics. Even successful war, Justi warned,

> has the most unhappy consequences for the subjects. The export trade is suppressed and hence the manufactures do not find sufficient potential buyers so that in turn a considerable number of workers are pushed into great misery. Usually, an increase in prices of alimentary goods is running parallel to this.[19]

War could destroy the beneficial fruits of even the longest and most prosperous reigns.[20] The lessons of Louis XIV's failed experiment in 'universal empire' were clear. Justi agreed with Melon's position in the *Political Essay upon Commerce* that under modern conditions the 'spirit of conquest and the spirit of commerce mutually exclude each other in a nation'.[21] Justi was shocked by the brevity of peace in

17 *Psammitichus* II, 261.

18 Kingsley Martin, *French Liberal Thought in the Eighteenth Century* (London: Phoenix House, 1962), p. 63.

19 *Vergleichungen*, p. 138.

20 Even when war was led successfully it destroyed the 'fruits which the long-time care of wise princes had planted for the accommodation and welfare of their states' (*Psammitichus* II, 261).

21 Jean François Melon, *A Political Essay upon Commerce*, translated by David Bindon (Dublin and London: Woodward and Cox, 1739), p. 123. Melon, like

Europe between the War of the Austrian Succession and the outbreak of the Seven Years War in 1756. In his writings between 1756 and 1763 his criticism of military conflict grew stronger. He was astonished that the disadvantages and the uncertainty of victory in modern wars could not deter the European princes from following 'their urge for conquest, honour and fame'.[22]

In his mirror-of-princes novel *Psammitichus* Justi offered an exhaustive account of the peaceful effects of trade. *Psammitichus* presented Justi's chief ideas on modern monarchy by using the literary device of an idealised fictional past. The novel told of the gradual realisation of a commercial monarchy in ancient Egypt by the virtuous pharaoh Psammitichus. Justi, like Fénelon in *Telemachus*, portrayed Tyre as an example of a virtuous commercial state. With the example of Tyre, he tried to demonstrate that the introduction of power politics into the realm of free international trade was bound to fail, as it would undermine a state's economic strength. This followed the assumption that it was impossible to conquer the wealth of a trading state because once conquered, its commerce would 'disappear and its eminently mobile wealth would escape capture'.[23]

As outlined in *Psammitichus*, Tyre was not a fully sovereign state, but dependent on the neighbouring Assyrian Empire. Each year, Tyre paid a tribute to the Assyrian king and was also obliged to assist Assyrian military operations with its navy. Surprisingly, the asymmetric relations between the small, yet opulent republic of Tyre and the territorially vast, yet commercially underdeveloped Assyrian Empire were extraordinarily stable. Their relationship constituted a balance of powers, which was based on the economic limits that for-

Justi later on, drew attention to the principle that the strength of a state was 'not to be measured by the extent of its territory, but by the number of its inhabitants, and the usefulness of their labour' (Melon, *Essay*, p. 142). Furthermore, he directly linked the economic prosperity of his time (1733) to the relative peacefulness in Europe in contrast to the less happy days during the extensive warfare before the Peace of Utrecht. Melon, like Montesquieu, hoped that trade would eventually replace military conflict with peaceful commercial competition.

22 *Vergleichungen*, p. 140.

23 Hont, 'Free Trade and the Economic Limits to National Politics', p. 48.

eign trade imposed on international politics. Why, the followers of Machiavellian power politics would ask, did the Assyrians prefer the loose vassalage of Tyre to full conquest? And why did wealthy Tyre accept the yoke of Assyria instead of regaining its sovereignty? Justi answered that both sides saw the economic benefits of the *status quo*, which could be destroyed by a lengthy and risky war.

The Tyrians saw that an opulent, but small republic in the vicinity of a powerful territorial empire only had the choice between dependency and eternal war. Endless war, however, 'would inevitably cause the cessation of trade and the downfall of the state, even though the latter would thus escape dependency upon the Assyrians'.[24] The Tyrians accepted dependency on the Assyrian Empire as the lesser evil. Conversely, the Assyrian monarchs had no real interest in the political subjugation of Tyre. The Assyrians, as a Tyrian merchant explains in *Psammitichus*, could

> easily see that it is of greater advantage to them to let us live according to our own laws, whereby commerce will continue to flourish and whereby they [i.e., the Assyrians] will have our capacities at their service, while if subdued by despotic government we would soon lose our trade and [economic] power.

A wise absolute monarch, the Tyrian merchant concluded, 'would have a small neighbouring trading nation rather as a friend and confederate [...] than as a subject'.[25] Under the laws of Machiavellian power politics (which overruled commercial interests) lasting peace between a small republic and a large territorial empire was impossible. By contrast, awareness of the imperatives of commerce created the possibility of a symbiotic, peaceful coexistence between even such diverse powers as Tyre and Assyria.

The hero of the novel, the Egyptian pharaoh Psammitichus, endorsed the new principles of foreign policy, as driven by commercial interests. He was the archetype of a virtuous prince who refrained from warfare for the sake of domestic economic advancement. When the Arabian king Jenys attacked the Assyrian Empire from the

24 *Psammitichus* I, 188.
25 *Psammitichus* I, 188.

east, Psammitichus was tempted to join the war and start a simultaneous attack on the Assyrians from the south. News of Jenys's military successes encouraged Psammitichus in such plans. This was a convenient moment to cause the downfall of the mighty neighbour. Weakened by Jenys's attack the Assyrians would be unable to halt an additional Egyptian invasion and would have to accept a peace treaty dictated by Egypt. The invasion could be justified as a pre-emptive strike, for if the Assyrian Empire was not effectively weakened it could remain a threat in the future. A war between Assyria and Egypt at some point seemed a foregone conclusion. Hence was it not wiser to act and solve the problem at this most opportune moment?

Against all odds, Psammitichus controlled his ambitions and refrained from attacking Assyria. He saw the fallacy in initiating war: 'He recognised', Justi wrote, 'that only defensive wars were just wars' and that even defensive wars turned into unjust wars once the military capabilities of the opponent had been neutralised. Further military operations amounted to exacting revenge and pursuing territorial gain.[26] According to Psammitichus, a just king could never shed the blood or endanger the life of his subjects except when defending the country against invasion. Taking into account the destruction and misery of previous wars, Psammitichus calculated that war against the Assyrians could lead to no lasting gain.

In *Psammitichus* Justi repeatedly highlighted the economically devastating effects of warfare. Although Psammitichus had won a lengthy war against his rivals in Egypt, the country had suffered severely. Fighting

> halted the wise designs of Psammitichus for population growth, for the flourishing of commerce and manufactures, and all in all for the furtherance of Egypt's welfare, and almost fully destroyed the beneficial fruits of previous years.

The war reduced the Egyptian population by 200,000 heads. Commerce and manufacturing had declined sharply. Governmental designs for the cultivation of the land and the commencement of trade and

26 *Psammitichus* II, 7.

industry had been interrupted, as the funds originally assigned for these purposes had been used to finance the war.[27] Observing the desolation of his country, Psammitichus promised to prevent all future wars and started to redouble his efforts for reconstruction, encouraging agriculture, trade, and manufacturing.[28] In order to establish a suitable framework for trade and industry Psammitichus cut taxes and contributions in kind by half and abolished those which had proven disadvantageous to the freedom of his subjects. In addition, he saved budget surpluses and cut all manifestations of courtly luxury.[29] Psammitichus's exemplary behaviour led to Egypt's rapid economic recovery in the novel.

Justi did not comment on the issue of war and international trade merely in the literary context of *Psammitichus*. His assumptions, he stressed, were not the product of abstract theoretical speculations, but had been confirmed by history. Throughout his writings, he repeatedly illustrated the failure of reason-of-state policies in Europe. Most of all, he regarded the sixteenth- and seventeenth-century Spanish, French, and Swedish attempts at military expansion as disasters and as evidence for his theory that economic policy – although initially ignored by statesmen – had gained increased importance for the European balance of power.

In Justi's view, Emperor Charles V had been an early example of the political ignorance of commercial power. Charles was 'a bad economist'. Despite his immense revenues (including gold and silver from America) his reign experienced constant financial deficits. His lack of money strongly influenced the outcome of his military operations. The number of mercenaries Charles was able to hire was restricted by his narrow budget. Charles's immense nominal political power stood in bizarre contrast to his limited military capabilities. His costly wars

27 *Psammitichus* II, 262.

28 Justi frequently highlighted Psammitichus's extraordinary dedication to peacekeeping. Even when Psammitichus is told that his wife Mykeris has been captured by the enemies, he does not let the urge for revenge get the better of his peaceful nature. Although Psammitichus knows the fortress in which Mykeris is held, he nevertheless dispenses with an attack on it, as he does not want to shed the blood of his subjects (*Psammitichus* II, 262).

29 *Psammitichus* I, 217.

against his adversaries were a serious strategic mistake, as they exhausted his economic strength and diminished his political power even further. Charles's policies were pre-economic, anti-commercial, and hence short-sighted.[30]

The relevance of economic capacity for political power became even more important after Charles V. Under modern conditions, Justi emphasised, the politics of military glory and territorial aggrandisement were bound to lead to national catastrophes. While based on hopes of enhancing the princely revenue and helping the military budget such policies undermined the very foundations of princely rule. Sharp tax rises with the sole objective of achieving a surplus for the treasury were perilous as they obstructed long-term economic advancement. Conquests ruined the countries that undertook them. Since all financial means in the hands of the prince were derived from the people it was of paramount importance to seek a country's economic success through external peace and with the help of a moderate, diligent tax policy that encouraged trade and industry. International standing could only be attained as a result of domestic economic growth, which, in turn, required moderate government.

Justi was convinced that he lived in an age of transition that was seeing a fundamental paradigm shift away from a feudal and military era into a free, commercial, and eventually more peaceful age. He was aware that such a transition would not be swift. Its opponents tried to slow down or even halt the entire process. European monarchs had not yet adopted, let alone understood, the new principles of commercial politics. Ignorant of the real sources of their power, most of them paid no attention to trade and blithely carried on with warfare abroad and the exploitation of their subjects at home.[31] With the outbreak of the Seven Years War in 1756, Justi's hopes for this transition faded. He predicted that the lessons of the new commercial age would only be learnt after a total collapse of Machiavellian power politics:

30 *Vergleichungen*, p. 140.
31 *Vergleichungen*, p. 226.

> This massive state of war in Europe will not cease until the highest point of misery will put an end to it, when all European subjects have been beggared and all governments declared themselves bankrupt.[32]

Louis XIV was the most recent and most infamous example of a systematic application of the principles of Machiavellian power politics under the altered conditions of modern international trade. Despite his early successes, Louis' experiment had failed and led to an economic and military disaster from which France was still suffering in the middle of the eighteenth century.[33] His unnecessary wars had exhausted France, impoverished its population, and annulled the commercial advances achieved by Colbert's policies. Louis only secured a few lasting conquests, whose benefits stood in no relation to the vast sums he had wasted on military operations and to the damage he had done to the economy. The memory of Louis' shortfalls was a painful reminder for contemporary rulers 'to see that it is to their very own advantage to make their subjects rich and happy'.[34]

Justi criticised French public opinion during the initial phase of Louis' military operations. Blinded by his early successes, French writers praised the king and rejoiced in his victories. Even respected authors like Boileau composed panegyrics about him that presented 'an offence against sanity and reason'.[35] This early enthusiasm stood in remarkable contrast to the public assessments at the end of Louis' reign. Upon Louis' death French authors no longer celebrated their 'glorious' king but instead lamented the wretched situation of their country. Faced with the opposition of all major European powers, France had suffered painful military defeats in the War of the Spanish Succession and had lost most of her commerce and manufactures. The blind hopes the French had placed in Louis had been crushed.

32 *Vergleichungen*, p. 227. Justi's view resembles Hume's and Smith's ideas on this topic as well as Kant's prediction that a good deal of warfare would take place before commerce could leave a lasting imprint on the modern world order.

33 *Gesammelte Schriften* III, 71.

34 *Polizeiwissenschaft*, p. 268; *Grundfeste* I, 701f.

35 *Vergleichungen*, p. 142. Justi also discussed the reign of Louis XIV in: *Physicalische und politische Betrachtungen*, p. 147.

The same happened in Sweden under Charles XII. At first, the 'nordic Alexander' impressed his subjects with a series of victories in the Great Nordic War and caused a national frenzy similar to the initial adoration of Louis in France. However, when finally faced with the sorry consequences of these conquests the Swedes became agonizingly aware of their self-deception. Struck by inflation, depopulation, starvation, and the looting of the Russian army, they soon condemned the imperialist policy of their king. At the end of Charles XII's reign, Sweden had lost its status as a great power. While seventeenth-century Sweden had been a strong and influential nation in Europe, not even the count of Mecklenburg respected its mid-eighteenth-century successor.

Contrary to France and Sweden, Denmark had understood that the rules of power politics and warfare had changed in the age of international trade, and declared neutrality in the Seven Years War. Justi praised the Danish restraint, for such neutrality stood in contrast to the country's bellicose past. In the previous hundred years, Denmark had missed no opportunity to fight Sweden in the hope of reclaiming its lost provinces of Schonen, Halland, and Bleckingen. Justi pointed out that it would have been relatively easy for Denmark to reconquer these provinces if the country had joined the Anglo-Prussian axis in the Seven Years War. Enfeebled by internal factions Sweden would have been unable to halt a Danish invasion. But Denmark decided against an attack. Owing to its hundred year-old conflict with Sweden, Denmark

> had learnt from experience that it is a principle of false politics to assume that one needs to recapture lost provinces, and that this principle ultimately serves no other purpose than to deprive the existing provinces of their people [...] and thus weaken them to the extreme.

Denmark had arrived at the conclusion 'that it is far more important to develop the domestic capabilities of the state than to re-conquer lost provinces'.[36] Like Psammitichus, who had deliberately foregone the opportunity to attack the Assyrian Empire after Jenys's attack and had

36 *Chimäre des Gleichgewichts der Handlung und der Seefahrt*, p. 992.

concentrated instead on the enhancement of Egypt's domestic development, Denmark chose to focus on the increase of its commerce. As Justi pointed out, these tactics turned out to be highly beneficial. By 1759, exports of certain commodities had risen sharply in comparison to pre-war figures.

The Danish decision to refrain from military operations epitomised the popular eighteenth-century belief that one could not capture markets by force and that the 'Machiavellian' empire by the sword was useless for economic success.[37] Avoidance of warfare, like Danish neutrality, and prudent commercial treaties, like the British Navigation Act, were far more important than territorial conquest.[38] English and Danish efforts to increase national political power through commerce were remarkably more sophisticated than the military efforts of contenders for 'universal monarchy', like Spain, France, and Sweden.

With these historical examples in mind, Justi warned against future wars. A state could acquire an immense wealth through conquest. But it could not last:

> [T]hese riches, instead of promoting the state's happiness, would inevitably lead to its decline since wealth that does not enter the state by commerce and does not require the industry of the citizens in their respective professions but instead simply flows into all parts of the body politic is the source for all those confusions that will cause the decline and complete destruction of the empire.[39]

Since commerce was the backbone of modern power politics, trade and industry had to stand 'at the centre of a nation's attention'. In this regard, commercial society had set clear limits to traditional power politics.

37 Cf. Hont, 'Free trade and the Economic Limits to National Politics', p. 70.

38 *Grundfeste* I, 536.

39 'Abhandlung von dem Wesen des Adels und dessen Verhältnis gegen den Staat, und insonderheit gegen die Commercien', in: *Gesammelte Schriften* I, 147–192, 177.

Justi's critique of the balance of power

Justi further elaborated his claim that foreign trade and domestic development were the modern alternatives to Renaissance 'reason of state' politics in his critique of the European system of the balance of power. The reciprocity of market exchange, Justi hoped, could effectively lower the risk of war. Like Voltaire and Frederick in the *Anti-Machiavel*, he believed that a durable and peaceful coexistence was at hand in a Europe made up by commercial states that adopted neo-Colbertist politics of growth instead of conquest. By contrast, the balance-of-power doctrine was a dangerous relic of the Continent's belligerent past.

With his two pamphlets, *Die Chimäre des Gleichgewichts von Europa* (1758) and *Die Chimäre des Gleichgewichts der Handlung und der Schiffahrt* (1759), Justi joined the great eighteenth-century European debate surrounding balance-of-power theories and its aim to break the dreadful cycle of half-hearted European peace treaties by setting international relations on a stable footing. The best-known contributions to this debate include writings such as Saint-Pierre's *Projet pour rendre la Paix Perpétuelle en Europe* (1713), d'Argenson's plan for the instalment of a central European court of justice, Rousseau's abstract of Saint-Pierre (1761) and Kant's *Perpetual Peace* (1795).[40]

It is barely surprising that a thinker like Justi, whose thought was driven by the goal of bringing an end once and for all to the backwardness of eighteenth-century Germany, was strongly opposed to the concept of a 'given', i.e., fixed, balance of power and the concomitant idea that maintaining the European status quo in terms of political and economic power relations provided the key to peaceful coexistence on the Continent. Apart from his theoretical intention to uncover the logical shortfalls and genuine inapplicability of the balance-of-power doctrine under the aegis of the new commercial age,

40 Cf. Heinz Gollwitzer, *Europabild und Europagedanke* (Munich: Beck, 1964), pp. 71–81.

his *Chimäre* pamphlets served the practical political purpose of publicly defending Anglo-Prussian interests in the Seven Years War against the attacks of Franco-Austrian pamphleteers. They claimed that Frederick's offensive warfare and the dominant English trade would destroy the traditional power equilibrium within Europe for ever.[41]

The literature on the balance of powers had grown rapidly in the decades after the Peace of Utrecht (1715) which firmly established the concept of international stability 'achieved through the workings of a system of conflicting or potentially conflicting forces' in the political thinking of Europe. The vast majority of writers thought of the balance 'in terms of something which *ought* to exist, something deliberately constructed by man and to be consciously fostered and safeguarded by him'.[42] Accordingly, contemporary discussions tended to focus on two issues: when – if at all – did the balance-of-power doctrine authorise pre-emptive action? In other words, was it in accordance with the standards of international law that a coalition of states attacked another state if the latter seemed to upset the balance, i.e., threatened to become too dominant on the Continent? Parallel with this, the debates focused on the question of adequate power measurement: how – if at all – could political, military, or economic capability of individual states be determined?

In the beginning of the eighteenth century thinkers such as Fénelon argued that rulers not only had a right but a duty to resist the excessive growth of the power of other states. In Prussia, Nicolaus Hieronymus Gundling took up this issue. In his *Erörterung der Frage ob wegen der anwachsenden Macht der Nachbarn man den Degen entblössen könne* (1716), Gundling discussed the question whether a state could rightfully attack a neighbouring state on the grounds that the latter was about to attain dominance which could upset the

41 For a list of Justi's pro-Prussian pamphlets during the Seven Years War see the bibliography at the end of this study.

42 Matthew S. Anderson. 'Eighteenth-Century Theories of the Balance of Power', in: *Studies in Diplomatic History – Essays in Memory of David Bayne Horne*, edited by Ragnhild Hatton and Matthew S. Anderson (London: Longman, 1970), pp. 183–198, p. 183 + 190.

existing balance of power. The experience of the War of the Spanish Succession led Gundling to answer in the affirmative. According to him, the *jus praeventionis*, 'was not allowed to private individuals "*in statu civitatis*", but applied to great lords [i.e., states] acting "*in statu naturalis*"'. This was true even if the side exercising that right had not been attacked but merely felt threatened by another state whose powers were growing. A ruler, according to Gundling, 'was entitled to draw his sword when the other party was on the increase or stepping out of the balance, as one nowadays puts it'.[43] States were justified in taking pre-emptive action that would otherwise be unlawful, under the condition that doing so contributed to the maintenance or restoration of the balance of power. They could intervene in the affairs of other states and even wage war in order to redress the balance. This rule, Gundling asserted, was in effect an extension of the law of self-defence.

Christian Wolff took a more sceptical stance. Rejecting Grotius' advocacy of punitive warfare, Wolff opposed the idea of intervention by one state into the affairs of another state on the grounds of the latter's domestic conduct. Wolff agreed that an equilibrium was 'especially useful to protect the common security', but warned that the preservation of the equilibrium could turn into a justification of wars.[44] What was crucial was not that a state's growth in power upset the balance of powers, but the method whereby this growth had been achieved. Dynastic acquisition and commercial or colonial advancements were, in contrast to offensive attacks and military conquest, legitimate means of strengthening a state even if they upset international power relations. Wolff, however, left a door open to a 'just' military intervention against states that were rising in power, particularly those that seemed to delight in war as such and appeared not to be 'influenced by considerations either of justice or utility as

43 Alfred Vagts and Detlev F. Vagts, 'The Balance of Power in International Law – A History of an Idea', *American Journal of International Law* 73 (1979), 555–580 (p. 561).

44 Vagts, 'The Balance of Power', p. 562.

commonly understood (for example, reason of state)'.[45] If such a state displayed offensive intentions, i.e., if it

> should manifestly be considering plans for subjecting other nations to itself [...] the other nations have the right, for the purpose of preserving the equilibrium, to overthrow the growing power by armed force.[46]

Emmerich de Vattel also regarded a power equilibrium as crucial to order and liberty in Europe. He equally distinguished between just and unjust pretexts of war, asserting that the legitimate growth of a nation constituted no legitimate reason to attack it. However, Vattel was far more indulgent in granting a legitimate right of warfare against a prospectively hegemonic power. If a country gave 'evidence of injustice, greed, pride, ambition or a desire to dominate over its neighbours', adjacent states could rightfully take warlike measures to frustrate those intentions.[47] In the absence of such evidence, neighbouring states were only allowed to counter a rising power through defensive alliances or 'gentle means'. Vattel conceded that the concept of a balance of power had become more and more complex in recent times. Increased international dynamism as a result of commerce and industry threatened to upset or even annihilate existing inter-state balances on a regular basis.

Among the mid-eighteenth-century German contributors to the debate, Ludwig Martin Kahle was probably the most fervent adherent of the balance-of-power idea. In *La Balance de l'Europe* (1744) Kahle highlighted the necessity and blissful effects of a European balance.[48] His treatise formed the main target of Justi's criticism in his first *Chimäre* pamphlet. Kahle regarded the balance of power as a just and

45 Richard Tuck, *The Rights of War and Peace: Political Thought and the International Order from Grotius to Kant* (New York: Oxford University Press, 1999), p. 190.

46 Quoted from Wolff's *Jus Gentium Methodo Scientifica Pertractatum* in: Vagts, 'The Balance of Power', p. 562.

47 Quoted from Vattel's *Le Droit des Gens* in: Vagts, 'The Balance of Power', p. 562.

48 Ludwig Martin Kahle, *La Balance de l'Europe considérée comme la règle de la paix et de la guerre. Traduit du Latin par Mr Samuel Formey* (Berlin and Göttingen, 1744).

useful instrument for settling international conflict. In his view, the balance could put a definite end to traditional reason-of-state policies (and the concomitant threat of universal monarchy) and further commercial activities by guaranteeing Europe's peace. Hence Kahle believed all the states in Europe were under a moral obligation to preserve the existing balance.

Yet Kahle's appeal to a moral obligation to defend the balance forced him to face a serious legal dilemma. The vagueness of the balance-of-power concept made it quite unsuitable to regulate political action on an international level. Kahle demanded that the European rulers dedicate themselves to the maintenance of the overall equilibrium. Just as the individual

> could be forced to sacrifice some of his personal wealth for the good of the community of which he was a member, so a ruler might justifiably be asked to give up territory, even territory to which he had every legal right, for the good of the European state system as a whole.

In Kahle's view, legitimate rulers sometimes had to 'renounce their rights to secure the maintenance of the equilibrium'.[49] However, as Justi was to point out, renouncing rightful claims on a territory in order to uphold the dubious and hazy concept of the European balance of power was tantamount to abandoning properly legal rights for subjective and arbitrary calculations of power.

Kahle also faced a further dilemma: the question of when and how to coordinate joint action against states that seemed to violate the existing balance of power. Kahle claimed that the preservation of the balance of power was a valid justification for interfering with national sovereignty rights. Breaking treaty obligations or invading neighbouring states justified intervention by other states. Kahle believed that the strengthening of a state by internal growth threatened the balance of power less than its growth by territorial conquest. But he nonetheless asserted that the sudden and rapid economic development of a state could provoke legitimate interference from its neighbours. A military campaign against a state violating the balance of power

49 Kahle, *La Balance de l'Europe*, p. 147.

because of domestic advancements would aim at the restoration of the lost balance, i.e., the re-establishment of the *status quo ante*. For the sake of keeping the European balance states could rightfully be denied the extension of their power or could even be deprived of current possessions:

> As a republic has a right to [...] dispose of all or some of its goods when the common welfare that one calls the supreme law cannot be preserved by any other means: for the same reason it is permitted to take certain parts of a nation from it when its excessive power becomes pernicious to others and when there are no other means to maintain the rights of the neighbouring people.[50]

Kahle's definition of the balance of power allowed preventative warfare and territorial reshuffling in order to defend a higher moral concept, even if a somewhat cloudy and vague one. Kahle's view of the balance of power, Justi argued, justified the very reason-of-state policies it was striving to overcome. This would mean 'that parties who were originally not involved in a dispute between two nations might be forced to participate in [it] and to apply reason of state against one of the disputing parties'.[51] Kahle's stance that states were obliged to participate in joint actions against violations of the balance contravened the system's original aim. Instead of keeping armed conflicts within regional limits, Kahle's interventionist doctrine automatically turned them into issues of continental relevance.

The balance-of-power doctrine gained a new relevance at the beginning of the Seven Years War when Franco-Austrian pamphleteers accused Prussia and England of overthrowing the established equilibrium. The Austrian government reprinted Gundling's *Erörterung* in 1757.[52] Gundling was a Prussian, but his doctrine about legitimate attacks against hegemonic powers was now used by Austrian pamphleteers to justify military action against Prussia, which was portrayed as corresponding to Gundling's idea of a malevolent power on the rise. The Austrians claimed that Prussia had become too pow-

50 Kahle, *La Balance de l'Europe*, p. 143.

51 Yvonne Podbielski, 'Republics, Morals, and Peace – Kant's Perpetual Peace in Its Historical Context' (Cambridge: Diss. Phil., 1996), p. 94.

52 (Frankfurt and Leipzig, 1757).

erful and had turned into a threat to its neighbours, particularly since it was ruled by a monarch who was obviously fond of the military. Because of its aggressive behaviour Prussia's power had to be reduced if the European equilibrium was to be maintained. The impact of this argument was considerable. During the Seven Years War British officials refrained from the use of balance-of-power terms to justify British aid to Prussia since it was clear that it was Frederick II who had disturbed Europe's balance with his attack on Austria.[53]

The *renversement des alliances* of 1755 had replaced the traditional Franco-Austrian rivalry with a new alliance and thereby upset long-held beliefs about the European balance of power. Thus a new question arose: which balance of power was to be preserved, the old or the new? Together with the new Anglo-Prussian alliance the *renversement* had marked a fundamental breakdown of the traditional European power system. It became clear that the concept of the balance of power and its concomitant doctrine of preventative warfare against states that upset it functioned only if the balance was static or slowly changing. The *renversement* had undermined this assumption. It seemed that the unpredictability of human affairs had made a stable balance of power a futile dream.

The stability of the balance became an even more pressing issue because of the rising dynamism of the new commercial age which seemed to accelerate the incessant fluctuations and movements that made up the reality of international relations. If the concept of a balance of power was to function at all in times of increasing trade, there was a need for clear criteria for power measurement (to provide objective grounds for initiating possible interventions). Many authors started to doubt whether traditional quantitative parameters, like territory and population, were accurate benchmarks for power measurement. But no agreed solution was found 'to the problem inherent in

53 Cf. Ernst Kaeber, *Die Idee des europäischen Gleichgewichts in der publizistischen Literatur vom 16. bis zur Mitte des 18. Jahrhunderts* (Berlin: Duncker, 1907), p. 124.

all balance of power theories: that of estimating with any accuracy the relative strength of different states at a given moment'.[54]

Justi's critique of the balance of power had a twofold aim: to demonstrate the impossibility of measuring power in the new commercial age and to prove that the idea of a just war against another state under the pretext of preserving the power equilibrium was a vain and dangerous illusion. In his two *Chimäre* pamphlets he offered probably 'the most penetrating attack ever made on the balance of power idea'.[55] Justi showed that the balance-of-power doctrine led to a logical dead end, promoting the very militarism it tried to prohibit.[56] In practice, the application of the concept was driven by envy and fear rather than by altruism. Instead of forming a stable basis for peace it figured as the cause of wars, death, and destruction.[57] In Justi's view, the balance theory merely served as camouflage for the self-interest or party prejudice of those who affected belief in it. It was 'nothing but the ideological justification adopted by statesmen eager to hide their real motives, motives usually described by the term "aggression"'.[58]

Justi opened his critique in *Die Chimäre des Gleichgewichts von Europa* with an historical explanation. History had shown that ninety per cent of past wars had been fought as a result of petty passions such as envy or the princely fancy for foreign conquest, without the survival of a state actually being at stake. Since its origin in the fifteenth century, the doctrine of balance of power was deployed as a

54 Anderson, 'Eighteenth-Century Theories of the Balance of Power', p. 185. Theories of power measurement were popular at the time, as, for instance, Bielfeld's comments in his *Institutions politiques* (The Hague: Gosse junior, 1760) show. Bielfeld divided the states of Europe into four classes in terms of their ability to wage war. In his view, Britain and France were the two dominant powers followed by Austria, Russia, Prussia, and Spain, of which the latter, though formidable, needed allies and outside support to wage war successfully. In contrast to this, states like Portugal, Sweden, and the Dutch Republic could only act as the auxiliaries of greater powers. Finally, there was a negligible class of small states in Germany and Italy.

55 Anderson, 'Eighteenth-Century Theories of the Balance of Power', p. 191.

56 *Chimäre des Gleichgewichts von Europa*, p. 10.

57 *Chimäre des Gleichgewichts von Europa*, p. 3.

58 Ernst B. Haas, 'The Balance of Power: Prescription, Concept, or Propaganda', *World Politics* 5 (1953), 442–477 (p. 463).

propaganda tool for justifying wars that were otherwise unjustifiable. It could be invoked to hide any kind of misbehaviour. In virtually all cases, the balance-of-power idea was used to cover military actions that had been started out of jealousy rather than for patriotic or altruistic reasons. The history of the concept was the history of base envy against flourishing states. Once any one European state had begun to rise in power, other states united against it and attempted to strip it of its head-start. Holland, Venice, or Sweden had never been in a position to aspire to universal monarchy. Nevertheless, they all were attacked by a league of European powers under the pretext of restoring the established equilibrium.[59]

Arguing against thinkers like Kahle, Justi pointed out that the classical European idea of the equilibrium of power between Austria and France (with England holding the balance) had ended with the rise of Prussia and Russia and the *renversement des alliances*. The idea of a balance of power could henceforth only mean that no single state should become more powerful than the remaining states in Europe put together. This latter scenario, however, was a practical impossibility. Further to underline the absurdity of the balance-of-power idea, Justi turned in the second chapter of *Die Chimäre des Gleichgewichts von Europa* to the contested issue of power measurement, and investigated the nature of the real power of states. If, he argued, practical policies were to be derived from the balance-of-power doctrine, the latter had to rely on a firm notion of power that could be objectively measured. Earlier thinkers looked at quantitative criteria such as the size of territory or population. Yet in Justi's view such an approach was entirely misguided. Under Phillip IV and Charles II Spain, with its vast colonial possessions, was by far the greatest territorial power of Europe. Its military and economic capabilities, however, were far inferior to those of France or England.[60] As for population size, Justi pointed to the hugely populous Persian and Roman Empires that were defeated by numerically inferior conquerors. Nor were large standing armies a reliable benchmark for assessing the real power of states. As Louis XIV's oversized military apparatus had shown, the immense

59 *Chimäre des Gleichgewichts von Europa*, p. 11.
60 *Chimäre des Gleichgewichts von Europa*, p. 32.

financial burden caused by large standing armies could effectively weaken a state.[61] Large armed forces were also more vulnerable than smaller, but better organised units. The debate about a European balance of power, Justi concluded, was bound to end up in chimerical statistical calculations.

At this point, Justi again put forward the famous eighteenth-century argument, popularised by thinkers like Voltaire and Frederick, that real power and princely glory were gained by domestic commercial growth and development rather than by external military conquest. Repeating the ideas of his Viennese inaugural lecture, he pointed out that the strength and power of a state depended on the perfection of its government. Justi's conclusion was that if a state modernised itself it could alter the balance of power far more dramatically than by following the old military route of territorial gain. As he claimed, there was not a state in contemporary Germany 'whose true power could not be doubled through wise [internal] arrangements'.[62]

According to the logic of the balance of power, a state that followed such a strategy would thoroughly upset the existing equilibrium and could become a target of legitimate attack by others. A state could thus be prevented from rising to power by domestic improvements. Contrary to Kahle, Justi believed that the doctrine of the balance of power hampered the economic advancement of the states of Europe as it tempted poorer nations to attack their more advanced and more successful competitors in the name of the balance rather than concentrating on their own development. The consistent application of the balance-of-power doctrine would prohibit internal reforms in the states of Europe and infringe their sovereignty. This would be an obvious act of injustice. As Justi remarked, it was like granting a fool the right to drug a sage in order to prevent him from making use of his superior intellectual faculties. Justi perceived

> the dependence of a free state upon another and more powerful state, the latter trying to prevent the former from adopting the proper measures for its

61 *Chimäre des Gleichgewichts von Europa*, p. 34.
62 *Chimäre des Gleichgewichts von Europa*, p. 94.

> happiness, as the greatest misfortune of a people, which should be avoided through the system of the balance of power. Yet such a coarse idea of universal monarchy, which aims at reducing all states to provinces of its own state, can scarcely ever be realised; however, the means proposed to avoid it are to be feared far more than the evil itself. If a balance of power were to exist in actuality then no slavery would be as hard, since each state would oppose every other state. Upon each new domestic arrangement, each internal improvement, the other states would be compelled to protest and interfere in order to prevent the first state from growing too powerful because of its domestic perfection. And the mutual dependence of such states would be far worse slavery than dependence upon one powerful neighbour. One state would object to one feature and the second to another feature of the internal improvement, and each state would concern itself more with the domestic business of its neighbours than with its own perfection.[63]

The result of such inappropriate and constant attention to the domestic affairs of neighbouring states was the frequent threat of military intervention in the name of the balance of power. However, if

> a state, which has grown more powerful internally, is attacked [...] in order to weaken it, such action is motivated least of all by concern for the balance of power. Such a war would be waged by the several states against the strong state for their own specific interests, and the rules of the balance of power would only be the camouflage under which these interests are hidden [...] States, like private persons, are guided by their private interests, real or imaginary, and not by a chimerical balance of power. Name one state that has participated in a war only to maintain the balance of power contrary to its interests or without a specific incentive.[64]

The true *raison d'être* of the balance of power was propagandistic. The concept was invoked to cover the egoistic interests of a particular state in order to fight another state in the name of a non-existing higher good. All countries 'used this construction to win allies [...] and conceal their passions beneath it'. When a statesman proclaimed that the balance of power had shifted, he actually wanted to say that

63 *Chimäre des Gleichgewichts von Europa*, p. 60. Quoted from: Haas, 'The Balance of Power', p. 464.

64 *Chimäre des Gleichgewichts von Europa*, p. 65.

his opponent had grown more powerful than was the case previously.[65]

Instead of stability and peace the fraudulent transformation of the balance of power into a doctrine of just war could produce instability and military conflict. The balance, Justi pointed out, became synonymous with the very kind of world order that it was supposed to prevent. The policy of envy that hid under the cover of the balance-of-power idea was bound to lead to the creation of oversized armies, excessive taxation, and increasing public debts.[66] Justi believed the consequences of the 'mutual slavery' caused by balance of power were already in existence in Europe. This was a particularly dangerous development since the growing commercialisation of Europe rendered reliable power calculations (as required for maintaining the balance of power) virtually impossible.

In the new commercial age, Justi asserted, power changed so rapidly that it could not be determined precisely at any given point in time.[67] The growth of domestic commerce could quickly enhance the economic and military capacities of a state. European states were in continuous rise and decline, making it impossible to justify military interventions on the grounds of the preservation of a balance. Since one could not constantly re-calculate the power of states or foresee their future growth (or actions towards their neighbours), the very idea of a stable balance of power in Europe had become obsolete.[68] A fixed balance was as illusory as full equality between states. Equality

65 *Chimäre des Gleichgewichts von Europa*, p. 116.

66 *Chimäre des Gleichgewichts von Europa*, p. 79. Justi held a view similar to d'Argenson who scornfully remarked in his *Mémoires*: 'Since the reign of Charles V one has only talked about the *equilibrium of Europe* to sacrifice for the sake of this chimera more people than during the entire Crusades' (René Louis Marquis d'Argenson, *Mémoires et journal inédit* (5 vols, Paris: Jannet, 1858), p. 360. Instead of the balance, he identified 'the national debt, the lack of economy and princely money' as 'the only guarantee for the general peace that we currently [1752] enjoy' (p. 373).

67 *Chimäre des Gleichgewichts von Europa*, p. 81.

68 Justi deliberately exaggerated this point. Except perhaps for Kahle, no writer of significance was willing to advocate interference in the internal affairs of a state merely in order to prevent it becoming stronger through better administration or a more sophisticated economic life.

among states or confederations was 'as impossible […] as the equality of wealth among the citizens of a republic'. Since antagonism was the driving force behind human actions there was a permanent need for inequality. Different jobs, different salaries, and different spending attitudes among the citizenry would always create a certain degree of inequality, which, however, was highly beneficial since it stimulated general industry through the common desire for material and social improvement. By contrast, a strictly imposed egalitarian structure would suppress 'all industry and incentives for work'.[69]

In Justi's view, a certain amount of inequality between European states was necessary to create a healthy competitive environment on the international stage. It was shortsighted to cling to the balance of power which would keep all European nations in a condition of relative weakness and underdevelopment. For that reason, Justi viewed free international commercial competition as preferable to the plans for a confederation or union of states in Europe (as suggested by Leibniz or Saint-Pierre) and rejected their proposals for the establishment of coercive supranational institutions. For in his view it would be impossible to agree on a universally accepted arbiter who would determine justly when a state had upset the equilibrium, and decide on a possible intervention.[70]

Justi's critique of the balance of trade

Justi further elaborated his ideas on international power relations in his second pamphlet, entitled *Die Chimäre des Gleichgewichts der Handlung und der Schiffahrt* (1759) – albeit in a different way. Having dealt with the question of the continental balance of power in the first *Chimäre* pamphlet, Justi now turned to the other great battlefield of the Seven Years War: the Anglo-French conflict in North America and the ensuing question of a balance of power in

69 *Chimäre des Gleichgewichts von Europa*, p. 96f.

70 *Chimäre des Gleichgewichts von Europa*, p. 106.

overseas trade and colonial possessions. Justi defended English policies against the growing number of French pamphleteers who feared an English tyranny over world trade and urged European powers to unite against what they saw as a disguised English attempt to achieve a 'universal monarchy' of the seas. While Kahle had been Justi's main target in his first *Chimäre*, in the second he attacked French and Austrian writers such as Mirabeau, Jacob Nicolas Moreau, Maubert de Gouvest, and Martin Hübner.

Mirabeau in his *Ami des hommes* (1756/57) had identified the continental focus of France's foreign policy as a fatal error. France was better advised to ensure that her naval trading routes remain free. Since trade was a common source of welfare for all European states, England's aggressive commercial expansion threatened the peace and tranquillity of the entire Continent. In order to avoid an English tyranny over the seas, to keep commerce free and to restore a reasonable balance of power, France, together with its continental allies, had to fight England in the New World. Jacob Nicolas Moreau in his *Mémoires pour servir à l'histoire de notre temps, par rapport à la guerre Anglo-Gallicane* (1757/58), Maubert de Gouvest in *La Voix d'un Citoyen d'Amsterdam* (1758) and Martin Hübner in *Politique Danois* (1756) echoed Mirabeau's worries about the lethal threat that could arise from English commercial supremacy.[71]

All these authors asserted that universal monarchy, though attempted by Charles V and Phillip II, was impossible to achieve on the Continent. Louis XIV (who, in their view, had been an excellent monarch) had never aspired to it. According to them, the myth of Louis's military threat to Europe was deliberately nurtured by the English to blindfold the continental states and distract attention away from England's own aspirations to world power. The English had made dangerous advancements in their aims for empire. Many European nations were under direct threat: for the Italian states, the English possessions of Minorca and Gibraltar in the Mediterranean posed a considerable danger; Spain was about to lose Florida to the English in the New World; in a serious violation of international law, the English

71 Justi (and later Kaeber) falsely attributed Hübner's pamphlet to Maubert (Kaeber, *Die Idee des europäischen Gleichgewichts*, p. 126f.).

had attacked French trade vessels; and Holland had been prohibited by England to trade under licence from the French. England was clearly seeking a total commercial domination of Europe – a goal which could be realised only if she possessed overwhelming naval power. For Moreau, Europe had become 'a meadow whose watering stream [commerce] belongs to a foreign master [England], who can deliberately fish in it or change its direction'.[72] Since good neighbours would help fight a fire in the house next door to them, the European powers were now obliged to support France in her military struggle against the commercial tyranny of England. A coalition of continental powers was called to wage a just war against the monopolist British and re-establish the balance of trade between the island nation and continental Europe.

Maubert believed that there had to be a balance between the peoples of Europe not only in political power but also in trade.[73] For him the balance of power and the balance of trade were one, as the former clearly relied on the latter. The supremacy of a single commercial power had to be avoided at all costs. Each state, Maubert asserted, had a legitimate claim to a just (even if not an equal) share of overseas trade. He demanded the establishment of a balance of commerce that included equitable access rights to the seas and a fair partitioning of the European imperialist colonial project, thus turning the economic equivalent of the balance-of-power concept into a truly global system.

To Justi, Maubert's demands for a balance of commerce appeared even more ridiculous than the advocacy of a balance of political power. He scathingly remarked that he had never imagined that the flawed balance-of-power concept would be applied to other issues, least of all to trade. Justi started his enquiry with an analysis of the fundamental principles of foreign trade. He laid particular stress on the circumstance that states, like private citizens, were free to determine whether they became involved in foreign trade or not. Two

72 Jacob Nicolas Moreau, *Mémoires* (2 vols; Frankfurt and Leipzig, 1757 and 1758), II, 69. Quoted from: Kaeber, *Die Idee des europäischen Gleichgewichts*, p. 134.

73 Kaeber, *Die Idee des europäischen Gleichgewichts*, p. 131.

different paths existed for economic development, both of which could lead to the happiness (*Glückseligkeit*) of a state. One was the path of self-sufficiency and isolation (*Absonderung*), the other one was the path of exchange and foreign trade (*Umgang und Commercien*). The path of self-sufficiency and isolation, for which Justi coined the expression 'the philosophical way', promised permanent internal stability, but only a meagre international profile. By contrast, the path of exchange and foreign trade was constantly ruptured by discontinuity and instability, but promised immense wealth and great international influence.[74]

To the former category of states belonged small *poleis* (like Sparta) and large empires (like China and Japan) which had deliberately chosen isolationist economic policies.[75] Such states carefully secured their frontiers (e.g., the Great Wall of China), strictly regulated all foreign exchange (like the Japanese with the Dutch), and had no inclination to influence other powers or the system of international relations in a substantial way.[76] Justi conceded that hardly any nation could be considered entirely free in this choice, as it depended on a country's geographical location and general 'spirit' whether it engaged in foreign trade, or not. France, for instance, would never be able to follow the virtuous path of isolation. Justi modelled his analysis of isolationist states on Montesquieu's descriptions of republics in *The Spirit of the Laws*. Isolationist states had to be governed by strict legal codes established by historical founding figures (like Confucius or Lycurgus). Austere asceticism and severe restrictions on luxury were the hallmarks of these states. Tight sumptuary regulations were needed to keep up industry and a warrior spirit and to create a culture of virtue and patriotism. Though generally critical of national economic self-sufficiency, Justi acknowledged that isolated states were capable of a relatively high degree of happiness

74 *Chimäre des Gleichgewichts der Handlung und der Schiffahrt*, p. 968.

75 *Chimäre des Gleichgewichts der Handlung und der Schiffahrt*, pp. 947–955.

76 *Chimäre des Gleichgewichts der Handlung und der Schiffahrt*, p. 949. Justi believed the Spartans had committed a fatal mistake when they aspired to become the supreme power in Greece.

(*Glückseligkeit*). His sympathies, however, rested with the other model.

Justi's stress on the freedom of states to engage or not in foreign trade was a polemical move against contemporary French and Austrian pamphleteers. In this he tried to reject the view of Moreau, Maubert, and Hübner that the states of Europe had a common destiny as parts of a 'common republic of powers' due to their geographical proximity and a shared historical heritage that commanded mutual duties and obligations such as the guarding of the balance of power and participation in joint warfare against nations that threatened it.[77] Pointing at the absence of a supreme, supra-national power in Europe, Justi defended the old Grotian idea that each European state actually remained a free agent in the state of nature. The emphasis on the sovereign choice of individual states with respect to their external commercial engagements also helped Justi in his vindication of the English Navigation Act. States that decided to follow the path of foreign trade (*Umgang und Commercien*) were free to determine with whom they traded, i.e., with which nations they would actually take up commercial relations. Thus any state had the right to close its frontiers and ports deliberately to a particular foreign power. Such a protectionist move, Justi asserted, was no offence to the excluded nation, as the latter was also free to close its border and domestic market in turn. Thus the English Navigation Act was in full accordance with international law.[78]

Justi highlighted profit as the driving force behind nations embarking on foreign exchange and trade. States, he pointed out, could engage in external trade only if their goods were cheaper than those of competing states. Foreigners would only trade with a state if they found no comparable goods for a better price anywhere else. Often the geographical location and the fertility of the land accounted for differences in price and quality of internationally traded goods. But first and foremost, it was the industriousness and skilfulness of a people that determined whether a state would be able to manufacture better and cheaper products than its rival. As Justi emphasised, the

77 *Chimäre des Gleichgewichts der Handlung und der Schiffahrt*, p. 1004.
78 *Chimäre des Gleichgewichts der Handlung und der Schiffahrt*, p. 934.

industry and skilfulness of the inhabitants of a country directly depended on the perfection of their government (*Vollkommenheit der Regierung*), i.e., on good economic policies.

Justi distinguished between the concept of a nation's own balance of trade (*Handlungsbilanz*) and an international balance of commerce between nations (*Handlungsbalance – Handlungsgleichgewicht*) as used by Moreau, Maubert, and Hübner. The former would either be positive (favourable) or negative (adverse) depending on whether a nation exported more goods than it imported (or not). Justi admitted that a negative national trade balance signalled a significant *de facto* loss for a state. However, if a particular state suffered from a negative trade balance this was not due to illegal acts of aggression by its partner trading nations. On the contrary, it implied that its inhabitants lacked a sufficient degree of industry and skills, probably exacerbated by the imperfect economic policies of their government. Given that a negative trade balance was a nation's self-incurred fault Justi stressed that an undeveloped nation could never rightfully accuse other trading nations of unfair commercial exploitation. A state accusing foreign nations of exploiting it was acting like an impoverished nobleman who tried to sue the tradesmen who had sold him the luxury goods that had ruined him.[79] It was not the tradesmen's fault that the nobleman was stripped of his wealth, but his own lack of insight. Similarly, it was not the ruthless behaviour of rival nations that caused the economic decline of a state, but its lack of preparedness for market competition.

Moreau and Maubert's concept of an international balance of commerce (*Handlungsgleichgewicht/Handlungsbalance*) implied that every state had a natural right to expect a (guaranteed) neutral national balance of trade (*ausgewogener Handelsbilanz*) with other states. But, as Justi emphasised, territorial differences and the different degrees of industry and skills made the economic equality of states an impossibility.[80] Following Moreau and Maubert's doctrine as a tenet of inter-

79 *Chimäre des Gleichgewichts der Handlung und der Schiffahrt*, p. 939.

80 Like international equality of political power, international equality of economic power was impossible to attain. Justi found it unimaginable that one nation, for the sake of preserving commercial equality, should be prohibited

national law would mean granting underdeveloped nations the right to obtain a perfectly balanced trade relationship with developed, flourishing commercial countries. States with a positive trade balance would thus appear as unlawful aggressors that exploited less developed nations.[81] Furthermore, economically less developed states that suffered from a negative national trade balance would be justified in attacking more developed nations by military means. In Justi's eyes, such a view was absurd. A less developed nation which accused a more developed rival power of exploiting it (i.e., imposing a negative national trade balance on it) was behaving like a loss-making merchant who claimed that his business rivals were obliged to share their profits with him despite the lower quality of his own products.

The idea of a guaranteed equality in international trade relations was fatal as it meant putting an end to international competition and destroying the main driving force behind human progress and development. It was a fundamental principle 'that commerce by nature must be fully free'. Limiting a nation's right to export was against the spirit of trade.[82] States had the right to isolate themselves by withdrawing from international trade. However, once they decided to enter into economic relations with rival powers they could not ask for a guaranteed gain or a neutral trade balance, but had to yield to the competitive pressure, i.e., accept that due to differences in industry and skills some states would gain more from international competition than others. If a nation wanted to rush ahead in the international race for economic development, then the only options available were domestic improvement or colonial expansion.[83] The French charges

from making use of its natural resources or the industry and skilfulness of its inhabitants (*Chimäre des Gleichgewichts der Handlung und der Schiffahrt*, p. 973). Moreover, establishing economic equality on an international level was unenforceable. As with political power, economic power could hardly be measured accurately in practice (*Chimäre des Gleichgewichts der Handlung und der Schiffahrt*, p. 976f.).

81 *Chimäre des Gleichgewichts der Handlung und der Schiffahrt*, p. 941.

82 *Chimäre des Gleichgewichts der Handlung und der Schiffahrt*, p. 973.

83 Colonial expansion was justified as long as it touched on territories that had not been affected by prior discovery, i.e., were in no way affected by existing international treaties.

against England of violating the international balance of commerce and aiming at universal economic tyranny were evidently void. Such claims, Justi concluded, were merely born of envy. Their true purpose was to direct attention away from the genuine causes of France's poor state of commercial development.

In the second chapter of *Die Chimäre des Gleichgewichts der Handlung und der Schiffahrt* Justi outlined why the idea of a universal supremacy over trade by a single nation, as feared by Moreau, Maubert, and Hübner, was a phantom.[84] Success in foreign trade would allow a state to acquire hitherto unprecedented material welfare. Echoing Melon's theory of the cumulative advantages of a competitively hegemonic state, Justi pointed out that a commercially developed nation could expect success in the fashion of a positive chain reaction: such a state would attract high numbers of foreign immigrants, which would result in accelerated population growth and give the state further potential for even greater economic output. In addition, the influx of money would increase its domestic circulation, which would lead to low interest rates. Low interest rates, in turn, would intensify private investment and foster agricultural improvement. As a result, a commercially successful state would grow stronger and stronger and could easily outperform all of its less developed rivals.

At the same time Justi drew attention to the self-balancing tendencies of international free trade. At a certain level of development, the positive economic chain reaction would come to a stop – with dramatic repercussions for the country's foreign trade relations. Justi took a position similar to Hume's theory of the natural limits of export trade. Justi stressed that even if a state's commercial advancement outstripped all others, it would never be able to dominate the trade of its neighbouring countries entirely. Rather, it would once again lose ground to them. In a developed state, the price of labour and commodities would rise to significantly higher levels than in poorer nations. The rise in the rich country's price levels would undermine its market positions. Its products would become too expensive for export so that at the peak of a country's commercial

84 *Chimäre des Gleichgewichts der Handlung und Schiffahrt*, p. 946.

development, a certain degree of decline would automatically set in.[85] The natural laws of markets did not allow unlimited economic growth by any single state. Hence it was foolish to attack a country because of its commercial success. Trade could never be used to establish lasting political hegemony. For Justi, this was the ultimate proof that the balance of commerce, as put forward by Moreau, Maubert, and Hübner, was merely a propaganda tool to promote reason-of-state policies in the area of trade.

While Maubert, Moreau, and Hübner called for joint European armed action against the threatening commercial expansion of England, Justi was intent on showing that warfare was an inappropriate means of redressing the balance of trade. War could not prevent a nation from achieving commercial domination and was fatal for the countries that tried to draw level with the more advanced state. It hindered the expansion of commerce and was likely to halt economic development.[86] The idea of an economically less developed nation (such as France) waging war against a more developed power (such as England) was inane in a double sense. Armed action against a great commercial power had only a slim chance of success. The less developed state was likely to lose militarily as much as economically.[87] The weaker aggressor was destined to suffer most from his own military adventurism.

In the past, French trade and naval power had suffered heavily in military conflicts with England. Justi was convinced that the call for a joint European military strike to deprive England of its commercial power was bound to end in disaster for France. Instead of offensive warfare, a nation (such as France) that wanted to progress economi-

85 Justi made the same point in *Steuern und Abgaben*, p. 162. For Hume's position see: David Hume, 'Of the Balance of Trade', in: *Political Essays*, edited by Knud Haakonssen (Cambridge: Cambridge University Press, 1994), pp. 136–149, p. 138f.

86 *Chimäre des Gleichgewichts der Handlung und der Schiffahrt*, pp. 957, 988 + 993. Justi stressed that commercial states generally loved peace (as it was advantageous to their trade), yet were ready to wage war if they felt their trade was threatened by unjust means.

87 In the end, it was economic power that would win the war (*Chimäre des Gleichgewichts der Handlung und der Schiffahrt*, p. 964f.).

cally was advised to push towards domestic growth while maintaining peaceful relations with its neighbours.[88] If two powers fought for commercial interest they were unlikely to gain from it. Instead, neutral powers would emerge as the real victors of such a conflict. The Anglo-French war presented an ideal opportunity for neutral states such as Sweden, Spain, and Denmark to increase their share of trade. Based on his own experience in Copenhagen, Justi held that the positive economic results stemming from Danish neutrality in the Seven Years War could already be seen throughout the country.

To conclude, Justi depicted the idea of the balance of powers, be it in political or economic terms, in both *Chimäre* pamphlets as a cynical device for the fraudulent justification of pre-emptive warfare and a continuation of earlier reason-of-state policies. Instead of creating peace and stability, as claimed by its proponents, balance-of-power thinking promised to condemn Europe to permanent war. Rather than presenting a feasible tool for putting international relations on a firm legal footing, the balance-of-power doctrine was a hollow concept that could be bent at will and used to invoke moral support for any kind of political action.

Justi saw no need for the establishment of coercive supranational institutions or regulations, as proposed by thinkers such as Leibniz, Saint-Pierre, or d'Argenson. He mistrusted the position of Moreau, Maubert, and Hübner who championed mutual obligations of states against rising (i.e., potentially dominant) powers which seemed to be striving towards universal monarchy. Since not even a predominant power, like England or France, could hope for substantial military aggrandisement in Europe and since a commercial empire was an illusion, such talk was born of envy rather than altruistic concern and would create an even more volatile world.

By contrast, free international commercial competition was capable of effectively mitigating the permanent state of war which the Continent had endured. Reinforced domestic economic growth could eventually stabilise the European state system. The growing impact of international commerce would force political leaders to acknowledge the uselessness of offensive warfare and joint pre-emptive military

88 *Chimäre des Gleichgewichts der Handlung und der Schiffahrt*, p. 989f.

actions against rising commercial powers. If a country did not opt for economic isolation, it was better off yielding to long-term market forces rather than continuing with traditional, shortsighted power politics. To bolster their international standing, the princes of Europe had to concentrate on domestic growth and peaceful relations with their neighbouring states. It was commercially-driven policies that could eventually end Machiavellian policies in Europe.

The best way to adapt to the freedom of international trade was by creating a constitutional framework that would be supportive of free commercial exchange and by applying viable economic policies that would bolster domestic development. Justi's concept of modern monarchy was his attempt to supply the German states with a constitutional framework that would help them to compete in the new global race for commercial excellence. Parallel to this, his reflections on economic policy (*Polizeiwissenschaft*) elaborated on the question of how modernised monarchical governments could successfully support domestic development. In the following chapters I shall analyse these two aspects of Justi's thought in greater detail.

Chapter Four
Modern monarchy

The economic shortfalls of despotism

Justi elaborated his political model of a modern monarchy with the imperative for commercial success in mind. Trade, he stressed, was beyond the reach of political control. Commercial success could not be imposed on a country by governmental fiat. Echoing Montesquieu's well-known argument in *The Spirit of the Laws*, Justi pointed out that the wealth of merchants by nature escaped the territorial control of politics. Markets were extremely flexible. They could not be kept captive within national borders but moved automatically to the most advantageous socio-political framework. In his *Vollständige Abhandlung von denen Manufakturen und Fabriken* Justi noted that

> the despot can force his subjects easily to undertake manufactures and factories in the same way as the whip of a guard in Algiers can make a slave practice a craft which he has never practised before. Yet neither the power of the despot nor the lashes of the guard will ever bring the imposed professions of these two wretched slaves to perfection; and manufactures that have been instituted by force will always remain in a poor condition. If manufactures and factories are to be led to perfection, genius, inclination, assiduousness, and diligence are required; and these are the fruits of liberty and of a just and mild government, but not of despotism.[1]

Commercial success required governmental moderation, security of private property, and a reasonable degree of civil, albeit not political, liberty.[2] The trust in the integrity and calculability of government actions determined the extent to which the inhabitants were willing to

1 *Manufakturen und Fabriken* I, 38.
2 *Manufakturen und Fabriken* I, 37.

invest and use their money. In direct reference to Book 5, Chapter 15 of *The Spirit of the Laws* Justi concluded that nothing is 'a greater impediment to [governmental] credibility than arbitrary and unjust power'.[3] Since all states 'in which a despotic and arbitrary power reins, and under which injustice and oppression rules, have thousand ways of stimulating distrust' the domestic economy in despotic states was necessarily underdeveloped.[4] For this reason, Justi was confident that under the altered circumstances of modern international trade all empires governed in a despotical manner would gradually lose their power.[5] In *Der Grundriss einer guten Regierung* he boldly predicted that all countries, 'in which unlimited power has deep roots, will sooner or later turn into vast deserts'.[6]

What is more, since under despotism social standing was a reward for flattery towards the despot, and not awarded on grounds of individual qualifications or merit, no incentive for honest labour would exist. In states where 'goods, rank, honour and life merely depend on the arbitrariness of the despot or his ministers', nobody would feel an inclination to acquire goods whose enjoyment was doubtful.[7] Czar Peter the Great of Russia was mistaken in his assumption that the construction of a formidable navy was the first and foremost step for turning Russia into a commercial nation. The Czar, Justi stressed, did not see that 'despotism is by far the greatest obstacle to commerce'. As a result, 'the most important measure that could have been undertaken for encouragement of trade [in Russia] would have been the abolition of despotism, for which he [Peter the Great], however, had a deep liking.'[8]

The principal problem in constructing a modern monarchical regime was to find feasible constitutional safeguards for it that would

3 *Grundfeste* I, 659.

4 *Grundfeste* I, 643.

5 *Psammitichus* I, 157.

6 Tyrannical empires would eventually become 'so weak that they cannot hold back any more external enemies' (*Grundriss*, p. 219).

7 Cf. *Grundfeste* I, 619. No entrepreneur would be willing to invest in manufactures and factories in a despotic state because of the immense insecurity created by random governmental interference.

8 *Chimäre des Gleichgewichts der Handlung und der Schiffahrt*, p. 980.

prevent a future decline into despotism. Justi was intimately familiar with French controversies over the nature of absolutism and shared their suspicion that absolute monarchies operated under the permanent threat of degenerating into ruthless despotisms. Without some form of constitutional checks, the selfish passions of the ruler could too easily produce economically disruptive policies. Apart from princely fancies, general prosperity was threatened by pitfalls such as ministerial despotism, war, and the economically destructive governmental thirst for revenue. Taking the French example into account, Justi was convinced that the absolutist regimes in the German countries required additional political protection if they wanted to push ahead with their modernising reforms without falling prey to the misfortunes that had wrecked France.

Justi as a critic of Montesquieu

Justi's theory of despotism was barely more than a summary of Montesquieu's arguments in *The Spirit of the Laws*.[9] But Justi differed from Montesquieu on the question of how despotic tendencies could effectively be suppressed in monarchies. In this respect, his ideas were diametrically opposed to Montesquieu's corporate model of monarchy. Justi was convinced that attacking corporate privileges (like those of the feudal aristocracy) was an essential precondition for commercial advancement. In his view, Montesquieu's neo-feudal model of monarchy was incompatible with the new requirements of modern international trade. Accordingly, he attempted to prove that it was possible to replace the traditional balancing role of the landed aristocracy in mixed constitutions with alternative constitutional ar-

9 Also his claim against Montesquieu that despotism was not a form of government in its own right, but merely the corruption of lawful government (*Natur und Wesen*, p. 142f.) was a standard objection of contemporary critics of *The Spirit of the Laws*. Rousseau, for instance, made the same point in the *Social Contract*.

rangements which would operate equally effectively as intermediary powers (*Zwischengewalten*), but without the political and economic suppression that he believed were the hallmarks of noble rule in the provinces.

The debate on commercial nobility

The French debate on commercial nobility in 1756 provided Justi with key arguments to develop his anti-Montesquieuian stand. Justi's involvement in the debate falls into the two-year interval between 1755 and 1757 that he spent in Göttingen as director of police and lecturer in the university. The debate was the predominant controversy of the year 1756 and 'perhaps the most heated clash of opinions on political economy in France between 1750 and the Revolution'.[10] The initial spark for it had been created by the publication of an anonymous treatise entitled *La Noblesse Commerçante* at the eve of the Seven Years War in early January 1756. Its author, the Abbé Coyer – a renowned and highly influential figure in the circle of writers grouped around Vincent de Gournay – had argued for the abolition of the law of *dérogeance* that threatened French nobles with loss of status if they engaged in commercial activities. Instead, Coyer had demanded political encouragement of noble enterprises in maritime, wholesale, and even retail trade, following English practice.[11] His ideas immediately caused a furore in Paris and scandalised the French reading public. The *Noblesse Commerçante* received numerous controversial reviews in the literary journals; in March 1756 the publication of the *Noblesse Militaire* by the Chevalier d'Arc marked the first elaborate attempt to refute Coyer's ideas.[12] D'Arc strongly defended the existing legal arrangements on political grounds. Noble commerce could destroy the

10 Leonhard Adams, *Coyer and the Enlightenment* (Banbury: The Voltaire Foundation, 1974), p. 33.

11 Gabriel François Coyer, *La Noblesse Commerçante* (Paris: Duchesne, 1756).

12 *Correspondance littéraire*, I, 486–500. Paul Auguste de Sainte Foix, Chevalier d'Arc, *La Noblesse Militaire ou le Patriote françois* (Amsterdam, 1756).

hierarchy of ranks in France and was an uncontrollable political risk at a time of war.

With the parameters of the debate established by the texts of Coyer and d'Arc, subsequent contributors widened the quarrel into a controversy on the nature of contemporary society and the political and economic status of the nobility in it. Within a year, Coyer's and d'Arc's texts had gone through several editions and no fewer than thirty independent pamphlets, written by key figures in Parisian intellectual life, had appeared on the subject. Many others, such as Mirabeau, referred to the debate in their extensive works.[13]

The debate quickly echoed throughout Europe. As early as October 1756, Justi published a German translation of both Coyer's and d'Arc's texts adding to it a brief treatise of his own.[14] Writing in exile in Tübingen, the Scot Sir James Steuart likewise commented on the debate in Book One of his *Principles*, which he first sketched in 1757. In England, John Brown referred to the controversy in his *Estimate of the Manners and Principles of the Times* (1757–58).[15] The issue turned out to be of lasting interest. Almost a decade after the original debate, the Viennese economist Joseph von Sonnenfels discussed the question of noble commerce extensively in 1765, while

13 In the *Ami des hommes* (1757), Mirabeau discussed Coyer's ideas at length and rejected them on both political and economic grounds. Victor Riquetti, Marquis de Mirabeau, *L'Ami des hommes, ou traité de la population* (6 vols; The Hague, 1758–62), II, 3–10. Coyer in his turn answered these responses and criticisms of his work, and he offered a more elaborate account of his ideas in the *Développement et défense du système de 'La Noblesse Commerçante'* (1757), which once more made the topic subject of heated discussions (Gabriel François Coyer, *Développement et défense du système de 'La Noblesse Commerçante'* (2 vols; Paris: Duchesne, 1757)). D'Arc had previously widened his views in the *Histoire générale des guerres divisées en trois époques* (2 vols; Paris, 1756).

14 'Von dem Wesen des Adels und dessen Verhältnis gegen die Commerzien', *Der handelnde Adel, dem der kriegerische Adel entgegengesetzt wird* (Göttingen: Vandenhoeck, 1756), pp. 243–288.

15 Sir James Steuart, *An Inquiry into the Principles of Political Oeconomy*, edited by Andrew S. Skinner (2 vols; Oxford: Oxford University Press, 1966), I, 70f. John Brown, *An Estimate of the Manners and Principles of the Times* (2 vols; London, 1757–58), I, 205–207.

in the following year Denis Fonvizin translated Justi's German edition from 1756 into Russian.[16]

The question of whether the nobility should participate in trade was far from being a new one, making the massive reactions to Coyer's treatise seem surprising. As the *dérogeance* laws, which allowed only maritime and wholesale trade to nobles, had remained principally unchanged since Colbert's days, the topic had been discussed quite regularly throughout the previous 150 years without ever attracting such wide and immediate attention.[17] In 1756, however, the advocacy of a commercial nobility had gained a wholly new political and military meaning which constituted a serious challenge both to the traditional hierarchy of ranks in French society, and even to the monarchy itself. This ensured that the topic gained a much broader attention than it had ever received before. Previous debates over the idea of a commercial nobility were far less concerned with the political role of the French aristocracy as such, but were primarily concentrated on the technical question of how to ease the wretched

16 Joseph von Sonnenfels, 'Versuch über das Verhältnis der Stände', *Politische Abhandlungen* (2 vols; Vienna, 1777), II, 122–125. Denis Fonvizin, *Torgujuscee dvorjanstvo protivu polozennoe dvorjanstvo voenomu* (St. Petersburg, 1766). A Spanish translation of Coyer's treatise from as late as 1781 gives proof of the lasting impact of the issue outside France.

17 For a detailed account of the French *dérogeance* laws see: R.B. Grassby, 'Social Status and Commercial Enterprise under Louis XIV', *The Economic History Review* 13 (1960–61), 19–38. For general overviews of the 1756 debate see: Edgar Deptire, 'Le système et la querelle de la "Noblesse Commerçante"', *Revue d'histoire économique et sociale* 6 (1913), 137–176 ; Jacqueline Hecht, 'Un problème de population active au XVIIIe siècle, en France: La querelle de la noblesse commerçante', *Population* [INED] 19 (1964), 267–289; John Mackrell, *The Attack on 'Feudalism' in Eighteenth-Century France* (London: Routledge, 1973), pp. 85–100. None of these interpretations has offered a detailed analysis of the contributors' writings and their indebtedness to Montesquieu. The European response to the debate has not yet been considered at all. Kiyoji Kisaki ('Controversy on the *Noblesse Commerçante* between Abbé Coyer and Chevalier d'Arc', *The Kyoto University Economic Review* 49 (1979), 48–79) and Jay M. Smith ('Social Categories, The Language of Patriotism, and the Origins of the French Revolution: The Debate over *noblesse commerçante*', *The Journal of Modern History* 72 (2000), 339–374) explore Coyer's and d'Arc's contribution in detail, albeit under a very different angle.

economic standing of impoverished French country nobles, the so-called *hoberaux*.[18]

By 1756, the debate's primary focus had shifted to the far more thought-provoking political question of whether the hereditary aristocracy in France (and other European monarchies) still fulfilled any significant constitutional function at all which would excuse their economically idle, extra-commercial standing. The advocacy of a commercial nobility was thus not confined anymore to the position of the *hoberaux* but had turned into a direct overall attack against the aristocracy as such: did the nobility still provide a vital constitutional function as a moderating intermediate power between sovereign and subjects that would in any way justify their elevated, hereditary, non-commercial standing? Or had they not been effectively deprived of their political power under absolutism and transformed into an idle, apolitical class representing the remainders of an obscure feudal past that stood in sharp contrast to the dynamism of the modern commercial age? If so, was it not appropriate from a political, economic, and military point of view to substitute them by a more personally defined elite in the state, not based on privileges and birth, but on individual skills and merit?

Coyer's theory of a trading nobility

In the *Noblesse commerçante* Coyer vehemently condemned Montesquieu's rejection of a commercial nobility and wondered about 'the

18 Supported by the existing regulations, a small number of wealthier nobles (many of whom had enjoyed recent ennoblement) had managed to amass large fortunes by investing into companies enjoying royal exemptions or monopolies. Some of them had even started to engage secretly into retail trade with the aid of employed agents. In the meanwhile, however, the economic situation of the growing number of poor country nobles (the *hoberaux*) had continued to deteriorate dramatically. For them, entry into wholesale trade was unthinkable due to the lack of capital, not to mention the lack of business-related knowledge and education. Cf. Guy Chaussinand-Nogaret, *The French Nobility in the Eighteenth Century*, translated by William Doyle (Cambridge: Cambridge University Press, 1985), p. 92.

dogmatic tone' that Montesquieu had adopted, contrary to his generally favourable descriptions of trade as an activity not to be hindered by moral prejudice.[19] Montesquieu had come to the conclusion that commercial activities were incompatible with the seminal political role of the nobility to function as an intermediate subordinate power that tempered political actions and guaranteed stability and moderation within the state, preventing it from declining into either princely despotism or a formation under the sway of popular fury.[20] In *The Spirit of the Laws* he had therefore strictly insisted on the removal of all threats to the economic infrastructure, which underpinned the traditional hereditary aristocracy, and had pointed out that the nobility must remain outside the levelling force of markets as the only way to preserve their exceptional social status in an age of general industry.[21] In his eyes, the economically paradoxical idea of a privileged nobility entering into commerce together with unprivileged people would endanger the political and constitutional balance in a most severe way, and could cause the complete destruction of monarchy, either by resulting in aristocratic tyranny as, for example, in Poland, or – after an eventual loss of the aristocracy's political function as an intermediate power – by establishing the direct communication of power between monarch and subjects and, hence, create despotism.[22]

In Montesquieu's view, England was in particular danger of undergoing such a development. Although Montesquieu admired the English constitution and the English system of free trade, he nevertheless thought that they created great political risks. The English usage 'that permitted commerce to the nobility' was one of the things that had 'most contributed to weakening monarchical government there'.[23]

19 Coyer, *La Noblesse Commerçante*, p. 114.

20 *Spirit of the Laws* 5, 11.

21 *Spirit of the Laws* 20, 21: 'It is against the spirit of commerce for the nobility to engage in it in a monarchy', and it is 'against the spirit of monarchy for the nobility to engage in commerce.' Economically, noble trade would be without 'any utility to commerce'. For this problematic see also: Donald A. Desserud, 'Commerce and Political Participation in Montesquieu's Letter to Domville', *History of European Ideas* 25 (1999), 135–151.

22 *Spirit of the Laws* 5, 8.

23 *Spirit of the Laws* 20, 21.

The result was that the English free state conspicuously lacked the moderating, stabilising, and anti-despotic authority of the nobility. Any further increase of the power of the Commons or any further political decline of the aristocracy could upset the balance of the country's mixed governmental structure as a whole making it end up in 'a popular state or else a despotic state' with a concomitant and possibly even fatal loss of liberty.[24]

For Coyer, however, the political dangers resulting from noble trade were marginal compared to its potential benefits for the national economy. The French nobles, he argued, having been deprived of their political power under the royal absolutist system, had long ceased to perform their task as an intermediate constitutional power. A comeback was impossible because they had turned into an indolent and apolitical class or, 'a paralysed corps without movements and actions, and – even worse – without ideas'.[25] Powerless and economically isolated due to the *dérogeance*, French nobles lived an idle and useless life.

Reversing Montesquieu's theory of a non-commercial nobility Coyer pointed out that, if at all, it was the sudden economic decline of the nobility in an age of rising general industry that could endanger the political stability of the country. Leaving the occupational profile of the nobility unchanged with the straightforward intention of preserving their superior standing within society would be irresponsible given that in a fully commercialised state any non-trading group, like the nobility, would inevitably be condemned to undergo rapid deteri-

24 *Spirit of the Laws* 2, 4.

25 Coyer pointed at the obvious anachronistic nature of the nobility's privileges: 'What would become of our privileges if we traded? [...] Why would you not keep them? You could, as in the past, sport your coat of arms and murmur against the middle classes who assume them; speak about your ancestors to those who do not question you [...] challenge to, or accept, a duel; keep your exemption of the *taille*, on condition that you pay under another name [...] pay your salutations to people and birth; hunt inconsiderately over the farmer's crops; beat and belabour those good people; and in case of need be decapitated, instead of perishing bourgeois-fashion by the rope' (Coyer, *La Noblesse Commerçante*, p. 163f.). According to Coyer's ironic description, most of the nobles did not do a lot more than walking 'around in great numbers in the towns and in the country not knowing what to do with their existence'.

oration in living standards and, hence, in socio-political influence. Trapped in poverty by their small fiefs, nobles would have no other option but to continue selling parts of their land to newly enriched bourgeois buyers aspiring to build their own private estates. Consequently, the ability to engage in commerce would have to appear to the nobles themselves 'like a plank of wood in shipwreck'.[26] Coyer hence demanded the abolition of 'this singular and Gothic law of *dérogeance*'. Restraining commerce by such a law was 'like constructing dykes along the Nile to prevent its floods from fertilising the land', or 'closing a mine because it had been found too rich'.[27] Embracing trade, on the other hand, would make the nobility not only shed its image as an idle and useless stratum of society, but it would also enable their transformation into a social group engaged in a stable and active occupation. Such a move would also generate vivid emulation among the nobles, enhancing their ambition for personal commercial success.[28] By enriching themselves in this way, trading nobles would also enrich the state. To realise these projected consequences most efficiently, Coyer demanded an official end to the governmental ban on nobles entering any sector of commerce, and he fervently rejected the traditional distinction between noble engagement in the wholesale and retail trades, which he thought were merely separated 'by a thin line' anyhow.[29]

For Coyer, England was the example to follow. He rejected Montesquieu's dark outlook about the future of the English free state. England had achieved two essential goals: national greatness and a healthy and rich aristocracy, both due to commerce.[30] For that reason, allowing trade by the nobility was an essential plank of any French project to imitate English economic success, a goal which Coyer thought was attainable. With his position, Coyer stands in a long line of eighteenth-century French attacks on the *dérogeance*-laws that

26 Coyer, *La Noblesse Commerçante*, p. 10.

27 Coyer, *La Noblesse Commerçante*, pp. 172 + 179.

28 Coyer, *La Noblesse Commerçante*, p. 184. Trade would also help the poor *hoberaux* to break out of their hopeless financial trap. Coyer depicted their misery at great length and declared it a national task to assist them.

29 Coyer, *La Noblesse Commerçante*, p. 178.

30 Coyer, *La Noblesse Commerçante*, p. 68.

were triggered by the comparative political and economic perspective that French thinkers began to take when looking at England. English inheritance laws still allotted the noble estate to the eldest son. However, younger sons were allowed to enter trade, accumulate large fortunes, and subsequently reclaim their titles – mostly in the form of privileges and prestige rather than landed property. In the light of the recent English economic successes French writers were naturally attracted by a practice that had both destroyed the negative overtones of commerce and established a *dérogeance*-free involvement of the nobility in wholesale and retail trade.[31]

In Coyer's view, a commercial nobility would also make a considerable contribution to extending French agriculture and generating population growth. The unrestricted allowance of trade would provide the nobles with a new incentive to cultivate more of their land with more efficient methods. By thus achieving economic autarky the nobles would also be able to sustain larger families. Coyer pointed out that in both Holland and England national commercial advances had caused such growth in population. Similarly, France's population could be doubled, and Coyer asked, 'if our king would count on 36 million subjects, which monarch could keep up with him?' In short, in an age of rising international economic competition, it had become insufficient for the nobility 'to defend the fatherland with their sword'. They also needed to have 'children for commerce'.[32] Most significant-

31 Coyer's praise of English noble commerce echoed the famous remarks by Voltaire in the *Letters Concerning the English Nation* (1733/34) who had directly contrasted the English practice of noble trade with the vain aristocratic attitudes in France and Germany where even the lowest nobleman would 'look down upon a trader with sovereign contempt', while the trader, 'by thus hearing his profession treated so disdainfully', would be 'fool enough to blush at it'. Yet what, Voltaire had asked, was the social use of an idle aristocrat 'powdered in the tip of the mode' compared to the industrious merchant 'who enriches his country, dispatches orders from his Compting-House to *Surat* and *Grand Cairo*, and contributes to the felicity of the world'? (Voltaire, *Letters concerning the English Nation*, edited by Nicholas Cronk (Oxford/New York: Oxford University Press, 1994), p. 42f.)

32 Coyer, *La Noblesse Commerçante*, pp. 87f. Coyer hereby echoed the quite common eighteenth-century theory of an alleged population decline in France. Cf. Hecht, 'Un problème de population active au XVIIIe siècle, en France'.

ly, increased noble maritime trade would contribute to the bolstering of French power. It was crucial for a flourishing export trade, and essential for colonial projects. Coyer again pointed at England: 'They have pushed their nobility into navigation. Let us bring ours there, too, and defend French commerce with the arms it is attacked with'; by transforming French nobles into 'lieutenants, captains, traders, and merchants covering the sea with their ships to recapture from England the balance of trade, which was in favour of us eighty years ago'.[33] All in all, the nobles would have to yield to the dictates of the new commercial age, in which greater wealth, a larger population and, in turn, greater consumption had emerged as the crucial parameters for the powerful standing of a country in the international arena: hence the need for them to start trading themselves.

D'Arc's reply

In contrast to Coyer, the Chevalier d'Arc was a follower of Montesquieu, fearing the levelling forces of markets. Like him, he believed that noble trade was likely to promote equality among the citizenry, which would finally destroy the monarchy and 'result either in republican government or outward despotism'.[34] D'Arc accepted that trade was necessary to sustain national power, but he refused to accept that the English model could be imitated in France.[35] He rejected Coyer's negative assessment of French commerce as being swamped by both the Dutch and the English. D'Arc worried for France not in commerce, but in war.

33 Coyer, *La Noblesse Commerçante*, pp. 101 + 103.

34 D'Arc had been educated at the famous Oratorian college at Juilly and afterwards entered the army. Having distinguished himself in the battles of Fontenoy and Lawfeld d'Arc obtained the Cross of Saint Louis, yet left the military service to fully devote himself to a literary career. Cf. Frank Sutcliffe, 'The Abbé Coyer and the Chevalier d'Arc', *Bulletin of the John Rylands University Library of Manchester* 65 (1982–83), 235–245. D'Arc, *La Noblesse Militaire*, p. 61. An application of Coyer's proposals would directly 'lead to the destruction of monarchy'.

35 D'Arc, *La Noblesse Militaire*, p. 20f.

Unlike Coyer, d'Arc believed that a country's international standing still depended first and foremost on a strong army rather than on a strong economy, which he did not regard as a strategic advantage *per se*. D'Arc thought that merchants were of little use for the defence of their country. Thus he saw it as important that the trading activities of the third estate remained limited. Traders were calculating, self-interested men whose only goal was 'to enrich themselves by offering their fellow citizens all those things that weaken their courage'.[36] They conspicuously lacked any patriotic spirit, and were always prepared 'to move into different climates' if they provided them with a more suitable location for personal gain. While military men had to 'sacrifice their fortune, their commodities, their leisure, even their life', merchants only knew 'how to undertake everything in order to accumulate wealth, opulence, and luxury in a country but nothing to preserve its liberty'.[37] Trade would only make French nobles destroy their military spirit and make them abandon their duty to defend their country.

D'Arc proposed the transformation of the French nobility into an exclusive caste of warriors who would leave trading activities to the common people. This was the most appropriate division of labour among classes in a modern commercial monarchy. Re-militarising the aristocracy and retaining the *dérogeance* was the key for employing all members of society most usefully and making the political order stable. D'Arc was convinced that great wealth would corrupt the nobles. He recommended luxury for the third estate and asked the nobles to leave their 'useless pomp to those who can be consoled by it for not being born noble'. Nobles were to live a frugal life and devote themselves entirely to the service of their country. A compulsory military duty for nobles could be introduced for a certain period of time fixed in advance, after which the nobles were to receive state pensions.[38] To expedite this project, d'Arc demanded a drastic increase in the number of officers in each infantry and cavalry regiment

36 D'Arc, *La Noblesse Militaire*, p. 31f.

37 D'Arc, *La Noblesse Militaire*, pp. 32 + 39.

38 Exceptions were only to be granted to large families who would be allowed to exempt one of their sons from the duty.

and the creation of purely noble corps, in which even the rank of ordinary soldiers was to be filled with nobles. To make the army competitive and efficient he proposed a system of emulation whereby common soldiers were to be granted the chance of ennoblement for great personal merit shown in battle.[39] All soldiers could aspire to such preferment, but the title was to 'die with the individual to whom it had been granted'.[40] The conversion of the traditional nobility into a military elite based on personal merit would justify the stripping of the title of any noble soldier who by the age of thirty could not prove his further utility for the state:

> The state feeds its members, therefore its members must serve the state. The idle, and therefore useless citizen is a criminal towards his fatherland and steals from it everything that he consumes. The gentleman is a citizen before he is a nobleman, and the only privilege which nobility brings is the choice of the important services, which the state can and should expect from him. The moment when he ceases to think thus is the moment when he ceases to be noble, and to take away from him the title of nobility is merely to fix him at the place which he has assigned to himself.[41]

D'Arc thus followed Montesquieu's theory of a non-commercial nobility and defended the *dérogeance* out of a deep conviction that keeping it was the only way to preserve the hierarchy of ranks and, with it, the political stability of the monarchy. While Montesquieu had stressed the importance of the nobility's financial and constitutional independence based on the income from their lands, d'Arc was far less concerned about this issue. On the contrary, open to commoners, largely dependant on governmental payments, and subject to a constant meritocratic control by the state, his noble military elite was no longer marked out by its idle, land-propertied standing, but by its direct service, usefulness and commitment to the common good.

39 D'Arc, *La Noblesse Militaire*, p. 102.
40 D'Arc, *La Noblesse Militaire*, p. 103.
41 D'Arc, *La Noblesse Militaire*, p. 108f.

Justi's involvement in the debate

In his essay 'Von dem Wesen des Adels und dessen Verhältnis gegen die Commerzien' ('On the Nature of Nobility and Their Relation to Commerce'), Justi took a clear stand in favour of noble trade and strongly demanded the commercial engagement of the nobility in the German territories. He criticised the aristocratic principle of heredity as an antiquated impediment to the maximisation of economic activities, which he thought was better replaced by more meritocratic structures. Like Coyer, he was convinced that a separate hereditary aristocracy was not an essential constitutional component in modern monarchies.[42] Historical experience had shown that the landed hereditary nobility had always suppressed the people. Instead of figuring as a moderating intermediate body that limited the authority of the monarch and protected the liberty of the people the nobility had acted as provincial petty tyrants and effectively helped the princely sovereigns of Europe suppress their peoples in an even more sophisticated manner. Justi therefore proposed the creation of a modern monarchy without a constitutionally established hereditary nobility, and quoted Japan, China, and Turkey as successful examples for such a governmental practice.[43] It was preferable to have no nobility than to have one in the traditional, feudal sense. Montesquieu's effort to save the aristocracy from the levelling forces of markets was imprudent. A continued limitation of trade to non-nobles, Justi argued, would only foster popular prejudices against trade, and would cause a serious general disregard of commercial activities.[44] Successful merchants would be misguided to imitate the noble lifestyle and give up their beneficial entrepreneurial activities once they had acquired sufficient wealth. Instead of continuing to promote economic growth they would turn into a noble-like idle, corrupted and decadent class of people.

42 'Von dem Wesen des Adels und dessen Verhältnis gegen die Commerzien', p. 265.

43 The contrast to Montesquieu could hardly be clearer. For Montesquieu, these states were lucid examples of despotism.

44 'Von dem Wesen des Adels und dessen Verhältnis gegen die Commerzien', p. 246.

The traditional hereditary aristocracy had failed in their role as a social and political elite. Thus Justi wanted to replace the nobility with a new kind of elite that would actively support the promotion of trade, industry, and general welfare. In his eyes, the conferring of new hereditary privileges was a fatal error.[45] Since it was highly uncertain whether the sons would be as outstanding as their ennobled ancestors, heredity would only make the new aristocracy vulnerable to future decline.[46] Heredity would give nobles the right to enjoy a distinct social standing without the permanent pressure and duty to excel, and would thus prevent them from serving the state in the most useful way. Moreover, a traditional hereditary aristocracy deprived the state of the possibility to reward with social distinction all citizens who performed exceptionally honourable and useful deeds.[47] Heredity thus prevented the maximisation of social emulation, which Justi regarded as the motor of economic advance.[48]

Justi requested the establishment of an individual meritocracy, or personal nobility, which would be free from the traditional criteria of birth and land. The traditional hierarchy of ranks was to be abolished. The only hereditary status to be preserved was that of the monarch. Elements of popular representation, especially on the local level, were also to be established. The new 'nobles' would be appointed for a lifetime only after an individual examination by the state, since all kinds of privilege 'which is not based equally on skills and merit, is an undue form of privilege and does not contribute to the welfare of the state'.[49] If, on the other hand, one wanted to preserve the traditional

45 'Von dem Wesen des Adels und dessen Verhältnis gegen die Commerzien', p. 251.

46 Justi's (and Coyer's) views have much of the biting irony, with which Joseph II was to attack the positions of the nobles during his reign. Cf. Edith Murr Link, *The Emancipation of the Austrian Peasant 1740–1789* (New York: Columbia University Press, 1949), p. 95.

47 'Von dem Wesen des Adels und dessen Verhältnis gegen die Commerzien', p. 259.

48 'Von dem Wesen des Adels und dessen Verhältnis gegen die Commerzien', p. 251.

49 'Von dem Wesen des Adels und dessen Verhältnis gegen die Commerzien', p. 253f.

hereditary nobility at all, Justi suggested a similar examination for them, which 'should be undertaken with each nobleman at the age of thirty'. If, Justi continued,

> he does not possess by then the required knowledge and skills, and if he is not advancing in great steps towards rendering useful services to the state, he should be personally declared unworthy of his noble standing. And if the same happened in three subsequent generations in the same family, the whole family should be deprived of their nobility.[50]

By combining the reform proposals of Coyer's and d'Arc's treatises, Justi became the most radical critic of a landed hereditary aristocracy in the entire debate. Justi thought that the disempowering of the nobility would bring about greater freedom and create a more just and lawful monarchy. He was also convinced that the elimination of the traditional nobility would help the economy. Even the best constitutional regime would fail in international competition in case it preserved its pre-modern institutional arrangements. Montesquieu's idea of the strictly non-commercial status of the nobility stood in strange contrast to his projected intensification of socio-economic competition. Justi, like Montesquieu, saw inequality as having a favourable effect on commercial activity. But he believed that social distinctions had to be attainable through personal merit and money, rather than remaining as fixed ranks defined by land and birth.

The separation of powers

Justi refined his critique of Montesquieu with a discussion of the separation of powers in 1758 in an essay entitled 'Abhandlung von der An-Ordnung und dem Gleich-Gewicht der Hauptzweige der obersten Gewalt' ('On the Arrangement and Balance of the Different Branches of the Supreme Power'). He agreed with Montesquieu that a balance between the different inner-constitutional powers was a prerequisite

50 'Von dem Wesen des Adels und dessen Verhältnis gegen die Commerzien', p. 252.

for good and moderate government.[51] If all three powers were united in the hands of a single person, liberty was lost in any form of government. Only exceptional virtue, wisdom, and justice in the person (or body) uniting the three powers could possibly save liberty. Yet Justi believed it fully illusionary to imagine a human being that would not be corrupted by such immense power. The human urge to enhance one's power could only be stopped by another power. Given the self-interested, passionate nature of man, the rule by an all-powerful individual would always result in tyranny and political serfdom.[52]

As with his views on despotism, Justi's rejection of unified executive, legislative and juridical power followed Montesquieu's claims. His polemic against Montesquieu focused on the balance between executive and legislative powers in monarchies that he believed a near impossibility.[53] England had managed to preserve stable relations between king and Parliament, but all other European kingdoms had lost the balance between executive and legislative power, result-

51 The essay was first published in 1758 in Justi's journal *Neue Wahrheiten* and also included in the second edition of the *Staatswirtschaft*. In the following years, Justi reprinted the ideas of the 'Abhandlung' with minor variations in his two major political works, *Der Grundriss einer guten Regierung* and *Natur und Wesen der Staaten*. The date of the article confirms that Justi only turned to a more careful dissection of Montesquieu's political claims after 1755, although he had been acquainted with *The Spirit of the Laws* since his early Viennese days. Calling Justi's remarks in this essay 'the heart of his constitutional thought', scholars such as Fenske, Würtenberger, Obert, Wilhelm, and Vierhaus mistook them as a proof of Justi's alleged republicanism.

52 In the same way, the unification of the three different powers under a single council also had to be avoided at all costs. If, for instance, an aristocratic assembly exerted control over all three powers at the same time, the state would have as many despots as there were members of the council. The unification of all three powers could also occur in direct democracies if the assembled people made the laws, executed them and dealt with them in juridical cases. Such practice would naturally lead to an unrestricted tyranny of the majority.

53 Justi, like Montesquieu, believed that the union between legislative and juridical power and the combination of executive with juridical power were as dangerous as the merging of all three powers. The former scenario would end up in the tyranny of the judges, who would be able to create their own laws. In the latter case, it would be an easy task for the ruler to govern despotically in the name of justice.

ing in either princely absolutism or aristocratic government. Ancient German liberty had gradually disappeared from Europe's monarchical regimes. Initially, 'the German and other Nordic tribes in Britain, Gallia, Italy, Spain, and Africa' had conceded to their kings 'only a moderate power'.[54] Kings held the executive power while legislative power had remained with the tribe. Over time, however, this practice (as described by Tacitus) had been lost. The legislative power of the assembly was gradually passed on to the king. No trace of the ancient German liberty was left in contemporary Spain, France, or Germany, where '[t]he lowest prince reigning over hardly more than ten thousand subjects, thinks it legitimate to rule with unlimited and despotic power'.[55]

A few European countries, however, took a different course. In their case, the nobility seized the legislative power and reduced the king to a representative figurehead without much political power. This led to the oppressive and ineffective aristocratic regimes in Sweden, Poland, and Hungary. Monarchies, Justi warned, had to be kept at all costs from taking this aristocratic path for it guaranteed commercial failure. The aristocratisation of a monarchy would inevitably lead to anarchy and political oppression.

Aristocracy and unfreedom

Justi's descriptions of aristocracy epitomise his dispute with Montesquieu.[56] Aristocracy figured importantly in *The Spirit of the Laws* as a distinct type of republican government in its own right.[57] Montes-

54 *Natur und Wesen*, p. 118.

55 *Vergleichungen*, p. 27.

56 *Grundriss*, pp. 137–140. A more exhaustive discussion of aristocracy can be found in: *Natur und Wesen*, pp. 166–189.

57 Cf. David Carrithers, 'Not so Virtuous Republics: Montesquieu, Venice, and the Theory of Aristocratic Republicanism', *Journal of the History of Ideas* 53 (1991), 245–268. Contrary to Carrithers, Nannerl O. Keohane has not perceived Montesquieu's views on aristocracy as being valuable in their own right (Nannerl O. Keohane, 'Virtuous Republics and Glorious Monarchies: Two

quieu neatly distinguished between democratic and aristocratic types of government and devoted separate chapters to each of them. Although he moved from his earlier sympathetic explication of the inner rationale of the Venetian constitution to criticising the tyrannical results of that same constitution when compared to the far more praiseworthy England, Montesquieu was generally positive about aristocratic governments and careful not to express pejorative judgements about them. As Judith Shklar remarked, Montesquieu's purposes in reconstructing the political experiences of aristocracies 'were far more scientific than programmatic'.[58] What mattered to Montesquieu was not the search for *one* ideal constitution but an appropriate understanding of the institutional, psychological, and legal peculiarities of each type of government in their context. In contrast to this, Justi's discussions of the distinct forms of government were normative from the outset.

According to Justi, the corrupt nature of aristocratic government lay in its crude mode of singling out a distinct corps of patricians for exclusive rule. The split of society into an impregnable ruling minority and a class of governed subjects was an inherently unjust process that presented a permanent offence to the people's dignity and self-perception. Inequality was far more unbearable in aristocracies than in monarchies since the superior status of the caste of noblemen was unlimited. By contrast, the elevated standing of nobles in monarchies was effectively mitigated as, there, nobles and people alike were subject to the supreme power of a king.

Justi agreed with Montesquieu that an essential requirement for aristocracies to function was self-moderation.[59] It was imperative for the survival of a hereditary patriciate to conceal the true extent of their power and create an impression of solidarity with the disenfranchised

Models in Montesquieu's Political Thought', *Political Studies* 20 (1972), 383–396).

58 Judith Shklar, *Montesquieu* (Oxford/New York: Oxford University Press, 1987), p. 79.

59 *Natur und Wesen*, p. 177f.

commoners.[60] By masking their dominance the nobles could reduce inequality within the state and make aristocracy somewhat less obnoxious. The nobles also were advised to pay higher taxes and restrict their private luxury. The latter point was particularly important since the joint effect of aristocratic political power and economic dominance could increase the oppression of the people even further. Venice was the best example of such camouflage policies. Its constitution had set tight restrictions to the outward presentation of aristocratic wealth in the city and only allowed ostentation in the nobles' country houses on the *terra firma*.

Taking into account the harsh inequality that characterised aristocratic rule, it was inconceivable for Justi that a people could have ever introduced this form of government deliberately. Historically speaking, he believed aristocratic government had emerged from brute force.[61] Justi portrayed the invasion of the Germanic tribes into the collapsing Roman Empire as the most famous historical example of a widespread instalment of aristocratic government through external subjugation. As Tacitus had remarked in his *Germania*, the German tribes were organised in a fairly liberal way, with kings ruling by leadership example (and with the approval of the tribal assembly) rather than by virtue of their power.[62] But after they subdued the native inhabitants of the former Roman provinces, the members of the conquering German tribes gradually transformed themselves into a new class of nobles. All the newly founded Germanic states became aristocracies, or, more precisely, aristocratic monarchies. This circumstance accounted for the weak standing of kings and the oppressive power of the feudal nobility in medieval times. Fortunately, Justi remarked, the oppressive local rule of the nobility had been overcome in the recent past. Only Hungary and Poland still demonstrated the ori-

60 *Spirit of the Laws* 5, 8: 'When they affect no distinction, when they mix with the people, when they dress like them, when they share with them all their pleasures, the people forget their weakness.'

61 Amassed wealth was a gentler mode of introducing aristocracy. In some republics, Justi believed a small group of wealthy and respected citizens had managed to exert increasing power over their fellow citizens within the body politic – a practice, which had eventually turned into a constitutional custom.

62 *Natur und Wesen*, p. 171.

ginal horrors of feudal tyranny, offering a repelling, yet truly representative picture of the defects of aristocratic rule.

Justi believed that aristocracies had to adopt extremely violent and oppressive means to remain in power, as they were prone to degenerate into democratic or despotic rule. Due to the horrendous inequality, the people would seize every opportunity to shake off their yoke and gain some share in political power.[63] As for the nobles themselves, their elevated position would nourish among their more ambitious members the desire to seize political power and establish a despotic regime. Such a *coup d'état* was likely to gather the support of the people, who would see it as protection from the oppression of the odious nobility.

To guard against popular uprisings and noble conspiracies, Justi agreed with Montesquieu that aristocracies had to introduce a 'hidden magistracy', i.e., a sophisticated system of secret intelligence as represented most infamously by the lion's mouth in Venice, into which anyone could anonymously deposit his personal accusations.[64] For Montesquieu the Venetian state inquisitors were 'formidable magistracies who through violent means lead the state back to liberty'. Though aware of their brutal methods, he had regarded their goal, i.e., the preservation of liberty, as admirable.[65] Justi believed the result of installing such a state-inquisition was political slavery. Living in an atmosphere of permanent mistrust and suspicion, inhabitants of aristocracies would never get to know true freedom. He drew a far darker picture of aristocracies than Montesquieu had done in *The Spirit of the Laws* and condemned the latter for praising Venice. Despite the longevity and apparent tranquillity of its constitution Venice, according to Justi, still represented an inherently oppressive regime.

Another means to preserve the delicate balance of power within aristocracies had an equally detrimental outcome. Justi referred to the

63 *Natur und Wesen*, p. 172.

64 *Spirit of the Laws* 5, 8.

65 *Spirit of the Laws* 2, 3. Otherwise, he pointed out, the subversion of the established constitution would become a real danger. Montesquieu believed it was not the task of the secret magistracies to subdue the populace but check the ruling patriciate, i.e., to guard the guardians and 'to preserve the aristocracy against the nobles'.

installation of a *liberum veto*. It was a device to block any attempt by individual noblemen (or a faction of nobles) to secure an excessively large share of power within the aristocratic assembly. But it only resulted in eternal discord and prevented the government from furthering the country's welfare. As in the case of Poland, a democratic aristocracy would naturally grow weaker and weaker, until it fell prey to foreign conquest.[66]

Given the devastating effects of both a hidden magistracy and a *liberum veto*, Justi regarded the strict separation of power as a *sine qua non* for abolishing the oppressive tendencies of aristocratic government. If the united body of aristocrats exercised the legislative, executive, and juridical powers simultaneously, it would exert a tyrannical regime, as, for instance, the thirty oligarchs had done in Athens at the close of the Peloponnesian War or the Decemviri in early republican Rome. Justi believed that contemporary Sweden would soon fall under the sway of such a violent, bloodthirsty regime, as there the once duly balanced constitution had fallen into the hands of the aristocracy. The Swedish *Reichstag* had united all branches of supreme power, so that the dominant faction within it was free to exercise arbitrary rule.

Justi suggested the creation of four different aristocratic committees as a remedy: these committees would deal with legislative, executive, juridical and economic matters respectively. Although the coexistence of these committees would slow down governmental procedures, Justi was convinced that this was a small price for making life in such an aristocracy 'at least somewhat more bearable'.[67]

66 *Natur und Wesen*, p. 130. Justi's rejection of the Polish government runs through all of his writings.

67 *Natur und Wesen*, p. 176. In addition to an inner-constitutional division of powers, office holders in aristocracies would have to rotate according to a strict time pattern. Brief office terms were crucial to avoid oligarchic concentrations of power. Moreover, it would be recommendable to leave military command, as in Italian city states, to foreign condottieri. Justi quoted Montesquieu's example of Ragusa where 'the head of the republic changes every month; the other officers, every week; the governor of the castle, every day' (*Spirit of the Laws* 2, 3).

Justi's attack against aristocratic government culminated in his rejection of the principle of heredity. He regarded a hereditary aristocracy as the worst form of government and in both *Der Grundriss einer guten Regierung* and in his *Natur und Wesen der Staaten* issued an emphatic call for a true nobility which would be attainable only 'through very courageous deeds, great virtues, extraordinary talents and skills, in short, by great and publicly known merits'.[68] In this way, the natural defects of aristocratic government could be overcome. Promotions would need to be awarded in public and would be allocated only on the basis of individual merit to a limited number of people for lifetime. Elected representatives of the people, who would meet every three years, would nominate candidates for personal elevation to nobility. Appointments would then be confirmed by a council of censors, which the people would elect from the already existing body of nobles. Only the most virtuous and senior members of the nobility – Justi suggested a minimum age of 55 years – would qualify for election as censors.

Governmental power would be divided between two supreme councils, the legislative and executive council, each of them staffed exclusively with 'noble' members. In order to gain membership to one of these councils, noble candidates would have to be elected by the people.[69] Every three years, one third of the council members would have to stand for re-election. Both councils would preside over a number of subordinate councils, such as a council of justice, a war council, a police council, a council of commerce, and a council of finance.[70]

With the help of the division of elective power between the people and the new nobility, the defects of aristocratic rule could be overcome. Purely aristocratic governments, by contrast, would continue to be 'full of mistakes and unable to further the happiness of the

68 *Natur und Wesen*, p. 186.

69 *Grundriss*, p. 199.

70 With the exception of the council of justice, whose members would also be elected directly by the people, the two supreme councils would staff these councils.

people and the entire state'.[71] Justi remained resolute in his condemnation of aristocracies, true to his conviction that a monarch always had less reason to suppress the people than the nobility did.[72] In contrast to this, Montesquieu never spoke of the aristocracy having inherent defects.[73] As with any other regime type (excepting despotism), aristocracy, in Montesquieu's view, could be either well administered or corrupted. For Justi, aristocratic governments were faulty by nature and had to be reformed.[74]

71 *Natur und Wesen*, p. 184.

72 *Natur und Wesen*, p. 173; *Psammitichus* I, 86ff.

73 *Spirit of the Laws* 2, 3. Montesquieu too had criticised the circumstances in Poland where, in his eyes, 'the peasants are slaves of the nobility'. However, on the whole, he spoke in a far more unbiased and favourable manner of aristocratic regimes.

74 In addition to his anti-Montesquieuian assertion that aristocracies were oppressive by nature, Justi polemically remarked that Montesquieu had committed serious errors while formulating his position. As many contemporary commentators on Montesquieu in the 1750s had pointed out (and as Rousseau was to point out two years later in *The Social Contract*), Justi claimed that Montesquieu's assertion that voting by lot was in conformity with the laws of democracy while voting by choice was 'in the nature of aristocracy' made sense only the other way around. Contrary to what Montesquieu had assumed, Justi held that it was safe and reasonable to introduce voting by lot only in aristocracies as, there, every eligible candidate would already have a sufficient educational background to fulfil his duties in office. Moreover, election by choice would give rise to the creation of powerful factions among the body of aristocrats, which, however, as Montesquieu himself had acknowledged with his advocacy of an 'inner magistracy', was a great danger in aristocratic government. Consequently Justi remarked that in voting by lot 'the possibility of seizing the most important posts of honour with the help of corruption and thus securing for themselves the way to a rebellion that would be detrimental for the republic would be closed to the most ambitious and agitated minds' (*Natur und Wesen*, p. 182). Finally, it would be irresponsible to open higher official posts to everyone in a democratically governed republic without the filtering process of an election (*Grundriss*, p. 204).

Justi saw democracy as unsuitable for large territorial states.[75] Democracy, he claimed, could only be found in some remote regions of the Swiss federation. The classical problem of democracies was the question of how effective internal power divisions could be introduced within them which preserved popular sovereignty in its entirety, but softened and mitigated it given that the populace was commonly dominated by shallow passions and had too 'little knowledge and wisdom' in political affairs.[76] In Justi's view, the solution of this dilemma was to leave legislative power entirely to the people while handing over executive power to elected ministers who would be in charge of foreign and military affairs. Since the democratically elected ministers would not possess their executive power by an *a priori* aristocratic standing (as it was the case with the monarch in monarchies and the aristocrats in aristocracies) they would be accountable for all their acts to the people and would even have to accept the people's right of decision in crucial questions concerning executive power, such as the declaration of war and peace and the issue of entering into federations and alliances.

Another delicate issue in democracies was the election of judges. To prevent the people from acting tyrannically as prosecutor and arbitrator, judiciary power would need to be exerted by elected representatives. In this context, Justi again referred to Sweden as the negative antithesis of good government. He pointed out that in the new Swedish constitution the *Reichstag*, which had originally pos-

75 *Grundriss*, pp. 140–142; *Natur und Wesen*, pp. 190–210.

76 *Grundriss*, p. 141. The problem of direct democracy's lacking internal power divisions is a standard issue in eighteenth-century thought after Montesquieu. Cf. Rousseau's *Social Contract* or Kant's *Perpetual Peace*: 'Of the three forms of sovereignty, *democracy*, in the truest sense of the word, is necessarily a *despotism*, because it establishes an executive power through which all the citizens may make decisions about (and indeed against) the single individual without his consent, so that decisions are made by all the people and yet not by all the people' (Immanuel Kant, *Political Writings*, edited by Hans Reiss (Cambridge: Cambridge University Press, 1991), p. 101).

sessed legislative power only, had recently gained immediate judicial power, too.[77] As to the organisation of popular assemblies, Justi recommended the introduction of a fixed minimum voter turnout in order to avoid undue manipulation of popular decisions by organised minorities. He also rejected a system of class divisions in democracies with regard to voting rights. *Tribus* practices, as in the Roman republic, where the united voice of the people accounted for only 1 of the 193 votes, violated the first and foremost principle of equality of democracies and hence were by nature aristocratic practices. Justi regarded further limiting of the power of the people as necessary. Taming the power of the people was the 'cliff at which all ancient democracies have shipwrecked'.[78] He suggested the establishment of a small supervisory council which would control the proceedings of the popular assembly, with a veto-right to defer decision. By forcing the people to reconsider some of their decisions, this supervisory board could moderate possible excesses of democratic legislation and policy-making.

Mixed regime-types

Mixed regime-types offered feasible safeguards against despotism and presented viable alternatives to 'pure' governmental forms.[79] Justi held that the more the different powers were isolated from one another and the more they stood in a balanced relation to each other, 'the more stable the state will be'.[80] However, numerous historical examples demonstrated that the establishment of a lasting equilibrium of the different constitutional branches in a mixed regime presented a near impossibility. Justi was primarily interested in constitutions that included a monarchical element.[81]

77 *Natur und Wesen*, p. 196.

78 *Natur und Wesen*, p. 209.

79 Justi's discussions of mixed regime-types can be found in: *Grundriss*, p. 142ff.; *Natur und Wesen*, p. 210ff.

80 *Natur und Wesen*, p. 211.

81 Nevertheless, he conceded that a mixture of aristocracy and democracy, as in republican Rome, was a workable model. Republican Rome was the most fa-

As mentioned above, he feared a gradual aristocratisation of monarchies. He believed that an aristocratic monarchy was vulnerable to the threat that the nobles would one day seize political power and establish a purely aristocratic regime. A mixed constitution, in which the executive branch would remain with the monarch while legislative power (most prominently, the financing of the army) would rest with the nobility, had a natural tendency to let the nobles gain an ever larger share of power, threatening to leave the king with nothing but an empty title. Justi referred to Poland, Sweden, and Hungary as the most infamous examples of countries that had taken this turn. Within them, the nobility's urge to limit royal power had in fact damaged their own welfare, as the ineffective aristocratic government had weakened the internal strength of these states, turning them into easy objects of foreign conquest. It was a natural consequence of aristocratic-monarchical regimes that the people living under them were not only 'deprived of all civil liberty', but usually experienced 'the true slavery of the nobility' as well.[82] This development had been confirmed by the historical experience of feudalism:

> The German peoples who founded aristocratic monarchies after the destruction of the Roman monarchy reduced the peasants to personal servants and regarded townpeople, who only emerged through gradual liberation from serfdom, with utmost contempt [...] until the towns, having become rich by commerce, were able to protect themselves against the arbitrariness of the nobility by federations and hence rose in respect.[83]

mous historical example of aristo-democratic government. But it had also revealed the inherent weakness of this constitutional arrangement. A durable balance of power between the people and the nobility could not be established. In the end, it was most likely that the people, as in Rome, ultimately undermined aristocratic power and destroyed the constitution. And since Rome had lost its balance regardless of its highly sophisticated constitutional system, who could seriously hope for a stable arrangement?

82 *Natur und Wesen*, p. 212.

83 *Natur und Wesen*, p. 213. This view bears strong similarities to Hume's *History of England* and Smith's detailed historical account of European trade in Book 3 of *The Wealth of Nations*.

Justi next turned to the constitutional mixture between monarchy, aristocracy, and democracy.[84] This model had been realised in England. The king had executive power, the people (or rather, the people's representatives) legislative power, while the nobility was in charge of juridical matters.[85] Justi believed that the very success of the English constitution rested on the fact that it had effectively kept aristocratic influence at a minimum. He was convinced that even the comparably small aristocratic share of power within the English constitution represented a considerable threat and warned that the nobility was always ready to expand their power vis-à-vis the king, trying to resume their mythic role as defenders of the oppressed.[86] The English would be successful in preserving their free state only as long as they managed to prevent any enlargement of aristocratic power and kept the nobility in their minimal role as arbiter between the monarch and the people. This was the task in which the other European nations had failed. Against the one successful model of England, Justi listed the numerous unsuccessful historical examples where the nobility had torpedoed the initially well-balanced, mixed constitution and enlarged their share of power to the detriment of both monarch and people as, for instance, in Sweden, Hungary, and Poland.[87]

The danger of losing the internal balance of power was reduced in a constitutional mixture of monarchy and democracy. A patriotic king, Justi believed, would experience less resistance from the people

84 *Grundriss*, pp. 148–151; *Natur und Wesen*, pp. 217–219.

85 'If these three powers were wisely arranged in the fundamental constitution of the state, so that one of them could do nothing without the other, and that one would always be capable to halt the other as soon as it tried to adopt undue means [...] it will be the most wise and happy government, under which humans can live' (*Natur und Wesen*, p. 218f.).

86 *Grundriss*, p. 151.

87 If England could be regarded as the best example of a constitutional mixture between the three different governmental elements of monarchy, aristocracy, and democracy, Sweden was the worst. There, the aristocracy had effectively taken over. *De iure*, Sweden, like England, still possessed all three constitutional elements: a monarch, a noble *Reichsrat*, and representatives of the citizens, the clergy, and the peasants. *De facto*, however, Sweden lacked a division of power as the governmental operations had come under the sole control of the noble *Reichsrat*.

than an impregnable caste of aristocrats. A democratic-monarchical government would be the ideal form of government.[88] In it, the people would hold the legislative power while the king would keep executive power. The people would enjoy full civil liberty and elect representatives who would deal with political and administrative issues.[89] The concept of democratic monarchy influenced Justi's model of modern monarchy strongly.

Monarchy

Justi was deeply aware of the inherent dangers and shortfalls of the kind of monarchical rule that Louis XIV or Charles XII of Sweden had practised. Given that kings and queens were human beings, governed by their passions, royal misconduct was the rule rather than the exception. The desire for military glory and territorial conquest that had guided Louis XIV was probably the most destructive urge among monarchs and was responsible for much of the misery in eighteenth-century Europe. Justi acknowledged that no form of government could 'as easily turn evil as monarchy', and regarded it ridiculous that peoples entrusted their welfare and security to the hands of a single person.[90]

Absolute monarchies had an inclination to abrupt changes in policies.[91] The shortsightedness and inconsistency that characterised the policies of European rulers were major obstacles to commercial advancement. Thus it was hardly surprising that all major trading states of the past had been republics. Tyre, Carthage, Marseilles, Venice, Genoa, the Hanseatic cities, and Holland had all enjoyed a dominant trade position at times when the rest of Europe suffered under princely arbitrariness and feudal oppression. With his theory of

88 *Natur und Wesen*, p. 214.
89 *Grundriss*, p. 145.
90 *Vergleichungen*, p. 5.
91 *Grundfeste* I, 772.

modern monarchy Justi sought to dislodge the assumption that small city-republics were by nature more compatible with commercial excellence than large territorial monarchies. In his view, the monarchical form of government was just as suitable for commercial success as the republican one. The example of the economic advancement in France under Colbert prior to Louis' military campaigns had shown that monarchies could easily attain as high a level of economic development as republics, provided they operated under the rule of law and granted their citizens a sufficient degree of civil liberty. Indeed, while republics usually required a long period of time to achieve commercial excellence, Justi was convinced that monarchies could do so much more rapidly.[92] The monarchical state, as 'the simplest and least artificial machine', allowed for the prompt execution of governmental orders and could generally be expected to react to political and economic changes much faster and more effectively than either democratic or aristocratic republics.[93]

Monarchical regimes possessed remarkable advantages. Justi adopted Montesquieu's fundamental assumption that commercial activities were far less problematic in monarchies than in republics, since the former did not rely on the public-spiritedness of their citizens. Monarchies could also live with virtually unrestrained inequality.[94] In the monarchical society of inequality everybody would strive for higher standing and greater social respect. Justi alluded to these Montesquieuian themes when he remarked in *Die Grundfeste* that monarchy was the proper form of government for emulation.[95]

92 *Manufakturen und Fabriken* I, 37; *Grundfeste* I, 772ff.

93 *Natur und Wesen*, p. 161. Similarly in: *Grundriss*, p. 135. Justi's view that thorough reforms of absolute monarchies could enable them to rival or even surpass the economic success of their republican competitors resembles Hume's hypothesis in the essay 'Of civil liberty': that 'if a prince or minister should appear, one endowed with sufficient discernment to know his own and the public's interest, and with sufficient force of mind to break through ancient customs, the economic difference between absolute governments and free ones, like Holland or England, could be lowered and eventually overcome' (Hume, *Political Essays*, p. 53).

94 *Natur und Wesen*, p. 144f.

95 *Grundfeste* II, 353.

How did Justi dismiss the objections that monarchy was a potentially unstable and dangerous form of government that could easily turn into the rule of a single, selfish individual? The problem, he asserted, was in the actual practice of monarchical rule in Europe and not in the monarchical form of government *per se*. With thorough reforms a modernised monarchical regime could be created that was secure against princely arbitrariness. Surprisingly, Justi did not advocate institutional barriers to curtail the power of the monarch as in the English constitution. The historical balance of the English constitution could not be copied in a different state. And as the failed Swedish experiment had shown, a stronger monarchical power was always preferable to a revived aristocratic oligarchy. Justi knew that the necessary reforms could only be implemented by a strong central power. His problem was the establishment of an unlimited royal authority which allowed no possibility for the monarch's abusing his power.

The debate about the historical origin of French monarchy

In developing his position Justi drew extensively on the theories that were developed in the eighteenth-century debates surrounding the historical origin of French monarchy.[96] Montesquieu himself had discussed these issues at considerable length in the final books of *The Spirit of the Laws*. Though seemingly marginal, books 28, 30, and 31 were in fact central contributions to the Old Regime's debate about the legendary Frankish conquest and its putative consequences, 'the French counterpart of the English discussions about the ancient constitution and the feudal law' and 'the most famous of the controversies to which the history of France has ever been subject'.[97] Participants in these debates have been branded (in nineteenth-century terminology) as proponents either of the 'aristocratic tendency' (*thèse nobiliaire*) or of the 'royalist tendency' (*thèse royale*). Supporters of

96 *Grundriss*, p. 175.

97 Harold A. Ellis, 'Montesquieu's Modern Politics – *The Spirit of the Laws* and the Problem of Modern Monarchy in Old Regime France', *History of Political Thought* 10 (1989), 665–700 (p. 669).

the aristocracy (among them, Montesquieu) argued in favour of a mixed regime, while proponents of the 'royal thesis' advocated a monarchy resting on broad popular support.[98]

Montesquieu's discussions in *The Spirit of the Laws* drew on arguments developed in the course of the famous controversy between Henri Boulainvilliers and the Abbé Dubos about French monarchy and the history that had produced it. Boulainvilliers's historical explanation of the beginning of feudal government in France, as outlined in his *État de la France*, presented a categorical rejection of absolutism. Once posthumous editions of his work started to appear in 1727, Boulainvilliers became turned into 'one of eighteenth-century France's leading aristocratic reactionaries' and into one of the fathers of eighteenth-century *thèse nobiliaire* thinking.[99]

Boulainvilliers drew a rosy picture of the 'mixed government' of medieval France, a regime in which 'crown' and 'nation' actually shared sovereignty. At the root of Boulainvilliers's anti-royalism stood his historical explanation of the Frankish conquest of Gaul. After the collapse of the Roman Empire, the Franks, whom Boulainvilliers regarded as the old nobility's ancestors, had conquered the Romans in Gaul and set up a German aristocratic state. The French kings originally were elected by the military aristocracy and had no right to legislate or govern without the Estates. The balance of the Gothic government was lost in subsequent centuries and ultimately abolished by modern absolutism. Boulainvilliers demanded that the Estates once more share in governmental power. The French king would have to respect again the fundamental laws of the ancient French constitution and take the advice of the Estates into account in all of his decisions.

Boulainvilliers's views were opposed by Jean-Baptiste Dubos in his multi-volume *Histoire critique de l'établissement de la monarchie*

98 Nannerl O. Keohane, *Philosophy and the State in France – the Renaissance to Enlightenment* (Princeton: Princeton University Press, 1980) p. 346.

99 Harold A. Ellis, *Boulainvilliers and the French Monarchy – Aristocratic Politics in Early Eighteenth-Century France* (Ithaca: Cornell University Press, 1988), p. 419; Kingsley Martin, *French Liberal Thought in the Eighteenth Century* (London: Phoenix House, 1962), p. 57.

française (1734). Dubos demolished Boulainvilliers' myth of a supposed Frankish conquest and the supposition that the conquering Franks had enslaved the defeated Gallo-Romans and established an aristocratic regime based upon the ancient liberty of the Germanic tribes. He boldly claimed that a Frankish conquest of Gaul had never taken place. The Franks and the Romans had, in fact, formed a strategic alliance. As Roman allies, the Frankish kings had taken over the exercise of Roman imperial authority. The Roman society had not been destroyed. The Merovingian kings simply exercised the same hereditary and absolute power as the Roman emperors had done before. They did of course consult the assemblies of the 'grands'. But the decision-making power always rested with the king, and not with the assembly. Thus the French monarchy had always been absolutist. In Dubos's view, Boulainvilliers's demand for a revival of noble power in France lacked historical provenance.

Montesquieu's commented on the debate in Chapter 1 of Book 30 of *The Spirit of the Laws*. He sought to revive and revise Boulainvilliers's account of the Frankish conquest and defend it against Dubos in order to discover in France's Germanic past the roots of modern French liberty. For Montesquieu, Europe's 'Gothic government' figured as 'the seedbed of modern politics and liberty in Europe [...] on both sides of the English Channel'.[100] It is worth quoting his eulogy of 'Gothic government' in *The Spirit of the Laws* at full length:

> Here is how the plan for the monarchies that we know was formed. On the subject one has only to see Tacitus on the *Mores of Germans*. The conquerors spread out across the country; they lived in the countryside, rarely in towns. When they were in Germany, the whole nation could be assembled. When they dispersed during the conquest, they could no longer assemble. Nevertheless, the nation had to deliberate on its business as it had done before the conquest; it did so by representatives. Here is the origin of Gothic government among us. It was at first a mixture of aristocracy and monarchy. Its drawback was that the common people were slaves; it was good government that had within itself the capacity to become better. Giving letters of emancipation became the custom, and soon the civil liberty of the people, the prerogatives of the nobility and of the clergy, and the power of the kings, were in such concert that there has never been, I believe, a government on earth as well tempered as that of each part of

100 Ellis, 'Montesquieu's Modern Politics', p. 695.

> Europe during the time that this government continued to exist; and it is remarkable that the corruption of the government of a conquering people should have formed the best kind of government men have been able to devise.[101]

Despite his praise of the English constitution Montesquieu was convinced that England's neo-German politics were no less exposed to the risks of despotism than France's. In both cases, the imminent danger had arisen from the gradual weakening and partial destruction of the intermediate power of the nobility. In constructing their modern government devoted to liberty, the English had unduly abolished the prerogatives of the lords, clergy, towns, and nobility and thus undermined the very institutions that sustained their liberty.[102]

French discussions of *The Spirit of the Laws* in the 1750s focused on this kind of 'Boulainvilliers–Dubos–Montesquieu debate' (Ellis). For its contemporary readers, *The Spirit of the Laws* was mainly a powerful defence of aristocratic positions. Since the hypothesis of the assumed antiquity of the French nobility (being older than the monarchy itself) and the positive view of the integrity of Gothic government (with its well-established balance between king and feudal aristocracy) were crucial for Montesquieu's argument that a strict hierarchy of ranks was necessary to rehabilitate the intermediary political power of the nobility, it was a standard move for French *thèse royale* critics to refute Montesquieu's political claims by attacking his historical explanations.

In France, Forbonnais was among the first to attack Montesquieu for his historical interpretation of the feudal government.[103] In a similar way, Claude Dupin in his *Observations sur un livre intitulé de l'Esprit des loix* (1750) saw no historical linkage between the ancient German tribes and the contemporary nobility in France. Dupin defended Dubos against Montesquieu and refuted the latter's claims that intermediary powers were essential constitutional elements of monarchy. As Dupin pointed out, one had seen (and could still see) numerous examples of well-functioning monarchies that operated

101 *Spirit of the Laws* 11, 8.

102 *Spirit of the Laws* 2, 4 + 20, 21.

103 Eli Carcassonne, *Montesquieu et le problème de la constitution française au XVIIIe siècle* (Paris: Presses universitaires de France, 1930), p. 129.

without hereditary nobility. The contemporary French nobility lacked any real political power, and there was no need for a revival of their political say. France could well operate like China, Persia, and Turkey (which rested on a firm legal foundation and were not, as Montesquieu had claimed, despotisms).[104]

Unlike most of Montesquieu's critics Justi did not question the correctness of Boulainvilliers's and Montesquieu's accounts of the historical development of French monarchy. Their explanations, he asserted in his *Natur und Wesen der Staaten*, were accurate. Their conclusions, however, were erroneous. Justi thus contested both Dubos's interpretation of the French past and Montesquieu's claims about the excellence and historical legitimacy of the feudal system. France, like all kingdoms founded by German tribes on the ruins of the Roman Empire, had indeed been a very limited monarchy. Yet ancient German liberty, praised by Montesquieu as the fount of English political liberty, was an irretrievable feature of the past, irrelevant to present-day constitutions. Tacitus' account of the Germanic kingdoms of classical antiquity in which kings had reigned only 'by example', but were dependent on the approval of a council of noblemen had unduly fascinated Montesquieu's mind. Happily, Justi stressed, virtually nothing was left of this mixed constitution. As Justi had already emphasised in previous discussions of aristocracy, countries like Poland and Hungary, where the feudal heritage was most alive, were subject to the worst forms of political suppression. Montesquieu's historical interpretation of feudalism merely served to disguise what the nobility really represented: a ruthless bunch of local petty tyrants.[105]

104 Despotism, Dupin remarked, was not a form of government in its own right, but merely the deterioration of a regime. Antoine Pecquet in his *Analyse raisonnée de l'Esprit des loix* (1758) took up the same aspect stating that despotism was simply the abuse of monarchy, i.e., the government of a single individual not bound by fundamental laws (Carcassonne, *Montesquieu et le problème de la constitution française*, p. 138f.). From contemporary critics of Montesquieu such as Dupin and Pecquet, Justi took over the idea that despotism was no form of government in its own right.

105 Justi's ideas bear some similarity to Diderot's position in the *Encyclopédie* (article 'Représentants') which, however, was drafted later. Diderot also agreed

Consequently, Montesquieu's demand in *The Spirit of the Laws* to limit royal absolutist power by reinvigorating the political voice of the aristocracy was a move into the wrong direction. It was a step backwards that would hamper trade and augment political oppression once again rather than safeguard civil liberty. Montesquieu had not understood that feudalism was by nature an unjust and suppressive system. His general admiration for *The Spirit of the Laws* notwithstanding, Justi was convinced that his French counterpart had fallen short in this particular aspect. Montesquieu had remained too feudophile (even in his praise of modern English liberty) and too blind with respect to the naturally oppressive function of a privileged caste, like the hereditary nobility.

By contrast, Justi viewed the customary limits that the aristocracy and other corporate groups, such as guilds and inns, placed upon the central monarchical authority as a corruptive influence that weakened the governmental administration and supported ruthless tyranny on the local level. Influenced by his experience of Haugwitz's administrative reforms and the European struggle for power in the 1750s, Justi pleaded for the systematic elimination of any influence that could be exerted by the provincial Estates on issues such as local governmental organisation or taxation. As the states of Europe needed effective, speedy execution of central government decisions, there was no longer room for local autonomy.

Absolutism was the living proof that the nobility was ineffective in checking the power of the monarch.[106] If it were really thus, absolute monarchies would have never come into existence. Yet they were not only in existence: the majority of them even operated in a lawful

with Boulainvilliers's historical explanations, but rejected his defence of the aristocracy. For the discussions of the 'Germanistic' and 'Romanistic' theories among the Encyclopédistes (particularly Diderot, Boucher d'Argis, and Jaucourt) see: Eberhard Weiss, *Geschichtsschreibung und Staatsauffassung in der französischen Enzyklopädie* (Wiesbaden: Franz Steiner, 1956), p. 29ff.

106 Montesquieu was mistaken in asserting that the '[i]ntermediate, subordinate, and dependent powers constitute the nature of monarchical government, that is, of the government in which one alone governs by fundamental laws'. His claim had been invalidated by the recent path of history. *Spirit of the Laws* 2, 4.

manner without relying any longer on the traditional hereditary aristocracy.

Justi scathingly pointed out that the French nobles had been incapable of halting Louis XIV's seizure of unlimited royal power. By no means had they been able to avoid the firm steps towards despotism that had been undertaken by Richelieu and Mazarin. Montesquieu had generally thought too much of France when making normative political statements in *The Spirit*.[107] Similar examples of the inherent weakness of the nobility could be found in other European countries as well as in the history of the more distant despotic regimes in Asia. As Justi pointed out in his *Vergleichungen*, Japan, Indostan, Siam, and Ceylon all had their hereditary castes of nobles which nevertheless remained fully ineffective against the all-dominant despotic power of the ruler. And what, Justi asked, should the nobility do 'once they are being suppressed and the ruler has united all arbitrary power in his own hands?'[108] New ambitious servants paid by the king for unconditional loyalty would gladly assume the nobility's place. Hence, Justi concluded, if Montesquieu 'states in his work from time to time that it is the nobility which keeps the unlimited monarchy from falling into despotism, he claims something for which he lacks profound evidence'.[109]

Representation

Despite his rejection of hereditary aristocracy, Justi agreed with Montesquieu that a monarchical constitution had to provide checks against unlawful princely actions. Since the aristocracy had 'an interest that is remarkably different from the true advantage for the people' the traditional Estates were not the right vehicle for this purpose. The nobleman

107 *Natur und Wesen*, p. 151.
108 *Natur und Wesen*, p. 154.
109 *Natur und Wesen*, p. 153.

> who himself does not pay any contributions and whose vote sometimes has the power and weight equivalent to a mid-sized town even though he owns only a few acres of land and ten peasants, votes freely to the detriment of the purse of his fellow citizens.[110]

Justi approved those German princes who no longer summoned their Estates. In abolishing them, princes had their own welfare, rather than that of the populace at large, in mind. But in doing so they nevertheless had done their countries a great service. The attention paid to the Estates was 'useless fuss'.[111]

Justi's condemnation of the nobility's representation and his apology for absolutism were essentially borrowed from arguments of French *thèse royale* thinkers such as Saint-Pierre, d'Argenson, or Voltaire. Saint-Pierre in his 'Observations politiques sur le gouvernement des rois de France' (1734) fully approved of Louis XIV's single-minded attempt to establish greater governmental centralisation in France and welcomed the fact that 'practically the whole power of the *grands* was destroyed' and 'wisely reunited in the ministry alone'.[112] Absolutism, though dangerously close to despotism, had freed the crown from the constraints of the ancient 'Gothic' constitution by destroying the intermediate power of the aristocracy and had subsequently achieved greater domestic order and security. In his plans for a political system that he himself termed 'aristo-monarchie' Saint-Pierre proposed to let the king hold the only hereditary office in the state and replace the traditional hereditary nobility with a pure meritocracy. Only a system rewarding individual merit would stimu-

110 *Grundriss*, p. 191.

111 *Grundriss*, p. 172.

112 Charles-Irénée Castel, Abbé de Saint-Pierre, 'Observations politiques sur le gouvernement des rois de France', *Ouvrajes politiques*, (16 vols; Rotterdam, 1734–41), IX, 270–280. Even though France was now 'governed in a manner more despotic', the absolutist reforms had nevertheless caused a far greater and more 'durable domestic tranquillity', which was 'much more desirable for subjects than less *despoticité* in government and a greater number of petty perpetual powers and despots ready to disturb tranquillity by their resistance and by their contrariety of their opinions about good and bad government' (Ellis, 'Montesquieu's Modern Politics', p. 680).

late men's selfish passions so as to yoke them to the service of the common interest.[113]

D'Argenson took up Saint-Pierre's genuine hostility towards the nobility and developed his own model of a reformed French monarchy in his *Considérations sur le gouvernement ancien et présent de la France* (1737). He painted a dark picture of both feudalism and hereditary aristocracy. The nobility would always be inclined to 'suppress their vassals'. Among themselves, they had a tendency to attack each other, committing the most atrocious of crimes. D'Argenson was convinced that aristocratic regimes inevitably degenerated into despotism, with one of the nobles becoming usurper, king, or tyrant over the rest. 'The great utility of a kingdom', he stressed, was 'to allow the citizens to live a life in peace and equality among themselves, while republics are constantly shaken by factions, intrigues, the rivalry both between nobles and plebeians and between the nobles themselves.'[114] Monarchies were also preferable to aristocracies and democracies as they generally promised greater promptness in implementing policy decisions.[115] In order to see 'the horrors of our feudal government so highly esteemed by M. de Boulainvilliers' he pointed at the inherent weakness of Poland. Such government was perhaps preferable to that of Nero. Yet in civilised times, 'we need no longer fear a Nero, and can rely on our enlightened Kings to do much good with unlimited power'.[116] True, d'Argenson admitted, supreme authority, which may be abused, was inherently dangerous. However, a divided authority, like that found in aristocracies, was even more so.[117]

113 Quoted from Saint-Pierre's *Ouvrajes* in: Keohane, *Philosophy and the State in France*, p. 370. See also: Thomas E. Kaiser, 'The Abbé Saint-Pierre, Public Opinion, and the Reconstitution of the French Monarchy', *Journal of Modern History* 55 (1983), 618–643 (p. 636).

114 René Louis Marquis d'Argenson, *Mémoires et journal inédit* (5 vols; Paris: Jannet, 1858), V, 313.

115 Nannerl O. Henry [Keohane], *Democratic Monarchy – The Political Theory of the Marquis d'Argenson* (Phd, Yale University, 1968), p. 46.

116 Henry [Keohane], *Democratic Monarchy*, p. 223f.

117 Moreover, aristocratic rule was undesirable since 'what is more cruel than to see oneself oppressed by people that have no other talents than being born

In his *Mémoires*, d'Argenson pointed out that the 'distinction of ranks and orders is excellent as long as it does not exceed the duration of life; it is heredity that makes distinction dangerous'.[118] The existence of a separate caste like the hereditary aristocracy was a clear example of unnatural inequality within the state.[119] He demanded that the state grant 'rewards rather for merit than for birth and recommendation'.[120] Inequality of talents and inequality of fortune were essential elements of vivid emulation and should not be restricted by hereditary privileges. A reformed nobility based on life peerage would include the very best in society and maximise socio-economic competition among the citizens.[121] Such a meritocratic nobility would be a suitable mixture between aristocratic and democratic elements within a monarchy.

Of course d'Argenson did not suggest the immediate abolition of the nobility. However, he strongly supported a considerable reduction of their economic and political power and calmly accepted their decline. D'Argenson was aware that people would say that the principles of his political thought were favourable to democracy and promoted the destruction of the nobility. 'But that', he admitted, 'is not an

noble and rich?' (D'Argenson, *Mémoires*, V, 305). Since its social organisation and institutions for transmission of power were exclusively based on inequality and heredity, the feudal system represented a denial of all established principles of good government. D'Argenson was aware that 'inequality in talents and assiduity will always work for inequality in economic status. But nothing should be done to perpetuate such inequalities hereditarily, to form a social or political caste' (Henry [Keohane], *Democratic Monarchy*, p. 109).

118 D'Argenson, *Mémoires*, V, 307.

119 D'Argenson, *Mémoires*, V, 304. With regard to the pro-aristocratic views of Boulainvilliers and his followers, d'Argenson pointed out that they had not the least idea 'about the damage caused by hereditary nobility'. If the magistrature in a state was exclusively reserved to the nobility, and if this nobility was hereditary and not based on individual merit, then the government would surely be bad. Feudal regulations and the venality of offices were imperfect means for efficient governmental administration. Influential posts such as ministers, intendants, magistrates, commanders, or essential prefects would have to be opened up to non-noble candidates as well.

120 D'Argenson, *Mémoires*, V, 316.

121 Henry [Keohane], *Democratic Monarchy*, p. 283.

objection: it is a confirmation of our conclusions.' He rejected intermediate legislative powers, whether of nobles or of parlements, and preferred the installation of assemblies made up of popularly elected representatives instead.[122]

D'Argenson viewed the monarchy as the one power strong enough to oppose the Church and abolish that system of privilege which was all that remained of corporate medieval life.[123] The King would be a superior umpire. Though not constrained by strong intermediate powers, the sovereign would recognise that his power originated from 'a contract between king and people' that demanded the observance of 'fundamental laws'. By appeal to natural laws and economic utility, d'Argenson denied the monarch the right to govern except in the interest of his subjects.[124]

Similar to d'Argenson, Voltaire also highlighted the need to curb the political power of the aristocracy and the clergy for the sake of good government. Deeply influenced by Dubos's exhaustive refutation of Boulainvilliers's aristocratic version of the French past, Voltaire perceived the venality of offices and the privileges associated with it as relics of feudalism and gigantic obstacles to reform.[125] Like d'Argenson, he was aware that absolutism abutted despotism.[126] However, while despotism was bad enough, aristocratic government, as in Poland, was a veritable catastrophe. The 'proud and lazy Polish

122 Cf. Henry [Keohane], *Democratic Monarchy*, p. 112, 117 + 197.

123 A further important proposal of d'Argenson that aimed at the limitation of the influence of the landed aristocracy was the reform of the suppressed, feudally dependent standing of the peasants. He pointed out that the existence of large fiefs was politically unjust (since it violated equality) and economically disadvantageous (Henry [Keohane], *Democratic Monarchy*, p. 123). For making a kingdom truly prosperous, he remarked, 'the lands need to be owned only by those who cultivate them' (D'Argenson, *Mémoires*, V, 314f.). Assigning individual peasants their own small pieces of lands would be a far more effective method of cultivation. It would triple the returns of the land and enhance the tax revenue significantly.

124 Henry [Keohane], *Democratic Monarchy*, p. 277.

125 Peter Gay, *Voltaire's Politics – The Poet as Realist*, (New York/London: Norton, 1967), p. 98.

126 Czar Peter the Great, for instance, was partly an absolute, and partly a despotic ruler.

nobles', he remarked, 'elect their kings and plot against them' and 'often sell their vote and rarely their affections'.[127] Aristocratic predominance made orderly government impossible and had reduced the Polish people to dismal servitude.

Borrowing the arguments of these French thinkers, Justi proposed alternative systems of representation on similar grounds. He admired the English system, but warned against its imitation on the Continent. In his *Grundriss einer guten Regierung*, he went farthest in developing a model of a monarchical state with strong democratic elements. Justi demanded that the legislative power in such a monarchy be left to a council of the elected representatives of the people who would replace the traditional representation of the Estates. Since 'every reasonable human being who has freedom and knowledge is capable of governing himself' he believed that 'a free and civilised people must rule itself to the extent that it is able to do so'. Every town and district of the land needed 'to name these representatives in a free election'. The people, he pointed out, 'are well capable of such procedure since even the lowest rank of people is able to recognise skills and merit in others'.[128]

Because 'all human beings are inclined to increase their power' the legislative assembly had to set constitutional limits to the executive power. As numerous historical examples had shown, it was hard to establish a durable equilibrium between legislative and executive power.[129] Justi opted for a legislative assembly that was comparatively weak vis-à-vis the executive power of the monarch. The monarch retained extensive veto rights and was also allowed to dissolve the assembly at any time. All important affairs of state, i.e.

127 Gay, *Voltaire's Politics*, p. 101 + 107.

128 *Grundriss*, p. 159.

129 According to Justi, it was the undue extension of legislative power that was responsible for the oligarchic monarchical regimes in Sweden and Poland where the king was virtually left with nothing but an empty title. Consequently, the peoples' representatives had to 'exercise all tasks that belong to the legislative, yet not the least thing that belongs to the executive power' (*Grundriss*, p. 161).

> the right to declare war and peace, to join alliances, the supreme command over the power of the state on sea and land, and all which belongs to this realm, must be left without restriction to the executive power of the king.[130]

Instead of active day-to-day management, the assembly was rather designed to supervise the general lawfulness of the king's conduct and draw his attention to popular grievances.

In his *Natur und Wesen der Staaten* Justi presented an even more pro-monarchical version of these proposals. There, the popular assembly was no longer referred to as legislative power but merely as a supervisory board designed to give critical, independent advice to the prince. Justi now labelled its members the people's tribunes (*Worthalter des Volkes*), who would be elected for life and would enjoy legal immunity.[131] These proposals were in line with Justi's desire to replace the hereditary aristocracy by meritocratic structures, ideally by life peers (*ein persönlicher Adel*).[132] For only a state

> in which nobody can possess noble status except those who have earned it due to personal distinction, will have the most certain and most powerful incentive to stimulate their citizen to virtue, skills, and great and glorious deeds.[133]

Justi's 'third way'

The initiative to modernise a monarchy could only come from the crown. Justi's critical discussions of governmental practices in Poland, Hungary, Sweden, and even England show to what extent his vision of modern monarchy, despite its constitutionalist grounding and its representative system, was based on absolutist principles.[134] Restrict-

130 *Grundriss*, p. 165.

131 *Natur und Wesen*, p. 156ff.

132 *Grundriss*, p. 190.

133 *Grundriss*, p. 191.

134 Like many contemporary thinkers, Justi believed that Poland would soon cease to exist since the practice of *liberum veto* had made consent in the assembly of

ing monarchical power was dangerous and came at a high price. Limiting royal power with the help of a powerful legislative assembly was no recipe for good government.[135] It could prevent despotism, but otherwise it had devastating effects. The legislative assembly could seize executive power and thus take control of the entire state. Foreign powers could easily bribe a member of the assembly who could then act against the nation's interests or engage in endless factional fights. Even England only functioned properly because of constant bribery.[136]

Justi perceived his own model of modern monarchy as a 'third-way' alternative (*einen dritten Weg*): a dialectical synthesis that combined the positive aspects of absolute monarchy, i.e., a strong central executive power, with the beneficial effects of limited monarchical rule in a mixed constitution.[137] Justi wanted a modernised version of absolute monarchy in which the monarch's constitutional standing was barely limited, yet in which 'the monarch by his own will must

nobles impossible. Similarly, Justi believed that Sweden had taken a wrong turn in limiting monarchical power after the disastrous wars of Charles XII. As a result of the constitutional limitations of royal power, the Swedish king had turned into a powerless puppy whose movements were controlled by the state council (*Reichsrat*). Justi pointed out that the country had only gained corruption and general decline by this move. The councillors (*Reichsraete*) were bribed by foreign nations to act on their behalf. This *de facto* loss of domestic sovereignty caused a substantial decline.

135 *Vergleichungen*, p. 28.

136 England represented the most sophisticated example of constitutional limitations of monarchical power. But in Justi's eyes, the English people paid too high a price for it. They could only prevent the absolutism of the early Stuart kings by civil wars and still paid dearly for their limited government. The costs for the taxpayers were substantial since the crown had to bribe MPs to achieve a stable majority in the House of Commons. To Justi, absolutism seemed preferable to parliamentary government as it outwardly avoided the patronage, influence peddling, and compromise that he thought were characteristic of English party politics. In contrast to this, France's bureaucratically organised system of governance seemed a more logical and efficient tool for implementing modernisation. Despite its shortfalls, French absolutism nevertheless represented many important features of political modernisation, particularly the centralisation of power as well as the structural differentiation and the rationalisation of authority.

137 *Vergleichungen*, p. 144.

make a moderate use of his power'.[138] Under such conditions, the monarch would have 'all the power to do good, yet no power to do evil'.[139] Justi consequently focussed on the question of putting absolute monarchs 'into such circumstances [*Umstände*]' and providing them with 'such incentives [*Triebfedern*]' that they used their power 'only to rule with diligence and wisdom and to make their people happy'. In this way, 'all disadvantageous consequences, which accompanied both unlimited monarchical power and limited forms of government' could be avoided.[140]

The Chinese model

A key feature of Justi's reform proposals was his frequent recourse to China as the best-known manifestation of unlimited, but moderate monarchy.[141] Justi 'produced one of the most systematic eulogies of China known to have been written during the period of the *rêve chinois*'.[142] Eighteenth-century sinophilism was a truly European phenomenon with a particular focal point in France, making Justi's references to China a further proof of how deeply his thought was

138 *Vergleichungen*, p. 145.

139 *Vergleichungen*, p. 173.

140 *Vergleichungen*, p. 8f.

141 Justi strove to rectify Montesquieu's judgement that China was little different from other Asian despotic regimes. Like many contemporary French critics of Montesquieu, most prominently Voltaire, Justi was eager to point out that China was not just another sample of 'oriental despotism' but rather a lucid example of rational, legal absolutism. In his eulogy of China he boldly referred to the country as having the 'most reasonable and wise constitution on our globe'. One of the crucial differences between China and European monarchies was precisely that the former did 'not know a hereditary nobility' (*Vergleichungen*, p. 466). The Chinese had duly recognised that birth and heredity were not principles that would lead to the maximisation of socio-economic emulation and good government. In China, personal elevations to the nobility, i.e., the chance for everybody to attain eminent social distinction, figured as one of the greatest incentives for loyal and virtuous service to the state.

142 Johanna M. Menzel, 'The Sinophilism of J.H.G. Justi', *Journal of the History of Ideas* 17 (1956), 300–310 (p. 300).

shaped by contemporary French thought. China was not only the model state of the Physiocrats. It was widely accepted as the best example of a highly civilised, enlightened, and successful absolute monarchy. This was more an idealised image than an empirical description. Many 'intellectual leaders of the seventeenth and eighteenth centuries praised the enlightened beneficence of China's philosopher-kings without knowing much about them'.[143]

Historical accuracy, however, was not the primary aim of European sinophiles. Most of them were aware that a precise picture of contemporary Chinese practices was impossible to attain given that the available sources were written by Jesuit missionaries or merchants who praised and criticised Chinese habits according to how the Chinese had reacted to their own dealings with them. What nourished Western writers' unbounded enthusiasm was the circumstance that, whether factual or purely fictional, the praise of a distant utopia like China could be used as an instrument for severe social, economic, and political criticism. The Chinese background served as an enabling device by means of which free criticism of contemporary ideas and institutions, political and religious alike, could be expressed without the fear of repression. Discussing China was 'a means of denouncing corrupt practices, inept government, religious dogmatism, economic ills, or urban luxury and artificiality without running afoul of the censors'.[144] The presentation of the Chinese Emperor as an ideal enlightened ruler governing humanely and justly for the benefit of his people was contrasted with the allegedly corrupt, militarily aggressive and economically suppressive absolute monarchs in Europe.

Justi's views on China were drawn from the works of Etienne de Silhouette and Jean-Baptiste Du Halde. Silhouette's *Idée générale du gouvernement et de la morale des Chinois* (1729) highlighted those elements of absolute rule in China that eighteenth-century *thèse royale* thinkers in France perceived as the foundations of modern monarchy: the absence of hereditary nobility, the efficiency of administration, the

143 Walter W. Davis, 'China, The Confucian Ideal, and the European Age of Enlightenment', *Journal of the History of Ideas* 44 (1983), 523–548 (p. 537).

144 Davis, 'China, The Confucian Ideal, and the European Age of Enlightenment', p. 523.

moderation of the ruler, and a developed infrastructure that supported inland trade. Silhouette stressed that the meritocratic schemes operating in China allowed promotion in governmental service on the basis of virtue and talent, resulting in a competent and highly competitive administration.[145] A further remarkable feature of Chinese imperial rule was the circumstance that the Chinese Emperor did not distance himself from his people despite his absolute power. Writing tablets placed at the palace gates allowed the people to note their grievances and concerns. In addition, the Chinese Emperor, according to Silhouette, was interested in stimulating the economic activities of his subjects. In order to raise the prestige of agriculture, the Emperor ceremonially ploughed a number of furrows every springtime and ordered his mandarins to engage in ceremonial ploughing as well.

Six years after the publication of Silhouette's *Idée* Jean-Baptiste Du Halde's *Description de l'empire de la Chine* (1735) emerged as the standard work on China in France and beyond. Melon, d'Argenson, Montesquieu, d'Argens, Voltaire, Marsy, and Quesnay all read it.[146] Translations into English and German secured its wide impact in Europe. Based on their reading of Du Halde, most French thinkers arrived at a highly positive evaluation of China. From Du Halde's descriptions, the reader obtains an idyllic picture of a peaceful, prosperous, and orderly land governed with fatherly tenderness by men of virtue and talent. The Marquis d'Argens, for instance, praised China's vast domestic trade built upon the exceptional quality of its roads and canals. Melon approved the Chinese procedure of inviting comments on the government and local administration from all citizens. Similarly, d'Argenson was influenced by Du Halde. Though d'Argenson believed that there were despotic tendencies in China at the local level, he was convinced that it was generally not a tyrannical state. In

145 Silhouette drew particular attention to the circumstance that the Chinese did not recognise a hereditary aristocracy in the traditional European way. The Chinese, Silhouette wrote, 'recognise no nobility but that of virtue, and no rank but that appertaining to a man's office. By this wise policy they make flourish that commerce which in most countries is ruined by the indolence of the nobility' (Lewis A. Maverick, *China – A Model for Europe* (2 vols; San Antonio: Paul Anderson, 1946), I, 30).

146 Maverick, *China – A Model for Europe*, I, 22.

particular, the way the Chinese absolute monarchy at the top of the state functioned was admirable.[147] By contrast, Montesquieu based his own ideas on China less on Du Halde but on the more critical reports of merchants engaged in the China trade. This explains his depiction of China as a despotic and fear-ridden state.[148]

Justi learnt about the Chinese activities of the Jesuits in his Viennese years when he established contacts with the Jesuit Father Frantz who was Joseph II's philosophy tutor. In his works (particularly in his *Vergleichungen*) Justi used the Chinese context to develop his own political ideas for European reform and to show the possibility of combining unlimited authority with moderation in its exercise. China held the key to solving the conundrum of how to create an omnipotent ruler who did not abuse his power. In seeking to elaborate a rationale for a moderate monarchy independent of traditional constitutional barriers, the Chinese model offered Justi an illustrious example of how to impose moral restraints on the unlimited authority of a monarch without, in effect, curtailing his power. The Chinese monarchy, Justi claimed, was the most efficient form of government known to men. In his own reform proposals he embraced those aspects of China that were most vividly debated in contemporary French discussions: the lack of a hereditary nobility, the absence of feudal suppression, the highly professional governmental bureaucracy with a council of ministers at its head that effectively limited the Emperor's power, the Chinese agricultural and educational system, and governmental policies for the advancement of inland trade.

147 Henry [Keohane], *Democratic Monarchy*, p. 225.

148 Basil Guy, *The French Image of China before and after Voltaire* (Geneva: Institut et Musée Voltaire, 1963), p. 204ff.

Chapter Five
Political reforms

Fundamental laws

Justi envisioned the enactment of a set of fundamental laws as the constitutional foundation on which a modern monarchy was to rest. Such laws were to limit the power of the monarch and his ministers, and function 'as an unmovable foundation and unalterable guideline in all of their acts and regulations'.[1] In his *Natur und Wesen der Staaten* Justi stressed that no 'monarch in the world, even the one with virtually unlimited might, can have power over the fundamental laws of the state' since 'how could they have power over that which is the very reason and origin of their own might?'[2]

Justi did not believe in the pseudo-historical doctrine of an original contract. The origins of the state were in those unconscious, unintended, 'invisible-hand'-like forces that drove humankind. The abstract theoretical concept of a contract, which would have united the people as if overnight under the constitutional roof of a state, could not have occurred to peoples in less developed stages of civilisation. States had grown organically in a lengthy evolutionary process: sometimes by the extension of patriarchal power or charismatic leadership, and occasionally by foreign conquest.[3] Slowly but surely (though

1 *Grundfeste* I, 773f. Similarly in: *Natur und Wesen*, p. 125: for all ministers of the government the fundamental laws would be 'the most exact guideline and the most sacred and unbreakable feature'.

2 *Natur und Wesen*, p. 99.

3 *Natur und Wesen*, pp. 37–40. In some cases, a wise lawgiver had founded governments. See also: Akio Ebihara, 'Justis Staatslehre und Wolffs Naturrechtslehre', *Zeitschrift der Savigny-Stiftung für Rechtsgeschichte – Germanistische Abteilung* 102 (1985), pp. 239–246. Ebihara first pointed out the fundamental difference between Justi's view and Christian Wolff's contractualism in *Vernünftige Gedancken von dem gesellschaftlichen Leben der Menschen und*

imperceptibly for the people), inter-human relations had grown from the family into larger clans, ultimately resulting in the establishment of states.[4] Justi's detailed account of the the gradual development of states in his *Natur und Wesen der Staaten* included the four-stages theory (hunting, pasturing, agricultural, commercial) that had been formed by Pufendorf and was to be popularised by Smith in *The Wealth of Nations.*[5]

Although no state had ever originated by a *de iure* contract of all citizens, Justi nonetheless claimed that *de facto* a tacit contract stood at the basis of modern statehood.[6] In other words, despite his de-

insonderheit dem gemeinen Wesen zu Beförderung der Glückseeligkeit des menschlichen Geschlechts (Frankfurt/M. & Leipzig, 1721).

4 *Natur und Wesen*, pp. 54–56.

5 *Natur und Wesen*, p. 12.

6 *Natur und Wesen*, pp. 98–102 + 123–127; *Grundriss*, p. 15. Justi's position on fundamental laws has led to profound confusion in the literature. Due to his claim that 'all power in the state originates from the people', recent interpretations erroneously assumed that he had propagated a proto-democratic attitude of popular sovereignty (*Volkssouveränität*) – similar to §20, 2 of Germany's present-day constitution (*Grundgesetz*). It was only a 'tiny step', they held, from Justi's ideas about popularly determined fundamental laws to a popularly elected constitutional assembly and modern republicanism. Cf. Uwe Wilhelm, 'Das Staats-und Gesellschaftsverständnis von J.H.G. von Justi: ein Beitrag zur Entwicklung des Frühliberalismus in Deutschland', *Der Staat* 20 (1991), 415–441 (p. 424); Thomas Würtenberger, 'An der Schwelle zum Verfassungsstaat', *Aufklärung* 3 (1988), 53–88; Marcus Obert, *Die naturrechtliche 'politische Metaphysik' des Johann Heinrich Gottlob von Justi (1717–1771)* (Frankfurt / M.: Lang, 1992). As I have outlined in the introduction, we should be careful of interpreting Justi's thought along these lines. Justi had no intention to overcome, let alone replace, monarchical reign by popular rule. Instead, his principal political aim was to ground the autocratic power of the absolute monarch on a firm legal and constitutional footing and limit it by a variety of reforms. Justi's model of fundamental laws was far from ideas about popular sovereignty based on democratic assemblies when compared to Rousseau's position on fundamental laws in the *Social Contract* (1762). Rousseau untied the knot that Justi and his predecessors had struggled with by cutting off fundamental laws from the contract metaphor. Rousseau did not deny that there were constitutional laws, and mentioned *loix fondamentales* in the *Social Contract*, which regulated the relations between sovereign and state. Yet Rousseau's point was that the concept of popular sovereignty 'admitted no such thing as laws con-

nunciation of an original contract he nevertheless explained modern states in contractarian terms as a transfer of the right to exercise the constituting power of the people (*Grundgewalt des gesamten Volkes*) on certain conditions to a superior body of sovereign authority (*tätige oberste Gewalt*). The preconditions for this transfer of power were embodied in the constitution of fundamental laws (*Grundverfassungen* or *Grundgesetze*). Once in existence, the fundamental laws could only be changed by the united will of the people, and not by the sovereign on his own, i.e., they were outside the jurisdiction of the supreme magistrate.[7] Yet once the sovereign (*tätige oberste Gewalt*) had been instituted by approval of the constituting power of the people (*Grundgewalt des gesamten Volkes*), introducing fundamental laws (a process that Justi believed had happened in the states of Europe centuries ago), the people also ceased to be legislators and became, in Justi's words, a mere 'contractual partner' in the exercise of power:

> If a people unite their powers and their will, and leave the use of the united powers to the united will, that is, if they establish a highest power, then this power rests in the beginning indisputably with the people, for it has been created by a union of their powers and their wills. A people can either exercise this power itself, make provisions for its use, or delegate it to others. The power by which a people makes provision for the exercise or delegation of sovereignty is called the *constituting power of the people* and differs from the soverign authority which is created only by the provisions of the former. The constituting power of the people is an integral part of the nature of the state, and always exists, even when there is the most absolute authority.[8]

The crux of the matter was the right of resistance: when the constituting power of the people had fallen dormant following the establish-

tractually established and contractually binding on the possessors of sovereignty. Not even the social contract carried such an obligation. The people as sovereign were superior to the state' (Rousseau, *Social Contract*, quoted from: Martin P. Thompson, 'The History of Fundamental Law in Political Thought from the French Wars of Religion to the American Revolution', *The American Historical Review* 91 (1986), 1103–1126, (p. 1126)). Designed for safeguarding absolute monarchy against arbitrary individual rule, Justi's theory did not endorse (let alone foreshadow) Rousseau's republican views.

7 *Natur und Wesen*, pp. 98–102.

8 *Grundriss*, p. 6f.

ment of sovereignty what could justify its awakening, i.e., their return to action? If it was dormant, as Justi asserted, and strictly prohibited from directly limiting or judging the policies of the sovereign, how could it awake at all? Was a simple violation of one of the fundamental laws by the sovereign sufficient to rouse the people to resist? And if so, who was to determine that the sovereign's action was a violation of the unwritten constitution? Sensing these difficulties, Justi tried to define clear-cut mechanisms for the re-activation of the constituting power of the people (*Grundgewalt des gesamten Volkes*) when confronted with the abuse of power by the sovereign (*tätige oberste Gewalt*).

The people always retrieved their basic constituting power upon the extinction of the royal family.[9] In this case, the people were authorised to elect a new ruler or even alter the form of government, as had happened in Sweden after the death of Charles XII. Alluding to the Glorious Revolution, Justi similarly believed the people were authorised to exclude a certain dynasty from the succession if the state was in danger of being converted into a dependent province of a foreign power or fall prey to religious oppression. He also conceded that in extreme cases, such as the threat of conquest or tyranny, the sovereignty of the people could dissolve the state, and power would revert to the people. Thus Justi did grant the people the right of resistance. Fundamental sovereign power could revert back to the people in an emergency. But he rejected such claims for all other cases. The people were never entitled to claim back the sovereign power upon their own initiative or on the grounds of their dislike of the current government. The English, Justi warned, erred when they tried, convicted, and executed Charles I, causing a civil war and leaving 'an eternal black mark on their history'.[10]

The idea of a king who was bound by fundamental laws and derived his power from a tacit or hypothetical contract with the people seemed to Justi as the best way to create a constitutional monarchy. In this way, the ruler had obligations towards his subjects without invoking divine right or traditional safeguards such as a mixed consti-

9 *Natur und Wesen*, p. 100.
10 *Natur und Wesen*, p. 102.

tution or a powerful hereditary aristocracy. The problem with Justi's model was that it was at the discretion of the monarch whether he actually ruled according to the fundamental laws or not.

Justi demanded that five core principles of good and moderate government (*eine gütige und gelinde Regierung*) be included in the fundamental laws. These were: civil liberty, sanctity of private property, independence of the judiciary, a steady level of taxation, and the prohibition of offensive wars.[11] The liberty of the citizen was the most important quality of all civil institutions 'and central for the great final cause of republics: the happiness of the state'.[12] A state that granted civil liberty was one in which the citizens had sufficient space and opportunities to pursue their passions, their self-interest and other particular intentions.[13] Since the ruler could not force his subjects 'to undertake successful business' it was best not to limit the range of their activities, but grant them full freedom to make deliberate use of their wealth.[14] The absence of freedom would have dramatic economic consequences. The lack of civil liberty, Justi warned, would suppress the courage of the people and their motivation for work.

Civil liberty implied religious toleration.[15] Pointing at Louis XIV's ill-advised religious policy, Justi believed governmentally imposed confessional unity effectively deported crowds of qualified workers and scared off potential immigrants.[16] Such restrictive policies, together with the far greater number of ecclesiastical holidays, were the reason for the less developed state of the Catholic countries in the south of Germany (in comparison to their neighbours in the

11 *Natur und Wesen*, p. 146; *Grundriss*, p. 233; *Polizeiwissenschaft*, p. 57; *Staatswirtschaft* I, 265.

12 *Natur und Wesen*, p. 125; *Grundriss*, p. 218f.

13 *Grundriss*, Vorrede.

14 *Staatswirtschaft* I, 377 + II, 77.

15 *Staatswirtschaft* I, 143 + 265.

16 *Natur und Wesen*, p. 410: 'The final aim of states is temporary happiness; yet the final aim of religions is eternal happiness.' P. 411: 'Laws and punishments, which force someone to adopt a certain religion, or which castigate someone on the grounds that he ceased to practice the religion or began to doubt it, are tyrannical and atrocious.' P. 450: 'Religious opinion does not form part of the final cause and duties of civil society.'

north). Justi put great emphasis on the importance of full freedom of conscience as a precondition for a flourishing economy.[17] The monarch, he maintained, could not legitimately curtail religious freedom.[18] Nobody, he asserted, 'must be accountable for what he tacitly believes for himself or because of the manner in which he serves God in his house'.[19] Though public worship could be restricted in certain cases, private service would have to remain free:

> No one can be charged on the grounds of his personal beliefs as long as he does not upset the state with them. And those religions that are publicly practised in other counties, must, in the name of tolerance, at least be granted the liberty to exercise their faith in private services at home.[20]

Although the government did not have power over the religious beliefs of its subjects, it did have an active role to play in the surveillance of religious groups.[21] Instead of aiming at the establishment of a single religion or confession, the government had to safeguard the peaceful coexistence of the different religious movements within its lands. In a well-governed monarchy, the administration supervised the life-style of the clergy, prohibited extremist sectarians, and ensured a reasonable amount of official holidays since too much work was detrimental to the overall productivity of workers.[22]

Moral perfection and contentment of the soul were not proper objects of the policing force of the state.[23] If they did not happen to hamper the overall aim of furthering a people's material welfare they could safely be left to the choice of the individual. No citizen could be punished on the grounds of some inward conviction as long as his or her external conduct was in accordance with the laws. Justi opted for a

17 *Grundfeste* II, 24.
18 *Natur und Wesen*, p. 148.
19 *Manufakturen und Fabriken* I, 34.
20 *Polizeiwissenschaft*, p. 58.
21 *Grundfeste* II, 22.
22 *Grundfeste* II, 38.
23 *Grundfeste* II, 101; *Staatswirtschaft* I, 55.

non-interference of government into private affairs. Family life had to be protected since

> governmental control of families could not happen without the investigation of the inner affairs of each family, which is the worst form of despotism and stands in contrast to all reasonable definitions of civil liberty.[24]

A further crucial characteristic of civil liberty was the freedom of movement. Justi condemned the widely established moving taxes (*An- und Abzugsgelder*) that were imposed on emigrants and immigrants in his days.[25] Such taxes would tend to keep foreign merchants out of a country and thus diminish the capital inflow. Instead, Justi recommended the encouragement of immigration of wealthy foreigners by granting temporary tax exemptions (for instance, for the first decade after immigration) or by providing alternative forms of subvention (e.g., furnishing immigrants with land).[26] The mildness or harshness of a particular government had a direct impact on the reproduction and migration of the citizens. Taking up Montesquieu's remark in *The Spirit of the Laws*, Justi pointed out that the more unjust and tyrannical a government was 'the more the people feel disgust at the idea of leaving behind unhappy offspring'. This behaviour pattern had been proven by the deliberate abortions of native Indians under the oppressive rule of the Spanish conquerors.[27] Justi sharply attacked the blindness of German princes concerning the intrinsic value of their population. German rulers did not undertake measures to halt emigration from their countries to Hungary or America. They did not perceive these movements as an outflow of human capital. In their

24 *Grundfeste* II, 103.

25 *Staatswirtschaft* I, 299; II, 395: 'It is advisable that a ruler prohibit by law that such moving taxes are levied.' Unregulated moving taxes were still quite common in Justi's days. In Habsburg Austria the moving taxes were first regulated in 1779 and not abolished until Joseph II's reign.

26 'Von der Accise und einer statt dessen einzuführenden neuen Gewerbesteuer', in: *Gesammelte Schriften* I, 380–439 (p. 388).

27 'Von der Accise und einer statt dessen einzuführenden neuen Gewerbesteuer', in: *Gesammelte Schriften* I, 380–439 (p. 388). The attempts at attracting foreigners were a vain undertaking for despotic governments. Justi argued that the population grew according to the extent that liberty existed in a state.

ignorance they even violated the basic laws of humanity and sold their own troops to foreign powers.[28]

The sanctity of private property was another vital feature of civil liberty. 'The sanctity of private property and the restraint from any interference in it' were among 'the most prominent principles of good government and should always be taken into account'.[29] The government had to ensure that the ordinary citizen was free from injustice, oppression and force and had true property rights over his belongings. Private property was not to be violated by governmental action. If, in a particular case, a compulsory purchase by the state of a certain piece of land or certain moveable goods seemed inevitable, appropriate compensation would have to be given to its original owner: 'If the supreme power claims its supreme property rights over private property in the name of the state, the proprietor must be reimbursed' for the damage caused by it.[30] Justi denied the monarch a supreme property right of the land, the so-called *dominium eminens*. The prince did not 'own' the country, but was merely installed to serve it.[31]

Justi underlined the importance of the rule of law and emphasised that civil liberty could only be established in a state in which the judicial institutions enjoyed an independent status.[32] He also counted

28 *Physicalische und politische Betrachtungen*, p. 74ff.

29 *Gesammelte Schriften* I, 619.

30 *Grundriss*, p. 246.

31 One needs to bear in mind that in most German territories of the time there was no legal distinction between the property of the state and that of the royal family. In the Habsburg territories, for instance, this distinction was not made until 1765.

32 Justi's stress on a separate judiciary reflects the efforts of Maria Theresa and Haugwitz to separate the courts from the administration. Maria Theresa identified this separation as the 'true corner-stone through which I may sustain the monarchy entrusted to me by God, for Whose further sturdy assistance we all hope, for the benefit and best interest of my prosperity'. She believed that a separation would give the sovereign an opportunity to examine the grievances of his subjects, to 'further a just and God-pleasing procedure between lords and subjects, and to watch carefully that the poor, and especially the subjects, are not oppressed by the rich, and especially by the lords'. Quoted from: Edith Murr Link, *The Emancipation of the Austrian Peasant 1740–1789* (New York: Columbia University Press, 1949), p. 47.

among fundamental laws the prohibition of tax increases except in emergency situations and the prohibition of offensive warfare – an issue which he increasingly called attention to after the outbreak of the Seven Years War.

Finally, he perceived the liberty of trade and industry and the concomitant duty of the government to support and encourage commerce as a fundamental law. Governmental trade policy was a highly sensitive issue. Nothing, Justi pointed out, 'needs to be treated as tenderly and carefully as trade'. The government had to be extremely vigilant not to scare away foreign traders and investors by imprudent conduct, since if a government 'terrifies foreigners once and gives them reason not to travel in our country, it will take a fair amount of time until one can attract them back again'.[33]

The politics of trade

Justi's concept of fundamental laws forms a link between his political theory and his economic ideas. Security of private property, religious freedom, a functioning jurisprudence, a stable, moderate tax level, peace, and sufficient space for private entrepreneurial activities all served the purpose of fostering a country's economic advancement. Since commercial success had become critical for national survival, Justi believed it was in the monarch's own interest to stay within the framework provided by the fundamental laws. Justi tried to prove this point with his concept of the mutual happiness (*gemeinschaftliche Glückseligkeit*) of the ruler and the ruled. The doctrine of mutual happiness was a critical element of Justi's theory of moderate absolute monarchy and persistently reappears in his writings.[34] Modern monarchical government differed from absolutism in that it did not only

33 *Gesammelte Schriften* I, 501. Justi acknowledged that some of these fundamental laws had already been implemented in the German states. The Hanoverian government excelled with its absolute guarantee of property rights and independent judiciary, while Frederick William I of Prussia had kept taxes and contributions stable during his entire reign.

34 'Betrachtung über das enge Band zwischen dem Regenten und den Untertanen', in: *Neue Wahrheiten*, 1758, 12, VI.

serve the selfish interests of the ruler, but took political and economic decisions with the public happiness in mind.[35] The monarch was not allowed 'to make his private will the will of the state'.[36] The *salus privata* of the ruler was no legitimate end in itself but merely was a by-product of the promotion and augmentation of the welfare of the general public. *Salus publica suprema lex esto* – the rule applied to the monarch himself.

For Justi, happiness was first and foremost identified by material wealth. Contrary to thinkers like Christian Wolff or Johann Friedrich Pfeiffer, who defined happiness (*Glückseligkeit*) not only in terms of the secure possession of material goods but also as moral well-being, Justi was content to leave the latter, which he termed philosophical happiness (*philosophische Glückseligkeit*), to individual choice. The 'philosophical definition of happiness' was not a political issue:

> The eternal blissfulness of the subjects does not fall under his [the monarch's] care. It is at the discretion of every individual subject. The ultimate end of republics only aims at earthly happiness.[37]

It was not the primary function of a state to promote moral happiness or religious bliss but to create a fundamental economic and legal framework in which the people could achieve material welfare. Justi defined an enjoyable life as a life above the minimal material requirements – without further hints as to moral conditions.[38] As the ultimate aim of civil society and government, *Glückseligkeit* was reduced to an external material condition of the subjects and allowed the state at best an indirect furtherance of morality.[39]

Justi's persistent assertion that the happiness of the prince and the happiness of his subjects were mutually dependent was not a naive appeal to the goodwill of the monarch, but pointed at the altered nature of commercially driven politics. His claim that short-term,

35 *Staatswirtschaft* II, 535: The ruler has no right to claim a distinct happiness that does not take into account 'the welfare of his people'.

36 *Natur und Wesen*, p. 316.

37 *Staatswirtschaft* I, 103.

38 *Staatswirtschaft* I, 33.

39 *Grundfeste* II, 15.

purely self-interested policies of the monarch (that were undertaken without the interest and welfare of his people in mind) were self-destructive underlines his inherently economic view of politics.[40] The fact that in the new age of international commerce the weakness of the subjects rebounded on the ruler was the ultimate proof that 'no prince can be called happy who does not rule over happy subjects'.[41] Since it was 'an undisputable truth that a people cannot achieve power and wealth if commerce does not flourish within their frontiers', a wasteful and chaotic economy would inevitably render the ruler 'feeble and weak'.[42] The state was no longer subject to the arbitrary will of the prince in so far as princely activities had also become subject to the universal rules of economics as the new driving force of human society. If only for his own sake, the prince had to act as representative of the collective interest.[43]

Justi pointed out that the new insight 'that the notions of uprightness and justice applied to all men and that a good government cannot distance itself from them without detriment and disadvantage to itself' was a key factor in dragging governments away from arbitrary conduct.[44] The doctrine of the mutual happiness had emerged as a powerful constraint on princely politics. For lasting political and economic success, the ruler had to distinguish 'his personal will very clearly from his will as a regent'.[45]

40 *Grundriss*, p. 238.
41 *Manufakturen und Fabriken* I, 85.
42 *Grundriss*, p. 257.
43 *Grundfeste* I, 519.
44 *Grundriss*, p. 281.
45 *Staatswirtschaft* II, 535; *Grundriss*, p. 224. The depersonalisation of the ruler's will as demanded by Justi reads like a crude version of what Kant later defined in *Perpetual Peace* as the republican *mode* of government in an absolute monarchy, i.e., the idea that a state 'may well *govern* itself in a republican way, even if its existing constitution provides for a despotic *ruling power*'. Though lacking the republican overtones of Kant's arguments in *Perpetual Peace*, Justi's mutual-happiness doctrine for modern commercial monarchies headed in the same direction. The similarity is even more evident when looking at their respective positions on war. Taking up Fénelon's adage that war 'ought never to be thought of but for the defence of liberty' Justi viewed the abstinence from waging unnecessary offensive wars as a fundamental law of monarchy. Based

To depersonalise the monarch's political will it was necessary to publish a detailed governmental programme (*Regierungsentwurf*) at the beginning of each reign, announcing all new regulations, prescriptions, and orders.[46] In addition, governmental regulations would have to be issued in the name of the law, and no longer with reference to the arbitrary will of the ruler. After all, Justi remarked, the greatest advantage of moderate states was that 'within them one is not dependant on the arbitrary will of the prince but on written law'.[47] Justi severely protested against the typical formulae ending legal documents and official royal edicts. It was despotic to finish legislative orders with idioms that directly spoke of the monarch's will, implying they had been ordered on the basis of the prince's deliberate decision. Hence phrases like 'By this we make known our will' or 'This is according to our will' would have to be replaced by idioms like 'This is in accordance with justice and the laws'.[48]

on his mutual-happiness doctrine no monarch had the right to wage an offensive war against a neighbouring country, as this was a decision that did not take into account the interests and happiness of the people who would suffer the consequences of military action (starvation, death etc.). Kant developed his famous proposal for universal republicanism in *Perpetual Peace* on similar grounds. According to him, the principal problem of ongoing warfare in Europe was the fact that monarchs themselves never suffered from its consequences: a monarch 'can thus decide on war, without any significant reason, as a kind of amusement, and unconcernedly leave it to the diplomatic corps (who are always ready for such purposes) to justify the war for the sake of propriety'. In contrast to this, the people themselves would always 'have great hesitation in embarking on so dangerous an enterprise' as war, for this would mean 'calling down on themselves all the miseries of war, such as doing the fighting themselves, supplying ensuing devastation, and, as the crowning evil, having to take upon themselves a burden of debt which will embitter peace itself and which can never be paid off on account of the constant threat of new wars' (Immanuel Kant, *Political Writings*, edited by Hans Reiss (Cambridge: Cambridge University Press, 1991), p. 100). In Kant's view, politics in the true interest of the people was best taken care of in genuine republics. However, the republican mode of government offered a feasible solution to do the same in monarchies.

46 *Grundriss*, p. 232.

47 *Grundriss*, p. 216. Apart from coinciding with the fundamental laws, all royal decrees had to match the actual standards of the civil laws.

48 *Grundriss*, p. 216.

The fundamental laws and the mutual-happiness doctrine only provided a rudimentary, yet insufficient framework for a third-way monarchy. Even with a clear legal code of fundamental laws, too much in a monarchy would still depend on the personal qualities of the ruler.[49] Considering the selfish nature of man and most people's mediocre intellect, Justi thought it was extremely dangerous to leave the supreme post in the state to the lottery of birth. He tried to reduce the risks with a twofold strategy: by restricting the range of governmental procedures into which the prince could interfere; and by ensuring that the prince was well prepared for those areas of political life in which his judgement still mattered.

Ministerial despotism and personal monarchical rule

The primary problem of modern monarchies was ministerial despotism. Often, Justi stressed, the monarch was hardly more than a representative figurehead while actual political power had shifted into the hands of omnipotent ministers who were in charge of governmental affairs and controlled the access to the king. This development was highly perilous. His all-powerful position allowed the prime minister (or *ministrissimus*, as Justi called him using a term popularised by Wilhelm von Schröder in his *Fürstliche Schatz- und Rentkammer*) to manipulate the monarch, turning him into a blind supporter of the minister's own goals and ambitions. Justi derived three lessons from his critique of ministerial despotism: first, the prince had to perform an active supervisory function to prevent ministers from seizing an undue share of political power; second, the prince had to be sufficiently well educated so that he could fulfil his supervisory role effectively; and finally, the monarch had to refrain from engaging in day-to-day politics, which was better dealt with if left in the hands of a professional body of civil servants.

Again, Justi followed French writers, particularly Saint-Pierre, d'Argenson and Montesquieu. Saint-Pierre in his *Discours sur la Polysynodie* (1719) (which led to his expulsion from the French

49 *Grundriss*, p. 135.

Academy) had severely criticised the ministerial system of France, calling it a vizirate similar to an oriental despotism. He denounced the unlimited power of seventeenth-century ministers like Richelieu and Mazarin and proposed instead a system of a plethora of subcommittees under the heading of a supreme council. Saint-Pierre hoped that such a plural committee system (*polysynodie*) would effectively overcome the ills of the current administration and create a more just and effective meritocratic bureaucracy.[50] Similarly, d'Argenson rejected the ministerial system of France, calling it a 'tyrannical oligarchy'.[51] D'Argenson blamed the ministers for being responsible for most of the evils attributed to monarchies. His ideal was 'a popular, egalitarian monarch, living among his people and doing without all the wasteful corrupt court'.[52]

Montesquieu highlighted the problem of ministerial despotism in Chapter 5 of Book 2 of *The Spirit of the Laws*. He lamented that monarchs were likely to turn 'lazy, ignorant, and voluptuous' and would abandon governmental responsibility altogether because of excessive courtly flattery. Princes fled their governmental duties by conferring executive power upon a single prime minister or, in Montesquieu's words, 'a vizir who will instantly have the same power as he [the king]'.[53] Once liberated from the burden of governance, such princes would dedicate their lives to the enjoyment of private fancies. Drunk with pleasures, they would forget about their governmental duties, thus paving the way for ministerial despotism.

Justi examined the problem of ministerial despotism in his fables and satirical essays, in *Psammitichus* and, most extensively, in *Leben*

50 Charles-Irénée Castel Abbé de Saint-Pierre, *Discours sur la Polysynodie* (Amsterdam: Du Villard et Chaugion, 1719).

51 Nannerl O. Henry [Keohane], 'Democratic Monarchy – The Political Theory of the Marquis d'Argenson' (Yale University: unpublished PhD thesis, 1968), p. 153.

52 Henry [Keohane], 'Democratic Monarchy', p. 159. D'Argenson hoped that a modified education with appropriate training would enable the king to pick and choose his closest advisors wisely and supervise their proceedings more effectively so that there would be no need for major action on the part of the king.

53 *Spirit of the Laws* 5, 2.

und Charakter des Grafen von Brühl.[54] The fable 'Der dicke Land-Edelmann und die mageren Pferde' ('The obese noble landowner and the skinny horses') is a metaphorical tale about the devastating consequences of an indolent king who handed the state's affairs over to an all-powerful prime minister.[55] The fable talks about a nobleman who transfers the supervision of his manor to a manager in order to dedicate more time to the enjoyment of his private pleasures. Predictably, the latter merely cares for his own good and has no interest in the running of the estate for his master's benefit. Having suffered from severe malnutrition, the horses decide to inform the nobleman about the defects of his estate manager. The proprietor patiently listens to the horses' concerns. In the end, however, he is too lazy to punish his manager and does nothing to relieve the distress of the animals. The fable's oustanding characteristic is its pessimism. Upon the nobleman's refusal to punish the manager or actively change the existing circumstances the horses do not turn angry or rebellious, but sadly accept the verdict and return to their stalls. Active resistance is out of the question.

Justi also voiced his advocacy of an active, supervisory rule of the monarch in a short satirical sketch called 'Psammitichus' (closely related to his novel of the same name).[56] The purpose of the story was to highlight the beneficial absence of powerful ministers during the active personal rule of Psammitichus in ancient Egypt. Justi set out by describing the complaints of Psammitichus's ministers. They recall the old days before Psammitichus's accession when they were able to plunder the public wealth and line their own pockets.[57] Psammitichus's active rule and his tight control of ministerial activities had put an end to the ministers' personal enrichment. Their selfish hopes were crushed. Instead of substantial personal gain, as they had hoped, their

54 Justi also dealt with the issue of ministerial despotism in his essay 'Ob ein Premierminister einem Staate zuträglich sey' (*Gesammelte Schriften* I, 235–247).

55 'Der dicke Land-Edelmann und die mageren Pferde', in: *Scherzhafte und Satyrische Schriften* III, 364. See also: Beatrice Roesch-Wanner, *Justi als Literat* (Frankfurt/M.: Lang, 1993), p. 98.

56 'Psammitichus', in: *Scherzhafte und satyrische Schriften* III, 413–417.

57 'Psammitichus', in: *Scherzhafte und satyrische Schriften* III, 413–417 (p. 413).

posts now demanded hard work and an obligation to contribute to the common good. Given the altered nature of the job, they expect that it would soon be difficult to find willing candidates for ministerial offices in Egypt. Justi concluded with the prediction that if kings, like Psammitichus, 'would start ruling not only by name, but in fact and in person, the attractiveness of the ministerial posts would soon diminish a great deal'.[58]

In *Leben und Charakter des Grafen von Brühl* and in the novel *Psammitichus* Justi further investigated the devastating effects of ministerial despotism and elaborated measures for its future prevention. Until recently it has remained unclear whether Justi was the author of *Leben Brühls*, a radical satire against the Saxon prime minister Heinrich Brühl.[59] However, personal remarks of the anonymous author and countless quotations that can also be found in Justi's other works give credible proof of his authorship.[60]

58 *Scherzhafte und satyrische Schriften* III, 417.

59 Contemporary sources also name Johann Christoph Adelung as a possible author. Choosing the genre of an epistolary novel was itself a critique of Brühl's policy. The anonymous author presented himself as a provincial postmaster who had secretly opened and copied the correspondence published in *Leben Brühls*. This was a satirical condemnation of Brühl's private espionage network (the *Cabinet Noir*) which proved invaluable during the struggle to get Frederick August II elected King of Poland: 'Brühl's agents, under the direction of a capable crook named Siepmann, opened the letters of the Polish magnates as well as of visiting foreigners, which they obtained from vantage points within the established courier service' (Robert L. Koehl, 'Heinrich Brühl: A Saxon Politician in the Eighteenth Century', *Journal of Central European Affairs* 14 (1954), 310–328 (p. 318)).

60 In several passages, the author of *Leben Brühls* refers to his personal acquaintance with Brühl and his time at the Saxon Court in Dresden. All these remarks relate to the years 1744–48 – when Justi lived in the Saxon capital as a novelist and journal-editor (*Leben Brühls* I, 18, 63 + 144). In the preface to the second volume the anonymous author refers to himself as a scholar (*Gelehrter*) living in Berlin (where Justi stayed at that time). Finally, numerous quotes from Montaigne, Loen, Plutarch, and Montesquieu, which can also be found in Justi's other works, as well as the general line of argument on ministerial despotism suggest his authorship (*Leben Brühls* I, 22 [Montaigne]; I, 39 [Loen]; I, 57 [Plutarch]; II, 66f. [Montesquieu]).

Abounding with amusing anecdotes and Saxon court gossip, Justi's *Leben Brühls* was designed to appeal to a broad literary public. As with the two *Chimäre* pamphlets, a significant reason for writing the book was to provide an eloquent apology for Prussia's war efforts, in this case the Prussian army's occupation of Saxony. At the close of the Seven Years War it was in Frederick's interest to sponsor the view that Brühl, rather than the long occupation by his Prussian troops, had ruined Saxony.[61]

Justi depicted Saxony as the most compelling example of the corruptive power of prime ministers over well-intentioned, yet mediocre monarchs. True to his pro-Prussian stand, he directly linked the devastating situation of Saxony to the excessive rule and influence of Brühl. Appointed 'silver page' to the Electoral and Royal Saxon Court at Dresden in 1720, Brühl had managed to rise swiftly in subsequent years.[62] With his bold move to take possession of the crown jewels upon Frederick August I's death in Warsaw on February 1, 1733, Brühl had secured himself a hugely influential position with the new Saxon Elector, Frederick August II. In June of the same year he was appointed minister. Three years later he became chief tax collector, and was made Count of the Holy Roman Empire. After the forced retirement of his main rival in the ministry, Sulkowski, in 1738, he rose to an uncontested position of wealth and power, a place he was to keep until his death in 1763. Brühl successfully managed to control Frederick August, whom he surrounded 'with an iron curtain of guards and pages to prevent unauthorised persons from getting to him with unpleasant complaints'.[63] He was not only in charge of the coun-

61 Accordingly, Justi also highlighted the 'barbarian destruction' of Dresden by Austrian troops.

62 Already by the late 1720s Brühl had become exchequer minister (*Kammerjunker*) and private secretary (*Kammerherr*) to Frederick August I. In 1730 he was entrusted with the oversight of the royal palaces and the inspection of forestry. In the following year Brühl was put in charge of the excise department and made director of domestic affairs. He was appointed to the Privy Council and became controller of the Evangelical Court Church. In 1732, the last year of Frederick August I's rule, he was named assistant to the tax director and soon hereafter president of the mining monopoly control board of Saxony.

63 Koehl, 'Heinrich Brühl', p. 323.

try's foreign affairs, trying to secure favourable alliances for Saxony in the rapidly changing concert of European great powers, but also controlled domestic policies. His ownership of large landed estates and various Saxon and Polish mines led to allegations of mixing public and private business and lining his own pockets.[64] Decorated with a grotesque number of titles and incomes Brühl's dominant standing in Saxony was represented by his luxurious palace with its legendary library and collection of Meissen china whose splendour equalled, if not surpassed, that of the royal court.

Brühl fitted ideally Justi's picture of ministerial despotism. In Justi's eyes, Brühl's rule was the opposite of an effective governmental administration that operated according to the principles of shared duties and limited responsibilities. Backed by his ridiculous surfeit of titles and positions Brühl had subverted the country's original monarchical constitution, setting up a tyrannical regime instead. The remarkable transformation of the Saxon government was the typical outcome of a monarch's abstaining from active self-rule, i.e., a king who 'entrusts the government to his minister and retires himself from the affairs of the state'.[65] Brühl, according to Justi, was only the latest (though clearly the most ruthless) representative in a long line of ministerial despots that included such illustrious figures as Lerna, the leading minister under Phillip III of Spain and first of the so-called *validos* (strong men or favourites through whom the Habsburg kings were to govern Spain until the end of the seventeenth century), as well as Richelieu and Mazarin in France.[66] All of them had followed the same strategy: to seize political power by gaining control of the king.

64 Due to his bold exploitation of public funds Brühl has met with harsh criticism in modern scholarship. None of the interpretations, however, denies that, despite his private enrichment, Brühl had been a hard-working administrator and an able, many-sided politician in his early years.

65 *Leben Brühls* I, 132.

66 In this context, Justi might have also thought of the French ministers Fouquet and Desmaretz. Nicolas Fouquet, Colbert's predecessor, had been accused of *lèse-majesté* for having usurped the Crown's authority. He was denounced and imprisoned for initiating a system of clientilism and for creating a corps of parasites who consumed the nation's resources. Nicholas Desmaretz, Colbert's nephew and the last ministry of Louis's 54-year reign, had a reputation for

Justi, like Saint-Pierre, held that the deception of the monarch was the principal vice of ministerial despotism. Powerful ministers would only allow selected information to reach the king.[67] Brühl had brought this strategy to a degree of perfection hitherto unknown. He had managed to render it 'impossible that any form of intelligence that could be disadvantageous to the minister reached the monarch'.[68] He carefully selected the servants that had direct access to the king. Private audiences were abolished. Brühl himself or one of his confidants would always be present, ready to interfere when necessary. Each time the king left his chambers, Brühl's servants inspected the adjacent floors for agitators who might try to approach the king without prior permission.

Access to the king (*Zugänglichkeit*), however, was an essential requirement for good monarchical government. To fulfil his supreme supervisory function the monarch had to remain approachable for all of his subjects. This was the only way for him to learn about popular grievances and attain a representative picture of the outward (i.e., popular) perception of his reign. To make sure that public grievances reached the monarch directly and were not suppressed or altered by the governmental administration, Justi pointed once more at the exemplary practices of the Chinese court as described by Silhouette and Du Halde. Justi stressed that there had been Chinese and Egyptian monarchs 'who installed a bell that could be rung by everybody who wanted to speak to them'. And, he added, 'one knows about rulers [...] who left banquets as soon as they heard that bell.'[69] In this context Justi once more condemned the contemporary practice of

being unable to distinguish his private purse from that of the king. He had been involved in a scheme for reminting the nation's money in which the gold and silver content of coins was reduced and he pocketed the difference (Hilton L. Root, *The Fountain of Privilege – Political Foundations of Markets in Old Regime France and England* (Berkeley: University of California Press, 1994), p. 40 + 56).

67 Saint-Pierre, *Discours sur la Polysynodie*, p. 25 + 39.

68 *Leben Brühls* I, 125.

69 *Leben Brühls* II, 27. A similarly beneficial arrangement had been established in Indostan where public audiences allowed the king to receive a direct impression of popular grievances.

European princes of retiring for lengthy periods of time to provincial summer estates where they could quietly dedicate themselves to leisure and hunting, but were isolated from their subjects' needs.[70]

In order to rule effectively kings had to be well educated. They needed knowledge of their own to determine whether ministers had adequate qualifications for their positions. Under a knowledgeable king, the emptiness of a flatterer like Brühl would have quickly been uncovered.[71] To avoid the rise of a man like Brühl kings had to keep a healthy distance from their advisors and ministers, which would prevent them falling prey to courtly intrigues: in order to remove his rival Sukowski from court, Brühl, for instance, had conspired with the Jesuit father Guarini, confessor to the royal couple.[72]

Justi repeatedly emphasised the disadvantages of ministerial despotism. The *ministrissimus* not only damaged royal authority, but also undermined the efficiency of the entire administrative apparatus. Already Saint-Pierre had pointed out that, due to their excessive workload and responsibility, prime ministers could not rule properly. While jealously guarding and defending his usurped power, the all-dominant 'minister-regent' had to staff key posts in the administration according to personal loyalty rather than genuine merit.[73] For the same reason, Justi believed that prime ministers were bound to fail. Like the king himself, they would eventually become victims of the flatterers around them. Lacking unbiased information about the true state of the country they would be incapable of carrying out reasonable domestic policies that fostered agriculture, commerce, and manufactures. Because of his financial inexperience and his primary interest in personal gain Brühl had gradually ruined the country.[74] His policy of overtaxation had retarded the advancement of popular welfare. Brühl was,

70 *Leben Brühls* II, 28. Justi's repeated criticism of extensive visits to remote summer castles by contemporary rulers can also be found in his *Schreiben an das Publikum* and his *Vergleichungen* (*Vergleichungen*, p. 96).

71 *Leben Brühls* I, 57.

72 *Leben Brühls* II, 24. According to Justi, both Brühl and Guarini had abused their good standing with Frederick August II, urging him to withdraw his protection from Sukowski.

73 Saint-Pierre, *Discours sur la Polysynodie*, p. 35 + 49.

74 *Leben Brühls* I, 168.

in effect, a projector. He had acted like a Turkish pasha, ignorant of all sound principles of political economy.[75]

Personal rule

Under ministerial despotism the prime minister effectively replaced the monarch as the true sovereign. Although there was no danger in contemporary monarchies of a ministerial *coup d'état* in the way that the eighth-century Carolingian *maior domus* Pippin had plotted against the Merovingian rulers, the devastating consequences of ministerial despotism nevertheless disqualified it as a sound governmental practice. In Justi's view, the active, personal rule of the monarch was an effective preventative measure against it. Active rule, however, did not mean that the monarch developed political initiatives himself, or that he came up with proposals for legislation or economic policy of his own accord. Strong political ambition in the monarch was as dangerous as ministerial despotism itself, since the ruler's personal goals were likely to be dominated by the thirst for glory and military conquest. The proper role of the absolute ruler in Justi's reformed monarchy was that of an attentive, critical supervisor of governmental affairs. The monarch was expected to follow the course of day-to-day politics with avid interest, constructive criticism, and occasional suggestions for minor adjustments.

To do so effectively, the monarch had to be able to understand the edicts that were issued in his name.[76] Justi criticised the contemporary European rulers' ignorance of the principles of finance and trade. None of them had 'deep insights in public finance, commerce, or in the means and measures required for the cultivation of the land and the encouragement of industry and consumption'.[77] Monarchs also had to be acquainted with the economic situation of their country. To reduce dependence on ministerial reports the king had to travel the provinces of his country in person. In *Psammitichus* the Egyptian

75 *Leben Brühls* I, 152f.
76 *Vergleichungen*, p. 29f.
77 *Vergleichungen*, p. 57.

pharaoh did not leave the execution of his plans to ministers while locking himself up in a remote summer residence. Quite the contrary, he travelled the provinces extensively to receive a first-hand picture of the state of the country and adjusted his reconstruction plans and orders accordingly. During his journeys Psammitichus held public audiences to learn about the people's grievances and the mistakes of the local administration.[78]

Following the suggestions of Saint-Pierre and d'Argenson, in Justi's modern monarchy most of the work of governing would be done by aides and subordinates, and not by the ruler himself.[79] The right of final decision in political matters would remain with the monarch, but the governmental bureaucracy would narrow the actual range of options over which the monarch had to decide, before he was presented with a choice. The extent of princely self-rule proposed by Justi was designed as a synthesis of the two opposing notions of a politically active king on the one hand (who was likely to ruin the state with his selfish political initiatives) and the notion of an indolent and corrupt ruler on the other (who would abandon governmental business for a life in luxury and abundance, leaving the state in the hands of ministers). The prince would oversee everything and judge over political issues, yet do so without following his own personal interests.[80] Since the monarch's power was only restricted by the body of fundamental laws, much in a modern monarchy would still depend on the character, i.e., the goodness, wisdom, and moderation of the king. For this reason, Justi pleaded for further safeguards like a reformed education of the prince and a substantial recasting of the central administration.

78 The governmental 'intelligence journeys', as demanded by Justi, became an important issue in Austria under Joseph II. He ordered the heads of the local administration to take annual journeys through the provinces. On these travels, they were to act as the eyes and ears of the government at Vienna and had to pay particular attention to the general condition of the population and the state of agriculture, industry and commerce.

79 Henry [Keohane], 'Democratic Monarchy', p. 50.

80 *Manufakturen und Fabriken* I, 178.

Justi's great hope was that a reformed royal upbringing might do the job of imposing moral restraints on the unlimited authority of the monarch without, in effect, curtailing his executive authority.[81] His educational ideas were designed to temper the prince's egoistic inclinations by replacing his self-love with a disinterested pursuit of the common good.[82] Princely education had to instruct the future regent in the art of ruling (*Regierungskunst*) and help him to gain expertise in constitutional law, public finance, and economic policy-making (*Polizei*).[83]

Justi's views were deeply influenced by Fénelon. In *Der Grundriss einer guten Regierung* Justi asserted that his educational ideal was

> the Duke of Burgundy, who died as Dauphin of France and certainly had all these wise, noble, and just principles that are required to make the subjects happy and which could be owned by a prince who was taught by the author of the *Telemachus*.[84]

In contrast to educated princes like the Duke of Burgundy, Justi depicted Louis XIV once more in the darkest light. Though Louis had undoubtedly possessed some form of natural intellect, he was, by and

81 *Grundriss*, p. 135; *Vergleichungen*, p. 353: Princely education 'is of the utmost importance for the people and one can never be careful enough about it'.

82 *Vergleichungen*, p. 30. Fatherly love for their subjects had 'to be installed deeply in the young princes from their infancy onwards'.

83 Justi was a strong believer in the power of education. In his essay on the question 'Ob eine gute Erziehung allemal ihre Wirkung thun müsse' ('Whether a Good Education Will Render Its Expected Effects') he remained confident that a sophisticated educational programme would bring about the intended results, even though there was no guarantee for a positive outcome. As human history had shown, reasonable parents, among them the greatest sages, who had known exactly what a good education required, had nonetheless ended up with 'the most godless and malevolent children' ('Ob eine gute Erziehung allemal ihre Wirkung thun müsse', in: *Moralische und philosophische Schriften* II, 206). However, such developments were exceptional. In the vast majority of cases, a good education had brought about its expected effects.

84 *Grundriss*, p. 417.

large, 'one of the least knowledgeable princes to ever rule cultivated peoples'.[85]

Justi claimed that the education of princes had failed in the past (and still did fail at contemporary courts) because of the choice of incapable tutors.[86] Monarchs usually had no interest in their successors' upbringing and left their sons' fate to be decided by courtly jealousies and intrigues. Discord among the members of the royal family about the education of crown princes had time and again 'brought great misery upon civic constitutions'.[87] The mother of King Alfons of Portugal provided probably the most infamous example of the fatal consequences of such intrigues when she deliberately hampered the upbringing of her son to preserve governmental control for herself.[88] Accordingly, Justi believed that when

> history shows us so few truly great and wise kings the cause of it can be seen in the circumstance that there were so few royal fathers who had any interest in the education of their princes.[89]

By contrast, Philip of Macedon's appointment of Aristotle as tutor for his son Alexander was the most prominent example for a successful royal upbringing. Phillip's choice had effectively laid the foundation for his son's extraordinary success as a ruler.

The tutor's role was to instill in his charge a firm resistance to the corrupting influences of the court. Otherwise, the

> splendour, which surrounds them [the princes], the flattering and complimenting behaviour of everyone who approaches them, can have no other effect according to the nature of man (being in every respect a very proud animal) than to fill them with arrogance and pride and make them look down on their fellow humans as somewhat minor creatures. The natural appetite of man for

85 *Grundriss*, p. 345.

86 Justi laid strong emphasis on the improvement of the instruction and appointment process for potential teachers, pointing out that teachers must 'truly be the most knowledgeable, witty and clever men [...] if one keeps the welfare of mankind and each particular state in mind' (*Vergleichungen*, p. 355).

87 *Vergleichungen*, p. 377.

88 *Grundriss*, p. 353.

89 *Grundriss*, p. 351.

pride makes middle-class children quickly conclude that they are something better than the common people. Such prejudices are unalterable and have, particularly in the person of the regent, life-long effects, which are not advantageous to his subjects.[90]

Justi was painfully aware of the dominant role of self-interest in human behaviour. The combination of unlimited political power and princely arrogance was a dreadful threat. Overpowered by vainglory the prince would perceive his elevated position as a means to satisfy personal desires. Hence the selfish inclinations of the prince had to be successfully recruited for the service of morality by a sophisticated education long before he took the throne.

Ignorance made kings even more dangerous. To put an end to the remarkable ignorance of monarchs in the fundamental methods of governmental administration, princes had to be instructed in these matters. It was disgraceful that virtually no contemporary regent was acquainted 'with public finance, commerce and the means and techniques of how to cultivate the land and encourage the domestic economy [*Nahrungsstand*]'. Not even the heads of the best-run European states were familiar 'with the most elementary definitions and principles of economic sciences'.[91]

Justi discussed the education of princes most extensively in his *Vergleichungen* and in *Psammitichus*. While in the former work he described the various methods by which the heir to the Chinese throne was provided with strong incentives to act in the interest of general happiness, he presented in *Psammitichus* an idealised, pseudo-historical account of princely education in a moderate, yet constitutionally unlimited monarchy. What fascinated Justi was the circumstance that Chinese practices had apparently tempered the absolute monarch's power in a manner that matched his own political ideals. Among the main features of the educational process of the Chinese crown prince Justi highlighted the thorough instruction in modesty and courtesy. From childhood onwards, the prince was supervised at all times and continuously trained in adopting proper conduct towards relatives and

90 *Vergleichungen*, p. 123.
91 *Vergleichungen*, p. 57.

servants and people of different ages – an endeavour which extended to seemingly marginal issues like good table manners. Parallel to this, the prince was instructed in history and literature. Justi particularly praised the wisdom of the essay 'The Rules of Princes' which the Emperor Tai-tsong is supposed to have written for his son, and which exhorts the prince to modesty, self-sufficiency, parsimony, humility, industry, respect for learning and concern for agriculture, the main pursuit of his subjects.[92]

Next to Chinese practices Justi approvingly spoke of the model of royal upbringing in the African kingdom of Whidah. There the crown prince was removed from the court after his birth and raised in complete obscurity and anonymity in the remote province of Zinghe. The prince grew up as an ordinary citizen uncorrupted by courtly flattery. Nobody was allowed to reveal to him the secret of his royal birth. The crown prince lived in a new family with his tutor figuring as his 'official' father. Thus it had happened that after the death of the late king the royal messengers had found and hailed the prince as their new ruler while he was guarding his (alleged) father's pigs.[93] Justi regarded such modest upbringing as a feasible method to shield the prince from youthful corruption at court. Although he did of course not recommend this practice for imitation at European courts he used it to reinforce his claim about the outmost importance of combating the typical princely arrogance. Justi pointed out that a direct confrontation with the daily life and problems of ordinary subjects in the way that the Whidahian crown prince experienced it during his youth would always keep alive in the ruler an avid interest for the common good.[94]

Justi made the ancient Egyptians in *Psammitichus* struggle with the same dilemma that motivated his political philosophy: the attainment of a stable, unlimited monarchical regime as the political basis

92 *Vergleichungen*, pp. 348–352. As Menzel has pointed out, the essay referred to is probably T'ang T'ai Tsung's *Ti chien* (Mirror for emperors), which is part of the *Liu chien chü* (Collection of six mirrors) (Johanna M. Menzel, 'The Sinophilism of J.H.G. Justi', *Journal of the History of Ideas* 17 (1956), 300–310 (p. 305)).

93 *Vergleichungen*, p. 104.

94 *Vergleichungen*, p. 122f.

for subsequent economic advancement. The ancient Egyptians of the novel had recognised both the need for a strong, virtually unlimited ruler and the dangerous proximity of absolute monarchy to despotism. Due to their long (and largely positive) experience with monarchical rule they came to the conclusion that 'the good order, the tranquillity, the security, and welfare of the Empire required them to grant great power to their kings'. However, as they were equally convinced by their intimate knowledge of human nature that 'great power was likely to be abused', they attempted to realise a project similar to Justi's 'third way'. Their reform projects focused on the education of the prince, as they believed that abuse of power stemmed largely from 'the evil inclinations and passions of kings', which were the result of their poor education.[95]

True to Justi's own *thèse royale* advocacy of strong monarchical power, the Egyptians concluded that 'one must not reject a thing as such [i.e., monarchy] because of its possible abuses' and that

> one would not be able to limit the power of kings without opening the door to thousands of irregularities and grievances within the empire and without weakening the state in front of its enemies. Instead, they believed that one would have to fight the abuse of monarchical power at its root. Consequently, the subjects themselves would have to take care of the education of the king's son since their happiness or misery, their welfare or wretchedness directly depended upon him. Hence the only issue over which the king had no power was his son's education. And nearly all fundamental laws and constitutional arrangements of the state that lay beyond the reach of princely power had the aim of ensuring a wise education with all possible diligence so that the spirit of faction or undue self-interest could not exert any influence in its process, thus inspiring the young princes with noble thoughts and inclinations and true love for their future people and instructing them in that great science of governing one's passions.[96]

Justi approved of the Egyptian practice of prohibiting the kings' interference in the education of the crown prince. The task of the prince's upbringing was thereby laid in the hands of the people (who had the greatest interest in his positive development). Their responsibility for the heir's education, however, ceased with the prince's eighteenth

95 *Psammitichus* I, 155.
96 *Psammitichus* I, 155.

birthday. Subsequently, his father introduced him to governmental practice. Psammitichus paid great attention to this latter task. After his son Nekos had turned eighteen, Psammitichus never left him indolent and put him in charge of several minor tasks in the army.[97] Nekos was consigned to supervise the construction of a fortress, he was commissioned to secure unprotected parts of the Egyptian frontier, sent out to a remote province to test the practical application of a reformed tax scheme, and ordered to take care of a branch of Egyptian trade and manufacturing. During all these assignments Nekos was not allowed to develop any personal initiatives. His success or failure was solely measured according to the extent to which he followed the instructions that his father gave him. After Nekos had learnt obedience and order, Psammitichus began to assign him more creative tasks. He asked Nekos to compose memoranda on pressing political and economic issues and began to discuss his own policies with him. Having thus given Nekos sufficient first-hand experience in governmental affairs Psammitichus ultimately set out to share his reign with his son. At the age of sixty-six, Psammitichus started a joint rule that was to last until his death. In so doing, he successfully ensured the smooth transfer of power.

These practices stood in remarkable contrast to contemporary customs at European courts. It was

> a lamentable fact of virtually all monarchies that those who should support the prince usually take into account their own passions, particular interests, and secondary intentions rather than the true good of the state.[98]

Naturally, there was still an immense risk that corrupted or incompetent successors would come to power. For this reason Justi proposed that the personal qualities of the crown prince be checked by a council of sages that would determine whether the intellectual capabilities of the crown prince were sufficiently developed for commencing his rule.[99]

97 *Psammitichus* II, 446.
98 *Psammitichus* II, 450.
99 *Psammitichus* I, 156.

Justi's ideas on the education of the prince envisage a philosopher-king. Uncorrupted, polite, and modest, the king would be filled with a zeal for the promotion of the common good. Equipped with a strong, independent mind, he would not fall under the influence of one of his ministers. Justi favoured hereditary succession (if only on pragmatic grounds so as to preclude rival claims to the throne). However, the hereditary status of the prince was now only a necessary, but not a sufficient precondition for commencing his rule. Justi's advocacy of a council of sages that determined the personal qualities of the heir shows that the crown prince had to meet certain intellectual standards by the time of his succession. Once in power, the prince was obliged to live up to the high demands of his elevated standing by excelling in his 'post'.

Access to the king

Justi suggested further measures for the moderation, but not limitation, of absolute rule. He was convinced that the quality of personal rule greatly depended on the degree of the monarch's accessibility (*Umgänglichkeit*).[100] The monarch had to remain directly accessible to the populace at large. He had to possess intimate knowledge of his lands and subjects and could 'never be too approachable'.[101] Frequent and direct contact with his subjects would remind him that he did 'not live for himself, but for the sake of the state'.[102] Such contacts were also crucial for the king to receive independent information about his country and frustrate the intrigues of ministers or favourites who aimed to separate him from his subjects (so that they in turn could run the state). Locked up in courtly isolation and manipulated by flatterers and ambitious ministers, the prince would be unable to exert a wise and diligent rule. Justi recommended the introduction of regular public audiences. In addition, a board of popular representatives (*Worthalter*

100 *Vergleichungen*, p. 84; *Grundriss*, p. 124.
101 *Vergleichungen*, p. 84.
102 *Vergleichungen*, p. 97.

des Volkes) would advise the king.[103] Instead of escaping to private retreats the health of the state required the king to be a public person who mostly stayed in the capital. Journeys to the provinces were to be undertaken not for private pleasures, but to receive first-hand impressions of the general state of the country.[104]

In Justi's view, the Siamese kings were among the most tyrannical rulers since their mysterious court procedures did not allow for public audiences and generally sought 'to persuade the common man that the kings were elevated above humanity'.[105] The distance between ruler and ruled enforced by the Siamese ceremonials greatly contributed to the fact that the Siamese subjects were 'held like slaves and know indeed no other sentiment than fear'.[106] Fortunately, such exotic rites had become rare in Europe. Shutting himself up in Prague's Hradschin and surrounding himself with magicians, astrologers and dubious quacks, the seventeenth-century Emperor Rudolph II was probably the last example of such an attitude.[107] Still, only few monarchs could be found in Europe who mingled frequently with their subjects or were reasonably well informed of their needs.

Major alterations in court ceremonial were necessary. The etiquette observed at most contemporary courts in Europe was still 'unnecessarily despotic'. Based on his own experiences in Vienna, Justi particularly criticised the stiffness of the Spanish etiquette at the imperial court. The obligation, for instance, to kneel during the entire audience with the Emperor needlessly hampered communication. Due to the number of prescribed genuflections and the ritual kissing of the monarch's hand, one could at best exchange a few distant words with the Emperor at audiences.[108] Justi praised 'enlightened' rulers who had

103 *Vergleichungen*, p. 341. Justi once more pointed to Chinese practices, like the drums in front of the imperial palace which citizens could beat to get attention, and the receptacle in which they could leave a statement of grievances at any time.

104 *Vergleichungen*, p. 96.

105 *Vergleichungen*, p. 90.

106 *Vergleichungen*, p. 90.

107 *Vergleichungen*, p. 94.

108 *Vergleichungen*, p. 25. Although Maria Theresa was far less attached to the established etiquette than Charles VI, most of the old rules, such as the practice

abolished such traditional, anachronistic practices. If the monarch managed to escape from his isolation through greater accessibility, he would also communicate more effectively with his ministers. Monarchs, however, also had to guard themselves against too close contact with their surroundings, as this would damage their dignity and ultimately their authority. Justi abhorred so-called *Kumpelkönige* (chummy kings) who undertook incognito pub crawls with their ministers or servants.

The reforms were designed to encourage public political criticism.[109] Justi believed that the opportunity for public criticism would exert a remarkably positive influence upon governmental conduct. With the help of ceremonial changes and greater accessibility of the prince, every citizen would be able to communicate his grievances easily and effectively to the sovereign. The prince was not legally bound to act upon such criticism. Nonetheless, it was a crucial part of modern monarchical prudence to offer the people a chance to voice their concerns freely.[110]

Reputation

Reputation could also be used as a constraint on the prince to act nobly and justly. The human aspiration to evoke admiration in others was so strong that it extended well beyond one's own lifetime. To be fondly remembered by posterity was a powerful and natural human wish. If wisely arranged, this drive could be used as a check on princely behaviour. In principle, Justi asserted, every monarch was horrified by the prospect of becoming an object of contempt after passing away. A *damnatio memoriae* as used by the Romans to wipe

of wearing black 'Spanish mantles', continued. The court's stiff traditions and habits were the reason for Joseph II's lifelong aversion to submissive ceremonials (Derek Beales, *Joseph II* (Cambridge: Cambridge University Press, 1987), p. 38). During his reign, Joseph even forbade the peasant to kiss the hands of the master, or to bow to earth before him. He considered this a particularly important reform, a visible sign that serfdom had been abolished.

109 *Vergleichungen*, p. 32.

110 *Vergleichungen*, p. 33.

out the memory of a despotic emperor was clearly in no ruler's interest. In his *Vergleichungen,* Justi eulogised the Chinese method of official record keeping as an ideal way to arrive at an unbiased account of a king's reign and thus impose on him a strong incentive for sound political conduct.[111]

In China, an imperial bureau of independent historians had been set up. Each of these historians composed ongoing diaries that commented extensively on all aspects of the emperor's reign. At regular intervals the accounts of imperial historians were sealed and locked up in a secret location so that they could not be accessed, altered, or manipulated at a later point in time. The accounts would not be published until after the death of the emperor, when they would offer an unbiased portrait of the emperor's rule, defying official governmental propaganda. Contrary to the Chinese practice, Justi believed that European monarchies knew nothing of the art of official record keeping. Instead of independent historians trying to create an impartial picture of the ruler, European courtiers humiliated themselves by publishing flattering accounts of even the most dreadful reigns.[112]

Administrative reforms

The systematic and innovative character of Justi's administrative reform proposals has earned him the title of a 'founding father of modern theory of administration (*Verwaltungslehre*)'.[113] To grasp the novelty of and intentions behind his ideas it is necessary to take their direct political relevance and their strong indebtedness to contemporary administrative reform projects in Prussia and Austria into account. Justi's proposals were not purely technical recommendations that focused on maximising bureaucratic efficiency. He did not regard

111 Similarly in: *Leben Brühls* II, 15.

112 *Vergleichungen*, p. 21.

113 Gustav Marchet, *Studien über die Entwicklung der Verwaltungslehre in Deutschland* (Munich: Oldenbourg, 1885), p. 327; Georg Christoph von Unruh, *Subjektiver Rechtsschutz und politische Freiheit in der vorkonstitutionellen Staatslehre Deutschlands* (Hamburg: Hansischer Gildenverlag, 1969), p. 11.

state officials as blind tools of arbitrary princely politics. Rather, they supplemented his overall political project of constructing a third-way monarchy.

The task of the reformed administration was to shift power away from the prince and effectively limit arbitrary interference with governmental procedures. In well-established monarchies, the king shared 'parts of his supreme power with several ministers and, most of all, with a permanent circle of state officials'.[114] Economically, the central administration was of vital importance for enabling accelerated commercial advancement. It was the administration's task to enforce the required modernising reforms and remove traditional obstacles to trade and industry such as feudal serfdom, the *Akzise*-tax, sumptuary laws, clothing regulations, or the corporate privileges of local guilds and inns. To implement competitive economic policies (*gute Polizei*) contemporary administrations first had to undergo severe reforms themselves.

Justi regarded administrative disorder as one of 'the most common defects of many states'.[115] As with the hereditary aristocracy and the guild system, the fundamental problem of contemporary administrations was the existence of quasi-hereditary rights. Favouritism ruled nearly everywhere. Posts were usually passed on from father to son, i.e., filled regardless of the individual ability of the candidate. Justi severely criticised the contemporary practice of appointing 'people to [administrative] councils by looking at their birth and rank rather than at their full knowledge or ability in the things they should adminis-

114 *Vergleichungen*, p. 91. Like French thinkers such as Saint-Pierre or d'Argenson, Justi designed a monarchy in which the ruler left 'the ordinary operations of the state in the hands of an administrative staff, selected on the basis of merit alone and organised into general departments of internal affairs, finance, and external affairs' (Thomas E. Kaiser, 'The Abbé de Saint-Pierre, Public Opinion, and the Reconstitution of the French Monarchy', *Journal of Modern History* 55 (1983), 618–645 (p. 630)).

115 'Ob die Pracht und Verschwendung einem Staate so nachtheilig sey, dass sie nothwendig verbothen werden müsse', in: *Gesammelte Schriften* I, 73–92, 89.

ter'.[116] Senior posts within administrations were usually held by people who demanded extraordinarily high payments, yet lacked expertise in the matters with which they had to deal. Predictably, they left the bulk of work to sub-officials and dedicated themselves to private pleasures. Justi ridiculed such policy with the dictum that posts were assigned to people 'rather than capable people to certain posts'.[117]

Justi had received a first-hand impression of the Haugwitz reforms in Austria, which had themselves been influenced by the administrative changes in Prussia under Frederick William I. In his administrative theory he took up the principal tenets of these reforms.[118] Yet while the actual administrations of Prussia and Austria at the time 'were a house whose foundations had been built over centuries and which had only received a new façade in the eighteenth century' Justi's proposals 'were designed from top to bottom by a single architect who was ready to destroy all ancient institutions that he could discover in order to replace them with something better'.[119] Justi firmly rejected the distinction between *Fiscus* and *Aerar*, i.e., the splitting up of the financial administration between the central government and the Estates. For him, as for Haugwitz, centralisation was the key to creating a more efficient administration.

The centralised bureaucracy should be organised as a pluralistic council system (*behördliche Kollegialverfassung*). With his plans Justi hoped to break up the vertical hierarchical structures that existed in most European administrations at the time. Justi's model of a council-based administration was deliberately set against the 'ministerial des-

116 *Staatswirtschaft* II, 671. It was 'an epidemic illness of states' that posts were assigned 'on the basis of favour, relations, intrigue' rather than staffed 'according to merit, abilities, and skills' (*Vegleichungen*, p. 465).

117 *Staatswirtschaft* II, 481. Justi criticised 'family relationships, bribes by ministers and mistresses, factions, intrigues, adulation and flattery' as the driving forces behind promotions in the civil service (*Vergleichungen*, p. 57). He pointed out that those upon whom the monarch confers the affairs of the state 'do not require his particular favour, but his respect for their merit and his firm conviction of their great diligence and abilities' (*Grundriss*, p. 225).

118 *Staatswirtschaft* II, 635; *Polizeiwissenschaft*, pp. 340–343.

119 Hans Haussherr, *Verwaltungseinheit und Resorttrennung vom Ende des 17. bis zum Beginn des 19. Jahrhunderts* (Berlin: Akademieverlag, 1953), p. 93.

potism' of France. All of his proposals served to prevent the unification of too much power in the hand of a chief minister (*ministrissimus*) while keeping administrative processes sufficiently quick, ensuring the prompt execution of orders.[120] The French system contained the intrinsic danger that individual ministers tended to expect a prince-like status within their departments.[121] In France, an all-powerful minister who was only answerable to the king and ruled over an army of subordinate civil servants and secretaries headed each of the different departments.[122] Yet such a centralised system 'was appropriate only for despotic governments'. It was 'not advisable to let crucial issues depend on the opinion and power of a single person', as no human could resist his own 'prejudices and particular intentions'.[123]

In theory, the French system promised the promptest execution of governmental orders and regulations. However, one could not hope for it to work in practice. Since everything depended on the ministers, the system would only work with altruistic state officials. This was a truly utopian expectation. Out of ten ministers there would be at best one who would use his tenure of office to exert a positive impact and foster substantial change. By contrast, most ministers would naturally turn into 'subordinate despots'.[124] The quality of governmental administrations within Europe still depended far too much on the personal talents of a few individual bureaucrats. The welfare of a certain pro-

120 *Grundfeste* II, 620.

121 Since in such a government 'the unlimited will of the prince is the supreme law, all others, to whom he assigns presidency over governmental affairs, will want to be as unlimited as the prince himself' (*Grundfeste* II, 621).

122 *Vergleichungen*, p. 53. Justi pointed out that governmental affairs in France, Denmark, Spain, and Portugal were run by the ministers and a supreme secretary of state who commanded several commissioners and sub-secretaries. All of the commissioners and sub-secretaries had to obey their superiors without being able to voice their ideas and concerns and thus influence the course of governmental policy. In other states, like Russia, different councils had only been introduced *pro forma* while real power remained with the ministers. For the sake of governmental efficiency it would be crucial that no minister exerted too much power. None of the ministers, for instance, would be allowed to send off *lettres de cachet* on their own authority.

123 *Staatswirtschaft* II, 638.

124 *Grundriss*, p. 217.

vince or department often relied on the random chance of whether its governor or minister acted in the interest of the general happiness or merely worked for his private ends. Justi concluded that

> [t]he characteristics of moderate states require that one recruits many civil servants of equal power and standing for the administration of the supreme power; and it is not even advisable to subdivide the affairs among them according to districts and provinces, but according to the nature of the work. In the same manner, one must not institute one single governor over a province or town who unites in his person all sorts of power. Several civil servants of equal power and authority will clearly put barriers to each other's doings and hence prevent the abuse of power, which is the inevitable consequence of unlimited might.[125]

Justi's ideas of administrative reform were influenced by French accounts of governmental techniques in China. In 1754 Justi translated Claude Lambert's essay entitled 'Excellent institution of the Chinese with regard to punishment and rewards of civil servants' (1749).[126] Justi pointed at the exemplary practice of the Chinese provincial administration where 'the council system [*kollegialische Verfassung*] is in force', ensuring that 'all officials and viceroys have colleagues at their side whose advice and consent was sought in directing governmental affairs'. Once more criticising Montesquieu, Justi took the existence of the council system as a further indication that China should not be classified as an oriental despotism.[127]

The growing economic complexity of commercial states required the creation of new government departments. The huge mass of data needed for managing the internal affairs of a commercial state could

125 *Grundriss*, p. 217.

126 Justi published the translation jointly with his own essay 'Die Nothwendigkeit einer genauen Belohnung und Bestrafung der Bedienten eines Staates' ('The need for strict rewards and punishment schemes for civil servants') (in: *Gesammelte Schriften* I, 102–114). Again, Justi was not really concerned with historical accuracy. Rather, he highlighted those aspects of Chinese life which he perceived to be underdeveloped or missing in contemporary European monarchies.

127 *Vergleichungen*, p. 53.

no longer be handled by a few individuals.[128] It was 'virtually impossible' that a single individual could administer 'so many different affairs with sufficient success and efficiency at the same time'.[129] Not even the most diligent and talented minister could fulfil his duties in complex commercial states if he did not delegate substantial areas of responsibility. In the same way as the division of labour had led to speedier and more efficient production in the manufacturing sector, greater specialisation would improve the proceedings of the governmental bureaucracy. The departmental councils would not only assist their respective ministers with ideas. They would also hold them back 'from many hasty and detrimental decisions'. In departmental councils that operated by majority vote the minister could have little 'room for being swayed by self-interest and passions'.[130]

Similarly to the reforms of Frederick William I in Prussia and Haugwitz in Vienna, Justi suggested the setting up of a general directory or supreme council of government.[131] The council was to be chaired by a vice-president or supreme chancellor. Justi was against the monarch actively participating in the discussions of his council. The king was to be a nominal figurehead. He would be kept informed about the decisions taken and would be asked for final consent only. The council was to restrain the monarch (who chaired it) from taking arbitrary decisions. He would act as a supreme controller, yet would not come up with active political initiatives himself.

The general directory was to be subdivided into five or six departments. Pointing at the need for centralisation, Justi stressed that

128 *Vergleichungen*, p. 54: No single minister could 'ever possess such a range of abilities and knowledge to understand all proceedings in his department'.

129 *Grundriss*, p. 218.

130 *Vergleichungen*, p. 54.

131 Justi explicitly refuted the practice of most German territories where different administrative councils existed separately from each other. Due to the close ties between all governmental affairs, particularly between financial, commercial, and political issues, Justi believed a supreme council was needed, in which all matters concerning the welfare of the state as a whole were discussed and decided upon (*Grundfeste* II, 616). Such a council was 'the most useful institution' for the administration of all governmental affairs (*Staatswirtschaft* II, 654 + 663).

the different departments of the general directory had to be organised by functions instead of being divided by territory or region. Justi was critical of the fragmentary nature of the Haugwitz reforms that united the government of Austria and Bohemia under the central *directorium generale*, but left out Hungary, Transylvania, and the Habsburg possessions in Italy and in the Netherlands.

Justi proposed separate departments for the police (*Polizei*), finance, commerce, justice, war, and – depending on the mineral resources of a country – mining. Each department was to be run by a committee that would meet four times a week. It would be made up of six to eight councillors and would be chaired by a president and a vice-president. Each of the six to eight departmental councillors was to specialise in a particular topic.[132] In this way, expertise and a fruitful emulation could be established that would animate the councillors to excel in their particular areas of work.

The heads of department formed the supreme council that would, like the Prussian General Directory and the Viennese *Directorium*, deal with all political and economic matters of general importance. The presidents, vice-presidents, and two further members of each departmental council would meet twice a week in the general directory to discuss administrative issues and take decisions by a majority vote. Final decisions would then be confirmed and executed by the monarch's privy council.[133]

The governmental administration would be divided into three different levels: local, regional, and central. On the regional level, administrators would be responsible for creating statistical tables and communicating the data gathered to the central authorities.[134] The regional departments were also responsible for exploring new land for cultivation and spreading technical expertise within their districts.[135] For that purpose Justi recommended the appointment of regional

132 For instance, in the *Polizei* department one councillor would specialise in the encouragement of agriculture, another in the improvement of fire insurances, and yet another in the relief of the poor, etc. (*Polizeiwissenschaft*, p. 342).

133 Justi demanded that each of the councillors have a full cameralistic educational background.

134 *Staatswirtschaft* I, 231.

135 *Staatswirtschaft* I, 230.

inspectors for agricultural affairs, whose task was to instruct peasants in new techniques of tilling. Justi demanded the realisation of the council system on all levels of the administration and condemned the traditional post of a city superintendent in major towns – an office that was usually hereditary and gave virtually arbitrary power. On the municipal level, each 'general police-director, police-lieutenant, or other supreme director of police in a great town' had to be assisted by a council in which he held the presidency, yet to which he was accountable for all his deeds and acts. The directors were allowed to execute spontaneous orders in emergency situations without the consent of the council. However, they would have to report to the council afterwards and seek retrospective approval. The council, Justi pointed out, 'will not halt the necessary action and efficiency of the police directory. Yet it will moderate significantly the passions of the director and will hold him back from many injustices.'[136]

The council system was a compromise between constitutional checks and balances and the avoidance of slow and inefficient government modelled on the parliamentary system of England.[137] In order to function properly, it had to be safeguarded by additional measures. Justi suggested adding to each council an independent arbiter who did not take part in administrative proceedings. His only function was to safeguard the correctness of the council's proceedings and report any abuse. Without such control, Justi believed that bureaucrats would work fairly because of to their sense of honour and justice. But keeping in mind the inherently selfish nature of man he feared that such sentiments were insufficient to guarantee personal integrity for ever.[138]

The government also had to publish a regular official periodical. This in-house journal would contain 'useful essays' on technical questions related to agriculture, commerce, finance, and natural sciences and would spread knowledge of recent developments and in-

136 *Grundfeste* II, 622.

137 'Abhandlung von der An-Ordnung und dem Gleich-Gewicht der Hauptzweige der obersten Gewalt, worauf die Glückseligkeit und Freiheit der Staaten hauptsächlich ankommt', in: *Gesammelte Schriften* II, 3–25, 8.

138 *Vergleichungen*, p. 59.

novations among civil servants.[139] This was particularly important since civil servants usually held a degree in law and were unfamiliar with the new economic procedures of modern commercial states.[140] In addition, the bulletin would advertise vacant positions, appointments, and promotions within the administration. Contrary to the contemporary practice of keeping silent about the misbehaviour and subsequent punishment of state officials the periodical would also announce official censure within the civil service.[141] With such a step, Justi hoped to motivate state officials to excel in their posts.

Further measures had to be taken in order to transform the civil service into a body of qualified professionals. Following contemporary French critics such as d'Argenson, Justi rejected quasi-hereditary posts and the venality of governmental appointments.[142] In *Der Grundriss einer guten Regierung* he dealt at great length with the question of whether a ruler could give consideration to birth in conferring posts, rewards, and favours to civil servants.[143] Justi insisted that only individual capability and skills were just selection criteria.[144] It was a mistake to look at social standing and birth. True merit was an individual achievement. It was against reason for a state to pay 'a family for their possible future services in advance for eternity'.[145] Taking up his attack on heredity from the 1756 debate Justi pointed out that nobles were not automatically more suitable for administrative posts

139 *Grundfeste* I, 671.

140 Justi, like many other contemporary thinkers in Germany, was convinced that jurisprudence (and – to a lesser extent – philosophy) no longer provided state officials with sufficient theoretical background knowledge to fulfil their tasks. In his view, state officials needed rather commercial acumen and familiarity with the basic principles of public finance.

141 *Vergleichungen*, p. 60.

142 D'Argenson believed that '[o]ne needs to suppress the venality of appointments, elect popular magistrates, limit the power of the intendants and, above all, ensure that all pieces of land are owned by those who can actually cultivate them' (Simone Meyssonier, *La Balance et l'Horloge – La genèse de la pensée liberale en France au XVIIIe siècle* (Montreuil: Les Editions de la Passion, 1989), p. 119).

143 *Grundriss*, p. 371ff.

144 *Grundriss*, p. 366.

145 *Grundriss*, p. 379.

than other candidates.[146] Hence all positions within the governmental bureaucracy had to be opened up to every member of society irrespective of wealth and birth.[147]

To guarantee that the bureaucratic elite treated its members according to clear-cut criteria of merit and ability, Justi sketched out a new recruitment and promotion system. He demanded entry tests for all candidates that wanted to work for the governmental administration.[148] In order to assemble statistical material, fundamental insights into political economy were required for all positions. Only civil servants who had enjoyed a higher education and had given previous evidence of their skills were to be appointed to senior positions. To maintain the quality of administrative work Justi advocated secret quality controllers who would test the functioning of the governmental bureaucratic apparatus in undercover missions and report their findings directly to the king. In addition, the individual performance of each civil servant would be evaluated every three years.[149] Justi even

146 *Vergleichungen*, p. 465.

147 Justi's advocacy of meritocratic schemes (contrary to hereditary rights) was a typical element of eighteenth-century theories of modern monarchy. Kant, for instance, later extended the positions of thinkers like Justi, proclaiming in 'Theory and Practice' that it was a universal principle of good government that 'every member of the commonwealth must be entitled to reach any degree of rank which a subject can earn through his talent, his industry and his good fortune. And his fellow subjects may not stand in his way by *hereditary* prerogatives or privileges of rank and thereby hold him and his descendants back indefinitely […] Thus no member of the commonwealth can have a hereditary privilege as against his fellow subjects; and no one can hand down to his descendant the privileges attached to the rank he occupies in the commonwealth, nor act as if he were qualified as a ruler by birth and forcibly prevent others from reaching the higher levels of the hierarchy […] through their own merit […] [H]e may not prevent his subordinates from raising themselves to his own level if they are able and entitled to do so by their talent, industry and good fortune […] He can be considered happy in any condition so long as he is aware that if he does not reach the same level as others, the fault lies either with himself (i.e., lack of ability or serious endeavour) or with circumstances for which he cannot blame others, and not with the irresistible will of any outside party' (Kant, *Political Writings*, p. 75ff.).

148 *Vergleichungen*, p. 491.

149 *Vergleichungen*, p. 49.

suggested the introduction of an 'up or out' system. State officials that failed to receive a promotion every three years would be dismissed.[150]

Since most members of established chivalric orders were not appropriate models of uprightness and integrity, Justi suggested the introduction of a new order for government officials.[151] Membership in this order could not be attained with the help of money or personal favours, but would be based on merit alone.[152] The idea behind this new order was to make manifest the novel working principles of the central administration, to enhance ambition, and to further the work ethos of its members. Justi regarded this step as necessary since all efforts that had been undertaken so far for the realisation of greater regulation and emulation within governmental administrations were hardly more than 'petty games, in which even the most ignorant person can easily rise'.[153] The prince had to be aware of 'the ambition and vanity of his civil servants and reward them only with those titles and dignities that correspond with the position that they actually hold'. Justi warned that if 'a titlemania started within a state' it would quickly turn into 'a poisoning sickness for all civil servants'.[154] Distinctions of merit and standing would be blurred once people managed to attain titles that were inappropriate to their individual skills.

Finally, Justi was concerned with the internal managerial problems and decision-making processes of the administration. Financial transactions within the administration would have to be carried out according to exact regulations while prescribed deadlines would standardise acts and payments. In this way, Justi hoped to overcome

150 *Vergleichungen*, p. 457. Justi's suggestions foreshadow the lists of conduct that Joseph II introduced to the Habsburg administration. These lists, designed to check on the zeal and aptitude of the bureaucracy, quickly became infamous as a vicious weapon by which a tyrant spied on his officials. They asked after rank, name, age, years of service, martial status, number of children, special knowledge and aptitudes, religious conduct, attitude towards superiors and colleagues, and financial standing.

151 'Die Notwendigkeit einer genauen Belohnung und Bestrafung der Bedienten eines Staates', in: *Gesammelte Schriften* I, 102–114.

152 Membership was to be conferred on an individual person for lifetime only.

153 'Die Notwendigkeit einer genauen Belohnung und Bestrafung der Bedienten eines Staates', in: *Gesammelte Schriften* I, 102–114, 113.

154 *Grundriss*, p. 358.

the usual delays in administrative proceedings, many of which he believed to stem from favouritism.[155] Civil servants in the provincial outposts of the administration would be obliged to compose regular reports on proceedings in their districts.[156] As a general rule, they would have to serve in districts that lay at considerable distance from their birthplace so that they would not have any family relations or friendship connections within them.[157] Moreover, in order to prevent government officials from exerting petty despotic power in their departments or districts a rotation scheme would ensure frequent changes of offices and duties.[158]

The aim of Justi's administrative ideas was to establish a general working order of government in which little space was left to individual whim. The monarch would no longer be in a position to select officials according to his fancies. The council system and the meritocratic appointment schemes would turn the administration into a bulwark against princely arbitrariness, reducing 'the authority of the ruler to that of rubberstamping bureaucratic decision-making'.[159] Within the administration itself, tight control, rotation of office, and shared responsibilities would render the rise of ministerial or local despots impossible.

155 *Staatswirtschaft* II, 626.
156 *Vergleichungen*, p. 426.
157 *Vergleichungen*, p. 416.
158 *Vergleichungen*, p. 445.
159 Hubert C. Johnson, 'Theory of Bureaucracy in Cameralism', *Political Science Quarterly* 79 (1964), 378–402 (p. 394).

Chapter Six
Economic policy (*Polizei*)

Justi believed it was the state's duty to create a stable and competitive economy. The ultimate aim of government had to be the creation of free markets. Justi was fond of emphasising the crucial role of independent, private economic initiative. Yet private initiative could only develop its full potential once institutional obstacles to commercial and entrepreneurial activity had been removed. For this reason, the state had to abolish monopolies, urban guilds, sumptuary laws and protective tariffs. This was to be achieved with the assistance of *Polizeiwissenschaft*.

The eighteenth-century term *Polizei* must not be confused with modern conceptions of *Polizei* (police) or with the nineteenth-century notion of *Polizeistaat* (police state). The term did not, like today, refer primarily to the upkeep of internal security. In the eighteenth century, this task was rather ascribed to the realm of politics (*Staatskunst*). By contrast, *Polizeiwissenschaft* was concerned with economic policies. According to Justi, the wider meaning of *Polizei* included everything that was undertaken 'for the cultivation of the land and the encouragement of consumption [*Nahrungsstand*]'.[1]

1 *Grundriss*, p. 157; *Manufakturen und Fabriken* I, 52. The broad meaning of the word in German is reflected in the *Prussian General Legal Code* of 1794 where *Polizei* includes building regulations, fire protection, public health, and relief for the poor. The limitation of the meaning of *Polizei* 'to the maintenance of peace and order, "law enforcement" in a narrower sense' only occurred in the course of the nineteenth century (Cf. G.W.F. Hegel, *Elements of the Philosophy of Right*, edited by Allen W. Wood (Cambridge: Cambridge University Press, 1991, p. 450). As Keith Tribe has shown, Heinrich Bensen in his *Versuch eines systematischen Grundrisses der reinen und angewandten Staatslehre für Kameralisten* (1799) was among the first to argue that *Polizei* was exclusively concerned with public safety (Keith Tribe, *Governing Economy. The Reformation of German Economic Discourse 1750–1840* (Cambridge: Cambridge University Press, 1988), p. 161f.). See also: Marcel Raeff, 'The Well-Ordered

Justi wanted to reduce the role of the state from that of actually guiding economic affairs to that of simply providing a suitable legal and political framework within which economic affairs might safely be left to guide themselves. The majority of his suggested policing efforts were limited to a period of transition. Justi saw that domestic markets in the German states were too immature to provide start-up capital for new ventures or to sustain them. However, he was disenchanted with the inefficient management of state-owned companies and with the practice of subsidising new industries over a long period of time. Accordingly, his proposals for the sponsoring of private economic undertakings and the setting up of privileged corporations by the government were designed as temporary measures that would help to realise the ultimate goal of unrestricted competition. Once a sufficient level of commercial and industrial development had been reached, government support had to be withdrawn to let the economy approximate the ideal of free trade. Again, Justi's ideas mirror the policies applied in Habsburg Austria at the time.[2] Although the Habsburg government owned enterprises, lent large sums to other enterprises, created monopolies, guaranteed sales, issued quality ordinances, recruited foreign skilled workmen, and employed other direct and indirect means to encourage economic progress, 'it wanted above all to create conditions for autonomous development'.[3]

The short view and the long

In his works on *Polizeiwissenschaft*, Justi repeatedly warned against quack advisers whom he termed 'pseudo-cameralists' (*unechte Ca-*

Police State and the Development of Modernity in Seventeenth- and Eighteenth-Century Europe: An Attempt at a Comparative Approach', *The American Historical Review* 80 (1975), 1221–1243; Reiner Schulze, *Policey und Gesetzgebungslehre im 18. Jahrhundert* (Berlin: Duncker & Humblot, 1982).

2 Charles W. Ingrao, 'The Problem of "Enlightened Absolutism" and the German States', *Journal of Modern History* 58 (1986), 161–180 (p. 176).

3 Hermann Freudenberger, 'State Intervention as an Obstacle to Economic Growth in the Habsburg Monarchy', *Journal of Economic History* 27 (1967), 493–509 (p. 494).

meralisten) and 'projectors' (*Projekte- oder Plusmacher*). Such 'experts' threatened a country's welfare and blackened the reputation of the new science of political economy. *Plus-* or *Projektemacher* could exert an equally disastrous impact on the national economy as ministerial despots. Their sole aim was to enhance the revenue of the prince to enable him to live out his private passions and amusements.

> In doing so, the country might be exhausted, the subjects might be suppressed, the domestic economy might be ruined – all this counts little to him [the false cameralist] if only he gains approval of his master and possibly even furthers his own interests.

By contrast, a true cameralist had to draw revenue 'without damaging the state. Either he takes it from the surplus wealth of the subjects or he tries himself to stimulate new surpluses and the spread of wealth'.[4]

Justi was quick to highlight how his thinking diverged from that of 'projecting' (*Plus-* or *Projektemacherei*). His ideas had met with fierce opposition among government officials in Vienna, Copenhagen, and Prussia who viewed him precisely as one of those daring projectors that he himself tried to decry. His advocacy of unconventional measures that stood in sharp contrast to traditional arrangements and threatened the established social, political, and economic position of many seemed highly risky to government and church functionaries. Since his opponents often referred to the disastrous effects of the speculative bubble of Law's System under the Regency in France, Justi was keen to distance himself from John Law's failing and named him, alongside the German thinker Loen, as one of the most harmful *Projektemacher* of recent history.[5]

4 *Staatswirtschaft* II, 32.

5 Justi lamented that Law's coinage tricks (*Münztricksereien*) had done great damage to the French economy and had tainted the reputation of financial advisers to such an extent that its repercussions could still be felt in his own days. Cf. 'Gedanken von Projecten und Projectemachern', in: *Gesammelte Schriften* I, 256–281, 273f. Similar ideas can be found in Justi's essay 'Abhandlung von dem so genannten Plusmachen, oder der schädlichen Art, die Einkünfte des Staates zu vermehren', in: *Gesammelte Schriften* III, 409–438, 432.

How did Justi differentiate his *Polizei* from projecting (*Projektemacherei*)? He claimed that in the same way as an enlightened monarch should not merely focus on his self-interest, but on the happiness of the people at large, so sound political economists should aim at the welfare of the entire country instead of promoting the personal fancies of the ruler.[6] Justi criticised the Prussian jurist Darjes for claiming in his *Erste Gründe der Cameral-Wissenschaften* (1756) that the primary aim of the cameral sciences was 'to preserve, augment and administer the annual income of the prince'.[7] Pseudo-cameralists were advocates of short-term Machiavellian aims to secure political and financial advantages to the prince at the expense of popular welfare, using such policies as political oppression, expropriation, re-coinage, arbitrary tax rises, or even war.

These policies were self-destructive. Generating a financial surplus by sharp tax rises or re-coinage was contrary to sound monetary theory. A sudden tax rise could yield a rapid temporary increase in revenue. Yet it would damage trade and industry so severely that the overall revenue would soon decline again and even fall below the initial level. High taxes suppressed the incentive to work and drew entrepreneurial talent and capital away from industry to government and the court. Taxes always had to be adjusted to the productive output of a country.

Hoarding reserves was an equally harmful and old-fashioned means of raising revenue. Apart from exhausting the country, hoarding money in the treasury did not make economic sense. *Plusmacher* still stuck to the old conception of gold and silver as primary forms of wealth. Yet, Justi claimed, those 'who believe that the wealth of a nation depends on how much gold and silver resides within it, err'.[8] Money as such was intrinsically worthless:

6 *Staatswirtschaft* I, 323; II, 22.

7 Joachim Georg Darjes, *Erste Gründe der Cameral-Wissenschaften* (Leipzig, 1756), p. 17.

8 *Grundfeste* I, 428.

> The wealth expressed in gold and silver is only a relative wealth of the state, which comes from commerce and dealings with other nations, and is hence necessary only because of that.[9]

The possession of gold and silver was not to be confounded with wealth as such:

> A country which possesses all sorts of goods in abundance will always be immensely rich even if not a single pound of silver or gold can be found within its frontiers. Even more, with its surplus of goods it will be able to obtain everything from foreign nations that it could otherwise obtain with gold and silver.

Industry, trade, and exchange figured as the real wealth of nations. Even a country 'with a soil of gold would have little or no circulation at all, if it did not produce goods'.[10]

Like Montesquieu, Justi raised the Spanish paradox. Charles V mistook nominal governmental power for actual political capability and the possession of gold and silver for national wealth. Spain's attempt to amass gold and silver in fact created a major outflow of capital.[11] The Spaniards, as Justi remarked quoting Montesquieu's phrase in *The Spirit of the Laws*, had merely acted as Europe's donkey by transporting gold and silver from America to the Continent. Mining projects represented vain attempts to render a country rich and powerful. A few people would profit from mining, while the majority of the inhabitants would remain in poverty.[12]

Money had to be seen as a practical invention that facilitated exchange.[13] In a rich country, money circulated quickly among the entire population. Louise Sommer was mistaken in her assumption that Justi was not concerned with the distribution of wealth within a state.[14] For Justi repeatedly stressed that a wide distribution of wealth

9 *Grundriss*, p. 89.

10 *Grundfeste* I, 614.

11 *Grundfeste* I, 429; I, 432; I, 581.

12 *Grundfeste* I, 474f.

13 Justi's historical accounts of the introduction of coinage can be found in: *Grundsätze der Polizeiwissenschaft*, p. 160; *Grundfeste* I, 595.

14 Louise Sommer, *Die Österreichischen Kameralisten in dogmengeschichtlicher Darstellung* (Aalen: Scientia, 1967. Originally: Vienna, 1920), p. 313.

was preferable to a massive accumulation of capital in the hands of a few, pointing out that

> it will surely be heavily disadvantageous for the happiness of the majority of the people and the general welfare of the state […] if the wealth of a country is united in the hands of a few, or when a certain caste or class of the people, be it spiritual or temporal, attracts all wealth.[15]

Under the altered conditions of modern international trade, the economic dominance of a certain class of people could easily become a source of political dominance and repression. A separated, impermeable class of wealthy citizens would naturally 'suppress the remaining parts of the people' who would 'contribute very little to the power of the state'. Analogously, the great wealth of the clergy in Catholic countries hampered the state 'in an extremely disadvantageous way'.[16]

For Justi a more equal distribution of wealth was central for national economic success. A single merchant holding one million florins in his hands, he pointed out in *Die Grundfeste*, was far less beneficial than ten merchants owning 100,000 florins each.[17] In *Der Grundriss einer guten Regierung* he repeated that ten merchants owning altogether two million florins had three times more influence 'on the furtherance of consumption (*Nahrungsstand*) than if these two millions were owned by an individual merchant only'.[18] It was evident, Justi concluded, that if a hundred families were economically well off they would have a far greater economic power and productive output than if the equal amount of wealth was concentrated in the hands of merely six or eight persons. Consequently, a good government worked for the wide distribution of wealth in the nation.

Justi shared Seckendorff's maxim that money was the sinew of all things (*Pecunia est nervus rerum gerendarum*). The ready availability of capital determined the extent to which governmental and private entrepreneurial action was possible and thus had an immense influence on national economic success. However, Seckendorff and

15 *Grundriss*, p. 239; *Grundfeste* I, 647.
16 *Grundriss*, p. 239.
17 *Grundfeste* I, 534.
18 *Grundriss*, p. 240.

his followers, as Justi was eager to point out, had an excessively narrow view of monetary matters. Rather than having the country's economic advancement at large as their single objective, these earlier economists, like contemporary projectors and entrepreneurs, aimed at amassing gold and silver reserves in the hands of the prince. In so doing, they failed to consider the economic damage done by hoarding such money.[19] As private savings only drew capital away from where it was most needed the prince was best advised not to amass moneyed wealth.[20] Long-term growth was preferable to windfalls, the pet idea of projectors. They wanted to establish new monopolies and privileged trade companies. But their idea of a tight supervision of the domestic economy was bound to render the private commercial activities of citizens even more difficult.

Projectors also held outdated views about the coinage. The damage caused by secret re-coinage (*Münztricksereien*) was enormous. In Justi's view, coinage was a further example of the tight limits that economic laws had imposed upon monarchical whim. In the past, many princes had perceived the right of coinage as an opportunity for creating financial gain. But such plundering could backfire as the fraud usually did not pass unnoticed for long. Once noted, the currency's value declined sharply, and the concomitant loss of confidence caused a dramatic outflow of capital from the affected country. As with taxation, governments could no longer regard fiscal policy as a way of 'making money', but had to see it as a means of furthering national economic prosperity.

19 Contrary to previous cameralistic literature, which dealt extensively with the princely treasury and dedicated lengthy consideration to the central role of the royal court for a country's economy and internal organisation (for instance, Schröder's *Fürstliche Schatz- und Rentkammer*), Justi did not speak of the prince and the princely treasure as central institutions of the state. The princely treasure, in Justi's view, was merely the private budget of the ruler, which was separate from the government's general budget. Further to highlight the strong link between ruler and ruled Justi used the term republic (*Republik*) when speaking about the state, notwithstanding its particular form of government, and talked of citizens (*Bürger*) and civil constitutions (*bürgerliche Verfassungen*), rather than subjects (*Untertanen*) and monarchies (*Monarchien*).

20 *Grundfeste* I, 616.

Despite his official condemnation of John Law, Justi did not regard him as 'some type of unprincipled pseudo-alchemist who attempted to implement a fundamentally unsound scheme for reforming the French economy and its finances'.[21] His view was that Law's financial innovations had failed not because the ideas behind them were fundamentally flawed, but because he and his political backers lacked caution and because too many 'invisible hands had found their way into the public purse'. Despite mistakes in implementation, Law had clearly grasped the fundamental underutilisation of resources in the French economy. He had been concerned about the unemployment and underemployment of the labour force in France, about the fields that lay fallow, and about capital that was hoarded rather than invested in productive economic activity. Justi agreed with Law's strenuous advocacy of paper money. And, like Law, he identified a monetary system characterised by excessively high interest rates and unduly reliant on the use of gold and silver as the circulating medium of exchange as the chief causes of weak national economic performance. Justi proposed to demonetise gold and silver and replace specie with paper credit banknotes as the new medium of exchange. Paper money was an appropriate way to facilitate exchange and to boost circulation. It could work, however, only under tight supervision. Paper money functioned as long as its value was guaranteed so that people could put their trust in it and accept it as a full replacement of specie.[22]

Luxury and sumptuary laws

One of the most hotly contested issues at the time was the question of the moral and economic repercussions of luxury. Justi's position on whether the government had to direct or limit private consumption was closely connected to his thoughts about social emulation as a way

21 Antoin E. Murphy, *Richard Cantillon – Entrepreneur and Economist* (Oxford: Clarendon Press, 1986), p. 128.

22 *Grundfeste* I, 618.

to maximise commercial and industrial activity. Justi defended Melon's advocacy of unlimited luxury against the more critical claims of Montesquieu or Rousseau.[23] As with his advocacy of commercial nobility, Justi hoped that luxury would create a more egalitarian society and believed that this was its greatest social benefit.[24]

Justi unequivocally stated that 'luxury is immensely beneficial for the domestic consumption (*Nahrungsstand*)'.[25] The 'happy consequences of luxury', he claimed, far outweighed its possibly dangerous moral effects.[26] Under contemporary circumstances excessive wealth and consumption could no longer be judged from a moral standpoint alone. Modern states were strengthened economically and militarily by their luxury which therefore had to be tolerated as a necessary evil for economic success, even though it intensified selfish behaviour. The desire to better oneself by pursuing luxury goods was a most

23 For a concise overview of the eighteenth-century luxry debate see: Istvan Hont, 'The Luxury Debate in the Early Enlightenment', in: *The Cambridge History of Eighteenth-Century Political Thought*, edited by Mark Goldie and Robert Wokler (Cambridge: Cambridge University Press, forthcoming). Justi discussed luxury in a number of essays: 'Ob die Pracht und Verschwendung einem Staate so nachtheilig sey, dass sie nothwendig verbothen werden müsse', in: *Gesammelte Schriften* I, 73–92; 'Betrachtungen von der Üppigkeit', in: *Gesammelte Schriften* II, 35–49; 'Von der Üppigkeit, der Verschwendung und andern Missbrauch der Güter', in: *Polizeiwissenschaft*, pp. 217–238 (largely identical with 'Von der Üppigkeit, der Verschwendung und andern Missbrauch der Güter'); 'Von der Üppigkeit', in: *Grundfeste* II, 331–370; *Steuern und Abgaben*, pp. 200–203.

24 Terence Hutchison is mistaken with his assertion that Justi was 'an opponent of luxury' (Terence Hutchison, *Before Adam Smith – The Emergence of Political Economy 1662–1776* (Oxford: Basil Blackwell, 1998), p. 250). Hutchison mistakenly drew his verdict from Justi's comments on the expenditures of the ruler and his government (cf. *Vergleichungen*, p. 63f.). Justi heavily criticised courtly splendour and demanded that only 'necessary expenditures for the support of the state' be undertaken from public funds. Government expenses 'should not be increased by imaginary wants' (*System des Finanzwesens,* transl. Monroe, p. 381). With these admonitions Justi intended to counteract the danger of tax-rises caused by lavish public authorities. However, he did not argue against private luxury.

25 *Manufakturen und Fabriken* I, 160.

26 *Vergleichungen*, p. 63.

powerful stimulant to increase public consumption, the effects of which would benefit everyone.[27] Splendour and lavishness were a folly, Justi noted, but 'it is evident that this folly is beneficial for a great number of other people who live on [...] it'.[28]

Luxury rendered wealthy citizens idle and kept them away from active public service. However, the rich were immensely useful for the common good.[29] In satisfying their excessive needs, the rich created a demand for luxury goods, from which certain branches of the market, artisans and craftsmen most of all, benefited. In this sense, Justi remarked, 'fortunately the personal interest of every human always corresponds to the welfare of the community as a whole'. Justi's position was quite close to the views of Bernard Mandeville in *The Fable of the Bees*. Given the beneficial effects of luxury one had even 'less reason to determine a certain point of wealth which must not be exceeded, or to claim that one could ever have too much wealth'.[30] If the rich ruined themselves by luxury it remained their private family problem, provided their money stayed within the country.

Justi went on to show that if luxury were to be abolished the incentive for work and commercial activity would be lost. Artisans would emigrate and the work ethic would suffer. If all people restricted their consumption to necessities, an immense amount of exchange dealings and commercial transactions would grind to a halt, and even those transactions which were necessary for a simple life would be reduced. States without luxury would only be able to nourish half the number of people they had previously supported. Their impoverished inhabitants would live on the edge of starvation, leading to a steady decline in military power. Thus 'frugal' countries would become easy prey for conquest by neighbouring states.

Apart from highlighting the economic benefits springing from luxury consumption, Justi drew attention to the practical difficulties

27 *Grundfeste* I, 570.

28 'Ob die Pracht und Verschwendung einem Staate so nachtheilig sey, dass sie nothwendig verbothen werden müsse', in: *Gesammelte Schriften* I, 73–92, 82.

29 *Polizeiwissenschaft*, p. 223: 'The fools who dedicate their life entirely to luxury are useful to the common good without knowing it and without receiving merit for it.'

30 *Staatswirtschaft* I, 429.

with suppressing luxury. Justi held that it was not a legitimate objective of legislation to force the citizens to live a life according to a strict moral or religious code. His positive acceptance of commerce and luxury was based on the idea that it was not the task of the government to suppress human vainglory as long as it did not directly harm others.

Justi claimed that it was simply impossible to arrive at a proper definition of luxury.[31] There was no categorical classification of what could legitimately be regarded as superfluous splendour or excessive wealth.[32] Luxury was relative and could only be judged within its respective social and economic contexts.[33] A detailed prohibition of luxury goods would result in a harmful augmentation of state control over private economic affairs. Such augmentation was a serious infringement of the privacy of citizens. The state could not 'legally force anyone to declare all details of his fortune'.[34] Commerce would not flourish under constant governmental meddling. Even if it could, it would be impossible to recruit the enormous number of officials who would be needed for the enforcement of anti-luxury regulations.[35] As Justi explained, the people 'love their freedom so much that they do not want to be limited in their narcissistic actions. And a state taking steps to limit these acts will hardly grow in population and wealth.'[36] For these reasons, he rejected the punitive taxes on silverware and even held that state-run lotteries, which were condemned by many contemporary critics as corruptive, were highly profitable for the public good.[37]

Justi furthermore objected to the widely held assumption that unlimited luxury-consumption drove people into financial ruin. It was simply not the government's task to 'direct all activities of private

31 *Grundfeste* II, 332.

32 *Staatswirtschaft* I, 411 + 429.

33 *Staatswirtschaft* I, 283ff.

34 'Ob die Pracht und Verschwendung einem Staate so nachtheilig sey, dass sie nothwendig verbothen werden müsse', in: *Gesammelte Schriften* I, 73–92, 75.

35 *Staatswirtschaft* I, 284.

36 *Staatswirtschaft* II, 378. The same sentence can be found in: *Steuern und Abgaben*, p. 201.

37 *Staatswirtschaft* II, 438f.

persons and hold back those who openly run into their misery'.[38] Even the strictest sumptuary laws and prohibitions would not turn an incapable entrepreneur into a diligent economist.[39] At best, the government could attempt to direct luxury into channels that were more profitable. Justi believed that this was the case if luxury goods were produced at home.[40] Although he regarded general import bans on certain goods as too rigid, he nevertheless approved duties and import taxes on foreign luxury products. As for the public display of luxury, Justi condemned dress codes that prohibited certain clothing to lower classes. A just and effective law against luxurious dress was economically useless and unenforceable in practice. Nobody, Justi stressed, could exactly determine the actual value of clothes that are being worn. And to distinguish different ranks or castes within societies with the help of signs would have 'many dangerous consequences and would generally be of no use at all'.[41]

Justi was strongly opposed to Montesquieu's claim in *The Spirit of the Laws* that sumptuary laws were appropriate for republics (most of all, in democracies) so that wealth there would be almost 'as burdensome as poverty'.[42] The choice between a frugal, virtuous republic and a commercial, 'vicious' monarchy, as depicted in the tale of the Troglodytes in Montesquieu's *Persian Letters*, was a dangerous illusion. There was no escape for any state from the growing international economic pressure in Europe, be it republican or monarchical. At the dawn of the modern commercial age the moralist's utopia of a virtuous, ascetic community had to be banished to the world of imagination. Republics, too, had 'to base their constitutions and institutions on the nature of man as he is' and could 'not assume certain characteristics in man that might have happened in another possible world if it had pleased God to give the people there the characteristics of angels'.[43] Luxury fostered self-interest and sup-

38 *Staatswirtschaft* I, 284.

39 'Ob die Pracht und Verschwendung einem Staate so nachtheilig sey, dass sie nothwendig verbothen werden müsse', in: *Gesammelte Schriften* I, 73–92, 85.

40 *Vergleichungen*, p. 63f.

41 *Polizeiwissenschaft*, p. 232.

42 *Spirit of the Laws* 7, 3.

43 'Betrachtungen von der Üppigkeit', in: *Gesammelte Schriften* II, 35–49, 49.

pressed the love for the common good.[44] Yet because of intensified commercial competition between the European nations no state, especially not a small republic, could afford frugality.[45] A frugal, non-commercial republic would soon fall prey to foreign invasion. The harsh sumptuary laws of contemporary city states like Geneva or Venice had been created out of the foolish wish to imitate the ancient Greek city states, from which, however, they differed in their general aims and features. Apart from being economically and militarily short-sighted, such an attitude was built on a historical misunderstanding of classical antiquity. Athens, as Justi pointed out, had gained strength by dedicating its efforts to commerce, and had never introduced severe sumptuary laws against luxury as, for instance, Sparta had.

Emulation

Justi was an enthusiast of meritocracy. He believed that individual skills and talent were raw material of virtually incalculable value for a dynamic modern society. In his view, social and geographical mobility in Germany and Austria was still too difficult. The inflexible and exclusive nature of traditional political and economic institutions blocked ambition for social advancement at all levels, hampering the free flow of capital and skills. Justi demanded the systematic breakup of the inflexible hierarchy of ranks. The protectionist atmosphere of the guilds and the stronghold of the nobility in the countryside had to be replaced with social competition.

Trade and industry required a wealthy mercantile class that possessed sufficient financial capital for large entrepreneurial investments. It was a prime objective of the state 'to have rich and powerful merchants'.[46] A country was only happy, if one could say of it, as was said of Tyre, that its merchants were princes. By contrast, miserable

44 *Vergleichungen*, p. 313.
45 *Vergleichungen*, p. 211.
46 *Manufakturen und Fabriken* I, 48.

and poor merchants denoted a wretched country.[47] Material wealth was the backbone of a flourishing mercantile class. Equally important, however, was the respect and standing that merchants enjoyed in society. To bolster their standing and make trade an honourable profession, the government had to confer titles and rewards on successful merchants and entrepreneurs.[48] After all, the driving force behind economic activity was not only fuelled by the aspiration for material returns, but also by the wish to gain social respect and distinction. True, Justi remarked, 'pride, ambition, and joy are celebrated by the possession of property'; yet we 'want to be more than what we used to be; we want ranks, titles, and honours'. Accordingly, 'one has to provide a certain consideration for the owners of factories and manufactures as a catalyst for these industries and for the economy in general'. Justi saw

> no obstacle to granting such people, who have made a considerable fortune and whose deeper insight, skilfulness, diligence, and efforts have accomplished manufactures and factories for the greatest benefit of the state, all kinds of titles and privileges.[49]

The granting of titles and honours was also an additional source of revenue for the state. In order to elevate the social standing of entrepreneurs Justi repeatedly quoted the exemplary practices in England where commerce had been successfully transformed into a socially well-regarded occupation.[50]

47 *Grundfeste* I, 591.

48 *Staatswirtschaft* I, 269f.; II, 400.

49 *Staatswirtschaft* I, 416.

50 *Polizeiwissenschaft* p. 198. As outlined above, Justi believed that a continued limitation of trade to non-nobles would only foster popular prejudices against trade, leading to a general low opinion of commercial activities. It is, as he remarked in his *Staatswirtschaft*, 'a very detrimental prejudice that the German nobles think their rank would be tarnished by commercial, industrial or other activities that would be useful for the state. This is the reason why those who have the greatest wealth [...] waste their time with hunting, gambling and other useless things and do not contribute anything, or hardly anything, to the welfare of the state. Not to mention that many of them gradually lose their fortune and ruin their families' (*Staatswirtschaft* I, 352).

In his fight against undue privileges hampering social emulation Justi particularly attacked the guild system. Apart from their 'ridiculous customs and ceremonies', he believed that the existing guilds and corporations failed to live up to modern economic standards in several respects. Like government administration, guilds suffered from the quasi-hereditary status of their members. They obstructed the promotion of technical skills and presented a substantial impediment to the advancement of domestic trade.

Justi particularly criticised the guilds' lengthy and complicated instruction processes and their rites for the admittance of master craftsmen. In his view, the guilds' instruction of their junior members was time-consuming, costly, unproductive, and unjust. Candidates for master's status commonly had to spend four years under the supervision (or rather, the arbitrary will) of a master craftsman to acquire skills which they could easily learn within three months. They were fully subordinate to their masters and had to create a final and costly, yet entirely useless, piece of work (the so-called masterpiece). The dependence of candidates on the approval of their masters naturally favoured sons of master craftsmen over equally skilled newcomers. Furthermore, masterships were often purchasable, and the son of a guild master typically paid less to enter a guild than other candidates did.[51] The guilds thus hindered the free choice of vocation among the citizens. In order to remove discrimination against novices in professions that were traditionally dominated by guilds, Justi suggested the setting up of independent governmental boards that would confer masterships on the basis of a standard examination that tested practical skills and techniques. In this way, the conferring of masterships could

51 *Staatswirtschaft* I, 252: 'I just want to mention the bad instruction that they [i.e., the masters] give to their apprentices who could learn in less than three months all that for which they now have to take three, four or more years of maidservant's work; the arrangements concerning the assignments of masterships are equally bad since – instead of ability and real skills – they require being the son of a master and constructing a costly, yet in common life useless masterpiece.' Cf. *Gesammelte Schriften* III, 394: 'They [i.e., the police] should not be complacent about craftsmen and their bribes for new masterships; nothing but ability and skills should be taken into account for the assignment of masterships.'

be liberated from undue favouritism, promoting the spread of technical skills and general learning.[52]

The guilds, like state-owned or semi-governmental trade companies, exerted a *de facto* monopoly.[53] They suppressed competition in many retail markets and existed for their own sake, rather than that of their customers. To prevent guild members undercutting each others' monopoly profits, guilds, for instance, controlled the expansion of output. The state, however, was only interested in real personal skills and true economic excellence and hence had to break up the established 'life-long, or even hereditary rights and privileges' of the guild system.[54] As the guilds showed a notorious unwillingness to fight these abuses themselves, a stronger governmental control of them was needed together with a long-term policy that aimed at overcoming their dominant, autonomous status.[55]

An effective way to reduce the influence of guilds and corporations (and expose them to greater competition) was to exclude them from new industries.[56] Justi stressed that it was imperative for the state to prevent the establishment of institutions or organisations that resembled the existing guilds or corporations within new manufactures. In so doing, it would be possible to push back the influence of guilds and exclusive rights in the wholesale trade.[57] Justi explicitly referred to the success of this procedure in Habsburg Austria. There, new industries, like the cotton manufacture in Schwechat (founded in 1726), were initially exempted from the guild regulations for a limited period of time and ultimately allowed to remain free.[58]

52 *Grundfeste* I, 551.

53 *Manufakturen und Fabriken* I, 226; *Grundfeste* I, 481.

54 *Staatswirtschaft* I, 254.

55 Justi preferred this option to a sudden prohibition.

56 *Grundfeste* I, 445 + 451.

57 *Grundfeste* I, 569.

58 Justi hoped that peasants, too, could become employees in manufactures and factories and thus shake off the yoke of feudal serfdom after a certain amount of time. Justi suggested six years of work. Such a move would reduce the exodus of unfree peasants and contribute to the economic advancement of the nation.

Institutional change was the most effective means to promote economic growth – far more effective than direct commercial involvement by the government, for instance, with the help of state-owned enterprises or subsidies to certain industries. The successful establishment of a trade or industry within a country depended primarily on the creation of a favourable institutional framework that left private commercial activities at liberty, allowing trade to evolve 'by itself'. In most contemporary states, however, institutional barriers still hampered trade 'from coming into being on its own accord'. In virtually all European states

> there are so many old and faulty laws and institutions [...] which were introduced by our forefathers out of lack of insight into the economy [*Nahrungsstand*], so that in every country numerous impediments exist that prevent the just relationship between all parts of the economy.[59]

Governments had to aim at a general liberation of trade through the abolition of restrictive practices that hindered the mobility of capital, goods, and labour (including foreign labour). Liberty of action in the markets for commodities and the factors of production would soon lead to strong economic growth. But Justi demanded protection tariffs for particular 'infant industries', which were as yet too undeveloped to face international competition.

In *Psammitichus* Justi presented his ideas of the removal of institutional barriers in an idealised form. He pointed out that the most remarkable characteristic of the Tyrian government was that it had never undertaken anything for the encouragement and enhancement of commerce. Nonetheless trade had always flourished extensively there. This had happened exactly because of the Tyrian government's neu-

59 *Grundfeste* I, 556. To introduce these changes effectively, the government itself needed to be reformed. Only after a radical restructuring of the governmental bureaucracy could the central administration become the driving force behind the envisioned removal of institutional barriers.

tral attitude towards trade. All that traders in Tyre expected from the government

> was that it did not put any barriers into their way, but left the merchants a free hand in all their doings and undertakings, which they regarded necessary for the enhancements of commerce and the growth of their profits.

All that the Tyrian government did with respect to commerce

> was to levy moderate custom duties on incoming and outgoing ships. Due to the great volume of Tyrian trade these moderate custom duties were a highly profitable revenue. Apart from this, the government hardly cared about commerce.[60]

Tyre's success proved that a flourishing commerce did not depend as much on the direct encouragement and support of the government as on the fact that no impediments and disadvantageous institutions existed in the state's constitutional framework. This was the real reason why so few empires and states enjoyed the fruits of commerce: despotic, self-interested and violent governments had simply put too many barriers in the way so that commerce could never find a smooth path within them.[61]

Justi highlighted the need for governments to foster industrialisation by removing institutional bottlenecks. Intervention in the economic sphere served to eliminate the obstructions that traditional society had created for itself over the course of decades, if not centuries. Apart from the acceleration of commodity flows the principal objective of this policy was the enhancement of social mobility and emulation. As Justi pointed out in his *Vollständige Abhandlung von denen Manufakturen und Fabriken*, freedom

> is the soul of commerce, and the state does everything it can for its support if it grants this freedom in so far as it is reasonable and not to the disadvantage of the true good of the state, and does not lay impediments in its way.[62]

60 *Psammitichus* I, 186.

61 *Psammitichus* I, 187.

62 *Manufakturen und Fabriken* I, 47 + 204.

If there were sufficient liberty in a state a flourishing economy would come 'into existence without great care of the government'.[63] Trade and industry required nothing but freedom and security to flourish 'by themselves'.[64]

Monopolies and industry

To safeguard the economic progress of a modern monarchy the prince himself was strictly prohibited from engaging in commercial activities.[65] Like Montesquieu in *The Spirit of the Laws* Justi pointed out that it would be too easy for a trading monarch to establish monopolies by declaring certain economic activities as *regalia*, i.e., exclusive privileges of the king.[66] Monopolies presented a serious threat to economic prosperity and were to be avoided by all means.[67] Justi carefully refuted possible arguments in favour of monopolies and showed that in the absence of competitors the monopolist – who lacked the pressure for cost-efficient production and fair pricing – would manufacture products inefficiently and sell them at inflated prices.[68] He pointed out that the 'more sellers there are who want to exchange their goods for money, the cheaper the goods will actually be sold'. In contrast to this, the monopolist

> who is sure that nobody else can undersell him, will never offer his goods at a cheap price; and he will never produce them in such an amount to dispose of them at a moderate price. He will limit the production according to the sales expectation in the particular town or country in which he holds the monopoly.[69]

63 *Grundfeste* I, 434.
64 *Grundfeste* I, 741.
65 *Manufakturen und Fabriken* I, 85.
66 *Staatswirtschaft* I, 226; II, 62f.
67 *Staatswirtschaft* II, 330 + 397: 'Nothing is more contrary to sound principles and the encouragement of trade and industry than monopolies.'
68 *Manufakturen und Fabriken* I, 148.
69 *Manufakturen und Fabriken* I, 149.

A country in which several monopolies existed could never expect to achieve a strong position in international trade. The monopolist would probably be incapable of selling his products abroad and would 'hinder the export trade and act to the detriment of all inhabitants in the state'.[70]

The government's role in economic affairs was to guard against the creation of monopolist structures and to keep economic competition among the citizens on an equal and fair footing. The plurality of factories in all branches of the market would maximise economic growth. It was the only way to guarantee the fair pricing of products and create employment: where many single entrepreneurs compete, 'the envy and hate that they feel against each other has no detrimental effect'. Rather, their envy has 'the happy effect that they strive to exceed each other in industry, innovative power and with help of their improved goods' to win the largest share in the market. And if some entrepreneurs succeeded in making their fortunes in this manner their examples 'will be great incentives for others to imitate them, and the multiplication of manufactures and with it the confluence of goods will develop by itself'.[71] This, Justi summed up, 'is what the government has to wish for'.[72] Since 'a single monopoly takes away employment that could nourish a thousand families' the government was not to grant a monopoly or exclusive privileges at any point in time to any kind of manufacture or factory.[73] Ideally, '[n]ot even the smallest branch of industry' would 'be left to a single person'.[74]

Justi knew that this theoretical ideal of free trade was difficult to accomplish in practice, particularly in economically underdeveloped countries like the German states. The government had to help. Only a

70 *Grundfeste* I, 754.

71 *Manufakturen und Fabriken* I, 150.

72 *Grundfeste* I, 752. It was the supreme principle of good government not to trade actively itself and hinder the establishment of any forms of monopoly. Nothing, Justi pointed out, was 'more contrary to the reasonable principles of the nature of civic constitutions than the government taking over certain kinds of industry and trade'. The government itself was not allowed to run monopolies or monopolist businesses.

73 *Gesammelte Schriften* III, 408.

74 *Polizeiwissenschaft*, p. 184.

few entrepreneurs in underdeveloped countries would be willing to take the exorbitant risks necessary for large industrial or commercial endeavours without the benefits of monopoly protection. Besides, infant industries needed governmental protection from cheap imports.

In the states of the Holy Roman Empire initial state investment was required in a number of sectors. There, the government was practically obliged to grant monopoly rights. In other words, new privileges were needed to overcome the legacy of old privileges. This could descend into a vicious circle.[75] Hence Justi demanded that monopolies be conceded only for a limited period of time. The government also had to reserve its right to revoke them when necessary, since once a certain level of economic advancement was reached the assignment of monopolies would do more harm than good.[76] If certain branches of the market were allowed to remain monopolistic for ever, they would never develop their full potential.[77]

The government could best encourage trade and industry by indirect ways. The monarch only had to set up 'certain factories and manufactures at his own cost if nobody else showed interest in undertaking them'.[78] In such cases the government was indeed compelled to establish a monopoly. But in order to absorb the cost of these initiatives, state investment needed to be restricted to a couple of years. As soon as the relevant branch of the market became well established, government support had to be withdrawn. Ultimately, all these

75 Such a vicious circle had actually happened in France: 'Colbert intended the privileges extended to particular merchants and to particular industries to be temporary measures. After an initial start-up period, the privileges were to be rescinded [...] Having fostered an industrial environment of royal patents, monopolies, and franchises, the Crown had to grant additional monopolies in order to develop new industries. A potential investor would not venture his capital without assurances of protection or special concessions similar to those granted to already-existing industries [...] To encourage large enterprises, the government generally had to provide investors with monopolies, subsidies, and tariff protection' (Hilton L. Root, *The Fountain of Privilege – Political Foundations of Markets in Old Regime France and England* (Berkeley: University of California Press, 1994), p. 120).

76 *Grundfeste* I, 757.

77 *Grundfeste* I, 755.

78 *Staatswirtschaft* I, 227.

undertakings had to be taken over by private management. Nearly all of Justi's suggestions concerning the establishment of new industries in the German states (for instance, silk manufactures) followed this pattern of initial governmental investment with subsequent privatisation and market liberalisation.

The principal problem for policymakers was to determine precisely when it was that monopolies had outlived their economic usefulness. The monopolists always tried to keep their privileges as long as possible. But if the decision for liberalisation was delayed too long, trade could be hampered. On the other hand, if a particular sector of the market was opened up to competition too soon, disaster could await both the investors and the government. Justi recommended a model that was successfully applied in Austria under Maria Theresa: the monopoly privilege of several Austrian cotton manufacturers expired in the early 1760s. Naturally, they desired a renewal. However, while in 1752, when the earlier term had come to a close, the manufacturers had been successful in their application for an extension, a decade later the government refused their request. Though many of them faced a more troubled existence afterwards, the move turned out to be a success in the long run. In subsequent years the Austrian cotton industry enjoyed steady growth.[79]

Justi formulated his ideas on government investment, temporary monopolies, and eventual privatisation most comprehensively in his essay 'Gedanken von der Aufhebung der Handlungsgesellschaften' ('Thoughts on the Dissolution of Trade Companies').[80] Justi, like Melon, pointed out that trading companies with exclusive privileges were indispensable for colonisation projects or other large economic endeavours which could not be funded by private investors. However, they violated the liberty of trade and hence presented only a temporary solution. Justi described the dissolution of the Danish West Indian Company in 1754 as an exemplary act for the privatisation of governmental or semi-governmental organisations. He thereby highlighted once more the inferiority of monopolistic productivity growth com-

79 Freudenberger, 'State Intervention as an Obstacle to Economic Growth', p. 500.

80 'Gedanken von der Aufhebung der Handlungsgesellschaften', in: *Gesammelte Schriften* II, 57–71.

pared to free market conditions. After a certain period of time, the existence of monopolistic trade companies would prevent the complete realisation of market potential in their sector. Furthermore, the shares of a company that enjoyed a *privilegium exclusivum* were normally in the hands of the government or under the control of a small group of wealthy investors. By opening up ownership of shares to the wider public (as part of the withdrawal of governmental ownership) a far greater number of citizens could directly benefit from the company's profits. The gradual withdrawal of governmental investment and shareholding in such companies could of course only take place under favourable market conditions. The company would need to be well established, i.e., it would have to have stayed profitable over a certain period of time. In addition, the market sector in which the company was active would need to show a fair potential for future growth so that private investors would build up rival companies that would compete with the former monopolist. Finally, governmental withdrawal from monopolist companies was only possible in a country with a considerable number of wealthy citizens who would be able to invest in newly established rival companies.

In several aspects, Justi's ideas on trade companies resemble Sir James Steuart's views of the statesman's constant superintendence of trade. Both thinkers pointed out that protection was essential in less developed states if industry was to be established. Like his Scottish counterpart, Justi believed that the state ought to monitor profit levels so that when the real value of commodities indicated that they were competitive abroad, trade could be liberalised domestically and internationally. Both Justi and Steuart held that 'the scaffolding must be taken away when the fabric is completed'.[81]

81 Andrew S. Skinner, 'Sir James Steuart: Economics and Politics', *Scottish Journal of Political Economy* 9 (1962), 17–37 (p. 32). See also: Sir James Steuart, *An Inquiry into the Principles of Political Economy*, edited by Andrew S. Skinner (2 vols; Edinburgh, 1966), I, 262.

Justi divided economic activity into three different areas: agriculture, manufacturing, and trade. Though agriculture presented an important segment in the general economic activity of a country, Justi made it clear that it had to be complemented by manufacturing and trade. Otherwise, the state risked suffering from a static economy.[82] The natural reward of a country that only had agriculture and pastoralism was a low population. Manufactures and factories were the key to large-scale economic advancement. Domestic industry was even more important than foreign trade. As the example of Japan had shown, a country could live well without external trade. But no state could flourish without manufactures and factories.[83] They did not only employ a good deal of people. Their employees also needed other people to satisfy their needs in turn. A larger number of manufactures and factories would thus give rise to a greater population and further urbanisation. Justi pointed out that in the more developed states of Europe like Holland, Britain, and France, the ratio between urban and rural population was far more weighted in favour of the towns than in German territories like Brandenburg or Saxony where, in his view, it was still balanced.[84]

In order to foster domestic economic growth the government had to establish and support new manufactures and factories until they were able to compete with foreign imports.[85] Priority in the foundation

82 *Manufakturen und Fabriken* I, 15.

83 *Manufakturen und Fabriken* I, 14.

84 *Manufakturen und Fabriken* I, 43. Justi strongly recommended the use of new machinery in manufactures and factories and proposed governmental schemes that rewarded technical inventions (*Manufakturen und Fabriken* I, 45; I, 137; I, 147; *Grundfeste* I, 568). He also underlined the importance of structural policy measures by the government (canals, roads etc.; *Grundfeste* I, 646). In so doing, the government had to make sure that manufactures and factories were not merely located in or around the capital. Otherwise, price levels between towns and provinces would become too disparate (*Manufakturen und Fabriken* I, 82 + 228).

85 *Manufakturen und Fabriken* I, 49.

and sponsoring of new manufactures and factories had to be given to those industries which offered the best opportunities for market satisfaction and employment to a large number of people. To assess these priorities correctly, the government had to gather meticulous data on the current economic situation in its territories.[86] The state-sponsored establishment of new companies was a costly task. Any government entertaining the hope of achieving this cheaply 'would have a vain expectation except when the country has great [natural] advantages over other states.'[87] In the absence of a geological or geographical headstart, the government had to find additional means to appeal to investors.

Justi did not propose that the state launch and run manufactures and factories entirely at its own risk. At best, the government could provide for the initial stage of development.

> Yet once they [manufactures and factories] are set up and running and can maintain themselves he [the monarch] must hand them over to private persons if he wants to act according to sound principles.[88]

For the foundation of large manufactures and factories it was generally cheaper (and economically preferable) that the government entered into public–private joint ventures, i.e., supported private entrepreneurs in establishing the desired business. Entrepreneurs would thus not only carry essential parts of the costs. Their aspiration for material gain (to be drawn from the new factory) would also give them a far greater incentive to economic excellence than a state-paid administrator would have who earned his salary regardless of the success or failure of the venture concerned.[89]

Justi carefully considered the question of how a government could best attract suitable entrepreneurs and how it should support them in the businesses they planned to set up. The government had a considerable number of options to direct foreign and domestic entrepreneurs into certain branches of manufacturing. First of all, it could

86 *Manufakturen und Fabriken* I, 73.
87 *Grundfeste* I, 446.
88 *Manufakturen und Fabriken* I, 87.
89 *Staatswirtschaft* II, 478.

offer land and buildings. In Justi's view, contemporary princes owned far too many edifices and castles and far too much land. These assets could either be sold, as Frederick William I had done in Prussia, or handed over to entrepreneurs under the condition of founding a particular factory.[90] The government could also provide entrepreneurs with free equipment and building materials. Alternatively, it could grant them a certain period of tax exemption (usually six years).[91]

The greatest risk for the government in attracting and sponsoring private entrepreneurs was that it could end up lining the pockets of adventurers and projectors who had no real interest in starting a sound business, but perceived governmental support schemes primarily as an opportunity for laying their hands on public funds. A careful scrutiny of entrepreneurs was essential. The government was never supposed to grant money, cash subsidies, credits, or loans to private investors, as it was highly questionable whether such money would ever be used for the establishment of a company (or whether it would not simply be spent on the entrepreneurs' private fancies).[92] Rather, Justi suggested that the government guarantee entrepreneurs preset premiums on items actually produced. It could also fix a certain price at which it would guarantee to buy manufactured pieces from them. In this way, the government could hedge the entrepreneurs' initial financial risk without giving them carte blanche for the use (and possible abuse) of public funds.

Justi was firmly convinced that it was too risky for the government to sponsor individual entrepreneurs.[93] He repeatedly stressed that a company 'that depends on a single man, is in many respects subject to far greater danger' than one run by a council of directors.[94] For this reason, Justi recommended that newly founded manufactures and factories be run under the joint administration of a board of shareholders, rather than under the directorship of a single

90 *Manufakturen und Fabriken* I, 79.

91 *Grundfeste* I, 449. The government could also attract potential investors by conferring titles of distinction on them.

92 *Manufakturen und Fabriken* I, 99.

93 *Grundfeste* I, 447 + 459.

94 *Grundfeste* I, 448. *Manufakturen und Fabriken* I, 92.

entrepreneur. The latter option, Justi underlined, was economically risky, as individual entrepreneurs commonly requested exclusive privileges from the government for their newly established enterprises. Besides, bearing in mind the inherently selfish nature of man, a council of shareholders seemed a far better option than single directorship.

Although individual ownership promised immediate economic success, as the proprietor would be driven by the expectation of profit, things could easily go wrong at a more advanced level. Success in business would make the entrepreneur dream of titles and honours. To achieve them, he would use company profits for private ends rather than for reinvesting them. Frequently, after the death of an entrepreneur, his heirs did not continue the business but sold it to their father's rivals. This usually led to the gradual decline of the business and the weakening of competition.[95] Thus ownership shared by a board consisting of six to eight people, one of them acting as president, was a far better organisational scheme than single managerial ownership.[96]

Justi's strenuous advocacy of government sponsorship of private companies complemented his fervent opposition to protectionism. The sponsorship for manufactures and factories aimed at the creation of companies that could successfully compete with rival producers both in the domestic market and abroad. Justi recommended export-driven policies that would enable manufacturers and traders to conquer foreign markets for their products. Isolationist countries had only a limited potential for economic growth. Isolationism failed to create high level of popular welfare. Since domestic consumption tended to stagnate the economic development of isolated nations would soon reach a plateau. Only exports could guarantee a constant growth rate.[97]

95 *Manufakturen und Fabriken* I, 92.

96 Here again, Justi's strong inclination towards committees and councils shines through.

97 *Psammitichus* I, 224.

Agricultural improvement was a crucial element in Justi's vision of national economic advancement. Much of a country's growth depended on progress in agricultural productivity. Since the landlocked character of most German states did not allow for naval and overseas trade, progress in the rural economy played a particularly important role in their attempts at commercial development. For Justi, agriculture included the entire inland development of a state, such as forestry, the construction of navigable waterways, and the reclaiming of land.[98] '[N]o part of a country's surface' was to be left uncultivated and useless.[99] Reclaiming barren lands and making them profitable was a real alternative to military conquest. Justi shared Melon's belief that a monarch who found the means for a better cultivation of his lands 'would do more service to the state than he who by a destructive and bloody war would add the same quantity of land to his country'.[100]

Justi was not a Physiocrat. Although he paid tribute to the economic contribution of agriculture, he nowhere linked productivity growth to that sector alone. The existence of a surplus in agriculture was an essential, yet not of itself sufficient, condition for a country's economic development. Long-term prosperity chiefly relied on the production of secondary goods that did not depend primarily on natural resources but on human inventiveness, imagination, entrepreneurship, scientific research, and the rapid circulation of wealth.

Justi's call for agricultural reform was motivated by his awareness of the sharply increased agricultural production in England and Holland, as described in French publications of the 1750s, most prominently in Ange Goudar's *Les interets de la France mal entendus* (1756). Justi became a fervent proponent of the English model. Agri-

98 An eminent example of the inland development of the land is Psammitichus's plan to construct a canal between the Red Sea and the Mediterranean (*Psammitichus*, II, 439).

99 *Polizeiwissenschaft*, p. 23.

100 Jean François Melon, *A Political Essay upon Commerce*, translated by David Bindon (Dublin and London: Woodward and Cox, 1739), p. 76.

culture began to flourish in England 'around seventy to eighty years ago', allowing the country to boast of having taken the cultivation of the land further than any other European nation.[101]

Next to English practices, Justi also admired the Chinese government's concern for agriculture and the welfare of the peasantry.[102] Justi was particularly attracted by Du Halde's description of the spring ploughing ceremony, in which the Chinese Emperor himself participated. This symbolic act positively underlined the general respect paid by Chinese society to agriculture. Justi furthermore praised the special prizes awarded by the Chinese mandarins to hardworking peasants. These practices stood in remarkable contrast to the unhappy lot of the European peasantry. Foreshadowing the reforms of Joseph II, Justi demanded that the peasants be liberated from carrying 'the entire burden of the whole state'.[103] Since it was 'that class of men [...] upon whom the power and prosperity of the state – yes! one could say the well-being of all other estates and classes of the people –' depended, a wise and benevolent monarch was best advised to follow the example of the Chinese emperors and alleviate feudal serfdom and corvées.[104]

Despite the increased amount of attention paid to the peasantry in the writings of seventeenth-century thinkers like Becher and Seckendorff and of early eighteenth-century cameralists such as Rohr, Dithmar, and Gasser, or Justi's contemporaries like Zincke, there was little suggestion in their works that improvement in basic agricultural practices would have to involve drastic changes in the social basis of agriculture itself. In contrast to them, Justi's ideas on the abolition of feudal serfdom were (like his attacks on the nobility and the guild system) an expression of his views on social levelling that lay at the basis of his political theory. Justi elaborated numerous reform proposals to make a more complete cultivation of the land possible.[105] In

101 *Abhandlung von der Vollkommenheit der Landwirthschaft und der höchsten Cultur der Länder* (Ulm and Leipzig: Gaumische Buchhandlung, 1761), p. 3.

102 *Vergleichungen*, pp. 293–304.

103 *Vergleichungen*, p. 306.

104 *Vergleichungen*, p. 307.

105 Justi developed his first ideas on agricultural reform in his *Kurzer systematischer Grundriss*, where he condemned feudal serfdom and demanded higher awareness for agricultural innovations, pointing out that a good farmer would

his view, the problem of agriculture primarily centred on the ownership of land. Only 'if the soil was in the hands of those who worked it, did it fulfil its real function'. This principle was being violated in three ways: by serfdom, compulsory service, and insecure tenancy. As long as they continued to exist, Justi saw no great hope that agriculture would flourish.

His trip to Denmark helped Justi refine his thoughts about agricultural reform. In May 1757 he had sent some of his writings on agriculture to the Danish minister J.H.E. von Bernstorff in Copenhagen with the remark that he planned to undertake a journey to Denmark. On Bernstorff's advice the Danish king then granted Justi financial assistance for his trip, whereupon he left Göttingen in July 1757 and spent the following nine months in Denmark. Justi used his time in Denmark mainly for travelling around the countryside. In his final report for the Danish government on how to convert the Jutland heath to agricultural production, Justi came up with a systematic plan for agrarian reform.[106]

Denmark, as he was quick to point out, used to follow a policy that was the exact opposite of what could make agriculture flourish. Although serfdom *(Leibeigenschaft)* had been abolished *de iure*, it nevertheless continued to exist *de facto*, as the individual farmers still depended on their former masters in many ways. The *Schollenband*, i.e., the prohibition against peasants leaving their rented allotments, was still in force. Justi severely criticised this prohibition as violating the fundamental right of freedom of movement and, in the final analysis, as an inducement for people to emigrate. The *Schollenband* caused peasants to abandon their fields in secret and seek a better status abroad. Secondly, hardly any of the Danish peasants owned the

not slavishly stick once and for all to a particular form of cultivating the land. He gradually extended these views in subsequent works.

106 'Alleruntertänigstes Gutachten wegen Anbauung der jütländischen Heiden', in: *Öconomische Schriften* I, 270–296. For Justi's Danish experience and its impact on his agricultural views see the Appendix and: Otto Clausen, *Chronik der Heide- und Moorkolonisation im Herzogtum Schleswig-Holstein (1760–1765)* (Husum: Husum Verlag, 1981); Wolfgang Prange, *Die Anfänge der großen Agrarreformen in Schleswig-Holstein bis um 1771* (= Quellen und Forschungen zur Geschichte Schleswig-Holsteins 60) (Neumünster: Karl Wachholtz, 1971).

land they cultivated. Usually they rented land from their former patrons in exchange for weekly services. For Justi the introduction of this system of labour-as-rent had been a grave economic error. The subordinate status of the peasants left them unmotivated, as the only reason for hard work and innovation was the realistic expectation of improving one's lot. Due to the unregulated, time-consuming service requirements and insecure ownership, the Danish peasants worked almost exclusively for the benefit of someone else. This was the reason for the endemic underperformance of Danish agriculture.

Adopting Goudar's principal tenet that private property was the most powerful incentive for work, Justi demanded the abolition of personal feudal dues and recommended a radical land reform. Only if peasants owned their land would they contribute to the commercial advancement of the state. England, for instance, would never have been able to bring its agriculture into its current flourishing state if the peasants had had to provide services as a kind of 'rent'.[107] The labour services were the 'sickness of our agriculture in Germany' and as long as they continued to exist there was 'no hope whatsoever for the rural economy and for the true cultivation of the land'.[108] Service took away from the peasants 'precious time and motivation to cultivate their land with due care'. Self-interest was the all-powerful motive for diligent tillage. A tenant would 'never apply as much industry and diligence to his piece of land as a proprietor would'.[109] In the final analysis, the servitude of the peasants was thus of limited utility even for the landowning lords themselves.

A first step in removing these substantial disincentives was the commutation of dues in kind into money payments (*Reluition*). Justi lamented that the tithe was also still paid in kind and suggested a cash contribution instead that would be levied against the value of the average annual crop of a particular field. These proposals went well beyond Maria Theresa's reforms, which had set 'legal limits, and in

107 *Abhandlung von der Vollkommenheit der Landwirtschaft*, p. 25.

108 'Verwandlung der Domänen in Bauerngüter', in: *Gesammelte Schriften* II, 390–406, 396.

109 *Polizeiwissenschaft*, p. 27.

some cases, even reduced the obligations of the peasantry', but had made 'no serious attempt to abolish these obligations'.[110]

Following the reform of dues and services, land ownership had to be transferred to the peasants to reduce their dependence on the lords. The free disposal of peasant property by the lord (*Freistiftlichkeit*) had to be abolished. From an economic point of view, this step was necessary since otherwise a peasant could not be sure whether, after his death, his progeny would be able to enjoy the improvements he had made on his farm. For this reason, even hereditary lease of the lands was far inferior to real property. Under hereditary lease the current proprietors would live in fear that the estate could be taken away from them or that it would not pass on to their daughters. This would greatly diminish their industry and eagerness to cultivate and improve it. Justi appealed to the landowners, pointing out that the status quo was equally disadvantageous for them: the surplus from rented lands was comparatively low, but it could be considerably enhanced if the landowners handed over property rights to their peasants and only reserved to themselves a certain amount of money contributions from the income of these lands.[111]

The village common presented a further obstacle that locked the peasants into property right structures which prevented the optimal allocation of resources. One could take it as a universal principle 'that land owned by private persons will be far better tilled than land that

110 Edith Murr Link, *The Emancipation of the Austrian Peasant 1740–1780* (New York: University of Columbia Press, 1949), p. 61.

111 *Grundfeste* I, 150: 'As long as the peasants do not have full property rights, they lack the most noble motive, the most effective incentive to cultivate their land to the best of their ability, for they must always fear that they or their children will be evicted. This confiscation is the privilege of the landowner as far as serfs are concerned, and often happens even to ordinary tenants. Such customs and rights, especially serfdom, are also in themselves so unjust and so contrary to the nature and character of the state that one can only be surprised that, in reasonable and enlightened times like our own, they can still exist [...] States, in which one estate or one class of people is subjected to another, have as monstrous a constitution as those which existed in the most barbarian times. Moral and reasonable epochs, like our own, cannot allow such institutions to continue without ignominy.'

belongs to the whole village or to several persons in common'.[112] In the *Staatswirtschaft* Justi argued for the enclosure of commons and the abolition of the collective grazing rights.[113] In his *Grundsätze der Polizeiwissenschaft* he declared it the best economic policy to transfer, as much as possible, the ownership of land into the hands of individual persons and leave nothing to the municipality or to a community. The commons had to be subdivided among the peasantry. In this context, Justi also attacked the traditional communal three-field rotation (*Dreifelderwirtschaft*), which he deemed unproductive due to the mutual dependence and the impossibility of reserving particular fields for the cultivation of certain kinds of grain.

In line with his criticism of communal property, Justi demanded the gradual abolition of the village as a corporate entity (whose creation he ascribed to the 'unfortunate law of the fist' of the Middle Ages). The village unit only prolonged the division of land into disadvantageous strips.[114] Ideally, the peasants should live scattered, each on their own lands (*Einzelhofsiedlung*). In his report on the colonisation of Jutland and in the second edition of the *Staatswirtschaft* Justi propagated a new form of rural village. The single farms should only be loosely united along a larger road so that the peasants were assembled closely enough to each other for mutual help and exchange, yet far enough from each other so that every house's backyard would offer direct access to one's own lands.[115]

Ownership alone, however, would not make for zeal and industry in cultivation. There was a vivid debate in the 1750s on what the ideal size of an agricultural unit should be to achieve maximum efficiency in production.[116] Laying strong emphasis on the independent farmer who owned his land and acted independently of social castes and cor-

112 *Polizeiwissenschaft*, p. 29.

113 *Staatswirtschaft* I, 523.

114 Cf. 'Untersuchung, ob die Einteilung in Felder und die Triftgerechtigkeit der Landwirtschaft vortheilhaftig sei', in: *Öconomische Schriften* I, 270–296; 'Vorschläge zu besserer Nutzung der gemeinen Triften und Weiden', in: *Öconomische Schriften* I, 465–476.

115 *Staatswirtschaft* I, 462.

116 Justi thought that thirty *Morgen* of 180 Rhenish quartersections each would be an adequate size.

porations, Justi believed that the smaller the amount of land owned by a single person was, the better it would be cultivated. The excessive amount of land owned by the Church or the nobility had emerged as a substantial impediment to agricultural advancement.

To effect a lasting improvement in agriculture, the government had to undertake a radical redistribution of land by splitting up large estates. Such redistribution would need to go hand in hand with a new land survey (*Cadastre*) that would clarify property rights and allow a more just taxation of the land. The primary aim of the survey would be to establish a clear distinction between peasant land and noble land so that the lord could not reclaim peasant land under any pretext. The survey would also serve the purpose of reassessing the soil in accordance with its geographical location and fertility, thus allowing a fair tax rate that would effectively prevent the overburdening of the peasants.[117]

Justi was sceptical about the realisation of his proposals. Implementing a land reform while respecting the non-interference into existing property rights which, as mentioned above, was among the fundamental, inviolable rights of Justi's modern monarchy was an extremely difficult task. There were two measures by which the government could bring about the intended transformation. First, a modified tax scheme could enhance financial pressure on great landowners. Justi suggested a levy on all lands not inhabited or cultivated by the owners themselves. Landowners who did not cultivate their land would be obliged to pay contributions three times higher than owners who sublet those parts of their property which they could not actively cultivate, to others. In this way, Justi hoped, one would gradually see 'the possession of the land fall into the hands of the peasants' without the invasion of property rights.

In order to break up large estates the monarch could furthermore set a positive example by splitting up royal domain lands and transferring them to independent peasants. As commercial states relied chiefly on the financial contributions of their citizens Justi argued that the transformation of domain lands into fully taxed property in private

117 *Staatswirtschaft* I , 321–399.

hands was a highly advantageous move.[118] By creating model farms on domain lands, one could encourage the imitation of this scheme by private landowners. Here Justi revised his earlier maxim (laid down in the *Staatswirtschaft*) that domain land must be inalienable.[119]

Justi's theories on agricultural reform generally offered a blueprint for the Josephist reforms and, together with their popularisation by Sonnenfels, did 'much to arouse the sympathy of the general public for the downtrodden peasantry'.[120] Many of Justi's suggestions were subsequently realised in the Habsburg territories: the idea of the transformation of domain lands (as advocated by Justi) was to prove influential on the system introduced in a few crown estates in Bohemia and Styria in the 1770s by the Austrian official Raab. Raab 'worked in an almost messianic fashion for the breaking up of large estates'.[121] His system included the commutation of services into money payments and the sale of small farms to individual peasant

118 'Verwandlung der Domänen in Bauerngüter', in: *Gesammelte Schriften* II, 390–406, 404.

119 The splitting up of royal domain lands was a much-debated issue in the 1750s. The police director of Berlin, Johann Albrecht Philippi, first advocated the idea in *Die wahren Mittel zur Vergrösserung eines Staates* in 1753. Justi's views draw on Johann Christian von Zech's *Die Verwandlung der Domänen in Bauerngüter, als das beste Mittel zur Bevölkerung, zur Macht und zum Reichtum eines Staates* (Berlin, 1759) (cf. Prange, *Die Anfänge der grossen Agrarreform in Schleswig-Holstein*, p. 658f.). Süssmilch adopted Justi's and Zech's ideas in the second edition of *Die Göttliche Ordnung*, which proved influential for Prussian policies under Wöllner (cf. Mittenzwei, *Preussen nach dem Siebenjährigen Krieg*, p. 193). In addition to the question of tenure, Justi's agricultural reform proposals focused on numerous technical innovations to improve the productive capacity of the land. His agricultural writings include practical and technical advice on all sorts of issues. For instance, he advocated year-round indoor-feeding of cattle and the introduction of natural hedges (as they had become common practice in Holland and England) to replace wooden fences and ease the emerging problem of timber shortage (*Grundfeste* I, 89). Moreover, Justi was a fervent advocate of compulsory agricultural insurance schemes (Cf. Peter Borscheid, 'Die Anfänge der landwirtschaftlichen Versicherung in Deutschland', *Zeitschrift für Agrargeschichte und Agrarsoziologie* 37 (1989), 37–55).

120 Murr Link, *The Emancipation of the Austrian Peasant*, p. 98.

121 Freudenberger, 'State Intervention as an Obstacle to Economic Growth' p. 498.

owners. With the subsequent extension of the system to many royal and secularised estates under Joseph II's reign, the Viennese administration hoped that the nobles might follow this good example. Furthermore, the law of 24 March 1770 stated that a part of the common pasture was to be allocated to each peasant who had hitherto had the use of it. A decree in 1772 limited the number of corvée days of peasants and enabled the commutation of dues in kind into money payments. And finally, on November 1, 1781, Joseph II enacted the abolition of personal serfdom wherever it still existed.

Taxation

Balanced taxation was an essential precondition for national commercial success. A well-designed tax scheme could profoundly accelerate domestic growth. By contrast, imprudently implemented levies would lead to political and economic disaster. Justi was aware of the growing impact of taxes. As is evident from his proposals for a higher levy on landowners who did not cultivate their fields themselves, he perceived the differentially weighted allocation of tax burdens as a significant tool for the practical implementation of his reform projects.[122] Many of his ideas on taxation and public finance clashed with traditional privileges and habits of feudal society, giving his views an immediate

122 In his writings, Justi offered several examples of the regulation of economic behaviour of the subjects by taxation – for instance, on viticulture: 'If one undertakes viticulture [...] or other parts of agriculture to such an extent that in so doing the cultivation of grain and other necessary products is affected, one needs to levy these former activities with high contributions and lower the taxes on the areas that one wishes to support and augment, and one will soon attain the intended effects' (*System des Finanzwesens*, p. 385). See also: Anton Tautscher, 'Die Steuer als Gestaltungsmittel der Volkswirtschaft bei den deutschen Merkantilisten', *Finanzarchiv* 9 (1943), 303–337.

political relevance and supplementing his idea of modern monarchy in several important ways.[123]

States derived their revenue from three different sources: the returns of princely (or governmental) domain lands, royal dues (*Regalia*), and the earnings from taxes and contributions. An ideal state, Justi observed, would be able to draw sufficient revenue from the first two sources and would not need to tax its inhabitants on a regular basis. Historically speaking, the first states had indeed managed to raise adequate sums from domain lands and dues on mining, coinage, forestry, hunting, salt trading, the postal system, and road tolls.[124] Over time, however, governmental mismanagement and emergencies had caused financial shortages. Each crisis, and warfare in particular, had forced governments to search for new ways to meet higher monetary demands. This had eventually resulted in the introduction of taxes and contributions.[125] Taxes were a Pandora's box. A good deal of injustice and oppression could have been avoided if governments had never had recourse to taxes and contributions. Permanent taxation had placed a powerful tool in the hands of the

123 Justi's thoughts on taxation can primarily be found in his *Ausführliche Abhandlung von denen Steuern und Abgaben* (1762) and *System des Finanzwesens* (1766), the latter of which led Inama-Sternegg to ascribe to Justi the merit for having developed 'the first system of financial theory' in the German-speaking world (Karl Theodor von Inama-Sternegg, 'Der Akzisenstreit deutscher Finanztheoretiker im 17. und 18. Jahrhundert', *Zeitschrift für die gesamte Staatswissenschaft* 21 (1865), 515–545 (p. 563)). Both works are in fact largely based on earlier essays published in *Neue Wahrheiten* and *Gesammelte Schriften* (see Table 3), particularly: 'Von Einrichtung der Steuern und Abgaben in einem Staat', in: *Gesammelte Schriften* I, 365–379; 'Von der Accise und einer statt derselben einzuführenden neuen Gewerbesteuer', in: *Gesammelte Schriften* I, 380–439. The most exhaustive treatment of Justi's tax theory still is: Joseph Grimmig, *Johann Heinrich Gottlob von Justi und Joseph Sonnenfels als Finanzwissenschaftler* (Bonn: Diss. Iur., 1949).

124 *Staatswirtschaft* II, 113–286. Justi strongly defended royal dues: 'On a country's surface (and below) there are always things which are not suitable for private ownership, either because their use must remain open to all citizens and no one can be excluded from them (which is an essential characteristic of private property) or because their dimensions are too large to be used or controlled by a single private person' (*Steuern und Abgaben*, p. 12f.).

125 *Natur und Wesen*, p. 58.

government and had opened the door to arbitrariness. Since governments had started taxing their subjects at their own discretion their insatiable thirst for money had become a threat to the health of states. Modern tax states operated under the permanent risk of self-incurred economic suffocation through overtaxation and concomitant political collapse.[126]

In his early writings, Justi still hoped modern states might be able to meet their expenses primarily from the income of the royal domains and dues (*Regalien*), and adhered to the traditional view that the prince was prohibited from selling royal land.[127] Under growing French influence, however, Justi reached the conclusion that it was vain to hope for a government that would still be able to operate without regular tax income.[128] Because of recent changes, such as the growing significance of manufacturing production and increased military budgets, the expenditures of states had to be paid for primarily in the form of moneyed contributions.[129] The concomitant risks notwithstanding, modern states were irreversibly built on regular taxation.[130]

Justi remained deeply sceptical of tax policies. Rising military expenses and public debts had turned the threat of harmful overtax-

126 In Justi's view, the decline and fall of the Roman Empire had given a warning example of the dramatic political repercussions of overtaxation. In late imperial Rome administrative mismanagement and the greed of public officials had led to such excessive tax rises 'that all free men lived in unspeakable misery, and therefore either gave themselves as serfs to anyone who would have them, or fled to the barbarians'. Permanent overtaxation, according to Justi, was the principal cause of the collapse of the Roman Empire, 'since all the provinces received the barbarians with open arms, regarding them as rescuers from their unspeakable affliction' (*System des Finanzwesens*, transl. Monroe, p. 384).

127 Initially Justi had counted this prohibition among the fundamental laws of monarchy.

128 *Vergleichungen*, p. 276.

129 'Von der Accise und einer statt derselben einzuführenden neuen Gewerbesteuer', in: *Gesammelte Schriften*, I, 380–439, 404.

130 After 1755 Justi therefore gave up his adherence to the principle that domain lands were not to be sold. As outlined in the previous chapter, he even demanded that domain lands be rented out permanently to independent freeholders.

ation, which he believed had destroyed the Roman Empire, into an acute problem for the European monarchies in his own days. Even if monarchs turned their back on the false preaching of projectors (and their tenet that taxation was a tool for 'making money' for the princely treasury) the inherently selfish nature of man left little hope for just tax policies:[131]

> Men are seldom prudent managers of their own property [...] How can we feel assured, therefore, that they will be good and prudent managers of property not their own, namely property of the state? How can we expect that they will restrain their natural tendencies to extravagance or avarice when managing the property of a stranger, when they never hold these tendencies within bounds in the case of their own property [...]? Once taxes have been resorted to, they have not the slightest compunction in abusing them. It costs them nothing, they can simply take it out of some other man's property; and only someone totally ignorant of human nature could deny that whenever a man has to take only what he needs out of the property of others, his needs will soon multiply enormously. Men are very ingenious in thinking up new needs when they have such an easy prospect of obtaining what they want. The natural result of once resorting to contributions is therefore bound to be that these taxes are steadily increased, and finally become an intolerable burden to the subjects, resulting in the ruin of both the subjects and the state itself.[132]

Offensive warfare, favouritism, and inefficient bureaucratic institutions caused a growing government thirst for revenue that threatened to undermine all policing efforts for commercial advancement.[133] In

131 Here again, Justi exposed his long-term, growth oriented view of government policies. Tax income was not an end in itself. Cf. *System des Finanzwesens*, p. 24 + 65.

132 *Steuern und Abgaben*, p. 15f. Similarly in: *Vergleichungen*, p. 272. Justi demanded that the general tax level stay below 25% (*Steuern und Abgaben*, p. 21).

133 *Steuern und Abgaben*, p. 21. Duties and customs, in particular, were not to be administrated by the financial council (*Cammercollegio*), but by the chamber of commerce (*Kommerziencollegio*) (*Manufakturen und Fabriken* I, 154). Otherwise, the risk that disadvantageous measures (like import bans) were adopted was too high. An import ban was 'a violent means, which limits the freedom of commerce and goes against the liberty of the subjects in hindering them from making free use of their fortune and the commodities of life and which leads to repressions in external states which likewise prohibit our country's products,

order to shield trade and exchange from governmental whim Justi sketched a plan for economically supportive tax policies that followed a set of fundamental rules and – echoing Montesquieu – took 'the genius, passions, beliefs and overall spirit of a people' into account.[134]

Justi feared that tax levels in Europe might soon jump to excessive rates of over 50%.[135] In the long run, such a move would dramatically diminish revenue, as it violated the pivotal principle of taxation: to keep up the citizens' ability to pay without, in effect, curtailing their wealth.[136] Justi believed that taxes had to be levied upon the subjects with complete equality and in just proportion. He was a fervent advocate of proportional taxation and defended his position on the grounds of the popular *Assekuranztheorie* ('assurance-theory') which was based on the contractual view of the state. The state had been founded for the protection of its members' lives and property. Under the contractual umbrella of the state, the life of each citizen had equal worth. Yet the inequality of material possessions justified graduated tax rates. Since wealthy citizens required greater protection, they had to pay a proportionally higher amount of contributions than their less

whereby ever new difficulties are created for trade' (*Manufakturen und Fabriken* I, 12). Strict import prohibitions led to higher prices and eventually caused monopolies (*Grundfeste* I, 528). In the worst case, they could lead to downright trading wars: 'We offend other people with the prohibition and suffer as a consequence just repressions and a decrease of our commerce' (*Manufakturen und Fabriken* I, 157). Duties were preferable to strict prohibitions (*Grundfeste* I, 554).

134 *Steuern und Abgaben*, p. 40; *System des Finanzwesens*, p. 367. Justi rejected Montesquieu's assertion in Chapter 13, 12 of *The Spirit of the Laws* that only free states (i.e., republics) could be levied taxed at high rates. Such an abstract statement, Justi remarked, was nonsense. Independently of the form of government, the level of taxation within a country always depended on its particular economic situation.

135 Justi held that 25% of income was already an excessive rate ('Von der Accise und einer statt derselben einzuführenden neuen Gewerbesteuer', in: *Gesammelte Schriften*, I, 380–439, 388).

136 Cf. *Staatswirtschaft* II, 287–297. If taxes were to fulfil an economically sound function, they were not allowed to attack the substance of the citizens' fortunes (*Steuern und Abgaben*, p. 23ff; *System des Finanzwesens*, p. 361).

fortunate fellows.[137] As the expenses for basic alimentary goods were – in absolute terms – roughly equal for the rich and poor, but in relative terms affected the latter far more, Justi argued for graduated, rather than mathematically proportional taxation.[138]

Taxes and fees had to be levied without infringement of the taxpayers' liberty and privacy. The intangible damage caused by a tax that violated civil liberties would outweigh any financial gain for the state. Infringements of civil liberties would scare off foreign investors and tempt inhabitants to emigrate.[139] Finally, taxes would have to be cost-effective, i.e., they had to be easy to collect, at minimal expense to the state and the subjects, and with minimum chances for fraud and

137 *Steuern und Abgaben*, p. 26ff.; 'Von der Accise und einer statt derselben einzuführenden neuen Gewerbesteuer', in: *Gesammelte Schriften*, I, 380–439, 390.

138 'Thus the more property a man has, the greater contribution he must bear; and this all the more justly, since it must be assumed that his earnings are always proportionately much larger. The point may be illustrated by an example. Martin, a merchant, has property amounting to twenty thousand dollars, and makes a profit of three thousand dollars. Christopher, another merchant, has property amounting to sixty thousand dollars, and makes at this rate nine thousand dollars a year. Let us assume that each of these merchants needs two thousand dollars a year for the support of his household, family, and servants; Martin, therefore, has only one thousand net earnings, while Christopher has seven thousand. Now if contributions are collected in exact proportion to property, and Martin pays two hundred dollars, while Christopher, having three times as much property, pays six hundred dollars a year, it is evident that Christopher nevertheless has to pay a much more moderate contribution than Martin; for the latter has only eight hundred dollars left to increase his property, while Christopher has six thousand four hundred dollars, that is, eight times as much, though he pays contributions that are only three times as great. There have, indeed, been states which have taken this circumstance into account, and increased the contributions proportionately, when the property exceeded a certain amount. But nowadays there is so little thought of this increasing in proportion to increases in property, that the system of contributions is so arranged in all states that the richest subjects always contribute least to the expenses of the state; and since nothing can be collected from the poor, all the burden of contributions falls upon the middle class' (*System des Finanzwesens*, transl. Monroe, p. 391).

139 *Steuern und Abgaben*, p. 39. This would cause a sequence of negative trends, including the decline of the population.

evasion on both sides.[140] Justi severely criticised the plurality of tax collectors in contemporary European states, which lead to arbitrary taxation, deception, and inefficiency:

> In certain neighbouring states there is no city too small not to have ten different collectors [so that] the expenses of public finance add up to the same amount as the revenue of the state that really flows into the exchequer.[141]

An excessive number of taxes was impractical since their administrative costs surpassed the revenue they created. Although Justi wanted to see the exorbitant number of contemporary taxes reduced, he rejected the idea of a single tax, such as Vauban's *Dixme Royal* or the Physiocrats' 'Impôt unique'.[142] A single tax, he objected, had no allocative functions and violated the principle of graduation.

Taxes could be levied in four different ways: by taxing immobile property, persons, commodities and manufacturing production. Justi demanded the establishment of a universal land tax (*Grundsteuer*), as he believed it best matched his claims for equality and cost-efficiency. For this reason, individual landed property had to be registered by the authorities in a new land survey. Taking the land's size, location, and soil quality into account, it would be easy to determine average earnings, on which the tax could then be imposed. In line with his anti-aristocratic thought, Justi attacked the exemption of land owned by the aristocracy:

> True to the principle which I have assumed above, i.e., that all who enjoy equal protection [from the state] also have to pay an equal amount of taxes according to the proportion of their fortune, I cannot approve of their exemption (or a lower contribution), particularly since the reason for their exemption, their service to the fatherland in war at their own expense, has long ceased due to [the introduction of] standing armies.[143]

140 *Steuern und Abgaben*, p. 42.
141 *Vergleichungen*, p. 287.
142 *Steuern und Abgaben*, p. 20; *System des Finanzwesens*, p. 451.
143 'Von Einrichtung der Steuern und Abgaben in einem Staat', in: *Gesammelte Schriften* I, 365–379, 371.

In contrast to the land tax, Justi opposed the taxation of merchant profits.[144] There was a danger of massive capital flight following a decision to introduce such a tax. Moneyed wealth could not be kept within political frontiers by governmental force. A tax on moneyed wealth would thus stimulate secret capital. To encourage commercial advancement, capital had to flow freely. Justi condemned the impediments imposed on the movements of owners of capital by the widely-established moving taxes (*Abzugsgelder*). These taxes were particularly onerous in Germany because of the patchwork character of the Holy Roman Empire. Justi therefore demanded the prohibition of *Abzugsgelder* on movements within the Empire.[145] The taxation of money income also proved difficult from a practical point of view. Mobile wealth could be easily hidden or transferred abroad. The frequent perjuries in declaring cash holdings showed that it was a near impossibility for government to assess the movable wealth of its subjects.[146] If it nonetheless tried, such an attempt would necessarily result in a violent intrusion of the citizens' private sphere, which would be 'unpleasant, burdensome, and damaging'.[147] Again here, Justi showed deep respect for the sphere of the individual and was opposed to what he perceived as an overextended governmental control of areas of life that were better left untouched.[148]

Justi furthermore advocated the introduction of a poll tax (*Kopfsteuer*) to include those citizens who did not own landed property.[149] The register for the poll tax would also function as census data, allowing the government to stay informed about population developments. Contrary to the land tax, Justi approved of the existing exemptions from the poll tax that applied to the nobility, the clergy, and scholars, and wanted them extended to children below 16 and old

144 'Von Einrichtung der Steuern und Abgaben in einem Staat', in: *Gesammelte Schriften* I, 365–379, 372.

145 'Von Einrichtung der Steuern und Abgaben in einem Staat', in: *Gesammelte Schriften* I, 365–379, 373.

146 *System des Finanzwesens*, p. 494.

147 *Steuern und Abgaben*, p. 95. Cf. 'Von Einrichtung der Steuern und Abgaben in einem Staat', in: *Gesammelte Schriften* I, 365–379, 374.

148 *Steuern und Abgaben*, p. 82.

149 *Steuern und Abgaben*, p. 79.

people above the age of 60.[150] As women and domestic servants could be expected to have less earnings and opportunities for material gain, they would only have to pay a reduced rate.[151]

In his discussions of consumption taxes Justi focused primarily on the *Akzise*, thereby entering the extensive controversy that raged in eighteenth-century Germany over this tax (the so-called *Akzisenstreit*).[152] True to his general belief that the tax system had to be based on direct property taxes (i.e., taxes levied in proportion to objects which were immobile and classed as private property of the taxpayers) while reducing or avoiding indirect taxes (particularly consumption taxes on basic commodities), Justi rejected the *Akzise*. Since it was levied on general-consumption goods like flour or salt, the *Akzise* hit the poor hardest. The unproportional and unequal nature of the *Akzise* clearly went against all sound principles of taxation.[153]

As with a tax on cash holdings, the levying of the *Akzise* caused a number of practical problems. The *Akzise* restricted the liberty of the citizens considerably and was 'disadvantageous for industrial and commercial advancement'.[154] The *Akzise* proceedings that forced merchants and travellers to lay their moveable belongings open to inspection and declare the goods intended for commercial transactions to local authorities was time-consuming and exposed them to the whim of tax collectors.[155] Justi criticised the inconsiderate, disrespectful way in which tax collectors treated merchants. Besides,

150 *Steuern und Abgaben*, p. 93. Justi criticised tax exemptions for indolent students: 'It is well known, how badly many students spend their time at universities and busy themselves with nothing but pleasures and amusements instead of learning something useful. Nevertheless, they are called scholars [...] without being useful to the state with science and erudition.'

151 *Steuern und Abgaben*, p. 83.

152 Cf. Inama-Sternegg, 'Der Akzisenstreit deutscher Finanztheoretiker'.

153 *Steuern und Abgaben*, p. 107; *System des Finanzwesens*, p. 465. Since consumption taxes 'were levied on things of general usage, which nobody can do without, one does not reach with them a kind of taxation that affects all subjects according to the proportion of their fortune' (*Steuern und Abgaben*, p. 31).

154 *Steuern und Abgaben*, p. 102.

155 *Steuern und Abgaben*, p. 103: the detailed inspections of travellers and their goods at the city gates caused 'many domestic affairs and circumstances [to be] uncovered, which could have remained secret without detriment for the state'.

their status gave the collectors extensive opportunities for fraud. The fierce governmental control that came with the *Akzise* was both politically harmful and economically counterproductive.[156] It hampered free capital flow within a country, and would create a general climate of suspicion and investigation which foreigners would try to evade. The *Akzise* was best replaced by an ability tax (*Gewerbesteuer*, technichally speaking a *Gewerbeertragssteuer*) on manufactures and factories, which would 'never be disadvantageous or detrimental'.[157] Working from the size and past performance of a company, one could calculate its prospective annual gains, which could then be levied according to a prescribed rate.[158] Supporting Justi's ultimate goal of political centralisation, such a tax would end local particularism, facilitate capital flow, and enable free inland trade.[159]

156 *Gesammelte Schriften* I, 503.

157 *Steuern und Abgaben*, p. 169; *System des Finanzwesens*, p. 17; 'Von Einrichtung der Steuern und Abgaben in einem Staat', in: *Gesammelte Schriften* I, 365–379, 370.

158 *System des Finanzwesens*, p. 469. The ability tax had to be instituted in such a manner 'that each enterprise is taxed according to its size, revenue, location [...] and consequently according to the amount of the resulting gain'.

159 *Grundfeste* I, 471.

Chapter Seven
Conclusion

This study has demonstrated that Justi's proposals for political and economic reform were addressed to very specific problems in the German states of his day. Yet contrary to widespread belief, they were not the result of a nationally limited cameralistic discourse, but the product of an age that was marked by intellectual controversies of a truly European scope. The analysis has shown how the narrowly nationalistic treatment of earlier studies prevented a comprehensive understanding of Justi's ideas in their appropriate context. In his works Justi answered the theoretical challenges set by seminal French publications in the 1740s and 50s and became an active contributor to the dominant debates of these years, such as the divide between the *thèse nobiliaire* and *thèse royale* camps on the historical origin of the French monarchy and the nature of feudalism, the pan-European controversy over the balance of power, the debates on commercial nobility and fundamental laws, the luxury debate as well as the rival views that were developed on China.

Justi's awereness of the pressure that a modern economy had begun to exert on politics formed the leitmotiv of his writings. He was convinced that his was an age of transition that witnessed a fundamental paradigm shift away from plain Machiavellian militarism towards an intensified, but potentially more peaceful, international race for commercial excellence. Market forces had gained a deciding role for the external standing and internal composition of states. National survival required governments to respond quickly and coherently to the challenges triggered by this transformation.

Justi's political economy was designed to expound the inner rationale of this transformation and highlight its far-reaching impact on the commercially underdeveloped German states. Pointing at the substantial risks and opportunities that the German states faced in their attempts to gain parity with England, Holland or France, Justi developed a comprehensive set of recommendations and guidelines that was to serve policymakers as a blueprint for reforms. His ideas on issues such as the changing nature of the European state system, despotism, the nobility, civil liberty, religious freedom, luxury, emulation, market liberation, agricultural reform, and taxation were all part of this project.

Justi launched a powerful tirade against the militaristic and anti-commercial spirit of his age. Modern commerce had revolutionised the European state system. The problem was that monarchs had not yet noticed, let alone understood, the new rules of the game. The failed attempts at conquest and hegemony of Charles V, Louis XIV and Charles XII of Sweden were poignant examples of this ignorance.

Justi believed 'reason of state' had managed to survive by reinventing itself in the guise of the 'balance of power'. The balance of power and, even more so, the idea of an international balance of commerce allowed the statesmen of Europe to continue their ruthless power politics while hypocritically claiming to serve a higher, though rather nebulous, moral goal. By invoking the balances of power and commerce to make their policies appear altruistic, contemporary rulers effectively used it to cover up their Machiavellian interests in territorial conquest and military glory, thus blighting the Continent with eternal war.

However, since economic power had become the backbone of political strength the true aim of any state, as Justi relentlessly stressed, could be nothing else than a pursuit of commercial success. Instead of joining the chimerical propaganda wars over the statistical power calculations that came with balance-of-power thinking, states were better off in concentrating on internal development and the expansion of their foreign trade. In this way, long-term commercially driven politics could gradually prevail over traditional short-term goals, reducing military conflict and creating a lasting peace for Europe.

Free international competition offered a real alternative to the military path as it eliminated the two dominant security threats that had tormented the peace of Europe in the past (and, with respect to the Seven Years War, still did so in Justi's own days). First, as commercial excellence depended upon civil liberty and moderate government, there were no unscrupulous shortcuts to push ahead in the struggle for economic dominance. Traditional ploys to enhance princely power, such as conquest, war, internal oppression, recoinage, or exorbitant tax levels had proven self-destructive since they effecttively hampered trade. As a result, any state desirous of pushing ahead in the competition for commercial power had to realise its political goals in consistency with the laws of economics. Secondly, the dynamism, extreme flexibility and balancing forces of trade would not allow for the tyrannical supremacy of a single state. Price mechanisms enabled even the least-developed countries to trade profitably with a more advanced competitor state, thus permitting them to strip the latter gradually, and at least partially, of its head-start.

To withstand increased competitive pressure in Europe, a drastic recasting of the internal configurations of contemporary states was required. They had to be consolidated from within in order to present a united front against foreign competitors. Justi shunned anti-commercial republican ideologies, which he deemed dauntingly outmoded in the new age of international trade. To survive in the midst of territorially vast and commercially aggressive monarchies, republics had to shed all remnants of their frugal, non-utilitarian ethos, which was in any case nothing more than a silly and anachronistic imitation of the distant past. Though perhaps lamentable from a moral point of view, modern commercial society was inevitably built on individual self-interest, vanity, unconstrained luxury and consumption.

Modern commerce had not only buried frugal republican utopias for ever in the realm of imagination. It also entailed the softening of the traditional hierarchy of ranks – with far-reaching consequences for the monarchies of the time. Justi berated Montesquieu for having failed to subscribe to this conclusion. In many respects, as Justi repeatedly emphasized, the traditional hereditary aristocracy as an order distinct from the people was a deplorable institution. A permanently stratified society resting on an assumption of natural inequality, as was found in aristocratic monarchies, inevitably connived at political oppression and economic misery. Aristocratically ruled monarchies, such as Poland, Hungary or Sweden were repulsive examples.

The right of the nobility to demand hereditary privileges had disappeared, since the functions for which these exemptions had originally been granted had ceased to exist. Absolutism was the living proof that the nobles were ineffective in halting the growing powers of the prince and performing the tempering intermediary role that Montesquieu had ascribed to them. Moreover, the nobles' military role had diminished with the advent of standing armies, and their commercially inactive status did nothing but foster general disrespect for trading and industrial activities. Like Montesquieu's opponents in France, Justi pointed to England as a model. England's feudal aristocracy based on birth and conquest was fusing successfully with a new aristocracy based on wealth, resulting in the creation of a more open social structure. Although a constitutional ideal, the limited English monarchy with its organically grown balance between executive and legislative powers was not to be imitated by continental nations. Within them, a more radical solution was needed. As their governments had come into sharp conflict with the Church and the anti-centralising interest of the old aristocracy (as it had happened to Haugwitz in Habsburg Austria), Justi believed the full strength of monarchical officialdom was required to diminish the forces of feudal and local privilege.

Justi was aware that in delivering the people from the special class and corporate loyalties by which they had so far been enchained, the existing hierarchy of ranks would be seriously weakened, giving the state the chance to grow rapidly at the expense of traditional associations like manors, communes, guilds and inns. While authority and power had been localised by the order of aristocratic society the dislodging of individuals from fixed social positions would pave the way for greater equality and centralisation. Although the disappearance of the magnates of aristocratic society and other intermediate institutions was beneficial from an economic viewpoint, it needed to be accompanied by substantial political reforms, as it would otherwise increase the risk of despotism in a grossly negligent way. Since all was lost under despotism, the principal concern of Justi's third-way model of monarchy was the establishment of a firm foundation of individual liberty within monarchies that had destroyed a good deal of their customary corporate structures.

The example of China showed that the creation of a moderate, absolute monarchy was possible. A clear set of fundamental laws, a modified education of the prince and an altered role of the king as a diligent supervisor of governmental affairs were prerequisites to the realization of this goal. The traditional estate summits had to be replaced by representative schemes. Justi was far from advocating the creation of a full-blown legislative assembly with far-reaching liberties vis-à-vis the executive power of the king, but rather envisioned a council of publicly elected advisers (*Worthalter*) who audited the lawful conduct of the prince. Meritocratic reforms could provide a further tempering agency against princely power. Altered rewards and promotion schemes could erase the usual favouritism and ineffectiveness of the administration, creating a self-contained bureaucracy that was able to function as a bulwark against monarchical whim. If the administration itself was restructured according to a council constitution in the style of Saint-Pierre's *Polysynodie*, day-to-day politics would be left in the hands of a professional body of civil servants with the prince acting merely as the representative figurehead.

The comprehensive policing efforts of the administration (*Polizei*) would play a vital role in national commercial advancement. The ultimate aim behind these efforts was the creation of a framework for far-ranging self-regulation. During the transitory period that preceded this goal, the government had to focus on the removal of traditional obstacles and on the state-sponsored initiation of manufactures and factories. In so doing, it had to guard carefully against overregulation.

Private luxury and consumption were among the areas that did not require governmental control. Pointing at the economically beneficial effects of self-interested actions Justi defended unlimited luxury against the moral prejudices of his day. In the same way as meritocratic schemes would unleash emulation by creating a higher degree of social mobility, unlimited luxury would stimulate ambition among the populace. Instead of a meticulous catalogue of sumptuary laws (whose enforcement was costly and potentially harmful to civil liberty) graduated taxation would serve as a far more sophisticated means to enable a wide distribution of wealth.

A further crucial aim of Justi's reforms was to break the dominance of local corporations and abolish the feudal serfdom of the peasantry. In so doing, the government had to be aware of substantial constraints and problems: it had to guard against furthering monopoly structures (by supporting dubious projectors) and violating the very foundations on which moderate rule and commercial success rested. Free market competition between private entrepreneurs in the manufacturing sector and a society of smallholders in agriculture were difficult to create. To avoid chaos, the guilds, for instance, could not be prohibited overnight. However, by excluding them from newly founded factories and depriving them of the right to confer masterships at their own discretion their influence could gradually be diminished.

The setting up of manufactures and companies caused a further dilemma. In order to open up new markets the government either had to run companies itself or grant the very guarantees and monopolist privileges to private entrepreneurs which it was trying to abolish in its fight against the guilds. For this reason, governmental help had to be granted for a limited period only. At all times, intrusions upon existing property rights had to be avoided. Hence expropriations were inappropriate in the agricultural sector. The transformation of this sector could only be achieved by the creation of model estates on crown lands and a substantially altered tax scheme.

Justi's political economy presents a grand scheme for the institutional reforms that had to be devised in the face of the immense political, social and economic challenges of his age. Contrary to previous assumptions, Justi was not a republican, but a partisan of the *res publica* in the monarchical form. His works not only foreshadowed the reforms of Joseph II and the Stein-Hardenberg reforms in Prussia: as this study has shown, they also revealed a number of lasting insights into the functioning of modern commercial societies.

Table One
Systematic overview of Justi's writings

Literary Writings & Journalism	**Political Economy (*Staatswirtschaft*)**	**Natural Scientific Studies**
PERIDOCIALS	↓	MINING
· *Ergetzungen der vernünftigen Seele*		· *Grundriss des gesamten Mineralreiches*
· *Neue Wahrheiten*		· *Die Kunst, das Silber zu affinieren*
· *Göttingische Polizei-Amts-Nachrichten*		·*Geschichte des Erdkörpers*
· *Fortgesetzte Bemühungen*		CHEMISTRY
SATIRES/NOVELS		· *Das entdeckte Geheimnis der sächsischen Farben*
· *Psammitichus*		· *Gesammelte chymische Schriften*
· *Leben Brühls*		
HISTORY/LAW		
· *Gesammelte historische und juristische Schriften*		

· *Staatswirtschaft*
· *Gesammelte Schriften*

POLITICS (*Staatskunst*)	**ECONOMIC POLICY (*Polizeiwissenschaft*)**	**PUBLIC FINANCE (*Cameralwissenschaft*)**	**TRADE THEORY (*Commerzienwissenschaft*)**
· *Grundriss*	· *Polizeiwissenschaft*	· *Steuern und Abgaben*	· *Manufakturen und Fabriken*
· *Natur und Wesen*	· *Grundfeste*	· *System des Finanzwesens*	
· *Vergleichungen*			

Table Two
Chronological overview of Justi's writings

1741	- *Deutsche Memoires* I - *Gespräche im sogenannten Reiche der Toten, zwischen Friedrich Wilhelm, Könige in Preussen und Churfürst von Brandenburg und Carl, Landgraf zu Hessen Kassel*
1742	- *Deutsche Memoires II*
1745	- *Die Dichterinsel* - *Ergetzungen der vernünftigen Seele* (–1748) - *De fuga militiae*
1747	- *Untersuchung der Lehre von den Monaden* - *Beweiss, dass die Universalmonarchie vor die Wohlfahrt von Europa und überhaupt des menschlichen Geschlechts die grösste Glückseligkeit wirken würde* - *Ursachen des Verfalls der Religion und der einreissenden Freidenkerei*
1748	- *Abhandlung von den Römischen Feldzügen in Teutschland* - *Dissertation sur la système des monads* - *Schrift über die Nichtigkeit aller Einwürfe und unhöflichen Anfälle gegen die Untersuchung der Lehre von den Monaden*
1750	- *Abhandlung von dem Zusammenhang der Vollkommenheit der Sprache mit dem blühenden Zustand der Wissenschaften* - *Das entdeckte Geheimnis der neuen Sächsischen Farben* - *Abhandlung von der Abtretung eines Reichs-Lehns in dem Frieden mit auswärteigen Mächten* - 2nd edition of *Deutsche Memoires* (first published in 1741)
1752	- French translation of *Das entdeckte Geheimnis der neuen Sächsischen Farben*
1754	- *Gutachten von dem vernünftigen Zusammenhange und practischem Vortrage aller Öconomischen und Cameralwissenschaften* - *Neue Wahrheiten* (–1758)

1755	- *Staatswirtschaft* I+II - *Anweisungen zu einer guten deutschen Schreibart* - *Abhandlung von den Mitteln, die Erkenntnis in den Öconomischen und Cameral-Wissenschaften dem gemeinen Wesen recht nützlich zu machen* - *Göttingische Polizei-Amts Nachrichten* - *Entdeckte Ursachen des verderbten Münzwesens in Deutschland*
1756	- *Grundsätze der Policeywissenschaft* - *Der handelnde Adel, dem der kriegerische Adel entgegengesetzt wird* - *Betrachtungen, welche Deutschland anietzo über die vereinigte Österreichische und Bourbounische Macht vernünftiger Weise machen muss* (unpublished)
1757	- *Rechtliche Abhandlung von denen Ehen* - *Grundriss des gesamten Mineralreiches*
1758	- *Die Chimäre des Gleichgewichts von Europa* - *Vollständige Abhandlung von denen Manufakturen und Fabriken* I - 2nd, enlarged edition of *Staatswirtschaft* I+II
1759	- *Die Chimäre des Gleichgewichts der Handlung und Seefahrt* - *Systematischer Grundriss aller Öconomischen und Cameralwissenschaften* - *Der Grundriss einer guten Regierung* - *Psammitichus I* - *Fortgesetzte Bemühungen zum Vortheil der Naturkunde und des gesellschaftlichen Lebens überhaupt* (–1761) - *Fabeln und Erzählungen von Thieren und sehr alten längst verrosteten Zeiten, bey deren Lesung man ganz sanft und süss wird einschlaffen können* - *Wohlgemeinte Vorschläge eines die jetzigen unglücklichen Zeiten beseufzenden Menschenfreundes* - 2nd, enlarged edition of *Grundsätze der Policeywissenschaft*
1760	- *Abhandlung von der Macht und Glückseligkeit und Credit eines Staats* - *Historische und juristische Schriften* I - *Moralische und philosophische Schriften* I+II - *Natur und Wesen der Staaten* - *Öconomische Schriften über die wichtigsten Gegenstände*

	der Stadt- und Landwirtschaft I - *Ökonomisches Wörterbuch* I - *Gesammelte chymische Schriften* I - *Die Grundfeste zur Macht und Glückseligkeit der Staaten* I - *Scherzhafte und satyrische Schriften* I+II - *Abhandlung von der Unverletzlichkeit der Waffen- und Kriegs-Verträge* - *Der enthüllte Österreichische Schriftsteller* - *Leben und Charakter des Königlich Polnischen und Churfürstlich Sächsischen Premier-Ministre Grafens von Brühl in vertraulichen Briefen entworfen* - *Psammitichus* II - *Schreiben an das Publikum von dem Verfasser der Briefe, so unter dem Titul: Leben und Character des Grafen von Brühl zum Vorschein gekommen sind* - *Untersuchung, ob etwa die heutigen europäischen Völker Lust haben möchten, dereinst Menschen-Fresser oder wenigstens Hottentotten zu werden* - Paul Jacob Marperger's *Montes Pietatis*, edited by Justi - French translation of *Leben und Charakter des Grafen von Brühl*
1761	- *Abhandlung von der Vollkommenheit der Landwirtschaft und der höchsten Cultur der Länder* - *Gesammelte chymische Schriften* II - *Gesammelte politische und Finanzschriften* I+II - *Vermischte Anmerkungen, welche verschiedene merkwürdige die Staatsklugheit, das Kriegswesen, die Sittenlehre die Öconomischen und dahingehörigen Cameral-Commercien und Policey-Wissenschaften, wie auch das Justizwesen betreffende Sachen abhandeln (oder: der Deutschen Memoires dritter Teil)* - *Beweiss, dass die bei denen Reichstäglichen Berathschlagungen über das bevorstehende Friedensgeschäfte von denen Evangelischen ergriffene itio in partes rechtmässig und in dem Westphälischen Frieden vollkommen gegründet sey* - *Vollständige Abhandlung von denen Manufakturen und Fabriken* II - *Die Grunfeste zur Macht und Glückseligkeit der Staaten* II - *Historische und juristische Schriften* II - *Leben und Charakter des Grafen von Brühl* II

	- *Moralische und philosophische Schriften* III - *Öconomische Schriften über die wichtigsten Gegenstände der Stadt- und Landwirtschaft* II
1762	- *Ausführliche Abhandlung von denen Steuern und Abgaben* - *Vergleichungen der europäischen mit den asiatischen und andern vermeintlich barbarischen Regierungen in drey Büchern verfasst* - *Abhandlung von denen Manufactur- und Fabriken-Reglements zur Ergänzung seines Werkes von denen Manufakturen und Fabriken* - *Der Teutsche Patriot* - *Erwiesene und ferner erläuterte Rechtmässigkeit der itionis in partes auf denen Teutschen Reichstagen*
1763	- *Ökonomisches Wörterbuch* II+III - *Zwei Preisfragen der Bayerischen Akademie der Wissenschaften* - *Leben und Charakter der jüngst verstorbenen Gräfin von Brühl* - French translation of *Die Chimäre des Gleichgewichts der Handlung und Seefahrt*
1764	- *Gesammelte politische und Finanzschriften* III - *Leben und Charakter des Grafen von Brühl* III
1765	- *Beantwortung der Preisfrage: Auf was für eine leichtere und sowohl in Ansehung der Zeit als des Holzes weniger kostbare, durch die Erfahrung bewehrte Art kann man aus den gewonnenen Kupfererzen Garkupfer erhalten* - *Die Kunst, das Silber zu affinieren* - 2nd edition of the *Grundriss des gesamten Mineralreiches* - *English translation of Leben und Charakter des Grafen von Brühl*
1766	- *System des Finanzwesens* - Russian translation of *Der handelnde Adel* by Denis Fonvizin
1767	- *Erörterung der Preisfrage, worinnen der Fränkischen Könige und der Herzoge von Baiern aus dem Agilofingischen Stamme wechselweise Rechte und Verbindlichkeiten bestanden haben* - *Abhandlung über die öconomische Preisfrage: Was tragen die Pflanzen selbst zur Zubereitung ihres Nahrungs-*

	saftes bey, und was ist bey ihrem ungleichen Wachsthum der Verschiedenheit des Erdreichs zuzuschreiben? - Dutch translation of *Die Chimäre des Gleichgewichts von Europa*
1769	- 2nd edition of *Anweisung zu einer guten deutschen Schreibart* - *Physicalische und politische Betrachtungen über die Erzeugung des Menschen und Bevölkerung der Länder* - French translation of *Grundsätze der Policeywissenschaft* by Marc Antoine Eidous
1770	- Russian translation of *Natur und Wesen der Staaten* by A. Volkov
1771	- *Von Getreydemagazinen, von Lebensmitteln und von dem Unterhalt des Vollkes* - *Geschichte des Erdkörpers* - 2nd edition of *Natur and Wesen der Staaten*, edited by Johann Godfried Scheidemantel (first published in 1759)
	Posthumous editions
1772	- Russian translation of *Die Grundfeste* by I. Bogaevakij
1773	- Dutch translation of *Natur und Wesen der Staaten*
1776	- *Von der Churfürstl. Pfälzischen Akademie zu Mannheim gekrönte Abhandlung über die Frage: Wie die Kupfererze mit Ersparung der Zeit und der Kohlen auf den Kupferhütten besser bearbeitet werden können*
1780	- 2nd edition of *Vollständige Abhandlung von denen Manufakturen und Fabriken*, edited by Johann Beckmann
1782	- 3rd edition of *Grundsätze der Policeywissenschaft*, edited by Johann Beckmann - Dutch translation of *Vollständige Abhandlung von denen Manufakturen und Fabriken* by Jacob van Manen Az
1784	- Spanish translation of *Grundsätze der Policeywissenschaft* by Antonio Francisco Puig y Gelabert
1789	- 3rd edition of *Vollständige Abhandlung von denen Manufakturen und Fabriken*, edited by Johann Beckmann
1791	- Spanish translation of *Grundsätze der Policeywissenschaft* by Miguel Geronimo Suárez y Núnez

Table Three
Identical passages in Justi's writings

Many of Justi's writings were first published either as independent pamphlets or articles in one of his journals. From 1760 onwards, Justi started to re-edit these writings in a number of essay-collections and used some of them again for the compilation of later treatises. A careful look at identical passages in Justi's writings says much about his working method. The tracking of the essay entitled 'Von Verwandlung der Bauerngüther' is particularly telling. Having read Siegmund Christoph Zech's *Die Verwandlung der Domänen in Bauerngüther als das beste Mittel zur Bevölkerung, zur Macht und zum Reichtum eines Landes* (Strassburg [i.e., Berlin], 1759), Justi's own essay appeared for the first time in 1760 in his journal *Fortgesetzte Bemühungen*. In the following year and in 1764, the essay was reprinted in two parts in *Gesammelte politische und Finanzschriften* and again incorporated in full length into *System des Finanzwesens* (1766). Apart from the literal repetitions listed below, numerous further, albeit more indirect, textual similarities can be found in Justi's writings.

Die Grundfeste

Pages:	**Title:**	**Identical with:**
I, 450–463	par. 503–522	*Manufakturen und Fabriken* I, 107–126

Historische und juristische Schriften

Pages:	Title:	Identical with:
I, 54–180	Abhandlung von den römischen Feldzügen in Deutschland	*Abhandlung von den römischen Feldzügen in Deutschland* (Leipzig, 1748)
II, 232–320	Abhandlung von der Abtretung eines Reichslehns	*Abhandlung von der Abtretung eines Reichslehns* (Vienna, 1750)
II, 323–592	Rechtliche Abhandlung von denen Ehen	*Rechtliche Abhandlung von denen Ehen* (Leipzig, 1757)

Moralische und philosophische Schriften

Pages:	Title:	Identical with:
II, 485–544	German translation of: *Dissertation sur le système des monades*	*Dissertation sur le système des monades* (Berlin, 1748)
III, 3–123	Ursachen des Verfalls der Religion und der einreissenden Freidenkerei	*Ursachen des Verfalls der Religion und der einreissenden Freidenkerei* (Berlin, 1747)
III, 181–360	Nichtigkeit aller Einwürfe und unhöflichen Anfälle gegen die Untersuchung von der Lehre der Monaden	*Nichtigkeit aller Einwürfe und unhöflichen Anfälle gegen die Untersuchung von der Lehre der Monaden* (Frankfurt/M./Leipzig, 1748)

Ökonomische Schriften über die wichtigsten Gegenstände der Stadt- und Landwirtschaft

Pages:	Title:	Identical with:
II, 246–310	Alleruntertänigstes Gutachten wegen Anbauung der jütländischen Heiden	*Neue Wahrheiten*, 1758, 2, XII

Gesammelte Schriften

Pages:	Title:	Identical with:
I, 33–46	Erörterung der Frage, ob es nach den Regeln der Staatskunst ratsam ist, den Verlust einer Schlacht zu leugnen	*Erörterung der Frage, ob es nach den Regeln der Staatskunst ratsam ist, den Verlust einer Schlacht zu leugnen* (Göttingen, 1757)
I, 102–114	Die Notwendigkeit einer genauen Belohnung und Bestrafung der Bedienten eines Staates	*Neue Wahrheiten* 1754, 2, V
I, 115–131	Vortreffliche Einrichtung der Sineser in Ansehung der Belohnung vor die Staatsbedienten (German translation from Claude François Lambert's article in the *Recueil d'observations curieuses* I, 19 (1749), pp. 345–363)	*Neue Wahrheiten* 1754, 2, VI
I, 147–192	Abhandlung von dem Wesen des Adels und dessen Verhältnis gegen den Staat und insonderheit gegen die Commercien	Von dem Wesen des Adels und dessen Verhältnis gegen die Commerzien, in: *Der handelnde Adel, dem der krieger ische Adel entgegengesetzt wird* (Göttingen, 1756), pp. 243–288.
I, 380–439	Betrachtung über die Accise benebst dem ausführlichen Vorschlage einer statt derselben einzuführenden neuen Art von Gewerbesteuern	*Neue Wahrheiten* 1754 6, I

I, 504–573	Kurzer systematischer Grundriss aller Öconomischen und Cameralwissenschaften (This treatise was Justi's first textbook for his lectures in Vienna, 1750–54) (continued in: *Gesammelte Schriften* II, 303–377)	*Neue Wahrheiten* 1754 2, VI; 3, I; 5, I
II, 3–25	Abhandlung von der An-Ordnung und dem Gleich Gewicht der Hauptzweige der obersten Gewalt, worauf die Glückseligkeit und Freiheit der Staaten hauptsächlich ankommt	*Neue Wahrheiten* 1758, 12, VI
II, 71–85	Ob die Kraft der Gesetze auf die Furcht ankommt?	*Neue Wahrheiten* 1758, 11, VII
129–175	Vienna inaugural lecture	*Abhandlung von dem Zusammenhang* (Vienna, 1750) Also in: *Auf allerhöchsten Befehl erstattetes Gutachten* (Leipzig, 1754)
II, 176–199	Gedanken von dem Ursprunge der Monarchien und Aristokratien	(Translation from Giovanni Cataneo's comments on Montesquieu's *Spirit of the Laws*)
II, 220–226	Kurze Betrachtung, über verschiedene grosse Helden der alten und neuern Zeit	(Translation from the *Lettres juives* by Jean Baptiste de Boyer, Marquis d'Argens)

II, 236–300	Beweis, dass die Universal Monarchie vor die Wohlfahrt von Europa und überhaupt des menschlichen Geschlechts die grösste Glückseligkeit würken würde	*Beweis, dass die Universal-Monarchie vor die Wohlfahrt von Europa und überhaupt des menschlichen Geschlechts die grösste Glückseligkeit würken würde* (Frankfurt, 1747)
II, 390–406	Verwandlung der Domänen in Bauerngüter (continued in: *Gesammelte Schriften* III, 438-448)	*Fortgesetzte Bemühungen* 1760, 3, XV
II, 406–572	Entdeckte Ursachen des verderbten Münzwesens in Deutschland	*Entdeckte Ursachen des verderbten Münzwesens in Deutschland* (Leipzig, 1755)
III, 219–248	Abhandlung von den Mitteln, die Erkenntnis in den Ökonomischen und CameralWissenschaften dem gemeinen Wesen recht nützlich zu machen	*Abhandlung von den Mitteln, die Erkenntnis in den Ökonomischen und Cameral-Wissenschaften dem gemeinen Wesen recht nützlich zu machen* (Göttingen, 1755)
III, 256–270	Betrachtung über die sogenannten genuesischen Lotterien	*Neue Wahrheiten* 1754, 2, VIII

Steuern und Abgaben

Pages:	**Title:**	**Identical with:**
103–109	par. 57–60	*Gesammelte Schriften* I, 390–396 (Parts of: V. Betrachtungen über die Accise, benebst einem ausführlichen Vorschlage einer statt derselben einzuführenden neuen Art von Gewerbesteuern, pp. 380–439)

171–189	par. 102–115	*Gesammelte Schriften* I, 416–432 (see above)

System des Finanzwesens

Pages:	**Title:**	**Identical with:**
83–94	par. 162–186	*Gesammelte Schriften* III, 409–438 (IX. Abhandlung von dem sogenannten Plusmachern, oder der schädlichen Art, die Einkünfte des Staats zu vermehren)
98–105	par. 189–207	*Gesammelte Schriften* II, 390–406 (III. Von Verwandlung der Domänen in Bauerngüther)
106–109	par. 211–216	*Gesammelte Schriften* III, 440–448 (X. Fortsetzung von Verwandlung der Domänen in Bauerngüter)
354–368		*Steuern und Abgaben*, pp. 1–44 (par. 1–19)

Table Four
List of original quotations

Chapter/ footnote:	Original quotation:
II, 27 & 37	*Natur und Wesen*, Vorrede Man kann mein gegenwärtiges Werk gleichfalls als einen Geist der Gesetze ansehen.
III, 4	*Grundfeste* I, 620 Die wenigsten Länder unsers Vaterlandes können von sich sagen, daß sie einen blühenden Nahrungsstand, und eine genugsame Menge Geldes in sich haben.
III, 7	*Grundfeste* I, 620 Ohngeachtet die natürliche Fruchtbarkeit der meisten Länder genugsam bekannt ist; ohngeachtet der ergiebige Boden noch ein und zwey mal so viel Menschen ernähren könnte; und ohngeachtet viele Teutsche Staaten eine vortheilhaftige Lage an den Meeren und schiffbaren Ströhmen haben; so lieget doch in den meisten Handel und Wandel sehr darnieder.
III, 8	*Polizeiwissenschaft*, p. 69 Teutschland, welches selbst ungleich besser cultiviert werden könnte, wenn man ernstliche Maaßregeln zum Aufnehmen der Gewerbe und Commercien ergriffe, giebt eine Quelle ab, woraus viele andere Länder bevölkert werden.
III, 9	*Manufakturen und Fabriken* I, 27f. Die Engelländer, Holländer und Franzosen haben in denen meisten Manufacturarbeiten einen so großen Vorsprung, daß ein neuanfangendes Volk sie schwehrlich einholen, geschweige ihnen den Absatz benehmen wird.

III, 11	*Manufakturen und Fabriken* I, 28 Frankreich hat in denen Manufacturen viel späther angefangen, als Engelland und Holland: und hat sie doch in einer gar kurzen Zeit zur Vollkommenheit und zu auswärtigen Vertrieb gebracht.
III, 13	*Grundfeste* I, 519 [H]eut zu Tage zweifelt so leicht niemand, daß die Handlung die Seele eines Staats ist, und daß dessen Macht und Glückseeligkeit größthenteils auf den Zustand seiner Commercien ankommt.
III, 15	*Natur und Wesen*, p. 74 Man hat endlich eingesehen, dass die Machiavellischen Grundsätze ganz und gar nichts taugen. Man hat aus der Erfahrung befunden, daß ein entvölkertes Land und auf das äußerste gedrückte Unterthanen einen Fürsten nicht mächtig machen; daß ein verarmtes und von Nahrung entblößtes Land auch die Armut seines Regenten nach sich ziehe.
III, 17	*Psammitichus* II, 261 Unseeliger Krieg! [...] wenn du am glücklichsten geführet wirst; so vernichtest du doch einen großen Theil der Früchte, welche eine vieljährige Vorsorge weiser Regenten zum Aufnehmen und Wohlfarth ihrer Staaten gepflanzet hatte.
III, 22	*Vergleichungen*, p. 140 Aber so viel schreckende Beyspiele auch der Spiegel der Geschichte denen Monarchen entgegen stellet; so gewiß überzeuget sie auch seyn müssen, daß der glücklichste Krieg vor Ihre Unterthanen betrübte Folgen haben wird; so ist doch dieses alles nicht vermögend, sie zu warnen, ihre Eroberungsbegierde, Ehr- und Ruhmsucht in Schranken zu halten.
III, 24	*Psammitichus* I, 188 Ein unaufhörlicher Krieg aber werde die Handlung des Staats ganz unfehlbar zu Boden stürzen, wenn sich auch derselbe dadurch der Abhängigkeit erwehren könnte.

III, 24	*Psammitichus* I, 188 Sie müssen leicht begreifen, daß es ihnen allemal nützlicher ist, uns nach unsern eignen Gesetzen Leben zu lassen, wobey sich der Flor der Handlung beständig erhalten wird, und wobey sie unsre Kräfte zu ihren Diensten haben werden, als daß sie uns ihrer despotischen Regierung unterwerfen, unter welcher sich unsre Handlung und unsre Kräfte bald verlieren würden. Ein weiser unumschränkter Monarch wird einen benachbarten kleinen handelnden Staat allemal lieber zu seinem Freunde und Bundesgenossen, der sich seinem Willen gemäß bezeiget, als zu seinem Unterthan haben wollen.
III, 26	*Psammitichus* II, 7 Er sah ein, daß alle Kriege, wenn sie gerecht seyn solten, nur Vertheidigungs-Kriege seyn müßten; und daß so gar ein bloßer Vertheidiguns-Krieg in der Folge ungerecht werden könne, wenn der Staat von dem angreifenden Theile keine Gefahr mehr zu besorgen habe, und dennoch aus bloßer Rachsucht und Eroberungs-Begierde der Krieg immer weiter getrieben würde.
III, 32	*Vergleichungen*, p. 227 Dieser ungeheure Kriegesstand in Europa wird also nicht eher aufhören, bis der höchste Punct der Noth demselben ein Ende macht, das ist, bis alle Europäischen Unterthanen an den Bettelstab gebracht, und die Regierungen selbst gänzlich verarmet sind.
III, 34	*Polizeiwissenschaft*, p. 268 Die Regenten [haben] eingesehen […] daß es ihr eigner Vortheil ist, ihre Unterthanen reich und glücklich zu machen […]
III, 35	*Vergleichungen*, p. 142 Boileau selbst, der vernünftige Boileau hat in so thörichten Hyperbeln von Ludewig dem XIV geredet, die alle gesunde Vernunft beleidigen.

III, 36	*Chimäre des Gleichgewichts der Handlung und der Schiffahrt*, p. 992f. Dänemark hat nun seit 100 Jahren, da es sich in alle wider Schweden entstandenen Kriege eingemischt hat, um Schonen, Halland und Bleckingen wieder zu erlangen, durch die Erfahrung befunden, daß es ein Grundsatz einer sehr falschen Staatskunst ist, daß man verlorne Provinzen wieder zu erobern suchen müsse: und daß dieser Grundsatz zu nichts dienet, als die annoch besitzenden Länder von Volk und Geld zu entblößen und auf das äußerste zu entkräften. Es ist überzeugt worden, daß es ein unendlich wichtigeres Augenmerk ist, die innerlichen Kräfte des Staats zu vermehren, als verlohrne Länder wieder zu erobern [...]
III, 39	*Gesammelte Schriften* I, 177 Alle Reichthümer, die nicht durch den Weg der Commercien in den Staat eingehen, die nicht den Fleiß der Mitbürger in denen Gewerben thätig machen und sich mithin in alle Theile des Staatskörpers ergießen, sind die Quelle aller Unordnungen, welche das Verderben und den gänzlichen Untergang des Reichs bald nach sich ziehen werden.
III, 50	'Von dem Wesen des Adels und dessen Verhältnis gegen die Commerzien', p. 252 Diese Untersuchung sollte mit einem jeden Edelmanne im dreysigsten Jahr seines Alters vorgenommen weren. Wenn er alsdann die erforderlichen Fähigkeiten und Geschicklichkeiten nicht besässe; wenn er sich nicht mit grossen Schritten auf dem Wege befände, dem Staate nützliche Dienste zu leisten; so sollte er vor seine Person des Adels unwerth erkläreth werden; und wenn sich der nämliche Fall in drey Zeugungen hintereinander in einer Familie ereignete; so sollte dieser Familie der Adel wieder genommen werden.

III, 36	*Chimäre des Gleichgewichts der Handlung und der Schiffahrt*, p. 992f. Dänemark hat nun seit 100 Jahren, da es sich in alle wider Schweden entstandenen Kriege eingemischt hat, um Schonen, Halland und Bleckingen wieder zu erlangen, durch die Erfahrung befunden, daß es ein Grundsatz einer sehr falschen Staatskunst ist, daß man verlorne Provinzen wieder zu erobern suchen müsse: und daß dieser Grundsatz zu nichts dienet, als die annoch besitzenden Länder von Volk und Geld zu entblößen und auf das äußerste zu entkräften. Es ist überzeugt worden, daß es ein unendlich wichtigeres Augenmerk ist, die innerlichen Kräfte des Staats zu vermehren, als verlohrne Länder wieder zu erobern [...]
III, 62	*Chimäre des Gleichgewichts von Europa*, p. 94 Ich kenne fast keinen Staat, dessen wahre Macht durch eine weise Einrichtung nicht noch einmal so groß werden könnte.

III, 63	*Chimäre des Gleichgewichts von Europa*, p. 60 Man siehet die Abhängigkeit eines freyen Staats von einem andern und mächtigern, der ihn verhindern will, die dienlichen Maaßregeln zu seiner Glückseligkeit zu ergreifen, als das höchste Unglück eines Volkes an, das man eben durch das System des Gleichgewichts zu vermeiden sucht; denn eine solche grobe Idee der Universalmonarchie, die alle Staaten zu wirklichen Provinzen ihres Reichs machen wird, kann schwerlich jemals in Erfüllung gesetzt werden; und dennoch ist das Mittel, das man dawider vorschlägt, weit ärger als alles, was man befürchtet. Denn wenn das Gleichgewicht in der That statt finden sollte; so würde keine Sklaverey so hart sein, als worinnen ein jeder Staat gegen alle übrigen Staaten stehen würde. Bey einer jeden neuen Einrichtung, bey einer jeden innerlichen Verbesserung würden ihn alle übrigen Staaten Einrede und Einhalt tun müssen, aus Furcht, daß die Macht dieses Staates durch die Vollkommenheit seiner Verfassung nicht allzu groß anwachsen möge; und die Abhänglichkeit von so vielen Staaten würde eine viel härtere Sklaverey seyn, als von einem einzigen mächtigen Nachbarn. Der eine Staat würde dieses, der andere jenes an der Vollkommenheit der innerlichen Verfassung abgestellt wissen wollen; und ein jeder Staat würde mehr mit der Aufmerksamkeit auf die innerliche Vergrößerung aller übrigen Staaten, als mit seiner eigenen Einrichtung zu thun haben.

III, 64	*Chimäre des Gleichgewichts von Europa*, p. 65 Jedoch, wenn man auch einen Staat, der sich innerlich zu stark vergrößert hat, nachdem man es wahrnimmt, mit Krieg angreift, um ihn zu schwächen; so wird solches nicht weniger als nach dem System des Gleichgewichts geschehen; Das wird ein Krieg seyn, den verschiedne Staaten ihren besonderen Interessen halber gegen ein mächtiges Reich erregen, und die Regeln des Gleichgewichts werden bloß der Deckmantel seyn, worunter man das Interesse verstecket, um sich Bundesgenossen zu verschaffen. Die Staaten werden wie die Privatpersonen durch nichts als ihr wahres oder eingebildetes Interesse geleitet; und sie sind weit entfernt, sich nach dem chimärischen Gleichgewicht zu richten. Man nenne mir einen einzigen Staat, der seinen Interessen zuwider, oder nur ohne ein besonderes Interesse, sich in einen Krieg eingelassen hat. Bloß um das Gleichgewicht zu erhalten.
IV, 1	*Manufakturen und Fabriken* I, 38 Es ist wahr, der Despote kann seine Unterthanen gar leicht zwingen, Manufacturen und Fabriken zu unternehmen, so wie der Prügel des Guardian zu Algier einen Sclaven gar leicht dahin bringen kann, ein Handwerk auszuüben, das er vorher nie gelernet hat. Allein die Gewalt des Despoten und der Prügel des Guardian werden die aufgezwungene Handthierung ihren beyden elenden Sclaven niemals in behöriger Vollkommenheit beybringen; und die mit Gewalt erzwungenen Manufacturen werden mithin eine schlechte Beschaffenheit haben. Wenn die Manufacturen und Fabriken zu ihrer Vollkommenheit gelangen sollen; so wird darzu Genie, Lust, Fleiß und Aufmerksamkeit erfordert; und dieses sind Früchte der Freyheit und einer gerechten und gütigen Regierung, nicht aber der despotischen Gewalt.
IV, 3	*Grundfeste* I, 659 Nichts ist aber eine so große Hinterniß des Credits, als eine willkührliche und ungerechte Gewalt.

IV, 4	*Grundfeste* I, 643 Alle Regierungen, worinnen eine despotische und willkührliche Gewalt das Zepter führet, und unter welchen Ungerechtigkeiten und Bedrückungen vorgehen, sind an tausend Arten, Mißtrauen zu erregen, sehr fruchtbar.
III, 65	*Chimäre des Gleichgewichts von Europa*, p. 116 [D]ie freyen Mächte haben sich dieses Lehrgebäudes nur bedienet [...] um sich Bundsgenossen zu verschaffen, und ihr besondres Interesse und ihre Leidenschaften, wodurch sie zum Kriege bewogen werden, darunter zu verbergen.
IV, 5	*Psammitichus* I, 157 Alle Reiche, die tyrannisch regiert werden, verlieren nach und nach alle ihre Stärke, so wie die Tyranney den Fleiß und den Muth der Unterthanen darnieder schlägt; und werden endlich so schwach, daß sie keinem auswärtigen Feinde Widerstand leisten können.
IV, 6	*Grundriss*, p. 219 Alle Länder, worinnen eine uneingeschränkte Gewalt tiefe Wurzel geschlagen hat, werden gar bald zu großen Wüsteneyen werden.
IV, 8	*Chimäre des Gleichgewichts der Handlung und der Schiffahrt*, p. 979f. Peter der Erste machte sehr gute Anstalten zum Aufnehmen der Handlung: und indem er sich vielleicht auf deren Wirkung allzusehr verließ; so übertrieb er die Anschaffung einer ansehnlichen Flotte, die vor den Zustand der russischen Handlung viel zu groß war. Vielleicht, wenn er länger gelebt hätte, vornehmlich aber, wenn er hätte einsehen lernen, daß die wichtigste Anstalt, die zum Aufnehmen der Handlung gemacht werden konnte, die Abschaffung der Despoterey wäre, die er aber sehr lieb hatte; denn die Despoterey ist die allergrößte Hinderniß der Commercien; so hätte er die Handlung und Schiffahrt der Russen mit seiner errichteten Seemacht in ein besseres Verhältniß haben setzen können.

IV, 54	*Natur und Wesen*, p. 118 Alle neuen Reiche, von deren Gründung wir in der Geschichte Nachricht finden und insonderheit diejenigen, welche von den teutschen und andern nordischen Völkern in Britannien, Gallien, Italien, Spanien und Afrika gestiftet worden sind, haben ihren Regenten nur eine gemäßigte Gewalt zugestanden.
IV, 55	*Vergleichungen*, p. 27 Der geringste Fürst, der kaum zehen tausend Unterthanen hat, glaubet zu einer unumschränkten und despotischen Gewalt berechtiget zu seyn.
IV, 66	*Natur und Wesen*, p. 130 [Die] Grundgesetze von Pohlen, die so beschaffen sind, dass ganz und gar nichts Heilsames zu Stande gebracht werden kann [...] taugen ganz und gar nichts.
IV, 68	*Natur und Wesen*, p. 186 Dieser persönliche Adel müßte nur durch sehr tapfre Thaten, durch große Tugenden, durch außerordentliche Fähigkeiten und Geschicklichkeiten, kurz, durch große und überall bekannte Verdienste erlanget werden können.
IV, 71	*Natur und Wesen*, p. 184 Wenn man alles dieses erwäget, was wir bis hierher von der Natur der Aristocratie vogestellet haben; so wird man mir leicht zugestehen, daß diese Regierungsform ihrem Wesen nach fehlerhaft und gar nicht geschickt sey, die Glückseligkeit des Volkes und des gesamten Staats vorzüglich zu befördern.
IV, 76	*Grundriss*, p. 141 Was aber der Güte der Regierung am meisten schadet, das ist, daß die größte Menge des Volkes, auf welche es doch hauptsächlich ankommt, wenig Klugheit und Einsicht besitzet.
IV, 78	*Natur und Wesen*, p. 209 Das ist die Klippe, woran alle Democratien des Alterthums gescheitert haben.
IV, 80	*Natur und Wesen*, p. 211 Je mehr diese beyden Gewalten vollkommen von einander abgesondert sind und je besser sie im Gleichgewichte mit einander stehen, desto dauerhaftiger wird der Staat seyn.

IV, 82	*Natur und Wesen*, p. 212 Es [das Volk] wird nicht allein gar keine bürgerliche Freyheit genießen, sondern gemeiniglich wird es unter der wirklichen Sklaverey des Adels stehen.
IV, 83	*Natur und Wesen*, p. 213 Alle aristocratisch-monarchischen Reiche, welche die teutschen Völker bey Zertrümmerung der römischen Monarchie stifteten, haben die Bauern als Leibeigene und die Bürger, die nur nach und nach durch Freylassung aus der Leibeigenschaft entstanden, in der äußersten Verachtung und Unterdrückung erhalten; bis sich die Städte, nachdem sie durch die Commercien mächtiger geworden, durch Verbindungen unter einander wider die Plackereyen des Adels schützten und in mehreres Ansehn setzten.
IV, 85	*Natur und Wesen*, p. 218f. Wenn diese dreyerley Gewalten in der Grundverfassung des Staats dergestalt weislich eingerichtet sind, daß eine ohne die andere nichts thun kann, und daß immer eine die andere zu verhindern im Stande ist, so bald sie üble Maaßregeln ergreifen will [...] so ist das die allerweiseste und glücklichste Regierung, unter welchen die Menschen je Leben können.
IV, 86	*Grundriss*, p. 151 Nichts aber ist so wahr, als daß die große Gewalt des Adels eine jede Regierungsform verdirbt, wo sie sich einmischt.
IV, 93	*Natur und Wesen*, p. 161 Der monarchische Staat ist eine sehr einfache Maschine, die am wenigsten gekünstelt ist.
IV, 96	*Grundriss*, p. 175 Montesquieu, [der] ein Franzos und Edelmann war, und zwar ein Edelmann, der noch das alte Vorurtheil vertheidiget, daß der Adel sich nicht in die Commercien einlassen müsse [...]
IV, 108	*Natur und Wesen*, p. 154 Was will er [der Adel] machen, wenn er einmal unterdrücket ist und der Beherrscher alle willkührliche Gewalt an sich gerissen hat?

IV, 109	*Natur und Wesen*, p. 153 Wenn er [Montesquieu] aber in seinem Werke hin und wieder zu verstehen giebt, daß es der Adel sey, welcher die uneingeschränkte Monarchie vor der Ausartung in die Despotery bewahre; so behauptet er etwas, worzu ihm tüchtige Gründe ermangeln.
IV, 110	*Grundriss*, p. 191 In einem Staate, wo ein erblicher Adel statt findet, hat der Adel allemal ein von dem wahren Nutzen des gesamten Volks ganz abgesondertes Interesse.
IV, 111	*Grundriss*, p. 172 Der Edelmann, der selbst keine Abgaben entrichtet, und dessen Stimme, ungeachtet er einige Hufen Land und zehen Bauren hat, zuweilen so viel gilt, als die Stimme einer ansehnlichen Stadt, votiret getrost auf den Beutel seiner Mibürger los.
IV, 128	*Grundriss*, p. 159 Da ein jeder vernünftiger Mensch, der Freyheit und Erkenntniß hat, sich selbst regieren soll; so muß auch ein freyes und gesittetes Volk sich selbst regieren, in so weit es darzu fähig ist [...] so ist es natürlich, daß es die gesetzgebende Macht durch seine Representanten ausübet. Diese Representanten muß eine jede Stadt und Bezirk des platten Landes durch eine freye Wahl ernennen; und hierzu ist das Volk gar wohl fähig; denn auch die geringste Sorte des Volks ist vermögend, die Geschicklichkeit und Verdienste einzusehen.
IV, 130	*Grundriss*, p. 165 Zu dem Ende ist es nöthig, daß der König alles besitzet, was zur vollziehenden Macht gehöret, ohne daß die gesetzgebende Macht den geringsten Antheil daran hat. Alle Staatsangelegenheiten, das Recht des Krieges und Friedens, der Bündnisse, der Befehl über die Macht des Staats zu Wasser und zu Lande, und alles, was in diesen Bezirk gehöret, muß der vollziehenden Macht des Königs uneingeschränkt überlassen seyn.
IV, 133	*Grundriss*, p. 191 Allein, eine Republik, in welcher niemand den Adel besitzen kann, wenn er nicht denslben durch seine eignen Verdienste erworben hat, wird die allergewisseste und mächtigste Triebfeder haben, ihre Bürger zu Tugenden, Geschicklichkeiten und großen und rühmlichen Thaten aufzumuntern.

IV, 137	*Vergleichungen*, p. 144 Sie ist wirklich an sich selbst die beste und thätigste Regierungsform.
IV, 138	*Vergleichungen*, p. 145 [D]er Monarch muß aus eigner Bewegung seine Gewalt allenthalben mit Mäßigung gebrauchen.
IV, 140	*Vergleichungen*, p. 8f. Es giebt noch einen dritten Weg, dessen sich die Völker bedienen können; nämlich, daß sie zwar ihren Königen alle uneingeschränkte Gewalt lassen; aber sie in solche Umstände setzen, und ihnen solche Triebfedern geben, daß sie aus eigner Bewegung alle ihre Kräfte anwenden, um mit Güte und Weisheit zu herrschen und ihre Völker glücklich zu machen. Alsdenn werden alle nachtheiligen Folgen, welche sowohl die uneingeschränkte Gewalt der Könige, als die eingeschränkten Regierungsformen zu begleiten pflegen, glücklich vermieden.
V, 2	*Grundfeste* I, 773f. Wenn demnach eine monarchische Regierung eine der größten Hinternisse wider den Flohr der Commercien und Gewerbe aus dem Wege räumen will; so muß sie vor allen Dingen gewisse Grundregeln festsetzen, die sie als einen unbeweglichen Grund und unveränderliche Richtschnur aller ihrer Maasreguln und Handlungen betrachten muß.
V, 2	*Natur und Wesen*, p. 125 [D]iese Grundregeln müssen vor alle ihre Ministers die allergenaueste Richtschnur und die heiligste und unverletzlichste Sache seyn.
V, 3	*Natur und Wesen*, p. 99 Kein Monarch in der Welt, er sey auch noch so uneingeschränkt, kann demnach eine Gewalt über die Grundverfassungen des Staats haben, und die Veränderung der Regierungsform, die Nachfolge in der Regierung und alle andere Grundverfassungen sind gänzlich außer den Gränzen ihrer Macht. Denn wie können sie über dasjenige einige Gewalt haben, was selbst der Grund und Ursprung ihrer eignen Macht ist?

V, 10	*Natur und Wesen*, p. 102 Die Engländer machten aus der Grundgewalt und Majestät des Volkes diesen höchst irrigen Schluß, als sie im vorigen Jahrhundert ihren König Karl den Ersten vor Gericht zogen, verurtheilten und denselben wirklich hinrichten ließen, aber dadurch einen ewig schwarzen Fleck in ihrer Geschichte verursachten.
V, 12	*Grundriss*, p. 218f. Zu der Glückseligkeit des Staats, als dem großen Endzweck der Republiken, wird auch die Freyheit des Bürgers erfordert.
V, 13	*Grundriss*, Vorrede Man würde allemal finden, daß ein jeder Mensch diejenige Regierung vor gut halt, unter welcher er Raum und Gelegenheit hat, seine Leidenschaften, seinen Eigennutz und besondere Absichten zu vergnügen.
V, 16	*Natur und Wesen*, p. 410 Der Endzweck der Staaten ist auf die zeitliche Glückseligkeit gerichtet; der Endzweck der Religion aber gehet auf die ewige Glückseligkeit.
V, 16	*Natur und Wesen*, p. 411 Gesetze und Strafen also, welche jemand zu einer Religion zwingen, oder wegen des Abfalls von einer Religion, oder der darwider geäußerten Zweifel bestrafen, sind allemal tyrannisch und grausam.
V, 16	*Natur und Wesen*, p. 450 Die Glaubensmeynungen gehören nicht unter die Endzwecke und Pflichten der bürgerlichen Gesellschaften.
V, 19	*Manufakturen und Fabriken* I, 34 Man mag aber die öffentliche Ausübung verschiedener Religionen zulaßen, oder nicht; so muß doch allemal in einem Lande, das blühende Manufacturen und Fabriken haben will, eine vollkommene Gewissensfreyheit stattfinden. Niemand darf wegen dessen, was er vor sich in der Stille glaubet, oder wegen der Art, womit er Gott in seinem Hause dienet, zur Verantwortung gezogen werden.

V, 20	*Polizeiwissenschaft*, p. 58 Es muß niemand wegen seiner Glaubensmeinungen, so lange er den Staat nicht damit beunruhiget, zur Verantwortung gezogen werden; und diejenigen Religionen, welche in andern Ländern öffentlich ausgeübet werden, müßen wenigstens die Freyheit haben, auf dem Fuß der Toleranz, in Privathäusern ihren Gottesdienst auszuüben.
V, 24	*Grundfeste* II, 103 Diese obrigkeitliche Regierung der Familien würde also nicht geschehen können, ohne die inneren Angelegenheiten einer jeden Familie aufzudecken, welches die ärgste von allen Despotereyen ist, und allen vernünftigen Begriffen von der bürgerlichen Freyheit widerstreitet.
V, 29	*Gesammelte Schriften* I, 619 Die Unverletzlichkeit des Eigenthums, und sich aller Eingriffe in dasselbe zu enthalten, muß eine der vornehmsten Grund-regeln einer weisen Regierung seyn, die sie niemals ausser Augen setzen muß.
V, 30	*Grundriss*, p. 246 Folglich, wenn die oberste Gewalt im Namen des Staats das Obereigenthum über Privatgüter ausübet; so muß denen Eigenthümern der Schade bis auf den Antheil, den sie an den gemeinen Lasten zu tragen haben ersetzet werden.
V, 33	*Gesammelte Schriften* I, 501 Es will nichts so zärtlich und behutsam tractirt werden, als das Handlungswesen. Wenn man die Fremden einmal abschrecket, und ihnen Anlaß giebt, daß sie eine Abneigung bekommen, in unsre Länder zu reisen; so ist eine gar lange Zeit erforderlich, ehe man sie wieder anreizen kann.
V, 34	*Gesammelte Schriften* I, 75 Man kann aber mit Recht niemand zwingen, die Beschaffenheit seines Vermögens zu entdecken.
V, 35	*Staatswirtschaft* II, 535 [D]er Regent [darf] keine von der Wohlfahrt seiner Unter-thanen abgesonderte Glückseligkeit verlangen […]
V, 36	*Natur und Wesen*, p. 316 [A]m allerwenigsten aber muß er [der Regent] seinen persön-lichen Willen zum Willen des Staats machen.

V, 37	*Staatswirtschaft* I, 103: Die ewige Glückseligkeit der Unterthanen ist nicht unter seiner Vorsorge begriffen. Diese hat sich ein jeder Unterthan selbst vorbehalten. Der Endzweck der Republiken ist bloß auf die zeitliche Glückseligkeit gerichtet.
V, 40	*Grundriss*, p. 238 Alle Regenten sind durch die Erfahrung überzeuget worden, daß ein armes Land auch die Armuth und Schwäche seines Fürsten nach sich ziehet.
V, 42	*Grundriss*, p. 257 Eine verschwenderische und unordentliche Wirthschaft macht auch allemal den Regenten schwach und unmächtig.
V, 44	*Grundriss*, p. 281 Allein in unsern erleuchteten und vernünftigen Zeiten hat man endlich genugsam eingesehen, daß die Begriffe der Redlichkeit und Gerechtigkeit allgemein vor alle Menschen sind, und daß sich eine Regierung niemals davon entfernen kann, ohne selbst zu ihrem Nachtheil und Schaden zu arbeiten.
V, 47 & 48	*Grundriss*, p. 216 Der größte Vorzug gemäßigter Staaten ist, daß man in denenselben nicht von den Willen des Regenten, sondern von vestgesetzten Gesetzen abhängt. Meines Erachtens ist es demnach in solchen Staaten gar nicht schicklich, daß die Canzeleyen, wenn sie im Namen des Regenten bey Justiz- und andern Angelegenheiten, wo auf die Gerechtigkeit der Sache gesehen werden muß, ihre so beliebte Endigungsformel gebrauchen: Daran geschiehet unser Wille, oder: Das ist unsre Willens Meynung. Diese Formeln sind nur einem Despoten anständig. In gemäßigten Staaten aber sollte es heißen: Das ist denen Gesetzen und der Gerechtigkeit gemäß.
V, 58	*Scherzhafte und satyrische Schriften* III, 417 Wenn die Könige ins Künftige nach dem Beispiel des Psammitichus anfangen sollten, nicht bloß dem Namen nach, sondern in der That selbst zu regieren, so würde die Herrlichkeit des Minister-Handwerks zu einem guten Teil wegfallen.
V, 65	*Leben Brühls* I, 132 [Ein König, der] seinen Ministern die Regierung anvertrauet und sich vor seine Person gleichsam zur Ruhe begiebt [...]

V, 68	*Leben Brühls* I, 125 Es ist fast nicht möglich, daß etwas zu Sr. Majestät dringen kann, welches dem Minister nachteilig wäre.
V, 69	*Leben Brühls* II, 27 […] und man weiß von Regenten unter diesen Völkern, welche mitten von der Tafel aufgestanden sind, sobald sie diese Glocke gehört haben.
V, 77	*Vergleichungen*, p. 57 Man nenne mir doch einmal einen Regenten, welcher in dem Finanzwesen, in denen Commercien, in den Mitteln und Maaßregeln zur Cultur des Landes und zum Aufnehmen des Nahrungsstandes eine große Erkenntnis besäße! [...] Die Regenten der am besten beherrschten Europäischen Staaten sind nicht einmal mit denen ersten Begriffen und Grundsätzen dieser Wissenschaften bekannt.
V, 84	*Grundriss*, p. 417f. Der Herzog von Burgund, der als Dauphin von Frankreich starb, hatte gewiß alle diejenigen weisen, edlen und gerechten Grundsätze, die erfordert werden, um die Unterthanen glücklich zu machen, und die ein Prinz haben konnte, der von dem Verfasser des Telemachs unterrichtet war.
V, 85	*Grundriss*, p. 345 Alles dieses wird durch das Beyspiel Ludewig des Vierzehenden in Frankreich genugsam bestätigt. Man kann nicht läugnen, daß dieser König diejenigen Fähigkeiten der Seelen besaß, die man einen guten natürlichen Verstand nennt. Allein, er war in der Erziehung dergestalt verabsäumet, daß er einer der ungelehrtesten Fürsten war, die je in der Welt unter gesitteten Völkern geherrscht haben.
V, 87	*Vergleichungen*, p. 377f. In denen bürgerlichen Verfassungen der Menschen haben die ehrgeizigen Uneinigkeiten der Königlichen Familien unaussprechliches Unglück angerichtet.
V, 89	*Grundriss*, p. 351f. Wenn uns die Geschichte so wenig wahrhaftig große und weise Könige zeiget; so ist die Ursache lediglich darinnen zu suchen, daß es so wenig königliche Väter gegeben hat, die eine wahre Sorgfalt vor die Erziehung ihrer Prinzen erwiesen haben.

V, 90	*Vergleichungen*, p. 123f. Der Glanz, der sie allenthalben umgiebt, das schmeichlerische und kriechende Bezeigen aller dererjenigen, so sich ihnen nähern, kann nach der Natur des Menschen, der in allen Betracht ein sehr stolzes Their ist, keine andre Wirkung haben, als daß sie mit Hochmuth und Stolz erfüllet werden, und sich angewöhnen, auf alle andre Menschen, als auf eine ungleich geringer Art von Geschöpfen herab zu sehen: Der natürliche Hang der Menschen zum Hochmuth läßt die Kinder mittlern Standes gar bald einsehen, daß sie mehr sind, als gemeine Leute; und die Eindrücke davon sind unauslöschlich, und haben insonderheit bey denen Regenten auf ihre ganze Lebenszeit Wirkungen, die ihren Unterthanen gar nicht vortheilhaftig sind.
V, 96	*Psammitichus* I, 155f. Sie urteilten, daß man wegen des Mißbrauches einer Sache nicht die Sache selbst verwerfen müsse, und daß man die Gewalt der Könige nicht einschränken könne, ohne zu tausend Unordnungen und Gebrechen im Reiche Anlaß zu geben, und den Staat gegen seine Feinde schwach zu machen. Allein, sie glaubten, daß man den Mißbrauch der königlichen Gewalt in seiner Quelle verstopfen müsse, und daß dannenhero die Unterthanen selbst vor die Erziehung der Söhne ihres Königs sorgen müßten, weil auf diese Erziehung ihr Wohl oder Weh, ihr Glück oder Unglück beruhete. Der einzige Punkt also, worüber der König gar keine Gewalt hatte, war die Erziehung seiner Söhne; und fast alle Grundgesetze und Verfassungen des Staats, worinnen der König nichts ändern konnte, waren dahin gerichtet, diese Erziehung weislich und mit aller ersinnlichen Vorsicht dergestalt zu veranstalten, daß der Parteygeist, die Nebenabsichten und der Eigennutz dabey keinen Einfluß haben konnten, und daß denen jungen Prinzen edle Gesinnungen und Neigungen, eine wahre Liebe gegen ihr künftiges Volk, und insonderheit die große Wissenschaft, ihre Leidenschaften zu beherrschen, beygebracht würde.

V, 98	*Psammitichus* II, 450 Es ist ein beweinenswürdiger Umstand fast bey allen Regierungen, daß diejenigen, welche die Regenten dabey unterstützen sollen, mehr ihre Leidenschaften, besondres Interesse und Neben Absichten, als das Beste des Staats vor Augen haben.
V, 102	*Vergleichungen*, p. 97 [Der Regent muß] nicht sich selbsten, sondern dem Staate leben [...] wenn er ein wahrhaftig guter Regent seyn will.
V, 105	*Vergleichungen*, p. 90 Der Grundsatz dieser tyrannischen Regierung ist, jedermann durch diesen stolzen Aufzug zu verblenden, und das gemeine Volk zu überreden, daß die Könige über die Menschlichkeit erhaben sind. Die Unterthanen werden als verächtliche Sclaven gehalten, und kennen in der That keine andere Empfindung, als die Furcht.
V, 114	*Vergleichungen*, p. 91 In wohl eingerichteten Königreichen, wo der Prinz vielen Ministern einen Theil seiner Gewalt überlässet, und besonders einer immerwährenden Gesellschaft von obrigkeitlichen Persohnen [...]
V, 116	*Staatswirtschaft* II, 671 Man hat in die Collegia Leute gesetzet, wobey man mehr auf Geburt und auf Gunst, als auf eine vollkommene Kenntniß und Fähigkeit in den Sachen, die sie verwalten sollten, gesehen hat.
V, 117	*Staatswirtschaft* II, 481 Allein so geht es, wenn man wenigstens durch die That auffordert, daß man die Personen gern mit Bedienungen, nicht aber die Bedienungen mit tüchtigen Personen versehen möchte.
V, 117	*Grundriss*, p. 225 [A]llein diejenigen, denen er [der Monarch] die Geschäffte des Staats anvertrauet, bedürfen nicht seine besondre Gunst, sondern seine Achtung gegen ihre Verdienste und seine vollkommene Überzeugung von ihren großen Einsichten und Fähigkeiten.

V, 122	*Vergleichungen*, p. 53 Man siehet aus der vorhergehenden Vorstellung von der Einrichtung der Sinesischen Monarchie, daß sowohl an dem Hofe, als in den Provinzen, die Collegialische Verfassung statt findet; und daß alle Staatsbedienten und Unterkönige Collegia zur Seiten haben, mit deren Beyrath und Beystimmung sie die Angelegenheiten besorgen müssen.
V, 124 & 125	*Grundriss*, p. 217 Die Eigenschaft gemäßigter Staaten erfordert es, daß man sich zu denen Geschäfften der obersten Gewalt vieler Bedienten von gleicher Macht und Ansehn gebrauchte; und es ist nicht einmal rathsam, die Geschäffte unter dieselben nach denen Ländern und Provinzen, sondern nach der Natur der Angelegenheiten zu vertheilen; eben so wenig als man über eine Provinz, oder Stadt, einene Bedienten setzen soll, der alle Arten von Gewalt in seiner Person vereiniget. Mehrere Bedienten von gleicher Gewalt und Ansehn werden allemal einander in Schranken halten, und den Mißbrauch der Gewalt verhindern, der bey einer unzertheilten Gewalt beynahe allemal die fast natürliche Folge zu seyn pfleget.
V, 128	*Vergleichungen*, p. 54 Ein Minister, wenn er auch zur Wohlfarth des Staats den besten Willen und Absichten hat, kann niemals einen so großen Umfang von Fähigkeiten und Erkenntniß haben, daß er alle in seinem Departement vorfallenden Geschäfte bis auf den Grund einsehen sollte.
V, 129	*Grundriss*, p. 218 [Es ist] unmöglich [...] daß ein einziger Mann so viele und mancherley Geschäffte mit genugsamen Erfolge und Wirksamkeit verwalten kann.
V, 130	*Vergleichungen*, p. 54 Sie werden ihn nicht nur mit ihrer Einsicht zu statten kommen; sondern ihn auch von vielen übereilten und schädlichen Entschließungen zurück halten. Er wird nöthig haben, einigen Betracht vor seine zugeordneten Räthe zu haben, und daher seinem Eigennutz und Leidenschaften nicht so viel Raum lassen dürfen.

V, 134	*Steuern und Abgaben*, p. 40 [Beim Maß der Steuerentnahme] muß auf die Natur, Lage, Fruchtbarkeit, Nahrung, die übrige Beschaffenheit des Landes und sogar auf das Genie, Neigung, Gesinnung und Geist des Volkes Bedacht genommen werden.
V, 136	*Grundfeste* II, 622 Diese Einrichtung wird die nöthige Thätigkeit und Wirksamkeit der Policey-Direction nicht aufhalten. Sie wird aber viel Leidenschaften des Directors mäßigen, und ihn von vielen Ungerechtigkeiten zurück halten.
V, 145	*Grundriss*, p. 379 Sollte es wohl der gesunden Vernunft gemäß sein, daß der Staat einer Familie die Dienste schon bis auf ewige Zeiten in voraus bezahlet?
V, 146	*Vergleichungen*, p. 465 Allein leider! Dieses scheinet eine epidemische Krankheit fast aller Staaten zu seyn. Die Bedienungen werden überaus selten nach Verdiensten, Fähigkeiten und Geschicklichkeiten, sondern nach Gunst, Ansehn, Anverwandtschaft, Cabalen, und kurz fast allemal noch Nebenabsichten vergeben; und es ist nur ein ungefährer Zufall, wenn diese Nebenabsichten zugleich auf einen Gegenstand fallen, der die erforderliche Erkänntniß und Fähigkeit besitzet.
V, 153	*Gesammelte Schriften* I, 113 Denn alles, was zur Zeit ähnliches davon eingeführet ist, sind Spielereyen, bey welchen der größte Ignorante leicht durchkommen kann.
VI, 4	*Staatswirtschaft* II, 32 Er muss nämlich das bereiteste Vermögen des Staats auf eine dem Staate unnachtheilige Art zu nehmen, und mithin entweder von dem Gewinnste der Unterthanen nehmen, oder selbst neuen Gewinnst und bereitestes Vermögen zu gründen suchen. Er muss demnach ausser dem alleräußersten Nothfalle die Substanz des Staatsvermögens selbst nicht angreifen und folglich so wohl nur einen mäßigen Theil des Gewinnstes erheben, als in dem Aufwande des Staats den Ausfluß des Geldes außer Landes verhindern.

VI, 4	*Staatswirtschaft* II, 33f. Es ist ihm [dem falschen Cameralist] genug, wenn er die Einkünfte des Regenten vergrößern kann, um ihn zu Vergnügung seiner verderbten Neigungen und Leidenschaften Geld zu verschaffen. Das Land mag dabey ausgesauget, die Unterthanen mögen bedrücket, der Nahrungsstand mag darunter zu Grunde gerichtet werden; dieses alles rühret ihn sehr wenig; wenn er sich nur ein vermeyntes Verdienst by seinem Herrn dadurch erwerben, mithin seinen eigenen Vortheil dabey befördern kann.
VI, 8	*Grundfeste* I, 428 [...] und diejenigen irren sich sehr, welche den Reichthum eines Landes auf die Menge des darinnen befindlichen Gold und Silbers setzen.
VI, 9	*Grundriss*, p. 89 Der Reichthum an Gold und Silber ist nur ein relativischer Reichthum des Staats, der sich lediglich auf die Commercien und den Zusammenhang mit andern Völkern beziehet und blos deshalb nöthig wird.
VI, 10	*Grundfeste* I, 614 Ein Land, dessen Boden aus Golde bestünde, würde wenig, oder gar keinen Umlauf haben, wenn es keine Güther in sich erzeugte.
VI, 12	*Grundfeste* I, 474 Es ist eine sehr eitle Einbildung, wenn man glaubt, dass wenn man Gold uns Silber habe, man alles erlangen könne, was zu glücklichen Lebensumständen erfordert wird.

VI, 15	*Grundriss*, p. 239f. Es wird allemahl der Glückseligkeit des größten Theils des Volks und der Wohlfahrt des Staats äußerst nachtheilig seyn, wenn sich der Reichthum des Landes nur in wenigen Händen befindet, oder wenn ein gewisser Stand oder Klasse des Volks den Reichthum allein an sich ziehet, dieser besondre Stand mag geistlich oder weltlich seyn. Diese reiche Klasse des Volks wird allemal das ganze übrige Volk unterdrücken; und dieser arme und unterdrückte Theil wird zu den Kräften es Staats sehr wenig beytragen [...] und in diesem Betracht ist der große Reichthum der Geistlichkeit in katholischen Landen dem Staate auf das alleräußerste nachtheilig [...] Zehn Kaufleute, die zusammen zwo Millionen reich sind, haben vielleicht noch dreymal mehr Credit Thätigkeit und Einfluß in die Beförderung des Nahrungsstandes, als wenn diese zwo Millionen ein einziger Kaufmann besitzet [...] Aus dem allen erhellet meines Erachtens gar deutlich, daß eine gute Regierung bemühet seyn muß, den Reichthum des Landes und dessen Wirkungen so viel möglich unter alle Einwohner zu vertheilen.
VI, 25	*Manufakturen und Fabriken* I, 160f. Überhaupt muß man sagen, daß die Üppigkeit, die mit denen Manufacturen und Fabrikenwaaren des Landes getrieben wird, eines der allwerwirksamsten Beförderungsmittel vor den inländischen Debit ist [...] In allen andern Fällen ist die Üppigkeit dem Nahrungsstande ungemein zuträglich.
VI, 26	*Vergleichungen*, p. 63 Ich habe die Üppigkeit überhaupt vor dem gesamten Nahrungsstand in meinen übrigen Schriften so überzeugend erwiesen [...]
VI, 28	*Gesammelte Schriften* I, 82 Wenn die Pracht und Verschwendung eine Thorheit ist, so ist es doch gewiß, daß diese Thorheit eine große Menge andrer Menschen vortrefflich zu statten kommt, die davon Leben und sich ernähren.
VI, 29	*Polizeiwissenschaft*, p. 223 Allein die Thoren, welche sich der Üppigkeit gänzlich ergeben, sind dem gemeinen Wesen nützlich, ohne dass sie es selbst wissen und ein Verdienst davon haben.

VI, 30	*Staatswirtschaft* I, 429: [Man hat keine] Ursache, dem Reichtum einen Punkt zu setzen, den er nicht überschreiten dürfe, oder zu behaupten, dass man zu viel Reichtum haben könne.
VI, 32	*Staatswirtschaft* I, 411 Allein ich glaube dem ohngeachtet, dass kein Grad des Vermögens zu bestimmen ist, bey welchem man stehen bleiben müsse.
VI, 35	*Staatswirtschaft* I, 284 Die Menschen aber zu Entdeckung ihres Vermögens anzuhalten, ist allen guten Grundsätzen zuwider.
VI, 36	*Staatswirtschaft* II, 378 Die Menschen lieben die Freyheit so sehr, daß sie auch in ihren eiteln Handlungen nicht eingeschränket seyn wollen; und ein Staat, der dergleichen unternimmt, wird schwerlich an Einwohnern und Reichthum wachsen.
VI, 36	*Steuern und Abgaben*, p. 201 Die Menschen lieben die Freyheit so sehr, daß sie auch in ihren eiteln Handlungen nicht eingeschränket seyn wollen; und ein Staat, der dergleichen unternimmt, wird schwerlich an Einwohnern und Reichthum wachsen.
VI, 38	*Staatswirtschaft* I, 284 […] denn die Regierung kann ja nicht alle Handlungen der Privatpersonen dirigieren, und diejenigen […] zurück ziehn, die in ihr Verderben hinein rennen.
VI, 41	*Polizeiwissenschaft*, p. 232 […] die verschiedenen Stände durch ein zu tragendes Kleinod, oder anderes Zeichen, kenntbar machte, welches aber viele bedenkliche Folgen und überhaupt wenig Nutzen haben würde.
VI, 46	*Manufakturen und Fabriken* I, 48 Es liegt dem Staate gar sehr daran, reiche und vermögende Kaufleute zu haben.

VI, 48	*Staatswirtschaft* I, 269f.: Endlich ist eine gewisse Achtsamkeit vor die Manufacturiers und Fabrikanten, als ein Beförderungsmittel dieser Gewerbe, und überhaupt des Nahrungsstandes anzusehen [...] Ich sehe nichts, was uns abhalten könnte, solchen Leuten, die durch ihre besondere Einsicht, Geschicklichkeit, Fleiβ und Mühe zum gröβten Nutzen des Staats wichtige Manufacturen und Fabriken zu Stande gebracht, und sich dabey ein ansehnliches Vermögen erworben haben, allerley Titel und Vorzüge zu ertheilen, eben so gut als wir sie hundert andern Personen [i.e., den Adeligen] zugestehen, die so wenig als ihre Vorfahren [...] etwas nützliches vor den Staat geleistet haben; sondern welche durch die unverdiente Gunst eines Regenten oder Ministers, durch gerichtliche Bedienungen, wobey sie die Unterthanen auszusaugen Gelegenheit gehabt haben, oder durch Wucher und andere stinkende Wege zu einer ansehnlichen Familie geworden sind, und denen wir doch gleichwohl Titel und Würde nicht versagen, wenn wir glauben, daβ sie sich darnach aufzuführen Vermögen genug haben.
VI, 49	*Staatswirtschaft* I, 416 Wir wollen mehr seyn, als wir zeither gewesen sind; wir wollen Rang, Titel und Würde haben.
VI, 50	*Staatswirtschaft* I, 352 Es ist eine sehr schädliche Meynung vor Deutschland, daß sich der Adel darinnen einbildet, sein Stand werde durch Commercien, Manufacturen, und andere dem Staate nützliche Unternehmungen verunehret. Dadurch geschieht es, daß diejenigen, welche öfters das meiste Vermögen haben, der Republik nützlich zu werden, ihre Zeit größtentheils mit Jagen, Spielen, und andern eiteln Dingen, zubringen, und zu dem Besten des Staats wenig oder gar nichts beytragen: zu geschweigen, daß viele nach und nach ihr Vermögen dadurch versplittern, und ihre Familien in den äußersten Verfall bringen.

VI, 51	*Staatswirtschaft* I, 252f.: Ich will itzo nur des schlechten Unterrichts erwähnen, den sie ihren Lehrlingen ertheilen, die dasjenige höchstens in einem Vierteljahre weit besser erlernen könnten, worüber sie drey, vier und mehr Jahre mit bloßen Absehen und Verrichtung aller Mägdearbeit zubringen müssen; desgleichen der üblen Einrichtung bey Ertheilung des Meisterrechtes, da es auf die Eigenschaft eines Meistersohnes, auf kostbare und im gemeinen Leben niemals brauchbare Meisterstücke, keinesweges aber auf Fleiß und wahre Geschicklichkeit ankommt.
VI, 51	*Gesammelte Schriften* III, 394 Am allerwenigsten sollte sie denen Handwerkern die Geldschneidereyen von denen neuen Meistern nachsehen; und nichts als die Fähigkeit und Geschicklichkeit sollte bey Erlangung des Meisterrechts in Betracht gezogen werden.
VI, 54	*Staatswirtschaft* I, 254: Der Staat [...] kann keine Ursache haben, warum er [...] immerwährende oder gar erbliche Rechte und Vorzüge ertheilen wollte.
VI, 59	*Grundfeste* I, 556 [...] so sind in jedem Staate so viel alte fehlerhaftige Gesetze und Einrichtungen vorhanden, welche unsere Vorfahren aus Mangel der Einsicht in den Zusammenhang des Nahrungsstandes angeordnet haben, daß es in keinem Lande an unzähligen Hinternissen wieder das gerechte Verhältnis aller Theile des Nahrungsstandes fehlet.
VI, 60	*Psammitichus* I, 186 Alles was der Kaufhandel von der Regierung zu Tyrus zu gewarten hatte, war, daß sie demselben keine Hindernisse im Weg legte, sondern denen Kaufletuen in allen Anstalten und Unternehmungen, die sie zu Ausbreitung der Commercien, und zu Vergrößerung ihres Gewinnstes vor dienlich erachteten, freye Hand ließ. Die Regierung begnügte sich einen mäßigen Zoll von denen ein- und ausgehenden Schriften zu nehmen, der jedoch in Ansehung der großen Wichtigkeit des tyrischen Handels überaus einträglich war, und bekümmerte sich übrigens um die Commercien wenig oder gar nicht.

VI, 61	*Psammitichus* I, 186f. Ich machte daraus den Schluß, daß die Ausbreitung und der blühende Zustand des Kaufhandels nicht sowohl auf die Unterstützung und Beförderung der Regierung, sondern hauptsächlich darauf ankäme, daß in dem Staate und dessen Zustande und Verfassungen keine Hindernisse und denen Commercien nachtheilige Einrichtungen und Beschaffenheiten vorhanden seyn müßten.
VI, 62	*Manufakturen und Fabriken* I, 47 Die Aufnahme der Commercien kommt nicht sowohl auf Beförderungsmittel, als auf Wegräumung der Hinternisse an.
VI, 62	*Manufakturen und Fabriken* I, 47 Die Freyheit ist die Seele der Commercien; und der Staat thut alles, was er zu Beförderung derselben thun kann, wenn er diese Freyheit, in so weit sie vernünftig ist und dem wahren Besten des Staats keinen Nachtheil verursachet, gestattet und ihnen keine Hinternisse im Weg leget.
VI, 69	*Manufakturen und Fabriken* I, 149 Der Monopolist, der versichert ist, daß ihm kein anderer den Kauf verderben kann, wird seine Waaren niemals wohlfeilen Preißes geben; und niemals wird er sie in solcher Menge verfertigen, daß er sich derselben mäßigen Preißes zu entledigen genöthiget sehe. Er wird die Verfertigung auf den Absatz in der Stadt oder in dem Lande einschränken, worinnen er das Monopolium hat [...]
VI, 70	*Grundfeste* II, 754ff. [...] so hintert er [der Monopolist] damit alle auswärtige Commercien, und fällt allen Einwohnern des Staats beschwehrlich.

VI, 71	*Manufakturen und Fabriken* I, 150f. Wo viele einzelne Fabrikanten mit einander eifern: so hat der Neid und der Haß gegen einander keine schädliche Wirkung [...] Ihr Neid hat vielmehr die glückliche Wirkung, daß sie einander durch ihren Fleiß, durch ihre Erfindungskraft und durch ihre bessere Waaren zu übertreffen suchen [...] Wenn es einigen gelinget auf diese Art ihr Glück zu machen; so werden diese Beyspiele eine große Anreizung vor andere seyn, eben diesen Weg zu erwählen, und die Vervielfältigung der Manufacturen und mithin der Zusammenfluß der Waaren wird von selbst entstehen.
VI, 72	*Grundfeste* I, 752f. Nichts ist allen vernünftigen Grundsätzen von dem Wesen der bürgerlichen Verfassungen so sehr zuwider, als die privative Anmaaßung der Regierung über gewisse Gewerbe und Nahrungsarten.
VI, 74	*Polizeiwissenschaft*, p.184 Kein Gewerbe, so klein es auch ist, und wenn es der Handel mit Federspuhlen ware, muß jemand allein überlassen werden.
VI, 78	*Staatswirtschaft* I, 227: Eben so sieht sich ein weiser Regent zuweilen genöthiget, gewisse Fabriken und Manufacturen auf seine eigene Kosten anzulegen, weil sie niemand unternehmen will.
VI, 87	*Grundfeste* I, 446 [...] würde eine sehr eitle Erwartung haben, wenn nicht das Land vor allen andern Staaten überaus große Vorzüge hätte.
VI, 88	*Manufakturen und Fabriken* I, 87 Allein so bald sie [die Manufakturen und Fabriken] in Gang gebracht sind und bestehen können; so muß er [der Monarch] sie an Privatpersonen überlaßen, wenn er guten Grundsätzen gemäß verfahren will.
VI, 94	*Grundfeste* I, 448 Ein Werk, das von einem einzigen Manne abhängt, ist in verschiedenen Betracht allemal weit größerer Gefahr unterworfen.
VI, 103	*Vergleichungen*, p. 306 Alle Last des ganzen Staats liegt gleichsam auf den Landleuten.

VI, 104	*Vergleichungen*, p. 307 Überhaupt siehte man nicht, warum nicht ein weiser und gütiger Monarch dem Beyspiele des Sinesischen Kaisers nachahmen [...] könnte.
VI, 108	*Gesammelte Schriften* II, 396 [Frohndienste sind] die auszehrende Krankheit unserer Landwirtschaft in Deutschland.
VI, 109	*Polizeiwissenschaft*, p. 27 Ein Pächter wird niemals so viel Fleiß und Sorgfalt aufein Grundstück verwenden, als ein Eigenthümer.
VI, 111	*Grundfeste* I, 150 So lange die Bauren nicht das vollkommene Eigenthum der Güther haben, die sie bewohnen; so fehlet ihnen der vornehmste Bewegungsgrund und die wirksamste Triebfeder ihre Grundstücke auf das beste zu cultiviren; weil sie immer befürchten müssen, daß sie, oder ihre Kinder, aus dem Besitz der Güther herausgesetzet werden möchten; als welches bey denen Leibeigenen Bauren dem Guthsherren allemal frey steheht, und auch bey denen, auf Meyerecht sitzenden, Bauren nicht selten geschiehet. Diese Gewohnheiten und Rechte, insonderheit aber die Leibeigenschaft, sind auch an sich selbst so unbillig und der Natur und dem Wesen eines Staats so offenbar entgegen, daß es die äußerste Verwunderung verdienet, wie sie in so vernünftigen und erleuchteten Zeiten, wie die unsrigen sind, annoch staat finden können. Die Freiheit des Bürgers und aller Mitglieder des Staats ist gleichsam die erste wesentliche Eigenschaft aller bürgerlichen Verfassungen; und Staaten, worinnen ein Stand, oder Classe des Volkes der andern mit Unterthänigkeit, oder Leibeigenschaft verwannt ist, haben eine so monströse Verfassung, die nur in denen allerbarbarischten Zeiten hat entstehen können, die aber gesittete und vernünftige Zeiten ohne Schande nicht fortsetzen können.
VI, 112	*Polizeiwissenschaft*, p. 29 Man kann es als eine allgemeine Regel ansehen, daß eine Oberfläche, die in dem Eigenthum der Privatpersohnen ist, allemal besser genutzet wird, als eine Fläche, die denen Gemeinden, oder vielen Persohnen in Gemeinschaft, zugehöret.

VI, 122	*System des Finanzwesens*, p. 385 Wenn man den Weinbau, den Wiesenbau und andre Theile der Landwirtschaft allzustark betreibt, daß dadurch dem Getreidebau und anderen nothwendigen Produkten Abbruch geschieht, so darf man sie nur mit großen Abgaben belegen und die Steuern auf Grundstücke, welche man gefördert oder vermehrt haben will, vermindern, so wird man bald den gewünschten Erfolg haben.
VI, 123	*Staatswirtschaft* II, 638 Es ist auch gewissermaßen gar nicht rathsam, seine wichtige Angelegenheit auf das Gutachten und die Verfügung eines einzigen Menschen ankommen zu lassen. Dieser Mensch kann mit Vorurtheilen und Absichten eingenommen seyn.
VI, 124	*Steuern und Abgaben*, p. 12f. Auf und unter der Oberfläche eines jeden Landes befinden sich allemal Dinge, die sich nicht wohl zu dem Privateigenthum schicken, weil ihr Gebrauch entweder allen Bürgern gemeinschaftlich verbleiben muß, und niemand davon ausgeschlossen werden kann, als welches letztere doch zum dem Wesen des Eigenthums erfordert wird, oder weil ihre Erstreckung zu groß ist, als daß sie in dem ausschließenden Gebrauch und dem Gewehrsam einer Privatpersohn seyn könten.

VI, 132	*Steuern und Abgaben*, p. 15f. Alle Menschen sind mit ihrem eigenen Vermögen überaus selten vernünftige Haushälter […] Wie kann man sich also von ihnen versprechen, daß sie mit einem fremden Vermögen, nämlich mit dem Vermögen des Staats, gute und vernünftige Haushälter seyn werden? […] Wenn die Quelle der Abgaben einmal eröfnete ist: so haben sie nicht den geringsten empfindlichen Bewegungsgrund, der sie von dem Mißbrauch derselben zurückhalten könnte. Es kostet ihnen ja nichts, sie können ja nur aus einem fremden Vermögen nehmen; und man müßte die Menschen gar nicht kennen, wenn man nicht zugestehen wolte, daß sich bey einem jeden, dem es weiter nichts kostet, als nur aus einem andern Vermögen zu nehmen, was er nöthig hat, die Bedürfnisse gar bald auf eine ungeheure Art vervielfältigen werden. Die Menschen sind sehr sinnreich, sich eingebildete Bedürfnisse zu erdenken; wenn sie eine so große Leichtigkeit vor sich ahben, ihre Bedürfnisse zu erlangen. Der natürliche Erfolg der einmal eröfneten Quelle der Abgaben kann demnach niemals anders seyn, als daß diese Steuern unaufhörlich vermehret werden, und endlich zu einer denen Unterthanen unerträglichen Last anwachsen, wodurch sowohl die Unterthanen las der Staat selbst in das Verderben gestürzet werden.
VI, 133	*Manufakturen und Fabriken* I, 12 Das Verboth der Einfuhre aber gewisser Waaren […] ist ein gewaltsames Mittel, welches die Freyheit der Commercien einschränket, der natürlichen Freyheit der Unterthanen Gewalt anthut, indem es den freyen Gebrauch ihres Vermögens und der Annehmlichkeiten des Lebesn hintert und welches in auswärtigen Staaten die Repressalien nach sich ziehet, daß die Einfuhre unsere Landesproducte gleichfalls verbothen wird, wodurch immer neue Schwierigkeiten in dem Kaufhandel entstehen.
VI, 133	*Manufakturen und Fabriken* I, 157 Wir beleidigen andre Völker durch das Verboth und leiden vermöge gerechter Repreßalien Nachtheil an unsern Commercien und dennoch wird der Endzweck den Absatz unsrer Fabrikwaaren zu befördern, nur schlecht erreicht.

VI, 141	*Vergleichungen*, p. 287 In manchen zum Theil benachbarten Landen ist kein Städgen so klein, wo sich nicht zehenerley verschiedene Arten von Einnehmern befinden [...] Die Unkosten des Finanzwesens belaufen sich in vielen Landen eben so hoch, als die Einkünfte des Staats sind, die wirklich in die Cassen eingehen.
VI, 143	*Gesammelte Schriften* I, 371 Nach dem Grundsatz, den ich oben voraus gesetzet habe, daß nämlich alle diejeneigen, so gleichen Schutz genießen, nach Proportion ihres Vermöges, auch gleiche Abgaben entrichten müssen, kann ich ihre Befreyung, oder gar geringen Beytrag zu den Abgaben, der Billigkeit nicht gemäß finden, zumal da die Ursache ihrer Befreyung, nämlich auf ihre eigene Kosten dem Vaterlande im Krieg zu dienen, durch die beständige Kriegsverfassung längst aufgehöret hat.
VI, 147	*Steuern und Abgaben*, p. 95 Überdies konnten die Abgaben auf die beweglichen Güther ohne eine Entdeckung des beweglichen Vermögens nicht statt finden, welches allen Unterthanen unangenehm und beschwerlich, und vielen unter ihnen schädlich fällt.
VI, 150	*Steuern und Abgaben*, p. 93 Es ist bekannt genug, wie übel viele Studirende ihre Zeit auf hohen Schulen zubringen, und statt dessen, daß sie etwas tüchtiges lernen sollten, sich mit nichts als vermeynten Vergnügen und Zeitvertreibe beschäftigen. Dennoch heissen sie alsdenn Gelehrte [...] ohne dem Staate im geringsten mit Wissenschaften und Gelehrsamkeit nützlich zu seyn.
VI, 153	*Steuern und Abgaben*, p. 31 [Weil eine Verbrauchssteuer] sich auf solche Sachen legt, deren Verbrauch allgemein ist und niemand entrathen kann, so erlanget man daduch ebensowenig eine Contributionsart, die alle Unterthanen nach der Proportionalität ihres Vermögens trifft.
VI, 154	*Steuern und Abgaben*, p. 102 Die Accise schränket die vernünftige Freyheit der menschlichen Handlungen gar sehr ein, und ist dem Aufnehmen der Gewerbe und des Nahrungsstandes nachtheilig.

VI, 155	*Steuern und Abgaben*, p. 103 [Viele] häusliche Angelegenheiten und Umstände [können] entdecket werden, die ohne Nachtheil des Staats geheim bleiben können, und die ein jeder ehrlicher Mann mit höchstem Verdrusse, und öfters mit Nachtheile seiner zeitlichen Umstände, bekannt gemacht sieht.
VI, 158	*System des Finanzwesens*, p. 469 [E]ine wahre Gewerbesteuer [muß] eine solche Einrichtung haben, daß ein jedes Gewerbe nach Größe, Umfang, Lage und Erstarkung und folglich auch nach Größe des daraus entstehenden Gewinsstes mit den Steuern belegt wird.

Bibliography

Works by Johann Heinrich Gottlob von Justi

Political and Economic Works

Abhandlung von dem Zusammenhang der Vollkommenheit der Sprache mit dem blühenden Zustand der Wissenschaften: Wobey zugleich zu Anhörung einer Rede von dem unzertrennlichen Zusammenhang eines blühenden Zustandes der Wissenschaften mit denjenigen Mitteln, welche einen Staat mächtig und glücklich machen, als mit welcher auf dem 16ten des Winter-Monaths in dem Kayserlich-Königlichen Theresiano das öffentliche Lehramt der Teutschen Beredsamkeit angetreten wird, alle hohe Beschützer und geneigte Gönner der Wissenschaften unterthänig und gehorsamst einladet Johann Heinrich Gottlob von Justi, ehmaliger Fürstl. Sächsischer Eisenachischer Witthumsrath, und bestimmter öffentlicher Lehrer der Teutschen Beredsamkeit und der Landes-Öconomie bey dem Kayserl. Königl. Collegio Theresiano (Wien: Joh. Thomas Trattner, 1750). Also in: *Gesammelte politische und Finanzschriften* II, 129–175.

Abhandlung von den Mitteln die Erkenntniss in den Öconomischen und Cameral-Wissenschaften dem gemeinen Wesen recht nützlich zu machen; Wobey zugleich zu seinen in diesen Wissenschaften auf den ...ten des Heumonats anzufangenden Vorlesungen ergebenst einladet Johann Heinrich Gottlob von Justi (Göttingen: Vandenhoeck, 1755). Also in: *Gesammelte politische und Finanzschriften*, III, 219-248.

Rechtliche Abhandlung von denen Ehen, die an und vor sich selbst ungültig und nichtig sind (de matrimonio putativo et illegitimo); wobey zugleich von dem Wesen der Ehe und dem grossen Einflusse der Ehegesetze in die Glückseligkeit des Staats gehandelt wird (Leipzig: Bernhard Christoph Breitkopf, 1757). Also in: *Historische und juristische Schriften*, II, 323–592.

Vollständige Abhandlung von denen Manufakturen und Fabriken (2 vols; Kopenhagen: Rothensche Buchhandlung, 1758 (I), 1761 (II); 2nd edition by Johann Beckmann: Berlin: Pauli, 1780; 3rd edition by Johann Beckmann: Berlin: Pauli, 1789; reprint: Aalen: Scientia, 1972; web edition: http://www.ub.uni-bielefeld.de/diglib/justi/vollstaendige/titel.htm).

Abhandlung von denen Manufactur- und Fabriken-Reglements zur Ergänzung seines Werkes von denen Manufakturen und Fabriken (Berlin and Leipzig: Verlag der Realschule, 1762).

Ausführliche Abhandlung von denen Steuern und Abgaben (Königsberg: Woltersdorffs Witwe, 1762; reprint: Wiesbaden: Gabler, 1977).

Abhandlung von der Abtretung eines Reichs-Lehns in den Frieden mit auswärtigen Mächten, worinnen zugleich erwiesen wird, dass die Herzogthuemer Parma, Placenc und Guastalla, ohngeachtet der in dem Aachischen Frieden an den Durchl. Infant Don Philipp beschehenen Abtretung, annoch wirkliche Reichs-Lehen sind (Frankfurt/Leipzig/Nuremberg: Peter Conrad Monath, 1750). Also in: *Historische und juristische Schriften*, II, 232–320.

Abhandlung von der Macht, Glückseeligkeit und Credit eines Staats (Ulm/Frankfurt/Leipzig: J.F. Gaum, 1760).

Abhandlung von der Vollkommenheit der Landwirthschaft und der höchsten Cultur der Länder (Ulm and Leipzig: Gaumische Buchhandlung, 1761).

Der handelnde Adel, dem der kriegerische Adel entgegengesetzt wird (Göttingen: Vandenhoeck, 1756). Also in: *Gesammelte politische und Finanzschriften*, I, 147–192. See also: translations.

Beweiss, dass die Unviersal-Monarchie vor die Wohlfahrt von Europa und überhaupt des menschlichen Geschlechts die grösste Glückseligkeit würken würde (Frankfurt, 1747). Also in: *Gesammelte politische und Finanzschriften*, II, 236–300.

Die Chimäre des Gleichgewichts der Handlung und Schiffahrt, oder: Ungrund und Nichtigkeit einiger neuerlich geäusserten Meynungen von denen Maassregeln der freyen Mächte gegen die zu befürchtende Herrschaft und Obermacht zur See, wobey zugleich neue und wichtige Betrachtungen über die Handlung und Schiffahrt der Völker, und über den höchsten Punkt der daraus entstehenden Macht und Glückseligkeit beygebracht werden (Altona: David Iversen, 1759). Reprinted in: *Teutsche Kriegs-Kanzley* (Frankfurt/Main and Leipzig, 1760), pp. 918–1024.

Die Chimäre des Gleichgewichts von Europa, eine Abhandlung, worinnen die Nichtigkeit und Ungerechtigkeit dieses zeitherigen Lehrgebäudes der Staatskunst deutlich vor Augen geleget und dabey allenthalben neue und rührende Betrachtungen über die Ursachen der Kriege und dem wesentlichen Grunde, worauf die Macht eines Staats ankommt, beygebracht werden (Altona: David Iversen, 1758).

Erörterung der Frage, ob es nach den Regeln der Staatskunst ratsam ist, den Verlust einer Schlacht zu leugnen, oder falsche Siege und Vorteile auszubreiten (Göttingen, 1757). Also in: *Gesammelte politische und Finanzschriften* I, 33–46.

Gesammelte politische und Finanzschriften (3 vols; Kopenhagen and Leipzig: Rothensche Buchandlung, 1761 (I+II) + 1764 (III); reprint: Aalen: Scientia, 1970).

Von Getreydemagazinen, von Lebensmitteln und von dem Unterhalt des Volkes (Frankfurt/M.: Andraeische Buchhandlung, 1771).

Die Grundfeste zu der Macht und Glückseligkeit der Staaten; oder ausführliche Vorstellung der gesamten Policey-Wissenschaft (2 vols; Königsberg and Leipzig:

Johann Heinrich Hartungs Erben, 1760 (I); Königsberg and Leipzig: Woltersdorffs Witwe, 1761 (II); reprint of both volumes: Aalen: Scientia, 1965).

Systematischer Grundriss aller Öconomischen und Cameralwissenschaften (Frankfurt and Leipzig, 1759).

Der Grundriss einer guten Regierung in fünf Buechern verfasset (Frankfurt and Leipzig: Johann Gottlieb Garbe, 1759).

Grundsätze der Policeywissenschaft in einem vernünftigen, auf dem Endzweck der Policey gegründeten Zusammenhange und zum Gebrauch academischer Vorlesungen abgefasset (Göttingen: Vandenhoeck, 1756; 2nd, enlarged edition 1759; 3rd edition, edited with notes and comments by Johann Beckmann 1782; reprints: Frankfurt/M.: Sauer + Auvermann, 1969; Düsseldorf: Verlag Wirtschaft und Finanzen, 1993).

Auf höchsten Befehl an Sr. Röm. Kaiserl. und zu Ungarn und Böhmen Königl. Majestät erstattetes allerunterthänigstes Gutachten von dem vernünftigen Zusammenhange und practischem Vortrage aller Öconomischen und Cameralwissenschaften, wobey zugleich zur Probe die Grundsätze der Policeywissenschaft mit denen darzu gehörigen practischen Arbeiten vorgetragen werden benebst einer Antrittsrede von dem Zusammenhange eines blühenden Zustandes der Wissenschafte mit denjenigen Mitteln, welche ein Staat mächtig und glücklich machen (Leipzig, 1754). Partly in: *Gesammelte politische und Finanzschriften* II, 129–175.

Natur und Wesen der Staaten als die Quelle aller Regierungswissenschaften und Gesetze (Berlin/Stettin/Leipzig: Rüdiger, 1760; 2nd edition, edited with comments by Heinrich Godfried Scheidemantel: Mitau: Steidel, 1771; reprint of second edition: Aalen: Scientia, 1969).

Öconomische Schriften über die wichtigsten Gegenstände der Stadt- und Landwirtschaft (2 vols; Berlin: Verlag der Realschule, 1760 (I), 1761 (II)).

Onomatologia Oeconomica Practica oder Ökonomisches Woerterbuch, in welchem die allernöthigste, nützlichste und durch sichere Erfahrung bewährte Haushaltungskünste zur Stadt- und Landwirthschaft gehörige unentbehrliche Anmerkungen, auserlesenste Vortheile und Handgriffe nach alphabetischer Ordnung deutlich und aufrichtig beschrieben werden (3 vols; Frankfurt and Leipzig: Gaumische Buchhandlung, 1760 (I), 1763 (II+III)).

Die Wirkungen und Folgen sowohl der wahren, als der falschen Staatskunst in der Geschichte des Psammitichus, Königs von Egypten und der damaligen Zeiten (2 vols; Frankfurt and Leipzig, J.G. Garbe, 1759 (I), 1760 (II); reprint: Aalen: Scientia, 1972).

Staatswirtschaft oder systematische Abhandlung aller Öconomischen und Cameral-Wissenschaften, die zur Regierung eines Landes erfordert werden (2 vols; Leipzig: Bernhard Christoph Breitkopf, 1755; 2nd enlarged edition: Leipzig: Bernhard Christoph Breitkopf, 1758; reprint of 2nd edition: Aalen: Scientia, 1963).

System des Finanzwesens, nach vernünftigen, aus dem Endzweck der bürgerlichen Gesellschaften und aus der Natur aller Quellen der Einkünfte des Staates hergeleiteten Grundsätzen und Regeln ausführlich abgehandelt (Halle: Rengerische Buchhandlung, 1766; reprint: Aalen: Scientia, 1969).

Vergleichungen der Europäischen mit den Asiatischen und andern vermeintlich barbarischen Regierungen in drey Büchern verfasset (Berlin/Stettin/Leipzig: Johann Heinrich Rüdiger, 1762; reprint: Königstein/Ts.: Scriptor, 1978).

Entdeckte Ursachen des verderbten Münzwesens in Teutschland, nach ihren ersten und wahren Quellen; wobey zugleich neue und wirksame Mittel dagegen vorgeschlagen werden, die ein jeder Reichsstand vor sich, ohne Mitwirkung des Reichs, und ohne Recesse mit seinen Mitständen, in Ausübung bringen kann (Leipzig: Bernhard Christoph Breitkopf, 1755). Also in: *Gesammelte Politische und Finanzschriften* II, 406–572.

Juridical, Historical, Literary and Natural Scientific Publications

Anweisung zu einer guten Deutschen Schreibart und allen in den Geschaefften und Rechtssachen vorfallenden schriftlichen Ausarbeitungen, zu welchem Ende allenthalben wohlausgearbeitete Proben und Beyspiele beygefüget werden (Leipzig: Bernhard Christoph Breitkopf, 1755; 2nd edition: 1769).

Die Dichterinsul nach ihren verschiedenen Landschaften und denen darinnen befindlichen Städten und Einwohnern sowohl als nach dererselben Gottesdienst, Staats- und Kriegsverfassung unpartheyisch beschrieben benebst einem Lob- und Heldengedichte (Leipzig und Wittenberg: Johann Friedrich Schlomach, 1745).

Fabeln und Erzählungen von Thieren und sehr alten längst verrosteten Zeiten, bey deren Lesung man ganz sanft und suess wird einschlafen können (Cologne, 1759).

Das entdeckte Geheimnis der neuen Sächsischen Farben benebst einigen Betrachtungen von dem Vorzug und der Theorie dieser neuen Färbekunst (Vienna: Kraus, 1750).

Gesammelte chymische Schriften, worinnen das Wesen der Metalle und die wichtigsten chymischen Arbeiten vor dem Nahrungsstand und das Bergwesen ausführlich abgehandelt werden (2 vols; Berlin: Verlag der Realschule, 1760 (I), 1761 (II)).

Geschichte des Erd-Cörpers aus seinen äusserlichen und unterirdischen Beschaffenheiten hergeleitet und erwiesen (Berlin: Christian Friedrich Himburg, 1771).

Gespräche im sogenannten Reiche der Toten, zwischen Friedrich Wilhelm, Könige in Preussen und Churfürst von Brandenburg und Carl, Landgraf zu Hessen Kassel (Frankfurt/M., 1741).

Grundriss des gesamten Mineralreiches, worinnen alle Fossilien in einem, ihren wesentlichen Beschaffenheiten gemässen Zusammenhange vorgestellt und beschrieben werden (Göttingen: Vandenhoeck, 1757; 2nd edition: 1765).

Historische und juristische Schriften (2 vols; Frankfurt and Leipzig: Johann Gottlieb Garbe, 1760 (I), 1761 (II); reprint: Aalen: Scientia, 1972).

Johann Heinrich Gottlob von Justi zeiget in dieser Schrift die Nichtigkeit aller Einwürfe und unhöflichen Anfaelle, welche wider seine Untersuchung der Lehre von den Monaden und einfachen Dingen zum Vorschein gekommen sind und leget denen Unpartheyischen den Ungrund der Monaden und einfachen Dingen fernerweit klar vor Augen (Frankfurt/M./Leipzig, 1748).

J.H. Gottlobs von Justi moralische und philosophische Schriften (3 vols; Berlin Johann Heinrich Rüdiger: 1760 (I+II), 1761 (III)).

Die Kunst das Silber zu affinieren: oder, das mit andern Metallen vermischte Silber wieder fein zu machen (Königsberg and Mitau: Johann Jacob Kanter, 1765).

Physicalische und politische Betrachtungen über die Erzeugung des Menschen und Bevölkerung der Länder (Smirna (i.e. Breslau): Neue Buchdruckerey, 1769). Published under the pseudonym Anaxagoras von Occident.

Scherzhafte und satyrische Schriften (2 vols; Berlin/Stettin/Leipzig: Johann Heinrich Rüdiger, 1760; 2nd, improved edition: 1765).

Ursachen des Verfalls der Religion und der einreissenden Freydenkerey (Berlin: Joh. Adam Rüdiger, 1747). Also in: *Moralische und philosophische Schriften* III, 3–123.

Prize-Essays

Abhandlung von den Römischen Feldzuegen in Teutschland oder wie weit der Römer Waffen in Nord- und Ost-Teutschland eingedrungen und was vor Denkmaale davon vorhanden sind, bey Gelegenheit der Aufgabe der Königl. Preussis. Academie der Wissenschaften auf das Jahr 1748 ausgearbeitet und mit vielen zur Erläuterung und besserem Verständniss der alten Geschichte dienlichen Anmerkungen versehen (Leipzig: Theophilus Crull, 1748). Also in: *Historische und juristische Schriften* I, 54–180.

'Joh. Heinr. Gottlobs von Justi Abhandlung über die öconomische Preisfrage: Was tragen die Pflanzen selbst zur Zubereitung ihres Nahrungssaftes bey, und was ist bey ihrem ungleichen Wachsthum der Verschiedenheit des Erdreichs zuzuschreiben? Lassen sich die verschiedene Güte desselben, und bey schlechten Erdreich die mangelnden Stücke, besondes in Absicht auf den Ackerbau, durch chymische Versuche auf eine brauchbare Art bestimmen?' In: *Abhandlungen der Churfürstlich-baierischen Akademie der Wissenschaften* (Munich: Akademische Buchhandlung, 1767), IV, 2, 55–96.

Johann Heinrich Gottlob von Justi, Königl. Preuss. Berghauptmanns, von der Churfürstl. Pfälzischen Academie zu Mannheim gekrönte Abhandlung über die Frage: Wie die Kupfererze mit Ersparung der Zeit und der Kohlen auf den Kupferhuetten besser bearbeitet werden können. Nebst einigen andern merk-

würdigen kleinen Schriften, die Chemie und Berghütten-Sachen betreffend (Leipzig: Paul Gotthelf Kummer, 1776).

Beantwortung der Preisfrage: Auf was für eine leichtere und sowohl in Ansehung der Zeit als des Holzes weniger kostbare, durch die Erfahrung bewehrte Art kann man aus den gewonnenen Kupfererzen Garkupfer erhalten (Munich, 1765).

'Erörterung der Preisfrage, worinnen der Fränkischen Könige und der Herzoge von Baiern aus dem Agilofingischen Stamme wechselweise Rechte und Verbindlichkeiten bestanden haben'. In: *Abhandlung der Churfuerstlich-baierischen Akademie der Wissenschaften* (Munich: Akademische Buchhandlung, 1767), IV, 1.

Zwey Preisfragen der Churfürstlich Bayerischen Academie der Wissenschaften über den Ursprung der alten Herzoge von Bayern und deren Verhältniss gegen die Fränkische Monarchie (Kopenhagen and Leipzig: Gabriel Christian Rothens Witwe, 1763).

'Untersuchung der Lehre von den Monaden und einfachen Dingen, worinnen der Ungrund derselben gezeiget wird; als die Ausarbeitung der Aufgabe, so die Königl. Preussische Hochpreissliche Academie der Wissenschaften zu Berlin, denen auswärtigen Gelehrten auf das Jahr 1747 vorgeschrieben hat'. In: *Dissertation qui a remporté le prix proposé par l'Academie Royale de Sciences et Belles Lettres sur le système des monades, avec les pièces qui ont concouru* (Berlin: A. Haude, and J.C. Spener, 1748), 1–43.

War Pamphlets, 1756–1763

Abhandlung von der Unverletzlichkeit der Waffen- und Krieges-Verträge, worinnen die, von dem Reichs-Hofrath unternommene, vermeintliche Vernichtung der Lieliensteiner Capitulation, und der Bambergischen Contributions-Verträge, desgleichen die Verletzung der Dresdner Capitulation und andrer Waffen-Verträge, aus ungezweifelten Grund-Sätzen das Natur- und Völker-Rechts beurtheilet werden. Als die Fortzetzung der Untersuchung, ob die Europäischen Völker dereinst Lust haben moechten, Menschen-Fresser, oder wenigstens Hottentotten zu werden (Philadelpia in Pennsylvania (i.e. Schwerin): Jacob Heinrich Lowe, 1760).

Betrachtungen, welche Deutschland anietzo über die vereinigten Österreichische und Bourbonische Macht vernünftiger Weise machen muss (Göttingen, 1756 [Unpublished]).

*Beweiss, dass die bey denen Reichstäglichen Berathschlagungen über das bevorstehende Friedens-Geschäfte von denen Evangelischen ergriffene itio in partes rechtmässig und in dem Westphälischen Frieden vollkommen gegründet sey: Nebst verschiedenen neuen und wichtigen Betrachtungen und Entdeckungen über das Betragen und die Absichten des Hauses Österreich und seiner meisten

Anhänger gegen die evangelische Religion ([No place of publication stated], 1761)

Erwiesene und ferner erläuterte Rechtmässigkeit der itionis in partes auf denen Teutschen Reichstägen durch die meisten Stimmen eines jeden Religions-Corporis; worinnen zugleich eine im Druck erschienen catholische Schrift, unter dem Titel: Gesetzmässige Beurteilung des Betragens, welches bey denen angestellten Reichs-Deliberationen zu Kayserl. Bevollmächtigung, in Nahmen des Reichs den Friedens-Congress zu Augspurg zu beschicken, von den widrigen Gesanntschaften geäussert worden; geprüfet und deren Ungrund klar gezeiget wird (Frankfurt and Leipzig, 1762).

Leben und Charakter der jüngst verstorbenen Frau Gräfinn von Brühl geborenen Gräfinn von Kolowart in vertraulichen Briefen entworfen ([No place of publication stated], 1763).

Leben und Character des Königl. Polnischen und Churfürstl. Sächsischen Premier-Ministre Grafens von Brühl in vertraulichen Briefen entworfen (3 parts; [No place of publication stated], 1760, 1761 & 1764).

Schreiben an das Publicum von dem Verfasser der Briefe, so unter dem Titul: Leben und Character des Grafen von Brühl, zum Vorschein gekommen (Hamburg and Leipzig, 1760).

Der enthüllete Österreichische Schriftsteller, oder Anmerkungen über die so betitulte Schrift: das entlarvte Preussische Friedensprojekt, welches unter dem Titul: Wohlgemeynte Vorschläge, auf was vor Bedingungen die itzo im Kriege befangenen Mächte zu einem dauerhaftigen und ihrem allerseitigen Interesse gemässen Frieden gelangen könnten u. heraus gekommen, und sehet, was es ist! (Vienna and Erfurt: Trattner and Jungnicolu, 1760).

Untersuchung, ob etwa die heutigen europäischen Völker Lust haben möchten, dereinst Menschen-Fresser oder wenigstens Hottentotten zu werden. Aus Veranlassung der jetzigen grausamen Art, Krieg zu führen, der gebrochenen Capitulation von Dresden, und verschiedener anderer Verletzungen des VölkerRechts, angestellet von einem ehemaligen Europäer, welcher sich nach Amerika begeben hat, weil er dereinst seine Nachkommen mit stinkenden Schaafs-Därmen nicht gerne ausgezieret wissen möchte (Philadelphia in Pennsylvania (i.e. Schwerin): Johann Heinrich Lowe, 1760).

Wohlgemeinte Vorschläge eines die jetzigen unglücklichen Zeiten beseufzenden Menschenfreundes auf was vor Bedingungen die jetzo in Krieg befangenen Mächte zu einem dauerhaftigen und ihrem allerseitigen Interesse gemässigen Frieden gelangen könnten zur Aufmunterung ganz Deutschlands (Friedensnah, 1759).

Note: Wolfgang Burgdorf (*Reichskonstitution und Nation. Verfassugsreformprojekte für das Heilige Römische Reich Deutscher Nation im politischen Schrifttum von 1648 bis 1806* (Mainz: Philipp von Zabern, 1998), pp. 133–174) argued that Justi was the author of the extensive comments in the German 1761 edition of Hippolithus a Lapide's *Abriss* (Philipp Bogislaus von Chemnitz [Pseudonym: Hippolithus a Lapide],

Abriss der Staats-Verfassung, Staats-Verhältnis und Bedürfnis des Römischen Reiches – Deutscher Nation: Nebst einer Anzeige der Mittel zur Wiederherstellung der Grund-Einrichtung und alten Freiheit nach dem bisherigen Verfall. Aus Bogislav Philipp von Chemnitz vollständiger lateinischer Urschrift; mit Anmerkungen welche die gegenwärtigen Umstände im Reich betreffen (Mainz and Koblenz, 1761)). However, it remains highly doubtful whether Justi was the author of the footnotes in this edition.

Edited works

Deutsche Memoires oder Sammlung verschiedener Anmerkungen, die Staatsklugheit, das Kriegswesen, die Justiz, Morale, Öconomie, Commercium, Cammer- und Policey- auch andere merkwürdige Sachen betreffend, welche im menschlichen Leben vorkommen, von einigen Civil- und Militairbedienten, auch von andern Gelehrten und erfahrnen Personen aufgezeichnet und hinterlassen worden (2 vols; Leipzig, 1741 (I), 1742 (II)).

Vermischte Anmerkungen welche verschiedene merkwürdige die Staatsklugheit, das Kriegswesen, die Sittenlehre, die Öconomischen und dahingehörigen, Cameral-Commercien und Policey-Wissenschaften, wie auch das Justizwesen betreffende Sachen abhandeln: oder der Deutschen Memoirs Dritter Theil (Vienna: Joh. Paul Krauss, 1761).

Montes Pietatis oder Leih-Assistenz- und Hilfshäuser, Leihebanken und Lombards, ingleichen von Leibrenten, Todten-Cassen und Lotterien. Mit vielen Anmerkungen und einem Anhange von Braut- und Witwen-Cassen (Leipzig and Ulm: Gaumische Buchhandlung, 1760). Original author: Paul Jacob Marperger.

Der Teutsche Patriot in etlichen physicalischen Vorschlägen zum gemeinen Besten mit einer Vorrede sr. Hochwohlgebohrn. des Herrn Berg-Raths von Justi begleitet (Berlin: Verlag der Realschule, 1762).

Edited Periodicals

Fortgesetzte Bemühungen zum Vortheil der Naturkunde und des gesellschaftlichen Lebens der Menschen (Berlin and Stettin: Johann Heinrich Rüdiger, 1759–61).

Ergetzungen der vernünftigen Seele aus der Sittenlehre und der Gelehrsamkeit überhaupt (6 vols; Leipzig: Bernhard Christoph Breitkopf, 1745–48).

Göttingische Policey-Amts Nachrichten auf das Jahr ... Oder vermischte Abhandlungen zum Vortheil des Nahrungsstandes aus allen Theilen der öconomischen Wissenschaften benebst verschiedenen in das Göttingische Policey-Wesen einschlagenden Verordnungen und Nachrichten (Göttingen: Johann Friedrich Hager, 1755–56).

Neue Wahrheiten zum Vortheil der Naturkunde und des gesellschaftlichen Lebens der Menschen (2 vols; Leipzig: Bernhard Christian Breitkopf, 1754–58).

French and Latin Works

Dissertation qui a remporté le prix proposé par l'Academie royale sur le système des monades avec le pièces qui ont concouru (Berlin: A. Haude and J.C. Spener, 1748).

De fuga militiae (Vitembergae: ex officina Schlomachiana, 1745).

Translations

Der handelnde Adel, dem der kriegerische Adel entgegengesetzt wird (Göttingen: Vandenhoeck, 1756). Original authors: Gabriel François Coyer and Paul Auguste de Sainte Foix, Chevalier d'Arc.

Die Kunst Papier zu machen: nach dem Text von Joseph Jerom François de la Lande übersetzt und herausgegeben von Johann Heinrich Gottlob von Justi (1762; reprint edited by Alref Bruns: Münster: Landschaftsverband Westfalen-Lippe, 1983; 2nd edition 1984; 3rd edition: 1993). Original author: Joseph Jerom François de la Lande.

'Gedanken von dem Ursprunge der Monarchien und Aristokratien', in: *Gesammelte politische und Finanzschriften*, II, 176–199. Original author: Giovanni de Cataneo.

'Kurze Betrachtungen, über verschiedene grosse Helden der alten und neuern Zeiten, aus dem Französischen der jüdischen Briefe übersetzt', in: *Gesammelte politische und Finanzschriften*, II, 220–226. Original author: Jean Baptiste de Boyer, Marquis d'Argens.

Schauplatz der Künste und Handwerke, oder vollständige Beschreibung derselben, verfertiget und gebilliget von denen Herren der Akademie der Wissenschaften in Paris in das Teutsche übersetzt und mit Anmerkungen versehen von Johann Heinrich Gottlob von Justi (4 vols; Berlin/Stettin/Leipzig: J.H. Ruediger, 1762–64 (I–III); Leipzig/Königsberg/Mietau: J.J. Kanter, 1765 (IV)). Original authors: Henris Louis Duhamel de Monceau, Charles Rene Fourcroy de Ramecourt, and Colonel Galon.

'Vortreffliche Einrichtung der Sineser, in Ansehung der Belohnung und Bestrafung vor die Staatsbedienten', in: *Gesammelte politische und Finanzschriften*, I, 115–131. Original author: Claude François Lambert (*Recueil d'observations curieuses*, Paris 1749, I, 19, 345–363).

De aart der wetten afgeleid uit de natur en het weezen der staaten (Amsterdam: J. Kok, 1773).

La Chimère de l'equilibre du commerce et de la navigation [...] *Traduit de l'Allemand par D.T.**** (Copenhagen and Leipzig: Rothensche Buchhandlung, 1763).

De chimere of hersenschim van het evenwigt in Europa, of Verhandeling de nietigheid van dit systema der Staat-kund ontvouwd wordt (S Grav.: P. van Cleef, 1767).

*Elementos generales de Policía escritos por el señor Juan Henrique Gottlob de Justi & c. y del idioma francés traducidos al Español con varias notas conduncentes a España, añadias por el propio traductor D. Antonio Francisco Puig i Gelabert (*Barcelona: por Eulalia Pferer, Viuda Impresora all Rey nuestro señor. Plaza del Ángel, 1784).

'Elementos de la policía general de un estado', in: *Memorias instructivas, y caminos sobre agricultura, comercio, industria, economica, chymica, botánica, historia natural* [...] XII, Memoria CXVI, Madrid, 1791, p. 377–496. Translator: Miguel Geronimo Suárez y Núnez.

*Élements généraux de police, démontrés par des raisonnements fondés sur l'objet et la fin qu'elle se propose. Traduis de l'Allemand par M.E.**** (Paris: Rozet, 1769). Translator: Marc Antoine Eidous. Not included: §§ 346, 347, 349, 354–359, 370 and Book IV.

Ezemesjacnyja socinenija k pol'ze I uveseleniju sluzascija (St. Petersburg, 1755–64).

The life and character, rise and conduct of Count Bruehl, Prime Minister to the King of Poland, Elector of Saxony; in a series of letters, by an eminent hand [...] *carefully translated from the German original* (London: printed for M. Cooper, in Pater-Noster-Row, and C.G. Seyffert, in Pall-Mall, 1765).

Osnovanie sily I blagosostojanija Carstv', ili podrobnoe nacertanie vsech' znanij I kasajuscichsja do gosudarstvennag blagocinija (4 vols; St. Petersburg, 1772–78). Translator: I. Bogaevakij. [*Die Grundfeste zu der Macht und Glückseligkeit der Staaten*]

Les sciences concernant la politique reduites en système (Halle, 1759).

Le secret des nouvelles teintures de Saxe avec quelques réflexions sur la théorie, & sur les avantages de ces nouvelles teintures. Traduit de l'Allemand sur l'original imprimé à Vienne 1751 (Paris: Durand, 1752).

Suscestvv izobrazenie estestva narodnych' ovscestv' I razlichnych' zakonov' (2 vols; 1802). [*Natur und Wesen der Staaten*]

Torgujuscee dvorjanstvo protivu polozennoe dvorjanstvo voennomu (St. Petersburg: Academy of Sciences, 1766). Translator: Denis Fonvizin. [*Der handelnde Adel, dem der kriegerische Adel entgegengesetzt wird*]

La vie et le caratère de M. le comte de Bruehl, premier ministre de Sa Majesté le roi de Pologne et électeur de Saxe (Paris, 1760).

Volledige verhandeling der manufatuuren en fabrieken. Met verbeteringen en aanmerkingen van Joh. Beckmann (Utrecht: J. v. Schoonhoven, 1782). Translator: Jacob van Manen Az.

Note: There exists a further Russian translation of *Natur und Wesen der Staaten* by A. Volkov (Moscow, 1770).

Periodicals

Allgemeine Deutsche Bibliothek (Kiel: Bohn, 1765–94).
Neue Berlinische Monatsschrift, edited by Friedrich Biester (Stettin: Nicolai, 1799–1811). Web-edition: www.ub.uni-bielefeld.de/diglib/Berlinische_Monatsschrift/
Giornale Enciclopedico di Liegi (Lucca, 1756–1760).
Göttingische Anzeigen von gelehrten Sachen, edited by the Königliche Akademie der Wissenschaften (Göttingen: 1753–1883).
Journal Encyclopédique, (Liège, 1756–75).
Journal oeconomique, ou, mémoires, notes et avis sur les arts, l'agriculture, le commerce (Paris: 1751–72).
Leipziger Sammlungen, edited by Georg Heinrich Zincke (Leipzig: 1744–61).
Observations sur la physique, sur l'historie naturelle et sur les arts (Paris: 1765ff.).
Schwäbische Nachrichten von Öconomie-, Kameral-, Polizey-, und Handlungs-, Manufaktur-, Mechanischen-, Bergwercks-Sachen, edited by Johann Jacob Moser (Stuttgart, 1756–57).
Tübingische Berichte von gelehrten Sachen, edited by Christoph Friedrich Schott. (Tübingen: Cotta, 1752–63).
Wöchentliche Hallische Anzeigen (Halle: 1731–1809).

Printed Sources

Adelung, Johann Christoph, *Fortsetzung und Ergänzung zu Christian Gottlieb Jöchers allgemeinem Gelehrten-Lexicon, worin die Schriftsteller aller Stände nach ihren vornehmsten Lebensumständen und Schriften beschrieben werden* (2 vols; Leipzig, 1784 (I) + 1787 (II); reprint: Hildesheim: Olms, 1960).
Arc, Paul Auguste de Sainte Foix, Chevalier d', *La Noblesse militaire ou le Patriote françois* (Amsterdam, 1756).

Argens, Jean Baptiste de Boyer Marquis d', *Lettres juives, ou Correspondance philosophique, historique & critique, entre un juif voyageur en differens etats d' Europe et ses correspondans en divers endroits* (The Hague: P. Paupie, 1764).

Argenson, René Louis Marquis d', *Mémoires et journal inédit* (5 vols; Paris: Jannet, 1858).

—— *Politische Schriften*, translated and edited by Herbert Hömig (Munich: Oldenbourg, 1985).

Becher, Johann Joachim, *Politischer Discurs von den eigentlichen Ursachen des Auf- und Abnehmens der Stätt, Länder und Republicken, in specie, wie ein Land volckreich und nahrhaft zu machen und in eine rechte Societatem Civilem zu bringen* (2nd edition; Frankfurt: J. D. Zunners, 1673).

Beckmann, Johann, *Vorrath kleiner Anmerkungen ueber mancherley gelehrte Gegenstände* (Göttingen, 1806).

Bensen, Heinrich, *Versuch eines systematischen Grundrisses der reinen und angewandten Staatslehre fuer Kameralisten* (3 vols; Erlangen, 1798–99).

Bielfeld, Jacob Friedrich, Baron von, *Institutions Politiques* (2 vols; The Hague: Gosse junior, 1760).

Boulainvilliers, Henri de, *Histoire de l'ancien gouvernement de France* (3 vols; The Hauge and Amsterdam, 1727).

—— *Essais sur la noblesse de France* (2 vols; Amsterdam, 1732).

Cantillon, Richard, *Essai sur la nature de commerce in general*, edited by Takumi Tsuda (Tokyo: Kinokuniya, 1979).

Cataneo, Giovanni de, *The Source, the Strength and the True Spirit of Laws ... in which the errors of M. de Montesquieu, and some other eminent writers, are occasionally considered. To which are added, Essays on the natural origin of political governments* (London: Lockyer Davis, 1753).

Coyer, Gabriel François, Abbé de, *Développement et défense du système de 'La Noblesse Commerçante'* (2 vols; Amsterdam and Paris: Duchesne, 1757).

—— *La Noblesse Commerçante* (Paris: Duchesne, 1756).

Darjes, Joachim Georg, *Erste Gründe für die Kameralwissenschaft* (Leipzig, 1756).

Du Halde, Jean Baptiste, *Description géographique, historique, chronologique ... de l'Empire de la Chine* (4 Vols; Paris, 1733). German translation: *Beschreibung des chinesischen Reiches und der grossen Tartarey* (Rostock, 1747–50).

Dubos, Jean Baptiste, *Histoire Critique de l'établissement de la Monarchie Françoise dans les Gaules* (3 vols; Amsterdam, 1734).

Fénelon, François de, *Telemachus, son of Ulysses*, edited and translated by Patrick Riley (Cambridge: Cambridge University Press, 1994).

Frederick II, King of Prussia, *Anti-Machiavell, Oder Prüfung der Regeln Nic. Machiavells von der Regierungskunst eines Fürsten. Mit historischen und politischen Anmerkungen. Aus dem Französischen übersetzt* (Göttingen, 1742).

Goudar, Ange, *Les intérêts de la France mal entendus dans les branches de l'agriculture, de la population, des finances, du commerce et de la marine et de l'industrie* (Amsterdam: Jacques Coeur, 1756). Translated into German by Johan

Albrecht Philippi, *Staatsfehler der mehresten Höfe im französischen Gemälde* (Berlin and Leipzig: 1766).
Grimm, Friedrich Melchior Freiherr von and Denis Diderot (eds.), *Correspondance littéraire, philosophique et critique* (6 vols; Paris: Longschamps, 1813).
Hörnigk, Philipp Wilhelm, *Österreich über alles, wenn es nur will* ([No place of publication stated] 1684; reprint: Düsseldorf: Verlag Wirtschaft und Finanzen, 1997).
Holst, Amalia, *Über die Bestimmung des Weibes zur höheren Geistesbildung* (Berlin: Heinrich Fröhlich, 1802; reprint: Zurich: Ala 1983; 2nd edition: 1984).
Humboldt, Wilhelm von, *The Limits of State Action*, edited and translated by J.W. Burrow (Indianapolis: Liberty Fund, 1993).
Hume, David, *Essays, Moral, Political, And Literary*, edited by Eugene F. Miller. Indianapolis: Liberty Fund, 1985).
Kahle, Ludwig Martin, *La Balance de l'Europe considérée comme la règle de la paix et de la guerre. Traduit du Latin par Mr Samuel Formey* (Berlin and Göttingen, 1744).
La Loubère, Simon de, *Du royaume de Siam*, (2 vols; Paris, 1691).
Lambert, Claude François, *Recueil d'observations curieuse* (2 vols; Paris: David le Jeune, 1749).
Lessing, Gotthold Ephraim, *Briefe, die neueste Literatur betreffend*, edited by Wolfgang Bender (Stuttgart: Reclam, 1972).
Lith, Johann Wilhelm von der, *Neue vollständig erwiesene Abhandlung von denen Steuern* (Ulm, 1766).
—— *Politische Betrachtungen über die verschiedenen Arten der Steuern* (Breslau, 1751).
Loen, Johann Michael von, *Der Adel* (Ulm: Gaum, 1752; reprints: Ann Arbor/London: University Microfiches International, 1980; Königstein: Scriptor, 1982).
—— *Der redliche Mann am Hofe* (reprint of 1742-edition: Stuttgart: Metzler, 1966).
—— *Des Herrn von Loen gesammelte kleine Schriften*, (4 vols; Frankfurt/M./Leipzig: Hutten, 1752; reprint: Frankfurt/M.: Athenaeum, 1972).
Mandeville, Bernhard de, *The Fable of the Bees – or Private Vices, Publick Benefits*, edited by F.B. Kaye (2 vols; Indianapolis: Liberty Classics, 1988).
Maria Theresia, *Politische Testamente*, edited by Josef Kallbrunner (Vienna: Verlag für Geschichte und Politik, 1952).
Marsy, François Marie de, *Histoire moderne des Chinois, des Japonais, des Indiens, des Persanes, des Turcs, des Russiens, etc. pour servir de suite a l'histoire de M. Rollins* (22 vols; Paris, 1755–71).
Melon, Jean François, *A Political Essay upon Commerce*, translated by David Bindon (Dublin and London: Woodward and Cox, 1739).
Mirabeau, Victor Riquetti, Marquis de, *L'ami des hommes, ou traité de la population*, (6 vols; The Hague, 1758–62).
—— *Traité de la monarchie*, edited by Gino Longhitano (Paris: Harmattan, 1999).

Monroe, Arthur Eli, *Early Economic Thought. Selections from Economic Literature Prior to Adam Smith* (Cambridge/Mass.: Harvard University Press, 1927).

Montesquieu, Charles Louis Secondat Baron de la Brède et de, *Considerations on the Causes of the Greatness of the Romans and their Decline*, translated by David Lowenthal (New York: The Free Press, 1965).

—— *Persian Letters*, translated by C.J. Betts (Harmondsworth: Penguin, 1991).

—— *The Spirit of the Laws*, translated by Anne Cohler, Basia Miller, and Harold Stone (Cambridge: Cambridge University Press, 1989).

Pfeiffer, Johann Friedrich von, *Berichtigungen berühmter Staats-, Finanz-, Policey-, Cameral-, Commerz- und ökonomische Schriften dieses Jahrhunderts* (6 vols; Frankfurt/M., 1781–84).

—— *Lehrbegriff sämtlicher öconomischer und Cameralwissenschaften* (4 vols; Stuttgart, 1764/65 (I); Mannheim, 1770–78 (II–IV)).

Philippi, Johann Albrecht, *Der vergrösserte Staat* (Leipzig: Breitkopf, 1759; reprint: Goldbach: Keip, 1998).

—— *Die wahren Mittel zur Vergröserung eines Staates* (Berlin: Haude and Spener, 1753).

Ramsay, Andrew Michael Chevalier de, *Les Voyages de Cyrus. Avec un discours sur la mythologie* (Paris: Gabriel François Quillau fils, 1727).

Rollin, Charles, *Histoire ancienne des Egyptiens, des Carthaginois, des Assyriens, des Babyloniens, des Medes, et des Perces, des Macedoniens, des Grecs* (13 vols; Paris, 1730–38).

Saint-Pierre, Charles-Irénée Castel Abbé de, *Ouvrajes Politiques* (16 vols; Rotterdam, 1734–41).

—— *Discours sur la Polysynodie* (Amsterdam: Du Villard et Chaugion, 1719).

Schröder, Wilhelm von, *Fürstliche Schatz- und Rentkammer* (Leipzig, 1752).

Seckendorff, Veit Ludwig von, *Teutscher Fürstenstaat* (Hanau, 1656).

Sonnenfels, Joseph von, *Gesammelte Schriften* (10 vols; Vienna, 1783–87; microfiche: Munich: Saur, 1990–94).

Smith, Adam, *An Inquiry into the Nature and Causes of the Wealth of Nations*, edited by R.H. Campbell and A.S. Skinner (2 vols; Indianapolis: Liberty Fund, 1983).

Steuart, Sir James, *Collected Works* (7 vols; London: Routledge/Thoemmes Press, 1995).

—— *Abhandlung von den Grundsaetzen der Muenzwissenschaft*, translated by Christoph Friedrich Schott (Tübingen: Cotta, 1761).

—— *An Inquiry into the Principles of Political Economy*, edited by Andrew S. Skinner with Noboru Kobayashi and Hiroshi Mizuta (4 vols; London: Pickering & Chatto, 1998). German translation: *Untersuchung der Grundsätze der Staats-Wirtschaft als ein Versuch über die Wissenschaft von der innerlichen Politik bei freyen Nationen*, translated by Christoph Friedrich Schott (5 vols; Tübingen: Cotta, 1769–72).

Süssmilch, Johann Peter, *Die Göttliche Ordnung in denen Veränderungen des menschlichen Geschlechts, Das ist, Gründlicher Beweiss der Göttlichen Vorse-*

hung und Vorsorge für das menschliche Geschlecht: nebst einem Versuch, die Verhältnisse der Sterbenden nach dem Alter und denen Kranckheiten zu bestimmen (Berlin: Gohls, 1742).

—— *Die Göttliche Ordnung in den Veränderungen des menschlichen Geschlechts, besonders im Tode: Durch einige neue Beweistuemer bestätigt und gegen des Königl. Gross-Britannischen Berg-Raths Herrn von Justi Erinnerungen und Mutmaassungen in zweyen Sendschreiben an selbigen gerettet* (Berlin: Haude and Spener, 1756).

Terrasson, Jean, *Abriss der wahren Helden-Tugend, oder, Lebensgeschichte des Sethos, Königes in Egypten: aus geheimen Urkunden des alten Egypten-Landes, und nach der französischen Übersetzung eines griechischen Originals verdeutsched von C.G.W* [= Christoph Gottlieb Wendt] (Hamburg: Thomas von Wierings Erben, 1732; also: Leipzig: Philipp Hertel, 1737).

Turgot, Anne Robert Jacques, Baron de l'Aulne, 'In Praise of Gournay', in: *The Economics of A.R.J. Turgot*, edited and translated by P.D. Groenewegen (The Hague: Nijoff, 1977), pp. 20–42.

Vincent de Gournay, Jacques Claude, *Traité sur le commerce de Josiah Child avec les remarques inédites de Vincent de Gournay*, edited by Takumi Tsuda (Tokyo: Kinokuniya, 1983).

Wolff, Christian, *Grundsätze des Natur- und Völckerrechts* (Halle: Renger, 1754).

—— *Vernünfftige Gedancken von dem gesellschaftlichen Leben der Menschen, und insonderheit dem gemeinen Wesen zur Beförderung der Glückseligkeit des menschlichen Geschlechts* (Frankfurt/M. and Leipzig, 1721).

—— *Gesammelte kleine philosophische Schrifften* (Halle: Renger, 1740).

Zech, Siegmund Christoph von, *Die Verwandlung der Domänen in Bauergüther als das beste Mittel zur Bevoelkerung, zur Macht und zum Reichtum eines Landes* (Strassburg [i.e. Berlin], 1759).

Zedler, Johann Heinrich, *Grosses vollständiges Universal Lexicon aller Wissenschaften und Künste* (64 vols; Halle and Leipzig: Zedler, 1732–54).

Zincke, Georg Heinrich, *Allgemeines Öconomisches Lexicon* (2nd edition; Leipzig, 1744).

Secondary Literature

Articles

Adam, Ulrich, 'Nobility and Modern Monarchy – J.H.G. Justi and the French Debate on Commercial Nobility at the Beginning of the Seven Years War', *History of European Ideas* 29 (2003), 141–157.

Anderson, Matthew S., 'Eighteenth-Century Theories of the Balance of Power', *Studies in Diplomatic History. Essays in memory of David Bayne Horne*, edited by Ragnhild Hatton and Matthew S. Anderson (London: Longman 1970), pp. 183–198.

Angermann, Ernst, 'Die Verbindung des "polizeistaatlichen Wohlfahrtsideals" mit dem Rechtsstaatsgedanken', *Historisches Jahrbuch* 74 (1955), 462–472.

Backhaus, Jürgen G. 'The Cameralists – A Public Choice Perspective', *Public Choice* 53 (1987), 3–20.

—— 'Christian Wolff on Subsidiarity, the Division of Labor, and Social Welfare', *European Journal of Law and Economics* 4 (1997), 129–146.

Bertrand, Valérie, 'La conception du commerce dans l'"Esprit des lois" de Montesquieu', *Annales Historiques de la Revolution Française* 269–70 (1987), 266–290.

Bödeker, Hans Erich, 'Das staatswissenschaftliche Fächersystem im 18. Jahrhundert', *Wissenschaften im Zeitalter der Aufklärung*, edited by Rudolf Vierhaus (Göttingen: Vandenhoeck & Ruprecht, 1985), pp. 143–162.

——, '"Staatswissenschaften" and Political Economy at the University of Goettingen: the Scottish Influence', *Transactions of the Eighth International Congress on the Enlightenment* 3 (*Studies on Voltaire and the Eighteenth Century* 305) (Oxford: The Voltaire Foundation, 1992), 1881–1884.

Bog, Ingomar, 'Ist die Kameralistik eine untergegangene Wissenschaft?', *Berichte zur Wissenschaftsgeschichte* 4 (1981), 61–72.

—— 'Mercantilism in Germany', *Revisions in Mercantilism*, edited by D.C. Coleman, (London: Methuen, 1969), pp. 162–189.

Bollnow, Otto Friedrich, 'Die philosophischen Grundlagen der Staats- und Wirtschaftslehren bei J.H.G. von Justi', *Finanzarchiv* 8 (1941), 381–402.

Borscheid, Peter, 'Die Anfänge der landwirtschaftlichen Versicherung in Deutschland', *Zeitschrift für Agrargeschichte und Agrarsoziologie* 37 (1989), 37–55.

—— 'Feuerversicherung und Kameralismus', *Zeitschrif für Unternehmensgeschichte* 30 (1985), 96–117.

Braeuer, Walter, 'Kameralismus und Merkantilismus. Ein kritischer Vergleich', *Jahrbuch für Wirtschaftsgeschichte* 1990, 107–111.

Braun, Hans-Joachim, 'Economic Theory and Policy in Germany 1750–1800', *Journal of European Economic History* 4 (1975), 301–322.

Carrithers, David W., 'Not so Virtuous Republics: Montesquieu, Venice, and the Theory of Aristocratic Republicanism', *Journal of the History of Ideas* 52 (1991), 245–268.

Crum, Frederick S., 'The Statistical Work of Sussmilch', *Publications of the American Statistical Association* 7 (1901), 1–46.

Davis, Walter W., 'China, the Confucian Ideal, and the European Age of Enlightenment', *Journal of the History of Ideas* 44 (1983), 523–548.

Delvaille, Jules, 'Ange Goudar et son projet pour la repopulation en 1756', *Revue d'histoire des doctrines économiques et sociales* 5 (1912), 1–28.

Desserud, Donald A., 'Virtue, Commerce, and Moderation in the "Tale of the Troglodytes": Montesquieu's "Persian Letters"', *History of Political Thought* 12 (1991), 605–626.

—— 'Commerce and Political Participation in Montesquieu's Letter to Domville', *History of European Ideas* 25 (1999), 135–151.

Dreitzel, Horst, 'Ideen, Ideologien, Wissenschaften: Zum politischen Denken in Deutschland in der Frühen Neuzeit', *Neue Politische Literatur* 25 (1980), 1–25.

—— 'Justis Beitrag zur Politisierung der deutschen Aufklärung', *Aufklärung als Politsierung – Politisierung der Aufklärung*, edited by Hans Erich Bödeker and Ulrich Herrman (Hamburg: Meiner, 1987), pp. 138–177.

—— 'Universal-Kameral-Wissenschaft als politische Theorie: Johann Friedrich von Pfeiffer (1717–1787)', *Aufklärung als praktische Philosophie. Werner Schneiders zum 65. Geburtstag*, edited by Frank Grunert and Friedrich Vollhardt, (Tübingen: Max Niemeyer, 1998), pp. 149–171.

—— 'Vom reichspatriotischen Konstitutionalismus zum nationalen Liberalismus. Zur Diskussion der landständischen Verfassung in der deutschen Aufklärung', *Aufklärung / Lumières und Politik – Zur politischen Kultur der deutschen und französischen Aufklärung*, edited by Hans Erich Bödeker and Etienne François, (Leipzig: Universitätsverlag, 1996), pp. 399–432.

Ebihara, Akio, 'Justis Staatslehre und Wolffs Naturrechtslehre', *Zeitschrift der Savigny-Stiftung für Rechtsgeschichte – Germanistische Abteilung* 102 (1985), 239–246.

Ellis, Harold A., 'Montesquieu's Modern Politics: *The Spirit of the Laws* and the Problem of Modern Monarchy in Old Regime France', *History of Political Thought* 10 (1989), 665–700.

Fenske, Hans, 'Gewaltenteilung', *Geschichtliche Grundbegriffe*, edited by Otto Brunner, Werner Conze, Reinhart Koselleck (8 vols; Stuttgart: Klett, 1972–97), II, 923–958.

Foucault, Michel, 'La technologie politique des individus', *Dits et écrits 1954-1988*, edited by Daniel Defert, François Ewald and Jacques Lagrange (IV vols; Paris: Gallimard, 1994) IV, 813–828.

Fournier, August, 'Gerhard van Swieten als Censor', *Sitzungsberichte der philosophisch-historischen Classe der k.k. Akademie der Wissenschaften in Wien* 84 (1876), 387–466.

Freudenberger, Hermann, 'An Industrial Momentum Achieved in the Habsburg Monarchy', *Journal of European Economic History* 12 (1983), 339–350.

—— 'State Intervention as an Obstacle to Economic Growth in the Habsburg Monarchy', *Journal of Economic History* 27 (1967), 493–509.

Haas, Ernst B., 'The Balance of Power: Prescription, Concept, or Propaganda', *World Politics* 5 (1953), 442–477.

Hecht, Jacqueline, 'Johann Peter Sussmilch: A German Prophet in Foreign Countries', *Population Studies* 41 (1987), 31–58.

—— 'Un problème de population active au XVIIIe siècle, en France: La querelle de la noblesse commerçante', *Population* [INED] 19 (1964), 267–289.

Hont, Istvan, 'Free Trade and the Economic Limits to National Politics: Neo-Machiavellian Political Economy Reconsidered', *The Economic Limits to Modern Politics*, edited by John Dunn (Cambridge: Cambridge University Press, 1990), pp. 41–120.

—— 'The language of sociability and commerce: Samuel Pufendorf and the theoreticcal foundations of the "Four-Stages-Theory"', *The Language of Political Theory in Early-Modern Europe*, edited by Anthony Pagden, (Cambridge: Cambridge University Press, 1987), pp. 253–276.

Ingrao, Charles W., 'The Problem of "Enlightened Absolutism" and the German States', *Journal of Modern History* 58 (1986), 161–180.

Inama-Sternegg, Karl Theodor von, 'Der Akzisenstreit deutscher Finanztheoretiker im 17. und 18. Jahrhundert', *Zeitschrift für die gesamte Staatswissenschaft* 21 (1865), 515–545.

Johnson, Hubert C., 'Theory of Bureaucracy in Cameralism', *Political Science Quarterly* 79 (1964), 378–402.

Kaiser, Thomas E., 'Money, Despotism, and Public Opinion in Early Eighteenth-Century France: John Law and the Debate on Royal Credit', *Journal of Modern History* 63 (1991), 1–28.

—— 'The Abbé der Saint–Pierre, Public Opinion, and the Reconstitution of the French Monarchy', *Journal of Modern History* 55 (1983), 618–643.

Keohane, Nannerl O., 'Virtuous Republics and Glorious Monarchies: Two Models in Montesquieu's Political Thought', *Political Studies* 20 (1972), 383–396.

Klein, Ernst, 'Johann Heinrich Gottlob Justi und die Preussische Staatswirtschaft', *Vierteljahrsschrift für Sozial- und Wirtschaftsgeschichte* 48 (1961), 145–202.

Klippel, Diethelm, 'The True Concept of Liberty. Political Theory in Germany in the Second Half of the Eighteenth Century', *The Transformation of Political Culture. England and Germany in the Late Eighteenth Century*, edited by Eckhart Hellmuth (Oxford: Oxford University Press, 1990), pp. 447–466.

Koch, Rolf Albert, 'Johann Heinrich Gottlob von Justis philosophisch Satiren', *Kant-Studien* 53 (1961–62), 490–506.

—— 'J.H.G. von Justis "Dichterinsel" und ihre Beziehungen zur Literaturkritik der Aufklärung', *Zeitschrift für deutsche Philologie* 91 (1972), 161–171.

Koehl, Robert L., 'Heinrich Brühl: A Saxon Politician of the Eighteenth Century', *Journal of Central European Affairs* 14 (1954), 310–328.

Komlos, John, 'Institutional Change under Pressure: Enlightened Government Policy in the Eighteenth-Century Habsburg Monarchy', *Journal of European Economic History* 15 (1986), 427–482.

Kurth, Lieselotte E., 'Historiographie und historischer Roman: Kritik und Theorie im 18. Jahrhundert', *MLN* (1964), 337–362.

Lluch, Ernest, 'Cameralism beyond the Germanic World: a Note on Tribe', *History of Economic Ideas* 5 (1997), 85–99.

—— 'Der Kameralismus, ein vieldimensionales Lehrgebäude: Seine Rezeption bei Adam Smith und im Spanien des 18. Jahrhunderts', *Jahrbuch für Geschichte* 2000, 133–156.

Maier, Hans, 'Ältere deutsche Staatslehre und westliche politische Tradition', *Politische Wissenschaft in Deutschland,* edited by Hans Maier (Munich, 1969), 133–152.

Mars, Francis L., 'Ange Goudar, cet inconnu (1708–1791). Essai bio-bibliographique sur un aventurier polygraphe du XVIIIme siècle', *Casanova Gleanings* 9 (1966), 1–64.

Martens, Wolfgang, 'Literatur und "Policey" im Aufklärungszeitalter. Aufgaben sozialgeschichtlicher Literaturforschung', *Germanisch-Romanische Monatsschrift* 31 (1981), 404–419.

—— 'Obrigkeitliche Sicht: Das Bühnenwesen in den Lehrbüchern der Policey und Cameralistik des 18. Jahrhunderts', *Internationales Archiv für Sozialgeschichte der Deutschen Literatur* 6 (1981), 19–51.

Menzel, Johanna M., 'The Sinophilism of J.H.G. Justi', *Journal of the History of Ideas* 17 (1956), 300–310.

Mittenzwei, Ingrid, 'Theorie und Praxis des aufgeklärten Absolutismus in Brandenburg-Preussen', *Jahrbuch für Geschichte* 6 (1972), 53–106.

—— 'Über das Problem des aufgeklärten Absolutismus', *Zeitschrift für Geschichte* 18 (1970), 1162–1172.

Murphy, Antoin E., 'Le développement des idées économiques en France, 1750–56', *Revue d'histoire moderne et contemporaine* 33 (1986), 521–541.

Perry, Geraint, 'Enlightened Government and Its Critics in Eighteenth-Century Germany', *Historical Journal* 6 (1963), 178–192.

Pribram, Karl, 'Die Idee des Gleichgewichts in der älteren nationalökonomischen Theorie', *Zeitschrift für Volkswirtschaft, Sozialpolitik und Verwaltung* 17 (1908), 1–28.

Raeff, Marcel, 'The Enlightenment in Russia and Russian Thought in the Enlightenment', *The Eighteenth Century in Russia*, edited by John G. Garrard, Oxford: Clarendon Press, 1973, pp. 25–47.

—— 'The Well-Ordered Police State and the Development of Modernity in Seventeenth- and Eighteenth-Century Europe: An Attempt at a Comparative Approach', *The American Historical Review* 80 (1975), 1221–1243.

Rétat, Pierre, 'De Mandeville à Montesquieu: honneur, luxe et dépense noble dans l'"Esprit des lois"', *Studi Francesi* 50 (1973), 238–249.

Riha, Tomas, 'German Political Economy: The History of an Alternative Economics', *International Journal of Social Economics* 12 (1985), 2–25.

Roscher, Wilhelm, 'Der sächsische Nationalökonom Johann Heinrich Gottlob von Justi. Ein Beitrag zur inneren Geschichte von Deutschland um die Mitte des vorigen Jahrhunderts', *Archiv für die Sächsische Geschichte* 6 (1868), 76–106.

Schmidt, Horst, 'Johann Heinrich Gottlob von Justi, ein vergessener Vertreter der deutschen Aufklärung des XVIII. Jahrhunderts, und Russland', *Wissenschaft-*

liche Zeitschrift der Martin-Luther-Universität Halle-Wittenberg; Gesellschafts- und Sprachwissenschaftliche Reihe 2/1961, 273–279.
Skinner, Andrew S., 'Sir James Steuart: Author of a System', *Scottish Journal of Political Economy* 28 (1981), 20–42.
—— 'Sir James Steuart: Economics and Politics', *Scottish Journal of Political Economy* 9 (1962), 17–37.
Sonenscher, Michael, 'Fashion's empire: trade and power in early 18th-century France', *Luxury Trades and Consumerism in Ancien Régime Paris: Studies in the History of the Skilled Workforce*, edited by Robert Fox and Anthony Turner, Aldershot: Ashgate Publishing, 1998, 231–254.
Tautscher, Anton, 'Die Steuer als Gestaltungsmittel der Volkswirtschaft bei den deutschen Merkantilisten', *Finanzarchiv* 9 (1943), 303–337.
Thompson, Martyn P., 'The History of Fundamental Law in Political Thought from the French Wars of Religion to the Amercian Revolution', *The American Historical Review* 91 (1986), 1103–1126.
Tribe, Keith, 'Cameralism and the Science of Government', *Journal of Modern History* 56 (1984), 263–284.
—— 'The Reception of Physiocratic Argument in the German States', *Économie et société* 29 (1995), 331–344.
Vagts, Alfred and Detlev F., 'The Balance of Power in International Law: a History of an Idea', *American Journal of International Law* 73 (1979), 555–580.
Venturi, Franco, 'Oriental Despotism', *Journal of the History of Ideas* 24 (1963), 133–142.
Vierhaus, Rudolf, 'Montesquieu in Deutschland. Zur Geschichte seiner Wirkung als politischer Schriftsteller im 18. Jahrhundert', *Deutschland im 18. Jahrhundert*, edited by Rudolf Vierhaus, Göttingen: Vandenhoeck & Ruprecht, 1987, 9–32.
Walker, Mack, 'Rights and Functions: The Social Categories of Eighteenth-Century German Jurists and Cameralists', *Journal of Modern History* 50 (1978), 234–251.
Wilhelm, Uwe, 'Das Staats- und Gesellschaftsverständnis von J.H.G. von Justi: ein Beitrag zur Entwicklung des Frühliberalismus in Deutschland', *Der Staat* 20 (1991), 415–441.
Würtenberger, Thomas, 'An der Schwelle zum Verfassungsstaat', *Aufklärung* 3 (1988), 53–88.
—— 'Die Planung im kameralistischen Staat', *Panorama der Fridericianischen Zeit*, edited by Jürgen Ziechmann (Bremen: Ziechmann, 1985), pp. 455–459.
Wysocki, Jürgen, 'Zur kameralistischen Theorie der Besteuerung von Grund und Vermögen unter Bezug auf die Reform Josefs II', *Studien zur Entwicklung der ökonomischen Theorie* II (Schriften des Vereins für Socialpolitik 115/II), edited by Fritz Neumark, Berlin: Duncker & Humblot, 1982, 131–156.

Monographs

Alem, André, *Le Marquis d'Argenson et l'économie politique au début du XVIIIe siècle* (New York: Burt Franklin, 1968; originally: 1900).

Balazs, Eva H., *Hungary and the Habsburgs 1765–1800. An Experiment in Enlightened Absolutism*, translated by Tim Wilkinson (Budapest: Central European University Press, 1997).

Baum, Detlef, *Bürokratie und Sozialpolitik, Zur Geschichte staatlicher Sozialpolitik im Spiegel der älteren deutschen Staatsverwaltungslehre* (Berlin: Duncker & Humblot, 1988).

Beales, Derek, *Joseph II* (Cambridge: Cambridge University Press, 1987).

Becher, Ursula A.J., *Politische Gesellschaft – Studien zur Genese bürgerlicher Öffentlichkeit in Deutschland* (Göttingen: Vandenhoek & Ruprecht, 1978).

Beer, Adolf, *Die Staatsschulden und die Ordnung des Staatshaushalts unter Maria Theresia* (Vienna, 1895).

Bleek, Wilhelm, *Von der Kameralausbildung zum Juristenprivileg* (Berlin: Colloquium Verlag, 1972).

Bonney, Richard (ed.), *Economic Systems and State Finance* (Oxford: Clarendon Press, 1995).

Borscheid, Peter, and Annette Drees (eds.), *Versicherungsstatistik in Deutschland, 1750–1985* (St. Katharinen: Scripta Mercaturae, 1988).

Brauleke, Hans-Joachim, *Leben und Werk des Kameralisten Philipp Wilhelm von Hörnigk: Versuch einer wissenschaftlichen Biographie* (Frankfurt: Lang, 1978).

Brechka, Franz T., *Gerhard van Swieten and his World* (The Hague: Nijhoff, 1970).

Brückner, Jutta, *Staatswissenschaften, Kameralismus und Naturrecht* (Munich: Beck, 1977).

Burgdorf, Wolfgang, *Reichskonstitution und Nation. Verfassungsreformprojekte für das Heilige Römische Reich Deutscher Nation im politischen Schrifttum von 1648 bis 1806* (Veröffentlichungen des Instituts für Europäische Geschichte 173) (Mainz: Philipp von Zabern, 1998).

Carcassonne, Ely, *Fénelon. L'home et l'oeuvre* (Paris: Boivin, 1941).

—— *Montesquieu et le problème de la constitution française au XVIIIe siècle* (Paris: Presses universitaires de France, 1930).

Carpenter, Kenneth E., *Dialogue in Political Economy. Translations from and into German in the 18th Century* (Boston: Baker Library, 1977).

Clausen, Otto, *Chronik der Heide- und Moorkolonisation im Herzogtum Schleswig-Holstein (1760–1765)* (Husum: Husum Verlag, 1981).

Dann, Otto and Diethelm Klippel (eds.), *Naturrecht, Spaetaufklärung, Revolution* (Hamburg: Meiner, 1995).

Dickson, P.G.M., *Finance and Government under Maria Theresia, 1740–1780* (2 vols; Oxford: Clarendon Press, 1987).

Dittrich, Erhard, *Die deutschen und österreichischen Kameralisten* (Darmstadt: Wissenschaftliche Buchgesellschaft, 1974).

Dreitzel, Horst, *Absolutismus und ständische Verfassung in Deutschland. Ein Beitrag zu Kontinuität und Diskontinuität der politischen Theorie in der frühen Neuzeit* (Mainz: Philipp von Zabern, 1992).

—— *Monarchiebegriffe in der Fürstengesellschaft – Semantik und Theorie der Einherrschaft in Deutschland von der Reformation bis zum Vormärz* (Cologne: Böhlau, 1991).

Ellis, Harold A., *Boulainvilliers and the French Monarchy. Aristocratic Politics in Early Eighteenth-Century France* (Ithaca: Cornell University Press, 1988).

Frensdorff, Ferdinand, *Über das Leben und die Schriften des Nationalökonomen J.H.G. von Justi* (Glashütten: Auvermann, 1970; originally: Göttingen, 1903).

Gay, Peter, *The Enlightenment. An Interpretation* (2 vols; New York/London: Norton, 1977).

—— *Voltaire's Politics. The Poet as Realist* (2nd edition; New Haven and London: Yale University Press, 1988).

Gollwitzer, Heinz, *Europabild und Europagedanke. Beiträge zur Geistesgeschichte des 18. und 19. Jahrhunderts* (Munich: Beck, 1964).

Gordon, Daniel, *Citizens without Sovereignty. Equality and Sociability in French Thought, 1670–1789* (Princeton: Princeton University Press, 1994).

Grimmig, Joseph, 'Johann Heinrich Gottlob von Justi und Joseph Sonnenfels als Finanzwissenschaftler' (Bonn: Diss. Iur., 1949).

Guy, Basil, *The French Image of China before and after Voltaire* (Studies on Voltaire and the Eighteenth Century 21) (Geneva: Institut et Musée Voltaire, 1963).

Haider-Pregler, Hilde, *Des sittlichen Bürgers Abendschule: Bildungsanspruch und Bildungsauftrag des Berufstheaters im 18. Jahrhundert* (Vienna: Jugend und Volk, 1980).

Haushofer, Heinz, *Die deutsche Landwirtschaft im technischen Zeitalter* (2nd edition: Stuttgart: Ulmer, 1972.

Haussherr, Hans, *Verwaltungseinheit und Resorttrennung vom Ende des 17. bis zum Beginn des 19. Jahrhunderts* (Berlin: Akademieverlag, 1953).

Henry, Nannerl O., see: Keohane, Nannerl O.

Herdmann, Frank, *Montesquieurezeption in Deutschland im 18. und 19. Jahrhundert* (Hildesheim: Olms, 1990).

Herrlitz, Hans-Georg and Horst Kern (eds), *Anfänge Göttinger Sozialwissenschaft: Methoden, Inhalte und soziale Prozesse im 18. und 19. Jahrhundert* (Göttingen: Vandenhoeck & Ruprecht, 1987).

Hont, Istvan, *Jealousy of Trade – International Competition and the Nation-State in Historical Perspective* (Cambridge/Mass. and London: The Belknap Press of Harvard University Press, 2005).

Humpert, Magdalene, *Bibliographie der Kameralwissenschaften* (Hildesheim: Gerstenberg, 1972; originally: Cologne: Schröder, 1937).

Hutchison, Terence, *Before Adam Smith: The Emergence of Political Economy 1662–1776* (Oxford: Basil Blackwell, 1998).

Ingrao, Charles W (ed.), *Early Modern Austria* (West Lafayette: Purdue University Press, 1994).

—— *The Habsburg Monarchy, 1618–1815* (2nd edition; Cambridge: Cambridge University Press, 2000).

Jenetzky, Johannes, *System und Entwicklung des materiellen Steuerrechts in der wissenschaftlichen Literatur des Kameralismus von 1680 bis 1840, dargestellt anhand der gedruckten zeitgenössischen Quellen* (Berlin: Duncker & Humblot, 1978).

Jeserich, Kurt G.A., Hans Pohl, and Georg-Christoph von Unruh (eds.), *Deutsche Verwaltungsgeschichte* (6 vols; Stuttgart: DVA, 1983–88).

Johnson, E.A.J., *Predecessors of Adam Smith* (London: King, 1937).

Johnson, Hubert C, *Frederick the Great and His Officials* (New Haven/London: Yale University Press, 1975).

Junkersdorf, Johann, 'Johann Heinrich Gottlob von Justi als Finanzpolitiker' (Königsberg: Diss., 1921).

Kaeber, Ernst, *Die Idee des europäischen Gleichgewichts in der publizistischen Literatur vom 16. bis zur Mitte des 18. Jahrhunderts* (Berlin: A. Duncker, 1907).

Kann, Robert A., *A Study in Austrian Intellectual History* (London: Thames and Hudson, 1960).

—— *Kanzel und Katheder: Studien zur österreichischen Geistesgeschichte vom Spätbarock zur Frühromantik* (Vienna: Herder, 1962).

Keohane, Nannerl O., *Democratic Monarchy: The Political Theory of the Marquis d'Argenson* (PhD, Yale University, 1968).

—— *Philosophy and the State in France: the Renaissance to Enlightenment* (Princeton: Princeton University Press, 1980).

Klein, Ernst, 'Johann Heinrich Gottlob von Justi: Ein Beitrag zur Abhängigkeit der cameralistischen Theorie von der staatswissenschaftlichen Praxis' (Halle: Diss. Phil., 1952).

Klingenstein, Grete, *Staatsverwaltung und kirchliche Autorität im 18. Jahrhundert* (Vienna: Verlag für Geschichte und Politik, 1970).

Klippel, Diethelm, *Politische Freiheit und Freiheitsrechte im deutschen Naturrecht des 18. Jahrhunderts* (Paderborn: Schöningh, 1976).

Klueting, Harm, *Die Lehre von der Macht der Staaten: das aussenpolitische Machtproblem in der 'politischen Wissenschaft' und in der praktischen Politik im 18. Jahrhundert* (Berlin: Duncker & Humblot, 1986).

Koch, Rolf Albert, 'Der Problemgehalt in J.H.G. v. Justis Satiren' (Halle-Wittenberg: Diss. Phil., 1950).

Koschwitz, Hansjürgen, 'Die periodische Wirtschaftspublizistik im Zeitalter des Kameralismus. Ein Beitrag zur Entwicklung der Wirtschaftsfachzeitschrift im 18. Jahrhundert' (Göttingen: Diss. Phil., 1968).

Krauss, Werner, *Perspektiven und Probleme. Zur französischen und deutschen Aufklärung* (Neuwied and Berlin: Luchterhand, 1965).

Kretschmayr, Heinrich, *Die österreichische Zentralverwaltung* (Vienna: Holzhausen, 1907).

Krieger, Leonard, *An Essay on the Theory of Enlightened Despotism* (Chicago and London: The University of Chicago Press, 1975).

—— *The German Idea of Freedom: History of a Political Tradition* (Boston: Beacon, 1957).

—— *Kings and Philosophers, 1689–1789* (London: Weidenfeld and Nicolson, 1971).

La Vopa, Anthony J., *Grace, Talent, and Merit. Poor Students, Clerical Careers, and Professional Ideology in Eighteenth-Century Germany* (Cambridge: Cambridge University Press, 1988).

Link, Christoph, *Herrschaftsordnung und bürgerliche Freiheit. Grenzen der Staatsgewalt in der älteren deutschen Staatslehre* (Vienna: Boehlau, 1979).

Link, Edith Murr, *The Emancipation of the Austrian Peasant 1740–1798* (New York: Columbia University Press, 1949).

Maier, Hans, *Die ältere deutsche Staats- und Verwaltungslehre (Polizeiwissenschaft). Ein Beitrag zur Geschichte der politischen Wissenschaft in Deutschland* (Neuwied: Luchterhand, 1966).

Marchet, Gustav, *Studien über die Entwicklung der Verwaltungslehre in Deutschland* (Munich: Oldenbourg, 1885; reprint: Frankfurt/M.: Sauer und Auvermann, 1966).

Martin, Kingsley, *French Liberal Thought in the Eighteenth Century* (London: Phoenix House, 1962).

Maverick, Lewis A., *China – a Model for Europe* (2 vols; San Antonio: Paul Anderson, 1946).

Meyer, Jean, *Le despotisme éclairé* (Paris: presses universitaires de France, 1991).

Meyssonier, Simone, *La Balance et l'Horloge. La genèse de la pensée liberale en France au XVIIIe siècle* (Montreuil: Les Editions de la Passion, 1989).

Mittenzwei, Ingrid, *Preussen nach dem Siebenjährigen Krieg. Auseinandersetzungen zwischen Bürgertum und Staat um die Wirtschaftspolitik* (Berlin: Akademie Verlag, 1979).

Müller, Hans-Heinrich, *Akademie und Wirtschaft im 18. Jahrhundert: agrarökonomische Preisaufgaben und Preisschriften der Preussischen Akademie der Wissenschaften (Versuche, Tendenzen und Überblick)* (Berlin: Akademie-Verlag, 1975).

Murphy, Antoin E., *Richard Cantillon. Entrepreneur and Economist* (Oxford: Clarendon Press, 1986).

Napp-Zinn, Anton Felix, *Johann Friedrich von Pfeiffer und die Kameralwissenschaften an der Universität Mainz* (Wiesbaden: Steiner, 1955).

Oberfohren, Ernst, *Die Idee der Universalökonomie in der französischen wirtschaftswissenschaftlichen Literatur bis auf Turgot* (Jena: Gustav Fischer, 1915).

Obert, Marcus, *Die naturrechtliche "politische Metaphysik" des Johann Heinrich Gottlob von Justi (1717–1771)* (Frankfurt/M.: Lang, 1992).

Pangle, Thomas, *Montesquieu's Philosophy of Liberalism* (Chicago and London: University of Chicago Press, 1973).

Pfannensteil, 'Rudolf Eugen, Johann Heinrich Gottlob von Justi, sein Leben und seine Lehre' (Würzburg: Diss., 1925).

Podbielski, Yvonne, 'Republics, Morals, and Peace: Kant's Perpetual Peace in Its Historical Context' (Cambridge: unpublished Diss. Phil., 1996).

Prange, Wolfgang, *Die Anfänge der grossen Agrarreformen in Schleswig-Holstein bis um 1771* (Quellen und Forschungen zur Geschichte Schleswig-Holsteins 60) (Neumünster: Karl Wachholtz, 1971).

Preu, Peter, *Polizeibegriff und Staatszwecklehre. Die Entwicklung des Polizeibegriffs durch Rechts- und Sozialwissenschaften des 18. Jahrunderts* (Göttingische rechtswissenschaftliche Studien 124) (Göttingen: Schwartz, 1983).

Pribram, Karl, *Geschichte der österreichischen Gewerbepolitik von 1740 bis 1860* (Leipzig, 1907).

Raeff, Marcel, *The Well-Ordered Police State: Social and Institutional Change through Law in the Germanies and Russia 1600–1800* (New Haven and London: Yale University Press, 1983).

Reinalter, Helmut (ed.), *Joseph von Sonnenfels* (Vienna: Verlag der Österreichischen Akademie der Wissenschaften, 1988).

—— *Der Josephinismus. Bedeutung, Einflüsse und Wirkungen* (Frankfurt/M.: Lang, 1993).

Remer, Justus, *Johann Heinrich Gottlob Justi: ein deutscher Volkswirt des 18. Jahrhunderts* (Stuttgart: Kohlhammer, 1938).

Roesch-Wanner, Beatrice, *J.H.G. von Justi als Literat* (Frankfurt/M.: Lang, 1993).

Root, Hilton L., *The Fountain of Privilege. Political Foundations of Markets in Old Regime France and England* (Berkeley: University of California Press, 1994).

Roscher, Wilhelm, *Geschichte der National-Ökonomik in Deutschland* (Munich, 1874).

Sandgruber, Roman, *Die Anfänge der Konsumgesellschaft. Konsumgüterverbrauch, Lebensstandard und Alltagskultur in Österreich im 18. und 19. Jahrhundert* (Sozial- und wirtschaftshistorische Studien 15) (Vienna: Verlag für Geschichte und Politik, 1982).

—— *Ökonomie und Politik. Österreichische Wirtschaftsgeschichte vom Mittelalter bis zur Gegenwart* (Vienna: Ueberreuter, 1995).

Sandl, Markus, *Ökonomie des Raumes. Der kameralwissenschaftliche Entwurf der Staatswissenschaft im 18. Jahrhundert* (Cologne/Vienna/Weimar: Böhlau, 1999).

Schefold, Bertram (ed.), *J.H.G. von Justis "Grundsätze der Polizeiwissenschaft"* (Düsseldorf: Verlag Wirtschaft und Finanzen, 1993).

—— *Philipp Wilhelm von Hoernigks "Österreich über alles"* (Düsseldorf: Verlag Wirtschaft und Finanzen, 1997).

Schelle, Gustave, *Vincent de Gournay* (Geneva and Paris: Slatkine, 1984; originally: Paris, 1897.

Schmidt, A., *Die Entstehung eines Eigensystems der Finanzwissenschaft* (Offenbach, 1937).

Schulze, Reiner, *Policey und Gesetzgebungslehre im 18. Jahrhundert* (Berlin: Duncker & Humblot, 1982).

—— *Die Polizeigesetzgebung zur Wirtschafts- und Arbeitsordnung der Mark Brandenburg in der frühen Neuzeit* (Aalen: Scientia, 1978).

Schumpeter, Joseph A., *History of Economic Analysis* (London: Routledge, 1954).

Senn, S.R., *The Economics of Sir James Steuart* (London: Bell, 1957).

Shklar, Judith, *Montesquieu* (Oxford/New York: Oxford University Press, 1987).

Skinner, Quentin and Martin van Gelderen (eds.), *Republicanism. A Shared European Heritage* (2 vols; Cambridge: Cambridge University Press, 2002).

Small, Albion, *The Cameralists – the Pioneers of German Social Polity* (Chicago: University of Chicago Press, 1909).

Sommer, Louise, *Die Österreichischen Kameralisten in dogmengeschichtlicher Darstellung* (Aalen: Scientia, 1967; originally: Vienna, 1920).

Stollberg-Rilinger, Barbara, *Der Staat als Maschine* (Berlin: Duncker & Humblot, 1986).

Stolleis, Michael (ed.), *Geschichte des Öffentlichen Rechts in Deutschland* (3 vols; Munich: Beck 1988–97).

—— *Staatsdenker im 17. und 18. Jahrhundert. Reichspublizistik, Politik, Naturrecht* (2nd edition: Frankfurt/M.: Metzler, 1987).

Tautscher, Anton, *Staatswirtschaftslehre des Kameralismus* (Bern: Francke, 1947).

—— Wirtschaftsgeschichte Österreichs auf der Grundlage abendländischer Kulturgeschichte (Berlin: Duncker & Humblot, 1974).

Thiele, Richard, *Thomas Abbts Anteil an den Briefen, die neueste Literatur betreffend*, (Halle, 1880).

Tribe, Keith, *Governing Economy. The Reformation of German Economic Discourse 1750–1840* (Cambridge: Cambridge University Press, 1988).

—— *Strategies of Economic Order: German Economic Discourse, 1750–1950* (Cambridge: Cambridge University Press, 1995).

Tuck, Richard, *The Rights of War and Peace: Political Thought and the International Order from Grotius to Kant* (New York: Oxford University Press, 1999).

Unruh, Georg-Christoph von, *Subjektiver Rechtsschutz und politische Freiheit in der vorkonstitutionellen Staatslehre Deutschlands* (Hamburg: Hansischer Gildenverlag, 1969).

Vierhaus, Rudolf (ed.), *Der Adel vor der Revolution* (Göttingen: Vandenhoeck & Ruprecht, 1971).

—— *Bürger und Bürgerlichkeit im Zeitalter der Aufklärung* (Wolfenbütteler Studien zur Aufklärung 7) (Heidelberg: Schneider, 1981).

Walter, Friedrich, *Die Geschichte der Österreichischen Zentralverwaltung in der Zeit Maria Theresias (1740–1780)* (Veröffentlichung der Kommission fuer Neuere Geschichte Oesterreichs 32) (Vienna: Holzhausen, 1938).

—— *Die theresianische Staatsreform von 1749* (Vienna: Verlag für Geschichte und Politik, 1958).

Weiss, Eberhard, *Geschichtsschreibung und Staatsauffassung in der französischen Enzyklopädie* (Veröffentlichungen des Instituts für europäische Geschichte 14) (Wiesbaden: Steiner, 1956).

Wilhelm, Uwe, *Der deutsche Frühliberalismus: von den Anfängen bis 1789* (Frankfurt/M.: Lang, 1995).

Würtenberger, Thomas, *Die Legitimität staatlicher Herrschaft – eine staatsrechtlich-politische Begriffsgeschichte* (Berlin: Duncker & Humblot, 1973).

Zielenziger, Kurt, *Die alten deutschen Kameralisten. Ein Beitrag zur Geschichte der Nationalökonomie und zum Problem des Merkantilismus* (Jena, 1913).

Index